The State and Justice

An essay in political theory

MILTON FISK
Indiana University

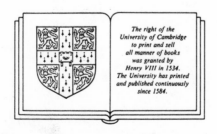

The right of the University of Cambridge to print and sell all manner of books was granted by Henry VIII in 1534. The University has printed and published continuously since 1584.

CAMBRIDGE UNIVERSITY PRESS

CAMBRIDGE

NEW YORK   PORT CHESTER   MELBOURNE   SYDNEY

Published by the Press Syndicate of the University of Cambridge
The Pitt Building, Trumpington Street, Cambridge CB2 1RP
40 West 20th Street, New York, NY 10011, USA
10 Stamford Road, Oakleigh, Melbourne 3166, Australia

First published 1989

Printed in the United States of America

Library of Congress Cataloging-in-Publication Data
Fisk, Milton.
The state and justice: an essay in political theory / Milton Fisk.
p.   cm.
Bibliography: p.
Includes index.
ISBN 0 521 37473 1.   ISBN 0 521 38966 6 (pbk.)
1. Justice.   2. Legitimacy of governments.   3. State, The.   I. Title.
JC578.F58   1989   89-1022
320'.01'1 – dc20   CIP

British Library Cataloguing in Publication Data
Fisk, Milton
The state and justice: an essay in political theory.
1. State
I. Title
320.1

ISBN 0 521 37473 1 hard covers
ISBN 0 521 38966 6 paperback

Contents

CONTENTS

Preface

Theories of the state gravitate toward either of two poles. Few of them have been able to settle in a middle ground. This is unfortunate, since, though most of them get something important right about the state, few of them incorporate the complementary insight associated with the other pole. At one of the poles the state is treated as an instrument for advancing some concrete social force: the economy, a dominant group, or technology. Many recent theories of the state try to avoid this pole through their emphasis on the state's ability to run counter to such social forces. These theories then set out from the autonomy of the state and move in the direction of the other pole.

The key factor associated with this other pole is the legitimating activity of the state. It legitimates its own rule and indirectly the dominant social forces of the nation. The state does a variety of things to gain acceptance. It secures its rule through economic activity, such as bolstering consumer demand; through political activity, such as funneling insurgencies into mainstream parties; and through ideological activity, such as fashioning the framework for public education. Different theories of the state have emphasized some of these legitimating activities over others, but rarely has any of them made its legitimating activity less of a mystery. No light is shed on either its basis or its limits.

Perhaps this failure could be remedied by a theory that blends the instrumental with the legitimating aspects of the state. Of course, we would have to be careful not to sacrifice state autonomy in the process of keeping legitimating activity from hovering above the ground without moorings. Moreover, it will not be enough to put these features of the two poles together and simply declare a synthesis, as a few theories of the state have already done. For the synthesis of the instrumental and the legitimating aspects of the state to make sense it must be worked out within an underlying theory.

Yet an underlying theory has been notably absent despite the

vii

rich outpouring about the state since the mid 1960s. The earlier attraction to the instrumental pole may explain this absence, for this pole encouraged an overly simple interpretation of materialist explanation, explantion of the sort that grounds events in socio-economic factors. In that interpretation, these factors determine, in the manner of causal antecedents, what the state will be and do. Such a determinist interpretation had to be dropped once the task was redefined as explaining autonomous state activities without abandoning materialist moorings altogether. There was, though, no plausible replacement for it. The emphasis on the pole of legitimation then took place in a virtual vacuum as regards promising guidelines for materialist explanation.

What is needed now, and what it is hoped this book will supply, is a synthesis of the instrumental, or the functional, and the legitimating poles within a nondeterminist conception of materialist explanation. While I follow the general approach of James O'Connor, Alan Wolfe, and Claus Offe in claiming that both the pole of function and that of legitimation are essential, I try to show, as they have not, how these poles can be integrated within a single theory. They rightly reject a determinist materialism, but their choice of no alternative leaves them with all the drawbacks of an unstructured empiricism.

Apart from the need for an underlying theory, there is also the need to pay attention not just to the functional but as well to the legitimating aspects of the state. The focus on legitimation brings into relief connections with certain liberal theories of the state. They treat the state as a defender of rights and hence as a promoter of justice that gets its legitimacy from this activity. With these theories as part of the general cultural background, it is not surprising that recent debates on justice – involving John Rawls, Ronald Dworkin, Bruce Ackerman, Allen Wood, Allen Buchanan, and John Roemer – have pointed to conclusions about the nature of the state. One aspect of these debates dealt with the issue of whether Marx's reluctance to appeal to justice placed him completely outside the liberal tradition with its conception of the state as a promoter of justice. Yet the interest among neo-Marxists in the legitimating role of the state, which leads it to promote a view of justice, opens up a point of contact with these debates and hence the liberal tradition.

It is, as I shall try to show, useful to conceptualize much if not all legitimating activity as the promotion of a pattern of justice. The state is able to rule only by establishing limits on benefits and losses, and such limits make a pattern of justice. This much of the theory of the state presented here is directly linked to liberal theories. These limits become the moral norms that, when widely disseminated, are the basis for the citizenry's acceptance of the rule of their state. The state will attempt to fashion these norms in a way that least disrupts its functional role, but the norms are also fashioned by pressures from those who suffer when there are no limits on benefits and losses. Part of the task of integrating the pole of function and that of legitimation into a single theory will be, in view of this connection with liberal theories of the state, to show how a state that functions for certain social forces can also be a state that promotes a just order.

Liberal theories of the state often tied themselves to a view of rights and justice that defied inclusion within a materialist view of the world. But the state as a promoter of justice need not be tied to a nonmaterialist conception of justice. Natural rights and contractarian justice can be left behind for more solidly based counterparts. Instead, the state can be thought of as defending a pattern of justice that has its roots, on the one hand, in pressures from groups of its citizens and, on the other hand, in the requirements of ruling.

The link tying state legitimation to justice gave me the idea earlier on that an appropriate subtitle for this book would be "An Essay in Political Ethics." The liberal theory of the state had been an exercise in political ethics and only recently ceased to be called that. And in the neo-Marxist theories of the state the dominant role of legitimation seemed to be a basis for categorizing them also as exercises in political ethics. Later I dropped the idea when I recalled that I would give roughly equal weight to the pole of function and the pole of legitimation. Moreover, I would be trying to show how these poles interact within the state. In contrast, certain liberal theories ignore the state's role of functioning for concrete social forces, as do the neo-Marxist or post-Marxist theories – such as those of Jürgen Habermas, Fred Block, Adam Przeworski, and Ernesto Laclau and Chantal Mouffe – that give special prominence to legitimating activity at the expense of function on the ground that otherwise state autonomy would be compromised. Still, I would insist that political ethics is an integral part of political theory, though not the only part. By settling for "An Essay in Political Theory" as subtitle I avoid the suggestion that I have been drawn so far toward the pole of legitimation that I have abandoned the functional role of the state.

The idea for this book took shape during a sabbatical in 1983 spent in Mexico. Early versions of some of the chapters were given in two different series of lectures that year, one at the National Autonomous University of Mexico and the other at the University of Louisville. After composing the first draft in 1984, I was aided in improving both conceptual formulations and arguments by students who read the book in my classes on political philosophy at Indiana University in 1985 and 1986. In addition, a number of friends and co-workers have made pointed criticisms, leading to revisions that gave the project greater depth. In this regard I owe thanks to Nancy Holmstrom, Harold Kincaid, Richard Schmitt, and Victor Wallis, all of whom took time to provide me with written comments. Betty Robertson put care and skill into typing and retyping the book until I had worked out most of the kinks. In concluding these acknowledgments, I pay my respects to the memory of Steve Zeluck (1922–85), from whom I learned much of my politics, both practical and theoretical.

MILTON FISK

Bloomington, Indiana

Introduction

Can the state rule without justice?

A friend of mine returned from the People's Republic of China several years before the market orientation began with an account of the situation there that on balance was favorable. On the negative side, she was put off by the close supervision of her activities by the officials. But there was an overriding positive side to things; she was convinced that the society's institutions encouraged the pursuit of justice. This she thought differentiated it from society in the United States, where it is not the pursuit of justice but the pursuit of economic power that is encouraged.

Her comparison stuck with me like a pebble in my shoe. It was not that I wanted to reverse the comparison by saying that in the United States the fundamental goal is justice whereas in China it is power. Moreover, what annoyed me was not that her comparison took sides, for I too was ready to grant that the Chinese Revolution had led to gains for the majority of the people of China along the dimension of basic needs. And I was also ready to consider the necessity of a better order for the United States. I was annoyed because I could not fit the comparison with what I had come to think about justice itself, which was that no stable state can rule without encouraging a pattern of justice. How had I come to this view?

1. Setting limits

It might be said that some nations fail to pursue justice because there is only one true justice and different nations pursue different things. Perhaps, then, a society has the choice of pursuing or not pursuing this true justice through its state institutions. If so, surely something predisposes one group of people to take it upon themselves to actualize this pattern of justice, whereas another group of people lack what it takes to be predisposed to it.

This line is reasoning lands us in a difficulty since it leads us to

1

ask an unanswerable question: What explains the fact that only some peoples pursue genuine justice? We might attempt to answer that they pursue justice in virtue of their intrinsic nature. They are intrinsically better than peoples who reject justice. There is, though, no reason to hold that the Chinese are intrinsically better people than North Americans or that, conversely, we are any better than they are.

This talk of an intrinsic predisposition to justice ignores history, and in the case of the Chinese it ignores that part of their history that was the Chinese Revolution. Perhaps, then, the answer to our question is that a people's peculiar history of domination and struggle against it determines whether or not they will pursue the one correct pattern of justice. The landlords and the big merchants had dominated the masses of poor peasants and the urban workers in China, and this order of things was ended only with the victory of the revolution in 1949. The context for the pursuit of justice was provided by the struggle against and ultimate destruction of the old order. In general, it is not intrinsic differences between peoples so much as differences in the struggles imposed on them that determine whether they are in pursuit of justice. The Chinese set up a new state that would try to realize the true pattern of justice revealed to them as a result of their domination by and struggle against the old order in a revolution that lasted a quarter of a century. In contrast, the alleged failure to pursue justice in the United States is explained by the fact that in the United States the struggle against the old order is weaker.

The fallback from intrinsic natures to historical struggles has its own problems. This is because there are both just and unjust revolutions. The former pursue the true pattern of justice, and the latter do not. The revolution itself gives no guarantees of justice. But if a favorable outcome for a just revolution were a matter of pure chance, then those who want justice would have no reason to fight in a revolution. To make a just revolution likely, we have to return to the original answer that some peoples are intrinsically better than others. It is thus a predisposition to pursue justice on the part of a noble people that is crucial to their making a new order just. We had, though, already rejected this answer.

Perhaps it is wrong to focus not on the role of justice but on its content. Yet we focus on its content when we insist on a particular pattern of justice – the true one – as a necessary condition for the pursuit of justice. The role of a pattern of justice is to set limits so

2

that a floor is put under the losses people can be expected to sustain and a cap is put over the benefits they can hope to win. To be in pursuit of justice is to try to set limits, whether or not they are true, correct, or genuine.

There is of course room for criticism of a particular set of limits. Such criticism will have support from groups that suffer from those limits. A new set of limits – a radical pattern of justice – will be implicit in such criticism. The Chinese revolutionaries had a glimpse of a just society when they rejected as inadequate the limits set by the old society. Everyone who struggles against the entrenched and arbitrary power of an existing order has a glimpse of justice. But to say this is not to say that the Chinese revolutionaries glimpsed true justice. They had found a pattern of justice that responded to the inadequacies of the prerevolutionary pattern in the circumstances of China at that time.

The pattern of justice the Chinese glimpsed was a program of land use and of industrial production that promised to end the abuses and suffering that had affected the vast majority. It was not a program that could be adapted to all circumstances. In particular, it was not a program that would meet the expectations of economic and political equality that are frequently articulated in advanced industrial democracies within the official trade union movements. Expectations of economic equality would be disappointed by the fact that in the People's Republic the range from top to bottom pay in many sectors and occupations remained as wide as or wider than in various industrialized capitalist countries.[1] And expectations of political equality would be disappointed by the fact that mass organizations were actually transmission belts from the Communist Party to the masses rather than vehicles by which the masses formulated policy.[2]

The pursuit of justice is not restricted to revolutionary situations. In the United States, for example, limits on losses and benefits are widely acknowledged, often enforced, and sometimes strengthened. They may not be true justice, but they are important because they originated when unrequited interest boiled over in outrage. Outrage alone did not set the limits because they had to wait for struggles and negotiations with conflicting parties. The compromises made in this process led to limits that were weaker than those who had been outraged would have liked. Still, they have the role of a pattern of justice, and insisting on these limits is the way the U.S. government pursues justice.

3

2. Stable rule

That may not seem controversial, but what I am about to say will surely seem so. The role of justice in a state is to set limits, but could a state decide to pursue no limits on losses and benefits? Is the role of justice optional for a state? Every state depends on force to rule, and some depend on it more than others. No state, though, can rely on force to such a degree that meaningful limits on benefits and losses are eradicated. Such a state would damage its ability to reproduce its society and would then lose the support it needs for stable rule. Every state that does not indulge a self-destructive impulse attempts to realize a pattern of justice.

In assessing this claim, it is well to keep three things in mind. First, the pattern of justice a state adopts will be one that serves its needs for stability in relation to the pressures it faces. If its justice is less strict than that of some other state, this is no reason for saying that it has no pattern of justice. Second, as we shall see in Part Two, a state's pattern of justice is more than the pattern of practices of its courts. Justice in the broad sense goes beyond the judiciary. A state's pattern of justice will also include the administering of distribution through executive agencies. Third, a pattern of justice may disarm dissent without eliminating dissatisfaction. So a pattern of justice may be seen as grudging and narrow even by those it makes governable.

Though required by the state, justice sets the state at odds with itself. Pursuing justice is one side of the state, but the other side is supporting a social order with its component economy. Of themselves, most economies place no limits on the way they benefit the dominant group within them. There is then a potential conflict between pursuing justice and supporting an economy. This conflict is the basis for the numerous ways in which the state is pulled in opposite directions. Through its pursuit of justice the state gains a normative dimension that coexists uncomfortably with its economic functioning. Familiar forms of materialist reductionism overlook the way the state is restricted from within by a normative conception of justice.

This normative dimension of a state is to be made sense of in terms of its citizens' social, economic, and political circumstances. We need only consider the fact that to be ruled a people needs a certain degree of cohesiveness made possible by limits on the behavior of conflicting subunits. Through the efforts of unifiers, these limits come to function as social or political norms. State rule by itself calls for limits on the degree to which a dominant minority can reduce the economic and political power of the majority. Without these limits, the state loses its legitimacy in the eyes of the majority and becomes vulnerable to insurrectionary efforts. (In addition to limits coming from pressures by dominated groups, there are also limits that unify factions within a dominant group and those that restrict actions on dominated groups among themselves.)

Why then is the normative dimension of the state not reducible to a material base? If a state's norms of justice help it to rule, then since the state functions to keep the social organism healthy, justice helps the state to function as it should. Suppose that the preeminent task in keeping the social organism healthy is that of keeping the society's characteristic economy flourishing. Then it will be tempting to conclude that rules of justice are no more than moral translations of economic laws.[3] Yet this is the kind of materialist reduction that I said fails to explain the normative dimension of the state. It fails because of the potential for conflict between the limits imposed by a pattern of justice that successfully legitimates the state's rule and the inequalities – of goods and of rights – that allow the economy to flourish. It is always an open question whether the pattern of justice needed to avoid ungovernability will conform to the requirements of keeping the economy flourishing.

To illustrate the idea that ruling requires justice, consider the hypothetical case of a society of purely self-interested individuals. A state for such a society cannot play a large role without trammeling individual self-interest. But it would not be respected at all if it failed to insure that the fewest possible obstacles to the pursuit of individual self-interest are allowed. The state's pattern of justice is then a pattern of limiting interference with self-interest. This state pursues the realization of a pattern of justice conforming to the libertarian ideal. The core of this pattern is equal liberty, since benefits and losses are limited only by the stricture that they not result from trammeling liberty.

The pattern of justice in contemporary Western society is, of course, more complex. The universal pursuit of individual self-interest is modified by the interests of organizations; the interests of enterprises and institutions become a basis for an acceptable subordination of individual self-interest. Still, limits are needed on how far organizations can subordinate individual interests. The state has the job of applying those limits if its rule is to be recognized as legitimate.

A pattern of justice emerges here that, on the one hand, allocates

5

decision-making power to those with demonstrated ability to build enterprises and institutions and to show loyalty to them.[4] There is no call for a devolution of decision-making power to the masses of the people. The same pattern, on the other hand, puts limits on the losses people are to suffer from enterprises and institutions. There is to be a safety net for those laid off by companies, for those hurt at work, and for those whose wages give them nothing for retirement. Together these factors constitute the elitist welfarism characteristic of the pattern of justice of many contemporary Western states.

3. Rationalism

What good, though, is the pursuit of justice if it is not true justice? The role of justice is to set limits, but we are interested in correct limits. My friend must have been saying that China was pursuing something closer to the true standard of justice. There are several points to be made about this. First, the method of pursuing true justice is fraught with familiar pitfalls. Second, the pursuit of justice can be quite important even if we lack the knowledge that it is true justice.

On the first point, which is about method, we note that national patterns of justice, such as those of China and the United States, can be discovered in the behavior of those nations. We can quarrel over what details belong to those patterns of justice, but we have some idea of where to go to try to settle these disputes. We simply look at the arrangements controlling political power and the distribution of resources. When it comes to true justice, however, we can only appeal to something philosophers have called reason. When there are disputes about this true standard, such as the dispute between Plato and Aristotle over justice, rational reflection is the only recourse. Certainly, we want to think straight about justice, and in this sense there is a need to be rational in disputes about justice and what it is. The rationalist, though, is making the stronger claim that reason can give us an assurance that a conception of justice – which may have historical roots in a concrete social situation – can be projected as the true standard.

An appeal to reason of this sort is akin to the kind of appeal to reason in the sciences that has long since been abandoned. Consider, for example, Kant's rationalism. He quite consistently fitted out the mind with an ability to know the basic principles of physics quite apart from confirmation in experience at the same time that he gave it an ability to know the basic principles of morality quite apart from confirmation in experience. Subsequent revolutions in science made it inappropriate to hold an apriorism in regard to physics. Yet the view of mind that makes apriorism appropriate for a given subject matter tends to make it appropriate for any other subject matter not fundamentally distinguished from it. Surely, it will be said, morals and physics are basically different. The problem is, though, that recent trends in moral theory point to the difficulty of distinguishing morality fundamentally from physics by any of the standard marks – subjectivity, unconfirmability, nondescriptivity, and egocentricity.[5] So once the rationalist method is abandoned in physics there is no firm basis for continuing to support it in morality.

Attempts have nonetheless been made to save the idea of a true justice by modifying rationalism. Rawls, for example, thinks that a back-and-forth process between critical reflection and our intuitive sense of what is right will lead us to an equilibrium in which we are satisfied that we have hit upon the universal principles of justice.[6] Even this modified rationalism is dubious. How do we show that there is but a *single* equilibrium point? A lot will depend on where – in terms of nation, culture, and class – we start. Each starting point will have an aura of assumptions that will not be removed by critical reflection in moving to equilibrium. If we start with the intuitions associated with a North American pattern of justice, it seems unlikely that equilibrium will be reached with a revolutionary Chinese sense of justice. So there is really no alternative to reverting to the dubious, unmodified rationalism if what we want is a single overarching standard of justice.

On the point about the importance of limits, we note that the rationalist expresses the connection between justice and the state by noting that most states are not pursuing a just order, that is, *the* just order. In the rationalist view, states as they actually exist generally have little to do with justice, for it is only the ideal state, or a state tending toward it, that pursues justice. An uncrossable gulf thus opens up in political ethics between justice and actual states. Pursuing justice becomes too tall an order for an institution that merely helps concentrate the power of a minority. However, if we do not insist on the rationalist view of justice, the gulf between actual states and justice closes up. Justice becomes an important aspect of any state. Each state can then be seen as an institution that organizes society along lines that set limits to the losses and benefits allowed to any group within it. This limit-setting feature of states is realized, in one form or another, in states of all epochs.

The focus of this book will be the form it takes only among contemporary states.

There is more, though, to the importance of justice than its being an aspect of the state. It is also the residue of struggles to end domination, and it is thus important as a partial fulfillment of the demands of the dominated. In addition to this official justice, there is also a radical justice based on unfulfilled interests. Radical justice is espoused by those who are unwilling to let popular demands go unmet simply to preserve stable rule. Official justice can be criticized from the perspective of radical justice even when the latter cannot claim to be true justice on a rationalist basis. Radical justice, then, serves a vital role quite independently of whether it is true justice. (Only in Part Five will my main focus be on radical justice.)

The view that justice is a set of limits serving governability is merely schematic. It tells us justice is a set of limits without specifying a specific set. Rationalist accounts strive for more specificity than is desirable here, where we want to identify the quite different sets of limits on benefits and losses enforced by distinct states as constituting so many patterns of justice. Furthermore, in the schematic view, there are no specific restrictions on the range of limits within which justice is to hold the benefits of the fortunate and the losses of the hapless. Instead, there is the general restriction that the limits on benefits and losses are to fall within a range that promotes governability in the circumstances in question. This restriction does, though, mark my view of justice as political rather than merely social. Even radical justice is political since it not only advances the interests of the dominated but does so in a way that limits the losses of other groups in order to promote stable rule.

Limits on losses and benefits are genuine norms. So our non-rationalist view allows us to preserve the normative element in classical rationalist theories of the state. Empirical political theory came to think it necessary to abandon the normative element, since this element suggested either the rationalist theory of the ideal state or a subjectivist view of political ethics. Thus an anti-normative tradition began that either, in the manner of behavioral science, adopted a positivist approach to the actions of the state or else, in the manner of structuralist Marxists, undertook to derive the state's actions from a limited list of relations within it while leaving little room for the agency of popular movements. In each case the normative component was effectively abandoned. But it is not necessary to abandon the normative element in order to steer clear of both rationalism and subjectivism.

4. Beyond group interest

Do we really need a normative dimension to avoid a one-sided view of the state? Let me recall a few truisms about ruling. They are truisms that ruling groups have twisted in order to entrench their domination. But it is dangerous to forget them when we think about the state. (These truisms should be interpreted in light of the materialist political theory of Part One.)

One of the things that qualify a group for ruling is its willingness to take an interest in the society as a whole. This calls for an effort to cross lines of conflict to win acceptance for a uniform set of limits on the benefits and losses of all conflicting parties. This effort leads to granting rights to a multiplicity of social tendencies and thus leads beyond an unrestricted class egoism. An adjustment of the various parts of the whole society into a recognizable order results from the application of such a set of limits.[7] The attempt to rule without setting such limits would give those who are deprived no hope of avoiding greater deprivation and would thus create a breeding ground for militant dissent. The normative dimension of the state – the pattern of justice it pursues – is a set of obligatory limits on benefits and losses that adjust the various parts of the society in the direction of cohesiveness.

From Aristotle came this idea that political stability is the reason the state is linked with justice. A political constitution that considers the common interest was for him a genuine constitution since it establishes a share – though not necessarily an equal share – in the goods of the society for members of all groups. Constitutions that consider only the personal interests of the rulers were for him perversions incapable of sustaining a stable rule.[8]

From Gramsci came the related idea that, outside exceptional circumstances, a group could not become a ruling group in the first place if its program were blatantly a self-interested one. To become a ruling group, a group cannot appeal to the nation simply to rally around its economic interests when it happens to be an economically dominant group, or to rally around its interest in religious authority when it happens to be a dominant priestly caste. It must present itself as a group concerned with the cohesion of society as a whole, without of course undercutting its own parochial interests while it sets the limits for benefits and losses needed to realize this cohesion. A group that can be seen by the society as advancing this cohesion is what Gramsci called a hegemonic group. There was for Gramsci a qualitative difference between a dominant group's interests considered by themselves and those same interests coordinated with a subordinate group's interests under the hegemony of the dominant group.[9] A hegemonic group curbs its interests within the pattern of justice it has adopted. And this qualitative difference is reflected in the difference between being merely a dominant group in the society – masters over slaves, priests over flocks, owners over workers – and being a ruling group.

We reach the conclusion that a normative dimension is not optional for states. A pattern of justice is inherent in states since they need a mechanism of stability and a ruling group to run them. The examination of the patterns of justice of states in regard to the general conditions in which they arise and are applied – their relation to the functions of states and to the conflicts of groups – I shall call *political ethics*. Any theory of the state that is not hopelessly one-sided will have political ethics as a component. Moreover, a political ethics cannot be developed without developing the other elements of a theory of the state, since one is led to these other elements from the general conditions of patterns of justice. Political ethics is then one route to a theory of the state, and it is the route I choose here.

Despite all this, the tendency remains to think of only the exceptional, the admirable, or the model state in terms of justice. U.S. defense secretary Caspar Weinberger put it bluntly in a debate in 1984 with British disarmament activist E. P. Thompson before the Oxford Union.[10] He said the Soviet Union makes a travesty of morality by identifying morality with Soviet power, whereas the United States distinguishes power from principle and operates in the world on the basis of principle. The comparison suffers from the same one-sidedness as that between China and the United States. It involves that one-sided view of states that results from considering them apart from their constitutive requirement for attempting cohesion. In the USSR no less than in the United States, ruling, at home and abroad, calls for putting limits on losses and benefits. (Weinberger's self-serving comparison reminds us that, at least in an age of imperialism, a state's pattern of justice will involve not just the coordination of domestic interests but also, as discussed in Part Four, the coordination of global interests, through setting limits on losses and benefits.) It is understandable that Weinberger's partisanship should lead him to reduce the pattern of justice of a state he regards with hostility to the interests of its dominant group. In sum, while we should be sensitive to the way a pattern of justice legitimates and leaves intact certain interests of a dominant group, we must not ignore the fact that the coordination of the interests of a dominant group with those of subordinate groups through the imposition of limits introduces genuine checks on the dominant group.

Getting to a theory of the state by the route of political ethics helps to build a bridge from pre-state to state societies. Headmen, elders, ritual kings, or bigmen in pre-state societies are engaged in various ways with justice. Some only assist in the effort to reach a compromise between two clans after, say, a member of one has killed a member of the other.[11] Others go a step farther, actually using their moral authority in a dispute to get the settlement they want. Still others act as instruments of distributive justice through feasts prepared by their loyal followers.[12] The patterns of justice applied by these headmen or elders are deeply rooted in their societies' views about the appropriate occasions for seeking compromise, for vengeance, for compensation through seizing property, and for distribution.

The roles of headmen or elders in social cohesion get carried over to the state and expanded there. These roles are expanded in several ways in the state. First, in the state the systematic use of physical force becomes available to political authorities for enforcing decisions that in many pre-state situations depended for enforcement on the action of social peers. Second, the pattern of justice advanced by the state is partly a creation of the state itself rather than just a reflection of the mores of the society. Third, in the state the possibility emerges for the first time of a conflict between the limits imposed by justice and the goals of the dominant group in the society, which goals the state functions to promote. This conflict is vital for understanding the state.

5. Form and function

The possibility of such a conflict between the state's justice and its promoting the goals of the dominant group makes it difficult to see how the state could be accounted for in terms of these goals alone. For the goals the state functions to promote may suffer a restricted realization or no realization at all in view of the set of limits on benefits and losses defining the state's justice. It is a mistake, then,

11

to treat the ruling class and the state through which it rules as omnipotent in regard to realizing the long-term interests of the socially dominant class.[13] There is instead a dialectic within the state between the requirements to be met for stable rule and the goals that ruling is to promote.

I shall employ the working hypothesis that preeminent among the goals ruling is to promote is that of reproducing the economy. It is through reproducing the economy that the socially dominant class retains its dominance. In view of this preeminence, I shall often speak of the state's function of reproducing the economy, instead of its function of reproducing the society, without thereby implying that other possible functions simply dissolve into this one.

There is no implication, though, that the state's justice lacks functional value altogether. If justice stabilizes ruling and ruling in turn promotes the economy, then indeed justice functions to promote the economy, or at least some restricted part of it compatible with justice. But the link between justice and the economy is indirect, being mediated by the state. We cannot then say without additional qualification that the justice of a capitalist state exists because it functions to reproduce a capitalist society. This would ignore the important fact that it has this functioning through the state. This cannot be ignored since it is because justice has this function indirectly that there is the possibility it might be dysfunctional in regard to aspects of reproducing capitalism. (Later, in Part Three, I shall explain this indirect functionality by saying that state justice plays a second-order functional role whereas state reproduction of the economy plays a first-order functional role.)

Yet another factor is involved in complicating a functional account of state justice. This is the pressure from dominated groups that normally serves as the source of patterns of justice. It is this pressure from below that forces a ruling group to show concern for the social totality. How, though, does this complicate the account? Any functional account needs to rely not just on goals but also on agencies. The agencies here are the dominated groups acting on the basis of their own values, values expressing not just their position in the economy but also their cultural position. When these values conflict with the demands of reproducing the economic system, such groups act on the basis of these values to press for limits on benefits and losses.[14] Clearly, then, the pressure that brings about a pattern of justice is not a mere reflex of the goal of economic reproduction. It is rather a response to that goal based on a set of values

12

reflecting the positions of the dominated groups. The limits coming from state justice are in part determined by the values of groups whose pressure threatens stable rule.

Very little illumination and a lot of confusion result, then, from saying that there is state justice because it functions to reproduce the economy. First, state justice may be in conflict with reproducing the economy. Second, state justice is never directly but only indirectly functional for the economy through the rest of the state. And third, state justice is in part a product of the values of dominated groups. For these reasons it is useful to think of justice as that part of the state that contributes form to the function the state has of reproducing the economy. Through this form limits are put on that function.

Part One

An outline of a materialist political theory

The best course would seem to be to deal directly with the questions raised in the Introduction. But to deal with them in a fruitful way requires some background. To explain patterns of justice, I shall use a form of explanation that refers to a basic level of social structure plausibly called material. So much, though, has gone under the name of materialistic explanation that the key concepts have long since lost any firm meaning. To move ahead requires that the concepts be redeemed. Only in Part Two will I return to questions about justice.

The view of explanation put forward in Part One posits two tiers. Historical narrative, replete with agents and their effects, belongs to one of the tiers. The other tier is less often appealed to, but it is perfectly obvious from a consideration of the natural sciences. It is the tier of structures lying behind sequences of agents and effects. It is inappropriate to speak of these structures as themselves agents, and it is important to distinguish the way structures determine things from the way agents do.

To call a form of explanation materialist will be taken here to be a claim about structure rather than agency. It is a kind of explanation that uses a material structure for its second tier, whatever the agencies might be. There is then no requirement that agencies ultimately be cut from the same cloth as the structure; so materialist explanation, in the sense used here, does not imply that everything is generated immediately or ultimately by material agencies of a designated kind. A direct application of this two-tiered view of explanation will be made in interpreting the idea that the state is relatively autonomous from the economy.

1

A challenge to materialism

In the 1960s the appeal to state autonomy became popular as a refutation of the materialist account of the state. This refutation focused on state activities that appear to go beyond the demands of any system that could plausibly be called material, whether environmental, technological, or economic. A pattern of justice itself would seem to contribute to state autonomy.

It is worth looking at this criticism from autonomy in order to see whether my plan to treat the state within a materialist theory is feasible. But instead of starting with justice, I shall take the case of the nuclear and conventional arms race between the United States and the Soviet Union between the 1950s and the 1980s. This will be theoretically – though certainly not politically – more manageable than the much broader case of justice itself. It has been widely noted that the spiraling arms production after 1949 is a challenge to a materialist view of the state because the spiral has climbed upward with a logic that seems to be its own. The arms race is, I shall show, a challenge to an atomist form of materialism but not to the form I shall adopt.

1. The independence of the arms race

Despite modest reductions in limited areas such as those called for by the Intermediate Nuclear Forces Treaty of 1988, the arms race looks uncontrolled and pointless in relation to interests outside itself. Thus it is hard to imagine tying it down within any materialist perspective: It is not called for to overcome environmental depletion, nor is its existence explained by the need for a more productive technology, nor, as we shall see, does it seem to have been prescribed to overcome the stagnation in either the capitalist or the communist systems. Of course, materialist accounts of a specific legal system or of the geographical boundaries within which a given state claims a monopoly of administration were never con-

16

structed from a mathematically precise formula. But the advantages provided even by less precise accounts in unifying our understanding of the state around a single familiar field – environmental science, technology, or economics – made it difficult to claim a decisive victory against materialism. That is why the seeming absurdity of the arms race from any of these perspectives constitutes such an interesting case against materialism.

E. P. Thompson has summed it up with the claim that the arms race, whatever its initial origins, has taken on a logic of its own, a logic that he thinks leads towards extermination.[1] He is particularly concerned to refute Marxist accounts of the arms race, even though he might credit such attempts with a reasonable degree of success in regard to military buildups in the prenuclear world. The production of large numbers of battleships just before World War I might have been explained by the expansion of private capital beyond national boundaries. Now, though, the appeal to imperialism fails, Thompson believes, because the offshore expansion of capital is not served by the development and deployment of ever more sophisticated nuclear systems.

For the foreseeable future, neither major power can launch a disarming attack on the other, and hence the continued strengthening of nuclear systems is not now warranted on the basis of either side's vulnerability to military defeat on a first strike. If one side should decide to use nuclear weapons, more than enough nuclear weapons would survive on the other side for a damaging retaliatory response. So from Thompson's perspective the arms race is a manifestation of irrationalism and thus fails to have an explanation through rational interests of the sort operative in traditional materialist political explanations.

The arms race becomes, for him, a matter of political posturing among states, a posturing that their citizens learn to accept, not because it serves important interests but because of cold-war ideology.[2] This in effect ascribes to one level of state activity a total independence from the rest of the society. Any moorings in the material world of environmental, technological, or class interests have been cut. The cohesiveness of all levels of activity that was provided by a materialist account is lost, and the social world fractures into a multiplicity of independent realms. In particular, the political posturing of the arms race has little to do with efforts by multinational financial and industrial enterprises to bind less developed nations into economic dependency.

2. Atoms versus contexts

How should we judge this refutation of materialism? On the side of content we need to ask whether it is true that the arms race is irrational, transcending all familiar interests. On the other side, the side of form, we need to ask whether the nature of a materialist account has been properly represented. If it has not, then even an "irrational" arms race might be within the reach of a materialist account. I happen to disagree with Thompson both in regard to content and in regard to form, but in order to stick to the topic of materialist method I will focus on the disagreement about form. (The question of content – of the irrationality of the arms race – will be dealt with in due course, in Chapter 19.)

A great deal of confusion has been created about the idea of explanation as a result of modern atomistic philosophy. Its underlying theme has been that explanations take place in terms of isolated factors rather than in terms of systems in which these factors were embedded. Thus what a person does is to be explained exclusively in terms of his or her preferences and interactions with other people without reference to the kind of social system to which they all belong. This denigration of the contextual element in explanation requires that factors in abstraction from any context be an adequate basis for explanation.[3]

This theme had a disastrous effect in political theory when it was used to interpret the modern materialist approach to political phenomena. In place of the divine right of kings, the materialist approach grounded sovereignty in the interests of property. In place of the Hegelian concept of freedom, the materialist approach grounded the modern state in the interests of commerce. On the atomist interpretation, the materialism of these modern explanations derives from their making mundane factors the causal agencies behind rights and institutions. The atomist interpretation rejects the view, to be adopted here, that materialism is a commitment to providing a mundane context for whatever agencies bring about sovereignty and the modern state. The effort to eschew divine rights and Hegelian concepts was misinterpreted by atomism, turning materialism into a thesis about what kinds of factors could act as causal agents. In particular, Marxian materialism was interpreted as the thesis that economic factors had to be adduced as either the immediate or the ultimate causal agencies for a satisfactory explanation of political phenomena.[4]

It is, I suspect, this atomist interpretation of Marxian materialism that is behind Thompson's refutation of materialism based on the irrationality of the arms race. He thinks he has shown that there are no economic interests that could be the immediate or ultimate causal agency for the arms race. He is not denying that military contractors profit enormously from the arms race. Surely they do, but it is far from clear that their interests alone could turn vast resources over to an arms race that so many perceive as both dangerous and futile. For him there is no collection of economic interests that together generate the arms race. In fact, he says that a reassertion within the power elites of the United States and the USSR "of the claims of rational self-interest" would end the arms race.

Outside the atomist perspective, materialism can be interpreted to mean something strikingly different. The requirement that there be factors of a specific mundane sort – environmental, technological, or class – that act as the immediate or ultimate causal agents for political phenomenon would be dropped. This would loosen up materialism to allow that the particulars acting as immediate or ultimate causal agents could belong to *any* ontological level, rather than being restricted to a specific mundane level. The political posturing that fuels the arms race would then be perfectly acceptable as a causal agency within a materialist account, even though it is itself outside the levels of mundane activity preferred in the atomist interpretation of materialism and even though this political posturing may not be traceable to an ultimate causal agency within these levels of mundane activity. There would of course have to be a trade-off in order to preserve materialism. Instead of restricting the levels to which immediate or ultimate agents belong, some other aspect of explanation – the contextual one – would have to be restricted. The atomist kind of explanation relies on isolated agents and thus lacks this contextual aspect. To preserve the materialist character of explanation of the nonatomist kind, this contextual aspect will have to be restricted to a selected level of mundane activity.

This broader view of explanation is elaborated in the next chapter, but it is worth fleshing out here Thompson's criticism of materialism to make clearer the failings of atomistic materialism. These failings will put my contextual interpretation of materialism in a more favorable light. This interpretation makes materialism compatible with the state's having autonomy in relation to those kinds of mundane factors that are picked out as the only immediate or ultimate causes by atomistic materialism.

19

3. Economist atomism

One of the commonest views of spiraling arms spending is that it functions to absorb what would otherwise be inevitable over-capacity, an inevitable ability to produce more than can be profitably sold. Without military demand, considerable productive capacity would go unutilized.[5] The Great Depression showed that the Western economic system had a tendency toward overcapacity strong enough to resist most corrective mechanisms. It was only the arms economies of the late 1930s that set the stage for economic recovery. And had an arms economy not been continued after World War II something similar to the Great Depression would have returned. On this account, today's arms race is the result, on the one hand, of the quite rational wish of the capitalist class to avoid permanent economic stagnation and, on the other hand, of the competitive instinct of the Soviet leadership to keep abreast militarily.

So interpreted, the arms race can be viewed like a dam used for flood control. There was a time when the valley flooded periodically, washing out roads, bridges, and houses. These events were the stimulus for building a dam upstream that would contain the spring runoff. The floods no longer occurred, and now there are funds for maintaining the dam so that they will never occur again. The dam and the subsequent funding for maintaining it came about because of those earlier floods in conjunction with a widespread interest in avoiding flooding in the future.

Likewise, the Great Depression was a stimulus to making the arms economy permanent. This stimulus along with an interest in avoiding industrial overcapacity generated the arms race we know today. The Great Depression got the thing going, and the interest in avoiding overcapacity in the future kept it going by winning large appropriations for military production from the U.S. Congress each year. Past economic events and present economic interests provide the materialist basis needed for the arms race.[6]

This analogy points to a difficulty with this economist interpretation of the arms race. We can see that the dam is needed even after it is preventing floods by noting the rise of the water level behind it every spring. There is, though, no obvious check for the effectiveness of an arms economy. We can only talk hypothetically about the overcapacity that *would* have resulted had it not been for the military utilization of capacity. There ought to be some way to have a concrete check on this counterfactual claim.

Can we check it by referring to recessions? Arms spending packs a punch in shortening recessions. But these downswings are short to begin with. It is chronic stagnation and the impact of a permanent rather than a merely cyclical arms economy on it that we are discussing here. We are then dealing with a period sufficiently long to allow for countervailing effects. These effects may even negate the tendency of permanent arms spending to absorb overcapacity.

A more promising way to check our counterfactual is to compare the situation in the United States with that in states that have stayed out of the arms race. Japan no doubt also faces a threat of overcapacity, but it has a low military budget. It has dealt with that threat in a nonmilitary way by aggressive market expansion through export promotion. So the threat of overcapacity, which is characteristic of the capitalist system, does not simply by itself generate high levels of military spending. Where there is the threat of overcapacity it is only one factor among other – possibly noneconomic – factors that become relevant to arms spending. In the twenty years between 1960 and 1980, Japan's military spending was 1 percent of its gross domestic product whereas for the United States it was 8 percent. This made it possible for the Japanese to increase their industrial capacity more rapidly by investing 33 percent of their gross domestic product as against 18 percent invested in the United States between 1960 and 1980. Despite Japan's growing industrial capacity, it enjoyed a high level of capacity utilization with low military budgets.

Moreover, the recession of 1981–2 did not affect Japan worse than it did the United States, even though Japan had not absorbed a sizable part of its growing capacity in a military economy. True, Japan had to rebuild its industrial plant after World War II, and this made any hypothesis about the dangers of overcapacity irrelevant for that initial period. But the comparison with the United States has validity during the more recent period in which Japan had become an economic power. None of this denies that the threat of overcapacity had some role in sustaining American arms production, but it played that role only while linked to other, possibly noneconomic, factors.

In fact, some of the other factors turn out to be political and ideological. In accounting for the arms race one can hardly leave out either great-power rivalry, which is a political factor, or the ideology of inevitable hostility between rival states. But if these factors are needed to complement economic ones in providing an adequate account of the arms race, economic atomism must be abandoned.

4. Theory of ideology

Adding the political and ideological means different things under atomist and contextualist interpretations. Within the atomist perspective accepted by Thompson, there seems to be a strong case for the view of multicausalism, understood as calling not simply for many particular causes but instead for many *kinds* of particular causes. So, instead of restricting causes to the economic, to the political, or to the ideological, one adopts the catholic attitude of admitting economic, political, and ideological causes.[7] Multicausalism is usually assumed by the critics of reductionist monocausalism to be the last word, but unless they embed multicausalism within contextualism they stand rightly accused of an unsystematic eclecticism. For the moment, though, I shall focus not on this criticism but on the introduction of the political and the ideological factors. I shall start by focusing on ideological factors, since as part of the multicausal explanatory account their presence often involves the presence of political factors as well.

It is interesting that the arms economy today in the United States is rarely justified by its advocates on purely economic grounds. There is generally an appeal couched in cold-war ideology, an ideology emphasizing national security in the face of what is conceived as the Soviet threat. For atomist materialists this appeal to ideology introduces literally nothing new, since ideology is only a product of material factors. Cold-war ideology is, with no ado, reduced to a product of the chronic crisis of late capitalism.

The problem with this reduction is that, if ideology were an artifact of the material factors that stimulate it, it would lack its referential flexibility. What am I calling its referential flexibility? First, an ideology relates people to real circumstances; the kind of relation involved is a referential one; an ideology is about the circumstances to which it relates us. Second, these circumstances need not themselves be economic but may be political or cultural, implying that ideology is flexible enough to relate us to any of a variety of domains.

This referential flexibility is illustrated by the cold-war ideology. Even if it is the economic crisis of late capitalism that triggers

22

cold-war ideology, that ideology goes beyond this crisis by relating people to the political reality of underlying conflict between the United States and the USSR. In our small world the interests of the two superpowers get in one another's way. The ideology thus relates us to a reality of political conflict.

Of course, the cold-war ideology relates us to this conflictive reality in a certain way, one that exacerbates tensions. The manner of the reference to circumstances fixes attitudes and behavior. This manner of reference is a feature not of the ideas of classical theory of knowledge but of a social practice or institution that as a concrete medium embodies symbolic content. In general, the way we are related to reality by an ideology reflects certain dominant interests, not necessarily compatible with our own. Yet this does not make that to which the ideology relates us any less real.[8] Exclusive concentration on the manner in which we are referred by ideologies to reality has led to the view that ideologies are constructed out of whole cloth. This ignores the referential aspect in order to bring the manipulative aspect into focus.

Because ideology is referential, it never enters into explanation alone. It always points beyond itself to the reality to which it relates people. Since cold-war ideology relates them to the political reality of conflict between the United States and the USSR, this reality is drawn into any explanation in which cold-war ideology is already one of the explanatory factors. Political conflict is introduced into the explanation of the arms race by the very fact that the cold-war ideology is a part of the explanation.

All this seems obvious from the general fact that we often do not even bother to include an ideological view explicitly in an explanation where we actually appeal to it; instead, we go directly to the reality to which it relates people. Consider an explanation of support for capitalism among workers on the basis of the ideology of the unity of interests between classes. As applied to the capitalist system, this ideology relates people to the real fact that the dispossessed must sell their labor to the possessors in order to live. Yet, rather than saying that support for capitalism within the working class comes from the ideology of the unity of interests of classes, we elide the explanation, going directly to the necessity of wage labor for the dispossessed.

It makes no sense to say that ideologies enter explanations generally only as linguistic or behavioral capacities, for it is not these that elucidate the actions people take under the influence of ideologies. Elucidating their actions will depend, in a crucial way, on what the referents of the ideologies are. Suppose we leave out the reference to a political rival in appealing to the cold-war ideology when explaining the arms race. We are left then with an objectless sense of being threatened and an unmotivated need to be secure behind an arsenal. It is only if there is a specific political rival to which I am related by the ideology that this threat and this need are made definite enough to elucidate my support for arms competition.

Let us examine in more detail how the use of cold-war ideology introduces more than the economist factor of crisis control. Cold-war ideology points realistically to a conflict between the dominant classes of the United States and the USSR; the dominant class in each nation derives its power from social relations that would be undercut by the dominant class in the other nation. Capitalists, for example, would undercut the state property on which the power of the Soviet elite is based. So the dominant class in each nation resists the spread of social relations of the kind promoted by the dominant class of the other. Moreover, cold-war ideology realistically points to the fact that neither form of society will ultimately flourish if the other flourishes, since flourishing calls for each to expand its influence globally. Having been backed into its corner of the globe, the Soviet economy, for example, is more vulnerable to encircling capitalist pressures. The state as an instrument of force is naturally called on to prevent a constriction of influence and to allow for flourishing. Direct or indirect military conflict can be avoided at the periphery of expansion only with utmost caution. All these aspects of underlying conflict to which people are related by cold-war ideology enter into the explanation of the arms race. (The ideology relates them to these possibilities of conflict in a manner that exacerbates tensions rather than promotes caution.) Yet these aspects of conflict are political factors that go well beyond a purely economist account of the arms race with its focus on preventing economic crises. These political factors are introduced into an explanation of the arms race along with its appeal to the ideology of the cold war.

Ideology is a dangerously misleading word if we ignore its many interpretations. First, for the atomist materialist the word will be taken to mean a set of beliefs and institutions entirely reducible to economic factors. The reduction is twofold: (1) ideology exists as a product of economic stimuli; (2) if it has a referential aspect, only the economic is referred to. So state competition as an element of truth in cold-war ideology would be incompatible with this interpretation of ideology, unless state competition is itself only the acting out of purely economic forces in political costumes. If the first reduction – one of cold-war ideology to an origin in economic stimuli – is troublesome, this fallback position that appeals to the second reduction – the one of the reference to a competition between states to a reference to a play of economic forces – is even more problematic. At stake in this competition are the power of states and that of their dominant classes. As we shall see, power of these kinds is best understood within an economic context, but it is not the same as an economic force (Chapters 10 and 12).

Second, the word still implies a reference to a reality, but not the twofold reduction. It is in this sense that I think of ideology. On the one hand, the production of ideological conceptions and institutions is more complex than is implied by the model of reduction to economic stimuli. Multiple kinds of causes are allowed at the root of ideology, among which may be ideological causes themselves. Ideology can then be an additional factor over and above the economic in explaining political phenomena. On the other hand, ideology refers people to realities that need not be limited to economic ones. It will, in spite of this, function to serve the economic and political interest of dominant groups. These interests affect the ways ideology refers people to various realities without undercutting this reference itself.

Third, yet others choose to think of an ideology as what can be described as a signifying practice. This description is neutral in several ways: There is no specification of partisan interests to be served, and thus ideology is not inherently a weapon in a struggle. There is no specification of the causal history of ideology, and thus it is not inherently based in social factors, whether of one or of many types. The ideological is simply the meaningful in so broad a sense that even a reference to reality need not be required. This view, though neutral in itself, is compatible with an idealist interpretation of ideology as a perfectly autonomous realm.[9]

5. Beyond atomist materialism

Let us return from the theory of ideology to the use of ideology in the explanation of the arms race. Just how effective has ideology been in fueling the arms race from the U.S. side? The political coalition in the United States that has pushed through arms budgets since World War II has been not only one of the most powerful but also one of the most stable coalitions.[10] It is striking both for its sectoral diversity and for its basic unity of outlook. This

25

phenomenon, as we shall see, is inexplicable from the economist perspective. It confirms the crucial role of ideology and, behind it, of the political rivalry between great states in explaining the arms race.

On the one hand, there are the economist forces represented in the coalition: the large corporate contractors, congressmen looking for investments for their constituencies, universities tied to military research, union officials whose members' employment is tied to military contracts, and the Keynesian academic, business, and political bloc that sees government spending as the way out of the tendency to overcapacity. Military spending at a high level is viewed by these forces as a correct economic policy. For the coalition to be large enough to be effective, a way must be devised of winning others to it who are not convinced of the arms policy mainly on economic grounds. The nonmilitary corporations, the congressmen from rural areas, the nonresearch segment of the education sector, workers outside the military sector, and the non-Keynesian economists need to feel their interests are being advanced if they are to go along with high levels of military spending. What forces can bring them along?

Since it is so powerful and stable, the arms coalition will also include, on the other hand, representatives of the Pentagon, the Defense Department think tanks, the hawks in the Congress, the International Department of the AFL–CIO, the Committee on the Present Danger, the president, and the liberal and conservative media. This segment of the coalition is based on a rivalry between states with conflicting economic systems. Winning the struggle with the rival is seen by this segment as calling for a military buildup. To promote this buildup it has used an ideology that emphasizes national security in the face of the Soviet threat. There are divisions within this militarist segment of the coalition on the imminence of the danger faced by the United States and on the wisdom of modest arms control and disarmament measures. This division affects the pace and the directions of the arms buildup. But this segment of the coalition has successfully prevented any long period of decline in the absolute amount of military appropriations. There were declines for several years after the Korean War and for five years beginning with the winding down of the Vietnam War. Such postwar fatigue aside, the pattern has been one of sustained and rising military spending.

The cold-war ideology calling for national security in the face of the Soviet threat has readily been adopted for use by the economist

26

segment of the coalition as a support for its own goals. The use of cold-war ideology has thereby unified the economist and militarist wings of the coalition, providing them with a shield from official and unofficial opposition to large arms expenditures. It would be a staggering job to try to show that the militarist segment of the arms coalition is nothing more or less than the creature of the economist segment. Admittedly, there are interactions and interlocks between the two segments. But it would take more than this to show that the articulation of a policy of national security is a product of the economic system in abstraction from all ideological and political admixture.

Even the concept of the state, which is needed for cold-war ideology, will never enter the consciousness of humans confined to an abstract economic existence. Behind this lies the fact that no economic force, however complex, will bring the state, rather than merely further economic forces, into existence. Yet, when cold-war ideology speaks of national security in the face of the Soviet state, it presupposes the political reality of a network of states, a reality that no amount of juggling with production and overproduction will generate.

A similar argument refutes attempts to explain arms races on the basis of economic imperialism without the admission of a political level. An economy can expand around the globe when it pleases and never need protection by a military, provided it runs up against no organized political force. At present the relevant political forces are states with their well-understood ways of either collaborating or fighting back. Two purely economic systems, a capitalist and a centralist one, may be bewildered by finding one another as they advance through a politically virgin continent. Once their bewilderment gives way to defending themselves systematically against one another they no longer act as purely economic systems. The argument from imperialism for an arms race cannot then be purely economic but must assume states, or at least some rudimentary political organization.[11]

I conclude, then, that the sort of criticism Thompson has initiated in regard to the nuclear and conventional arms race does irreparable damage to materialism of one sort. None of the mundane considerations that make an argument materialist gets very far in accounting for this arms race. He suggests that ideological and political considerations do play a useful role. His criticism opens up the possibility of explanations in which political, economic, and ideological factors are all relevant. As a consequence, a

27

successful materialist method cannot be one that limits the factors that act as stimuli to just a few kinds. Eclecticism is then called for when it comes to such causes. We must, though, go beyond this eclecticism in regard to stimuli and consider the nature of the contexts in which they act in order to get a genuine materialism.

2

A framework for the state

This chapter takes us farther down the road of the ontology behind social explanation. It would be nice if we could spare ourselves this discussion of basic entities and their interrelations. But those political theorists who take the easier way usually adopt an implicit ontology that they do not hesitate to use in rejecting views they disagree with. We saw a simple instance of this in E. P. Thompson's rejection of a materialist explanation of the arms race. His atomist ontology was needed if his criticism was to apply to materialism generally. In this chapter I propose an alternative to that atomist ontology.

1. A development in the theory of explanation

About the time I thought I was mastering the technicalities of the philosophy of explanation I came across an idea that made me think my efforts had been in vain. Much of the Anglo-American philosophy of the early 1950s was still under the spell of the great revolution in logic of the early part of the century. This meant that explanation was viewed as drawing the logical consequences of theoretical generalities. The ontological impact of this subsumptionist model was idealist in nature, since explanation started not with the world and its structures but with the rarefied realm of theoretical generalities. In a paper given in 1959, Wilfrid Sellars made the disturbing suggestion that all this was wrong.[1] There was a nice ring of commonsense Aristotelianism about his critique, for which I felt an affinity, but I was so disoriented by it that I was unable to put it to positive use right away. What Sellars had said was that explanation consists not of deducing empirical from theoretical generalizations but rather of showing that the structure of things is the basis for their obeying the empirical generalizations they do.

There was no assurance that a realist alternative would be one of the kind Sellars had proposed. Given the atomist tradition of

Anglo-American philosophy, the alternative might have been a strict empiricism. It might, that is, have been a rejection of the idea that an underlying theory can show how things obey the empirical generalizations they do in favor of the idea that the connections asserted in empirical generalizations are ultimate. In this way, explanation would reduce to noting that observable factors of a given kind tend to have certain other observable factors as preconditions. This resembles the atomist philosophy discussed in Chapter 1: Isolated factors stand on their own as causes of other factors, and, presumably, similar factors will have similar causal consequences. What Sellars was suggesting was not a return to this atomism of the earlier empiricist philosophers but the acceptance of a realism of a totally different sort. I take him to have been saying that factors of the sort recorded in an empirical generalization are connected as they are because they pertain to a system of a quite specific nature. These factors are no longer isolated but are embedded in the context of a system with a certain structure. Either the system or its inherent structure can be employed in explanation as a context for connections.

This appeal to context is no mere elaboration on the empiricist theme of dispensing with anything but factors in empirical generalizations. Yet that is what it would be if the context for connections were just one more circumstance along with others making up the antecedents of something to be explained. The appeal to context plays a different role in explanation. Context is not a second or third factor that gives a putative causal factor enough company to catalyze its acting as a cause. Positing a second or third factor is not providing a context; it is only adding more isolated factors. But adding factors is all the atomist philosopher knows how to do when called on to provide some context. Context for the atomist thinker is greater numbers and nothing more.

Yet, in the model of explanation proposed by Sellars, the context for generalities provided by a system or its inherent structure differs qualitatively, not just quantitatively, from the isolated factors recorded in a generality. The difference is that between a basis for a generality and a part of a generality, whereas a circumstance or a cause is part of a generality. The structure of salt is a basis for a generality linking immersion in water and dissolving, but immersion is only a part of that generality, not its basis.

We have here the clue we need to solve the problem facing materialism. In political theory, materialism has a rough time if it is interpreted to mean that explanations are to be given in terms merely of factors that are ultimately limited to some suitably materialist category – the economic, the technological, the environmental. Such an interpretation of materialism is, at the ontological level, *atomist* in that the factors appealed to in materialist explanations are in reality isolated from any *encompassing system* whose structure would control the kinds of connections these factors form among themselves. Moreover, it is, at the epistemological level, *empiricist* in that materialist explanation is taken to be possible on the basis of general claims about what factors are causally connected in the absence of an *overarching theory* that could be used to say how it comes about that these factors are causally connected with one another. In the absence of special restrictions, materialist atomism would dispose one to materialist empiricism, and conversely.[2]

The suggestion made by Sellars opens up the possibility of a materialism that is neither atomist nor empiricist. Such a materialism insists, on the ontological level, that causal connections between factors have systems as their context and, on the epistemological level, that the relevant feature of these systems is a structure that can be formulated in terms of a theory that is in fact a materialist theory. It is not necessary here to try to specify further the line between materialist and other kinds of theories.[3] An acceptable line would place the theory of real numbers on the nonmaterialist side and the kinetic theory of gases on the materialist side of the line. Likewise, the theory of the divine right of kings, as put forth by James I of England, would be nonmaterialist, whereas Jean Bodin's theory that the right of kings to govern comes from the patriarchal structure of the family, which was the predecessor of the state, was a materialist theory. My aim here is to respond to the challenge to materialism that came about solely because of the atomist and related empiricist interpretations of it.

2. Causal connections and structures

Focus for a while now on my claim about the importance of context. An immediate consequence is that causal connections are relative to systems. Strike a dry match in the presence of oxygen and it bursts into flame, but strike a dry wooden stick in the presence of oxygen and it does not burst into flame. The systems differ – a match versus a stick – and this makes a difference to the causal relationship. The difference is not to be described as a mere difference in circumstances accompanying the striking.

31

From the atomist perspective, though, the difference will always be described in this way, but then the benefit derived from treating it as I have suggested will not be forthcoming. The benefit lost is that of being able to say how it is that there is a causal connection in the first place. For if all we have are the circumstances surrounding the factor that plays the role of the cause, then we can at most say that this factor is a cause in those circumstances and not in some others. But we cannot yet say how this factor in those circumstances actually comes to function as a cause. The point of building theories has been precisely to say how factors in given circumstances do act as causes and in other circumstances lack efficacy. But if we follow the course of insisting that all the context there is comes from aggregating circumstances, then we take the road that ends with saying there is no deep structure to causation. This is the empiricist view that there is causation wherever repetition of an antecedent yields a regularity.

What feature of a system allows it to play the role of a context in explanation? A context is to provide an account of connections between events. A system's being of a certain kind is surely relevant to this role. So to say a system belongs to a certain kind contributes to an account of connections involving it. But it does so only because of the assumption that systems belonging to such a kind have a structure – known, partly known, or so far unknown – that would account for the connection.

Consider, for example, the consequences of a sudden increase in productive capacity within the economy as a whole. After World War II productive capacity increased rapidly in both the older industrial nations and the nations of the periphery and of the third world. Nonetheless, the 1970s saw the beginning of chronic under-utilization of the vast capacity generated within the capitalist segment of the world. Unemployment began to run at higher rates, the standard of living of the masses of the people returned to earlier levels, and efforts to reduce levels of poverty met with less success. We should avoid generalizing from this by claiming a universal connection between a rapidly increased productive capacity and a subsequent leveling off of welfare. What, though, can we claim?

Such a connection between increased productivity and a subsequent leveling off of welfare would be warranted for capitalist society in the recent period and as well for the 1920s and 1930s. But the connection would not have the same plausibility for an agrarian society of the feudal sort. Of course, rapid increases in productive capacity were not typical for European feudalism.

32

What, though, happened when productivity did increase rapidly from using new seeds, draining marshes, going to the three-field system, and migrating eastward? Was there subsequently an analogue of the contemporary leveling off of welfare?

Assume that the feudal towns are amply supplied with produce in the wake of one or more of these innovations and that hence prices move downward. The feudal lord or abbot is not going to pick up and move in order to produce where there are higher prices. For one thing, land is not yet a full-fledged commodity. It is more likely that there will be an intensification of work on the land in order to generate roughly the same revenue despite the lower prices. This intensification, which may lower prices even more, would take place whether the land is worked by serfs, hired labor, or lessees. Underutilization of capacity and increasing poverty would not result from improved productivity.

The estates of Christ Church Priory, Canterbury, intensified serf labor services when confronted with a decline of revenue from grain sales during an agricultural depression in Kent in the early fourteenth century.[4] The point of this intensification was to have revenues to cover the expenses of the feudal ruling class, rather than, as in capitalism, to have a rate of return worth investing for.

The two systems with these different causal connections are capitalism and feudalism. The former provides a context for causal connections from rapidly increased productive capacity to a deterioration of welfare, whereas the latter system fails to provide a context for such a causal relation. The difference is not that we call the systems by different names. Rather, each system has its characteristic structure, a structure that in the capitalist case includes the fact that productive factors, such as land, are marketable items and the further fact that labor will be allocated to production where it is most profitable. We study the economic structure of the two systems not to find distinctive causal agents but to find why one system makes possible a causal relation that the other does not.

3. The two tiers of the framework model

The difference between the atomist and the contextual approaches can be put by saying that explanation is two-tiered for the contextualist. Moreover, if with each tier we associate the idea of causation, then the contextualist has two sorts of causation. The first level is simply explanation by isolated factors. The factors that

33

make the causes at the first level of explanation shall be called *stimulus* causes since they induce, generate, provoke, call up, or create a need for something. They do not have to be antecedent agents and thus need not be what used to be called efficient causes. Some stimulus causes may instead be subsequent goals and thus may be what used to be called final causes. The atomistic type of outlook is not, then, limited just to antecedent causes but takes in situations involving teleology.

The second level of explanation is explanation by structures, which is not independent of the first level since structures do not explain factors in history directly but only why certain factors are caused by others. At this second level stimulus causes are replaced by what shall be called *structure* causes as the basic units of explanation. And the model of explanation that calls for both stimulus and structure causes can be dubbed the *framework* model of explanation since the structure of a system provides a framework for accounting for stimulus causation.

The atomist materialist is eager to say that material factors have priority over others at the level of stimulus causes, but the nonatomist materialist does not need to give priority to material stimuli. Nonatomist materialists can afford to take this open-minded stance since it is possible for them to maintain that the restrictions imposed by materialism apply only to the kind of structure appealed to in the system that provides the context. Such a contextual materialism will give rise to explanations by means of a materialist structure. It will account for stimulus causation involving causes of a psychological, religious, or cultural nature, causes that do not at all fit the atomists' narrow preconceptions of what is ultimately allowable in materialist explanations.

A materialist theory of this contextual sort is thus considerably more flexible than an atomist materialist theory. This will be true even for a more sophisticated atomist materialism than that refuted in Chapter 1. A more sophisticated version would hold that it is self-defeating to limit ultimate causes to ones of a specific materialist sort. But, it would add, there is still an asymmetry that gives primacy to materialist causes at the level of stimuli. The asymmetry is probabilistic in nature: Events that represent changes in factors of a materialist sort – environmental, economic, or technological factors – are *more likely* to stimulate changes that are both propagated and amplified through nonmaterialist sectors of society – gender, ideological, political sectors – than vice versa.[5] I seriously doubt that such an asymmetry will pass muster, but if it does there remains the obvious question raised by postempiricist thinking of the sort done by Sellars: What is it about the systems involved that accounts for this asymmetry of causation? Answering this question puts us on the second tier within the framework model, the level of structure causes.

We get a sense of just how important the distinction between structure and stimulus causes is from looking at the highest levels of the physical sciences. The special theory of relativity seems entirely empty if we approach it with the expectation that it will tell us what is going on in the world. If we work with it a bit we see how it can be used indirectly to tell us about what is going on. In its essentials, though, the theory tells us only about structures: the finiteness of the velocity of light and the sameness of the laws of nature in systems moving uniformly with respect to one another. It is within those laws, whatever they are, that forces and stimuli enter the picture. The physicist will already have plenty of experience with these forces and stimuli. The special theory of relativity is still important to the extent that it imposes general restrictions on what the physicist is to say about how these forces and stimuli act. There are, to be sure, other elements of structure that enter into physics when the physicist discusses a special area, such as atomic physics. But, by considering the most general levels of physics first, we see in the most striking way the distinction between structure causes and stimulus causes.[6]

Enough has now been said about the framework model to get an idea of what a political theory that uses it would be like. We are forced to speak in generalities until we have specified what kind of structure is to be used in explanations employing the framework model. Choice of the structure causes in any field is contentious business, as recent developments in the history of science precipitated by the work of Thomas Kuhn have made amply clear. One of the elements in a new scientific paradigm is a conception of what is to go into that second tier of explanation we have associated with structure causes. Usually there is no way of demonstrating to the satisfaction of all contending parties which specific set of structure causes should be chosen over all others. Debates in political theory about the structural level are every bit as intense as those in the physical sciences. The useful thing about these debates is not the metaphysical polemics between defenders of an old and a new paradigm. It is that they begin the process of fleshing out a paradigm so that one can judge how fruitful it might be in explanation.

With this in mind I propose to concentrate in this book on working out a paradigm for the theory of the state that, on the one hand, uses the two-tiered framework model and, on the other hand, adopts an economic structural level. By concentrating on working out this paradigm I shall, then, minimize polemics – over what structure causes to adopt – with idealists, technological determinists, the late Frankfurt School, positivists, analytical Marxists, or poststructuralists. Still, it has to be admitted that my political paradigm has two contentious parts: a formal part, which is the framework model itself as opposed to an atomist model, and a substantive part, which identifies the second tier as the economic structure as opposed, say, to the structure of signifying discourse. It helps in understanding how contentious these choices are to point out that different goals and values are associated with them. This needs bearing in mind when we consider the adequacy of any one of these choices. Criteria for the sort of adequacy in question are shaped by the goals and values of those supporting the different paradigms. The adequacy of our political paradigm will not then be a matter of an unmediated comparison with political reality.[7]

4. Materialist political theory redeemed

In ending this chapter I need to show how the framework model makes critiques like E. P. Thompson's of materialist political theory totally ineffective. The actions of the political coalition that supports funding the arms race are not reflections of purely economic interests. Rather, cold-war ideology, with its basis in a competition between states ruling over divergent social systems, is an integral part of the stimulus causation of the arms race. Indeed, the coalition's being motivated by this ideology is a stimulus cause of the arms race. Though it would not be given prominence by an atomist materialism, such a stimulus cause presents no problem within a materialist framework model. What, though, might the structure cause of the arms race be?

Enmity between national powers has existed before without anything approaching the military outlays made in this century. A number of things have contributed to making this possible, without adequately explaining it. There is a greater pool of financial resources to tap in order to run a military establishment.[8] There is also the greater sophistication of destructive technology, which has made the military an increasingly more machine-intensive and less soldier-intensive institution.

These facts are all ancillary to the United States becoming a global policeman. Why, though, has it adopted this role? The question for the United States had rarely been how to defend its borders. The question that emerged after World War II was rather how to realize a global dominance with the willing support of other major capitalist countries.[9] This involved opening the world to at least the economic interests of the United States and of those other capitalist countries. Only a global policeman could keep a large part of the world open. Resistance to opening the world to these interests has been dealt with differently from instance to instance; during the Nixon administration Chile was opened up by U.S. support for a bloody coup, whereas China was opened up in the same period through a policy of détente, aided by divisions within the communist bloc. Despite this variety, the existence of a military force capable of meeting challenges in small, medium, and large encounters at any place in the world is an essential element in the strategy of opening the world to the interests of the United States and its major capitalist partners.

With considerations like these before us, I propose the following hypothesis about the structure cause in the explanation of the arms race. The goal of opening the world to the economic interests of the major capitalist nations provides the context – the structure cause. The economic goal is, though, only part of the account of the arms race. It is only a structure cause, and structure causes do not operate without stimulus causes. Among the stimulus causes is motivation by the ideology of the cold war. The structure cause explains how this ideology could be a stimulus cause of the arms race.

It must not be thought that this account puts the entire onus of the arms race on the capitalist side. At the level of stimulus cause, a decisive role is given to the noncapitalist, or centralist, side in accounting for the arms race. Global economic dominance without an arms buildup would be easy were there no resistance. But there is resistance in several forms, including, on the one hand, resistance in the nationalist forms represented by the Popular Unity government of Chile and, on the other hand, resistance in the broader form represented by the entire Soviet bloc. This resistance introduces a political stimulus cause for arming that acts within the context of the economic structure cause, the opening of the world to capitalism.

The Soviet bloc resists being opened up to capitalism, not because of a mind-set of expansionist socialist internationalism, which J. Edgar Hoover delighted in trying to prove by pulling quotes out of Lenin, but because of international realities. A Soviet bloc that is geographically restricted and forced to enter the world market against a more powerful capitalist bloc cannot expect its own more centralized economy to flourish.[10] Its long-term well-being, like that of the capitalist economy, depends on resisting external pressure. Effective resistance leads the Soviet bloc to give political, and sometimes material, support to nationalist struggles against the Pax Americana. The risks of going all out in support of these struggles are high, with the result that Soviet support is often limited and vacillating.

Within the Soviet bloc, the need to mount an effective resistance to Western expansion has been the basis for a commitment to the arms race. Soviet military weakness would have invited the Western bloc to pick away at the Soviet bloc's periphery. The capitalist economy could then have forced the centralized economy into the corner. The arms race has to do, then, with more than the need of capitalism to open up the rest of the world. This expansionism is indeed a structure cause in a full explanation, but of itself it does not include the important stimulus of resistance by the Soviet bloc to Western expansion.

Would a political structure cause do as well as the economic one we chose? Instead of resorting to the economic level, why not appeal to competition between states? Clearly, competitor states will strive for military superiority and thus engage in an arms race. This feature of striving for superiority would seem to fit the role of a structure cause in the explanation of the connection between cold-war ideology and the arms race. Striving for superiority is extremely important for understanding why mere deterrent capability never suffices for competitor states. Why, though, do states compete for military superiority? They do not pursue superiority simply because they have big egos. Rather, military superiority is a goal linked to other goals that states pursue, such as the post–World War II goal of U.S. economic hegemony.

We get here a glimpse of the fact that there may be several structural levels, even when one has been selected as primary. This is useful in dealing with provisional explanations. An explanation with only provisional value will employ as a structural cause something that in another context is only an effect. The connection between cold-war ideology and the arms race may be explained provisionally by the principle of superiority. But ultimately, competing for superiority will itself be accounted for as the effect of some stimulus on the basis of the primary structural cause.

3

The revolt against theory

A conception of theory is part of the framework model of explanation. This conception has strong ties with a realist view of theory. Theory in the framework model operates with structures in order to be able to explain stimulus causation. However, we find in much recent social and political thought an antipathy for theory in this sense. How does the framework model fare against these anti-theoretical currents?

1. Politics and theory

What is the place of theory in our overall social existence? Gramsci's answer to this question merits our consideration. He started from the assumption that people would not organize around their interests, and ultimately use the state as an instrument for advancing their interests, if they saw no possibility in the way things are of their interests ever being realized. There is, then, a need for demonstrating the feasibility of realizing their interests within a certain conception of the world.[1] This conception of the world is a theory, and theoreticians are to be valued for the indirect role they play in getting people organized to pursue their interests.

Gramsci insisted that a movement of one class to take control of the state from another required a theoretical underpinning. The ruling class being challenged would have its own family of conceptions of the world. Part of the success of these conceptions was their identification of the goals of the ruling class as those of the society as a whole. To pursue alternative goals would require a reasonable alternative theory, which would present a picture of the world that makes it compatible with the successful pursuit of these alternative goals. An alternative theory is needed to counter the existing theories of the ruling class. Theory is, then, a prerequisite for ruling, and ruling is what politics, in the foreseeable future, is about. Only when domination is no longer as deeply rooted in our basic social forms as it is now will alternatives to the state and to a supporting theory for it be on the agenda.

In opposition to all this there is a growing movement against the whole idea of theory. It opposes theory for giving primacy to one area of reality and for dividing reality with a set of categories. This movement has a variety of forms, a poststructuralist form in France and a pluralist form, emphasizing the autonomy of non-class struggle, in the United States. The common theme is a commitment to empiricism, whose assumptions undermine the pretensions of theory. Our materialist theory of the state, for example, would be objectionable simply because theories pretend to unify more than they possibly can. Far from helping to realize goals, theories mislead people through their one-sided attempts to encompass reality.

There are a number of explanations for this antitheoretical movement. On the left at least, there is a growing trend toward accommodation with the existing ruling group and along with it a diminishing need to provide a theory that can be an integral part of a confrontation with that ruling group. But there is another explanation, on which I shall focus here, that has to do with method. The antitheoretical movement commonly makes the assumption that any theory is bound to be a device for explaining things through stimulus causation of a preferred kind. This assumption ignores the distinction I have made between the two tiers of explanation, one involving stimulus causes and another involving structure causes.

If this restriction of theory to a preferred kind of stimulus causes is in fact made, there is every reason to attack theory and to replace it with some other activity. One such activity is writing historical narratives in which the richness of the variety of stimulus causes seems to defy any unitary conceptual grasp.[2] Another alternative to theory is the development of models of interconnected factors that can be used to avoid monocausal interpretations of reality. The number of interconnected factors can grow like Ptolemaic rings, but the fact that there is a model serves to conceal the absence of any underlying unity.[3] These empiricist trends to substitute multicausalism for theory are very popular today.

There is a catch, though, that tends to make attacks on theory ephemeral. If Gramsci is right, a thoroughgoing antitheoretical attitude begins to undermine the feasibility of organizing people around their interests for political struggles. Theories that might give hope to an ascendant group and theories that have won wide support for an established group become equally suspect. We re-move any basis people have for believing their interests can be realized. The probable result of the spread of disbelief is that mass support either for change or for the existing order withers away. This eliminates pressures on the state to keep its actions within tolerable bounds, since there are no longer expectations, arising from legitimating theories, that the state will satisfy interests in response to pressures. The ensuing abuses of an unchecked state will overcome this passivity, however, and revitalize resistance. Once again people will look for a view of things that makes their struggle feasible. Theories will emerge that give plausibility to movements either to limit the ruling group or to transfer state power to an ascendant group. A wave of attacks on theory is likely then to be followed by a return to theory.[4]

2. Revising Marxist theory

The attack on theory by those who wish to revise Marxism in par-ticular supports itself on the fact that economic determination never occurs without political determination. This intertwining can be illustrated in Marxist theory itself in connection with its economic claim that commodities tend to sell at their value. Here value is roughly the time labor puts in on a commodity. Wage labor, which is a commodity, tends to sell at the value determined by the time labor puts in on its own reproduction. Let us then use wage labor to make our illustration more specific.

It is not inevitable that wage labor's tendency to sell at value will be perfectly realized, since political factors affect how it is realized. Otherwise, it would be realized in the way physical tendencies are realized, and wage laborers would then be zombies rather than human agents contracting for a wage. The political forces of capital, labor, and the state are active on a continuing basis alongside the tendency toward an equilibrium at which labor sells at its value. Slowdowns, strikes, lockouts, federal mediators, presidential back-to-work orders, gun thugs, scabs, minimum wage laws, and plant closings are the most visible part of the political repertoire affecting the way the law of value is realized.

It would seem to follow that there is no such thing as economic primacy in explanation, since if the economic plays a role at all it is in conjunction with the political.[5] There may still be situations in which economic factors can be usefully emphasized while political factors are slighted. This, though, can justify only a pragmatic

41

rather than a genuine primacy. But if not just economic primacy but any primacy in explanation were undercut, there would be no way to unify diverse areas and hence no theory.

Moreover, since economic factors never operate without factors from other categories it may seem doubtful that we are talking about anything definite when we speak about the economic factors of a situation. Where things are as intertwined as the economic and the political are, it seems less and less plausible to speak about two distinct categories. In the end those who reject primacy slide over to the position that it is best to junk all categories – those concepts defining a major line in reality – and to stick to expressions for everyday things like wages, living costs, strikes, and mediation. In the absence of any categories, the aim of rejecting theory is fully realized.[6]

There are, then, two strands to criticisms of theory from the perspective of these revisionist Marxists. There is the attack on primacy, and there is an attack on distinctions. Looking at each of them carefully weakens the force of their general perspective. The first attack, that on primacy in explanation, has to do with denying any category of reality the status of a foundation for the rest. The criticism of theory is supposed, then, to contain a strand that "deconstructs" the metaphysical opposition between primary and secondary categories. This deconstruction puts in place of the primary/secondary opposition a "series" of things of comparable status.[7] In the series there are then no privileged members, and outside it there is no source, ground, or cause. The series, whether in the form of a historical narrative or of a model of interrelated categories needs neither internal nor external grounding. The second attack, that on distinctions, has to do with denying that there are distinct sectors of reality which we put under different categories. Each sector turns out not to be distinct but to involve the others. The more we try to distinguish sectors of reality, the more we are forced to rely on their being intertwined. All distinctions will tend to destroy themselves. Never mind the surface sophistry of these two strands of the criticism of theory; examining them carefully will point to more fundamental flaws.

3. Distinctions and primacy

Consider the criticism of distinctions first. On its face, it is most implausible, for we are often perfectly aware of interconnections between things that we nonetheless keep apart. We recognize that keeping them apart is the basis for a fruitful way of proceeding. If seventeenth-century scientists had been so overwhelmed by the interconnection between force and mass that they flatly denied any distinction between the two, they would have put an obstacle in the way of a great number of insights about physical motion. The interconnection is quite real; masses in motion are always under the influence of forces, and, conversely, masses invariably generate forces that act on yet other masses. But the idealization of force-free uniform motion, as an expression of the inertial character of mass, would have to be abandoned if this interconnection were to require a melding of force and mass. This idealization was an integral and fruitful part of the new physics, which differentiated it from the earlier variants of Aristotelian physics.

There is a way, though, that the criticism of distinctions makes sense. This is the atomist way of saying that causation is in truth a myth, for there is no real ground for it between such distinct things as are usually picked out to be cause and effect. It is a myth that posits invisible threads holding things together, and there is no ground for these threads in the distinct things so linked. The causal threads are, if they are anything, only an imposition of mind on things. In response to this myth of causality, the atomist claims that, if there is any linking at all, it is within a unity that lacks distinctions.[8] Thus where things are interconnected they cannot be distinct.

This makes sense only so long as the framework model is ignored. My answer to this atomist philosophy is that, though it is true there is no causation between isolated factors, it is possible to have causation when the distinct factors nonetheless pertain to a common framework. Though a rapid increase of productive capacity does not of itself lead to stagnation, it is plausible that it should lead to stagnation in the capitalist economic framework. In a feudal framework the plausibility of the link is lost. Since the framework does not obliterate the distinctness of cause and effect mediated by it, we have a way of linking things that are distinct. But we have gotten it by dropping an exclusive focus on stimulus causation and allowing structure causation to enter in through frameworks. In a framework, the structure causes provide the basis for the link between cause and effect that the atomist could not find in distinct events.

It is now time to turn to the criticism of primacy. Even if we admit there are distinctions between areas picked out by our categories, it does not follow that one of these areas has primacy. The suggestion that one area does have primacy has led to the accusation of authoritarianism. To claim primacy for the economic and hence to give the political a secondary status is treated as tantamount to providing a cover for dictatorial rule; under cover of saying the political does not really matter since everything is a matter of economic necessity, a ruling party can act without any political check. Also, to claim primacy for the economic is treated as tantamount to making the feminist struggle pick up what crumbs it can get from the class struggle. Theory, as a process of working out from a postulated primary area, is condemned as phallocratic, even though there are feminist theories that postulate the primacy of a framework that brings together both gender and economic relations.[9] I am unmoved by these resounding condemnations of theory as authoritarian. The alleged authoritarian consequences simply do not follow. Moreover, the opponents of theory themselves have a knack for falling into authoritarian ways of supporting their own values when they find those values at odds with the values made feasible by some theory.

When we get beyond their antiauthoritarian rhetoric, the opponents of primacy have several serious arguments. First, there is an argument at a general philosophical level. This is the argument that there is no single area of reality that supplies all that is necessary for the stimulus causation of things we want to explain. Wages are not explained fully by the law of value; they are what they are also because of the element of organized struggle by workers, owners, and the state. Wage differentials between men and women are not explained by the law of value; they are also affected by the element of male domination. Colonial domination is not explained by the law of the accumulation of capital; it is also affected by the element of military force. Clearly, these failures are crucial for an atomist theory that postulates the primacy of the economic. It simply cannot survive these failures.

But everything is different for the framework model of explanation. The argument of the opponents of primacy is effective against atomistic materialism, but it has no validity against primacy in the framework model. The framework model does not say that the structure cause it appeals to is itself the only stimulus cause. Rather, it says that the structure cause can explain how it is that a stimulus cause can have the effect it does, no matter what the category to which the stimulus cause pertains. In the examples above, then, it is perfectly appropriate that organized struggle is one of the stimulus causes of wages, that male domination is one of the stimulus causes of wage differentials, and that military force is one of the stimulus causes of colonial expansion. However, the explanations based on these stimulus causes are effective only within the framework of structure causes of an economic sort – the law of price tending to value and the law of capital tending to grow through the investment of profits. The primacy given to these structure causes is a primacy at the level of structural causation, which does not carry over to primacy at the level of stimulus causation. So there can be political, gender, and military stimulus causes when the economic is given structural primacy. There is no reason to substitute an empirical "series" for theoretical primacy in order to have the flexibility to choose causes from any number of categories. Within the perspective that there is a primacy of structure causes, one already has this flexibility.

4. Human interaction versus theory

The poststructuralist type of critique of the framework model we have just considered has an empiricist bias that is not shared by the type of critique we are about to consider. This second attack on theory, understood in the sense of the framework model, rests on the distinction between the natural and the human. More specifically, it rests on a Habermas-style critique of natural science that appeals to themes from the rationalist-idealist rather than the empiricist tradition. By adopting the framework model, I stand accused of taking over a method appropriate to natural science in order to have a basis for a theory that is about human interaction. This sort of scientific imperialism never works because it leaves out something important about the human.

The framework model with its sophisticated two-tiered system of explanation may be useful for the natural sciences, but it fails to deal with the crucial inadequacy of the natural sciences in respect to human interaction. Natural science is adequate to the task of the technical control of nature, but humans are more than agencies seeking to control nature for present goals. The distinctive thing about humans is that they form communities with explicit standards of behavior which are applied and revised in a context of discussion. An interest in community, rather than in control over nature, is behind investigations that have little in common with natural science.[10] These investigations have been said to belong to the field of *interpretation* since they reflect on meaningful human behavior from within it. And interpretation is not theory as we encounter it in the framework model.

On the one hand, others have already pointed out that the alleged differences between natural science and interpretation become doubtful if we drop the atomist conception of natural science made familiar by modern positivism.[11] For example, the ideal of theory on the positivist account is a hypothetico-deductive structure allowing the deduction of conceptually neutral observation claims from a hierarchy of generalizations crowned with the axioms of the theory. In the first place, the conceptual neutrality of observation claims has become suspect. Instead, theories are held to condition our ways of viewing the world. In an analogous fashion, maxims of interpretation applied in generating a narrative about the politics of a period condition our way of viewing human behavior. In the second place, Sellars's insight cuts against the hypothetico-deductive view of theory by deemphasizing the deduction of lower-level from higher-level generalizations and emphasizing the appeal to structure causes to show how things come under the generalizations, or how they fail to do so. Using theory in this way is more often than not a matter of constructing an interpretive narrative for which there are no precise deductive prescriptions.[12] The sequence of events in such a narrative is skillfully, but not mechanically, laid within the framework of a structure cause.

On the other hand, it has also been pointed out that the contrast between technical interest and interest in community becomes doubtful once we abandon the intellectualist myth about natural science. According to that myth, natural science is a neutral instrument to be evaluated not by whether it advances certain preferred social interests but by its ability to meet standards set by the intellect itself.[13] In contrast, the standards of interpretation are not to be found beyond human behavior, of which interpretation itself is a part. Interpretation is not a neutral instrument but part of the process of discussion in which social standards are formulated. Interpretation both reflects and contributes to those standards.

In fact, natural science is also part of the process of reaching consensus on community standards of action. A scientific theory projects a picture of the world that would not be accepted without prior acceptance of certain community norms. And, once accepted, that picture shapes the adoption and rejection of further norms. Like interpretation, the scientific picture both reflects and contributes to those norms.

The theory of evolution both reflected standards of the competitive Victorian world and became an essential element in the further elaboration of social standards. The emergence and development of the theory of evolution were an expression of a technical scientific interest that was indissolubly part of an interest within a broader community to elaborate its standards. We can then say that natural science is itself an interpretive enterprise since it starts from a consensus on values and becomes a basis for modifying and elaborating them.

Likewise, James Maxwell's theory of electromagnetism reflected and contributed to the development of a consensus in the nineteenth century around the norm of progress. The prior development of communication by electrical devices and the generation of electrical power stimulated the theory. Yet it was this development of an electrical industry, first for communication and then for power, that in no small part shaped the idea of progress as a value. The theory could then contribute to this idea the notion that mathematical science is integral to progress. The intellectualist myth of science fractures the social world with a division of labor between theory formation and value formation. This rejection of the myth identifies theory formation as part of the process of the social reflection on values.

There is not, then, anything objectionable about carrying theory into the realm of human interaction. Once exaggerated claims on behalf of theory are dropped, there is no fundamental dividing line between theory and interpretation. One of those claims was the deductivist account of the application of theory. This had to be modified once we adopted the framework model of explanation. Instead, I introduced the claim that structure causes are woven into causal narratives without the benefit of a fixed set of logical rules for doing so. The other exaggerated claim was the intellectualist myth about scientific theory. Since theory in the natural sciences plays a part in a community's interpretation of its values, it is part of interpretation rather than something distinct from it.

5. Two forms of essentialism

An attack on essentialism provides a third way in which theory is rejected, a way that like poststructuralism rests on empiricism. Part of the problem is getting clear on what essentialism is. The kind of essentialism under attack by those opposed to theory is emanationist in nature, and they assume that there is no other kind of essentialism. Emanationist essentialism makes use of the metaphor of organic growth: An essence is self-empowered to develop all that needs to be explained. The state, for example, is part of the

47

unfolding of the economic essence of society, or of the moral essence of society. The problem is that in recording the so-called self-development of an essence one needs an undetermined number of props that do not come from the essence. These props are contingent from the perspective of the essence and are thus inexplicable. To that extent, essentialism of this kind is unhelpful; but what is the alternative?

Althusser criticized emanationist essentialism and put in its place a philosophy that had no room for essence of any kind.[14] The connections among state, ideology, and economy were not to be made by singling out any one of these as an essence from which the others flowed. There was at best only a contingent conjuncture of state, ideological, and economic structures that made up the social whole. The connections among these structures were then to be thought of in the spirit of an empiricist atomism.

At the same time, Althusser took a step that was in conflict with his atomism. This was the step of singling out the economic features of society for a special role. Not only did they interact with the state and ideology through stimulus causation, but they were to have the deeper role of being "determining in the last instance." In view of his critique of emanationist essentialism, being determining in the last instance could not be seen as the unfolding of an essence. Unfortunately, though, Althusser gave us no clear idea as to what it was.

Faced with this messy situation, some who read Althusser criticized him for returning to the essentialism he had rejected. If the economic is determining in the last instance, then the state in a capitalist society cannot function to undermine capitalism in a systematic way in the long run, even though it can take measures that may outrage the capitalist class. The state then seems to be little more than an unfolding of the capitalist essence of the society. But emanationism was unacceptable for reasons elaborated by Althusser himself. With no other essentialist model on the horizon, the critics were forced to return to Althusser's empiricist atomism, which had no room for determination in the last instance.

Take the case of property law. Suppose property law is determined in the last instance by the economy. Suppose further that we can make sense of this only as a form of essential determination. If the only form of essentialism is emanationism, then property legislation will follow from the course of the development of capitalism. But laws regulating corporations often had the effect not of being a spur to accumulation but of protecting investors in corporations

48

from the disastrous effects of their own speculation. Political struggles were behind such legislation, and without taking them into account an abstract logic of capital could do little toward unraveling how the legislation came about. Critics of essentialism and hence of Althusser's determination in the last instance would advocate, in place of such an essentialist history, a thorough investigation of each piece of legislation that picks out a variety of causes.[15] And surely this would also be my recommendation – if there were no essentialist alternative to emanationism.

The framework model is, though, an alternative form of essentialism, yet it rejects the idea that a structure cause explains events by an immanent development. Instead, I have built into the framework model the idea that stimulus causes are contingent in relation to a structure cause. For the structure cause explains how a stimulus cause has the effect it does without explaining either the stimulus cause itself or the effect it has. Before theory is rejected altogether on the basis of rejecting emanationist essentialism, this alternative provided by the framework model needs to be given a hearing, which poststructuralists have certainly not done.[16]

The structure cause is a form of essence explaining how things can enter into the connections they do. The selection of an economic structure cause in preference to a technological or a moral one is a commitment about what is essential for a system. But it is not a commitment to saying that everything else about a system flows from that structure cause. (This may have been what Althusser wanted without making it clear.) Property law does indeed have a varied legislative history that is not derived solely from a structure cause. But turning that legislative history into an illuminating causal narrative requires placing it in a framework that clarifies how the agents in that history could cause legislative innovations.

The revolt against theory is vulnerable simply because it is based on a limited view of the complexity of explanation. Within that limited view of explanation, theory inevitably fails to be useful. But these failures of theory are avoided when it is constructed for use in the framework model of explanation, in which stimulus and structure cause are distinguished.

4

State autonomy

In the Introduction I discussed the conflict within the state between justice and the economy. In Chapter 2 a materialist framework model emerged as a basis for political theory. In this chapter these two themes come together. Class struggle, based in the economic framework, shows up within the state as a conflict between justice and the economy. And this conflict is the key to what is called the autonomy of the state.

1. When justice and the economy collide

The meaning of the conflict between justice and the economy is that limits placed by the state on losses and benefits interfere with tendencies within the economy. In the extreme these limits threaten the very existence of the economy. Within the modern liberal democratic state one aspect of the overall conflict is the specific conflict between democracy and capitalism. Democracy is part of a pattern of justice because it limits loss of control by the many and limits monopolizing control by the few. The thrust toward more widely shared control encouraged by democracy conflicts with the restricted control encouraged by capitalism.[1] The state's liberal function of promoting capitalism and its democratic form fail to come together in a harmonious institution. So long as democracy remains a widely accepted condition for legitimate rule, this contradiction cannot be eliminated. Of course, people can be dominated without legitimate rule, but such an arrangement is likely to be unstable.

Since justice is a requirement of stable rule there is no guarantee in advance that the function for which ruling is adopted will be compatible with justice. In different periods the specific character of the limits imposed by justice will vary. But this variation does not guarantee that, as circumstances change, the incompatibility between form and function will be bridged.[2] In fact, the variation in the limits reflects the relative strengths of the contending social forces. When those who are pressing stricter limits on benefits and

50

losses are stronger, it becomes possible for the state's form of rule to be incompatible with its functioning for the economy.

The conflict between form and function helps ground the claim that the state has a certain kind of autonomy. If problems internal to the reproduction of the economy fully determine the behavior of the state, then the conflicts between the form of justice and the function of economic reproduction would never have occurred. In particular, the democratic thrust of the liberal democratic state would never have become a challenge to the state's role of encouraging the capitalist economy. Economic reproduction would have fashioned all the state's behavior including that part expressive of the thrust toward democracy.[3] In fact, the democratic thrust in such a state continually poses problems for the reproduction of capitalism. In general, justice in a state poses problems for the associated economy. And so, through its pattern of justice, a state enjoys autonomy in respect to demands arising out of the inertial thrust of its economic system toward reproduction.

To illustrate this in relation to a liberal democratic state, I chose an example from U.S. military history. Part of the modern democratic ideal was popular control of the military. The persistence of this ideal, even after economic changes that were incompatible with it, demonstrates the autonomy of the ideal and of the military institutions based on it. This ideal placed an emphasis on the militia as opposed to the large standing army. In the United States this emphasis took the form of a military federalism that gave the individual states responsibility for raising militias in the case of a national emergency. (Even at the time of the Spanish–American War, the call for 136,000 national volunteers was matched with a call for 125,000 state volunteers.) The state governors were rewarded with the distribution of numerous officers' commissions, and they had control over officers in the state units up to the regimental level. So it was not a purely democratic militia that was being counterposed to a regular army; it was a pork barrel for state politicians, which remained a thorn in the side of the growing group of supporters for a centralized military bureaucracy.

The rationale for the idea of the citizen soldier had been the view that the United States in the early days was a democracy of small property owners, each with an individual stake in protecting his holdings. As the country developed, it became apparent that this view of the society was incompatible with the inequality of property holdings, an inequality present from the start but increased by industrialism. (In 1810 the richest 1 percent of the population

51

owned 20 percent of the wealth, whereas by 1910 it owned 30 percent.) Yet the decentralism stemming from the petty-bourgeois conception of the society was so well entrenched that it would be difficult to displace. Military decentralism, in particular, would take three-quarters of a century to displace.

Two events in the last quarter of the nineteenth century indicated a contradiction between, on the one hand, the democratically rooted military with its collection of militias and, on the other hand, the demands of economic reproduction. The recognition of this contradiction was a recognition of the autonomy of the military in respect to the demands of economic reproduction. In an essay published in 1906, which won the Military Service Institution annual award, Lieutenant Colonel James Pettit wrote that the structure of American democracy made it "impossible to organize and discipline an effective Army from the point of view of the military." Experience was surely on his side even if political interests were still dragging their feet.

The first event was the Great Rail Strike of 1877, which pitted the new large-scale corporation against an increasingly restive proletariat. Was the militia system up to handling this product of the development of corporate giants? The failure of the militia system to reflect the needs of the changing economy points to the autonomy of the military in relation to the economy. In Baltimore half the militia quit rather than confront their fellow citizens on strike. One National Guard unit mutinied in Pennsylvania. In Altoona troops surrendered and fraternized with strikers. The strike was broken only when federal troops were brought into Chicago, prompting the *Chicago Tribune* to call for forming regulars into a permanent national police force, because in a federal regiment "the men have no sympathy with any class." In fact, the militias in the form of the National Guard, created in 1903, remained in the hands of the governors in peacetime, though they were made to conform to U.S. Army standards.[4]

The second event was the agitation for a permanent military presence in the empire spawned by the 1898 Spanish–American War. Militiamen called up to defeat the Spanish proved to have no stomach for sticking around to see that Cuban rebels or Philippine rebels were denied the fruits of their national liberation struggles against the Spanish. Yet the imperialist lobby had made it clear upon getting into the war that the world must be opened up to U.S. trade. In the Senate, Albert Beveridge of Indiana said, "American factories are making more than the American people can use;

American soil is producing more than they can consume. Fate has written our policy for us; the trade of the world must and shall be ours."[5] Imperialism calls for permanent preparedness, thereby undercutting the view that militarily it is sufficient to be able to call out the militias in time of crisis. Even so, in view of the autonomy of the military, it took a half-century from the time of the Spanish–American War for the national security state to crystallize through the National Security Act of 1947.

2. Autonomy and the framework model

Must we interpret this lag in functionality as a matter of autonomy? There seems to be a simpler interpretation that uses only the demands of economic reproduction. According to it the effect brought about by a stimulus cause can outlast that cause. The demands of the small-property-owning economy brought the militia system about in the first place. Then, once brought about, it continued to exist while the petty-bourgeois economy was integrated into the new monopolist system. Because of the initial impulse that gave birth to it, the militia system lasted through a transition period when monopoly entrenched itself and before a centralized military bureaucracy was created. On this interpretation, the persistence of the militia system was a symptom not of state autonomy but of the persistence of the effects of bygone economic stimulus causes.

It is precisely to avoid the limitations of an interpretation like this with its denial of state autonomy that I have been emphasizing the framework model of explanation. The framework model keeps the importance of the economic in view without having to claim that each aspect of the state is determined by the state's economic function. The limitations of the above denial of state autonomy are of two sorts.

First, the interpretation leaves the absence of a military that would function to reproduce the economy without any explanation. Even if the militias do persist, why aren't there, in addition, new military forms that could be relied on to reproduce the economy in the face of serious threats? The response might be that the lag in functionality is of no importance since we all know it can't become grave enough to imperil the reproduction of the economy. If, though, there can be a lag at all, why should it be impossible for it to imperil reproduction?[6] Perhaps the reason is that when a threat to reproduction begins to emerge the demands of preserving the economy become strong enough to force a change in the military, whereas when there is only minor trouble the demands of preserving the economy are too weak to force a change.

One implication of this is thoroughly implausible. It is that the military would never fail the economy in a crisis. An adjustment in military organization would always take place in the nick of time so that the preservation of the economy would not be seriously threatened. Determination in the last instance by the economy would miraculously make the military effective. No wonder, then, that in December 1975 conservative military leaders were able to crush the threat to Portuguese capitalism sparked by the Armed Forces Movement in the military. Why, though, was it not equally inevitable that Somoza's National Guard should crush the columns of Sandinista guerrillas before he fled Nicaragua in July 1979?

Lags in functionality do need an explanation. But the demands of preserving the economy, in the form of stimulus causes, do not provide one. In our framework model there is, though, a place for noneconomic stimulus causes. In the American example, one of them is the antipathy for a regular army due both to its association with monarchy and to the republican tradition of states' rights. The lag in getting a military appropriate for the economy can be explained by taking account of the impact of this conviction, against the background, of course, of an emerging monopoly economy.

Second, the above interpretation also fails to deal adequately with the changes that put an end to a lag in functionality. The making of the centralized military bureaucracy was a process involving the monopolist economy, on the one side, and a real but limited democratic form of rule, on the other side. Since it involved two sides it was not the result of monopoly alone. These conflicting forces faced one another at various levels, including that of political negotiations. Those who wish to negate state autonomy by relying only on the demands of economic reproduction have no room in their account of ending the lag in functionality for political negotiations with those representing the form, rather than the economic function, of the state. The change to a centralized military bureaucracy was in part determined by a long seesaw battle among military professionals interested in reform, the states' rights wing of the Congress, the president as commander in chief, the chairs of various congressional committees, and a few business executives.[7] The battle was lost by those parties in these negotiations representing a democratic military, though there was

54

no assurance ahead of time that the forces supported by monopoly would win.

The framework model not only leaves room for political negotiations in explaining the shift to a centralized military but also leaves open the possibility that their outcome is not made inevitable by the economy. The monopolist economy plays the role of a background for political negotiations between the partisans of the conflicting forces.

3. Incomplete autonomy defined

With this said in defense of autonomy, it is time now to make the idea of autonomy more precise. I have illustrated the idea of autonomy by noting the possibility of conflict between democracy and economic reproduction. But democracy is only one possible aspect of the state's form of rule. Here, then, is a general formulation by which I shall be guided throughout this book: *The state has autonomy in respect to the economy insofar as its form of ruling can be in contradiction with its function of reproducing the economy.* Autonomy, then, points toward possible contradictions. It is the possibility of contradictions between the form of ruling and the function of reproducing the economy that is the basis for the autonomy of the state.

The notion of contradiction here is to be specified in the following way. Welfare benefits, as an aspect of state justice, will modify conceptions of employer control over assets without necessarily imperiling the economic system. Such benefits will not then be said to be in contradiction with the system. Only system-threatening changes will be said to put justice into contradiction with the economy. If contradictions in this sense are possible within an autonomous state, then surely conflicts will also be possible that merely threaten accustomed privileges without imperiling the economy. Thus state autonomy will imply possible conflicts between form and function, in a sense that is weaker than contradictions, simply by virtue of implying possible contradictions to the economy.

Autonomy may be complete or incomplete. (Incomplete autonomy is more often called relative autonomy.) The state is never completely autonomous for two quite different reasons. It is incompletely autonomous because, first, within the state itself the form of ruling is paired with the function of reproducing the economy. The state's form is under the influence of that function, at the same time that it may conflict with it. Since both form and function are

55

internal to the state, this influence is an internal constraint on the state. Even when the function fails to shape the form sufficiently to prevent a failure of the function, the function can play a part in shaping the form. When an internal feature limits autonomy, I shall say that *from an internal perspective* the state lacks complete autonomy.

Those who flatly reject the idea that the state functions for the economy will not posit any shaping of the form of rule by the economic function of the state. They will say that from an internal perspective the state is completely autonomous. Thus Bowles and Gintis, for example, advocate in a 1982 article a completely autonomous state from the internal perspective. For them, since the state does not function to reproduce the economy, the state's redistributive activity will not be shaped in any way by a state economic function.[8] Thus for them there would be no conflict within the state in a capitalist society resulting from having a liberal democracy run in the interests of its workers. I fully agree that it could be run in the interests of workers but, I would add, only at the expense of a deep conflict within the state between serving workers' interests and functioning for the economy. (A reply to the denial of the state's economic functioning will be developed only in Part Three.)

The state is also incompletely autonomous because, second, its form of ruling is shaped – by whatever factor – within the framework of the economy. Here the second tier of explanation is introduced. With no escape from the economic framework, there is no complete autonomy in respect to an external framework. Hence Bowles and Gintis seem willing to admit that the state is restricted by existing in the context of a specific economy. The potential for a capital strike, daily media hostility toward labor, and inequality of democratic participation are devices close enough to the structure of capitalism to make up a contextual restriction of the state's autonomy. When the economy as a structure cause limits autonomy, I shall say that *from an external perspective* the state lacks complete autonomy. This means that, by whatever factors the state's form of rule is shaped, the framework for shaping it is the economy.

As defined above, autonomy is neutral as between complete and incomplete autonomy. Restrictions need to be added in order to pick out one of these kinds of autonomy. The state has *incomplete autonomy* in respect to the economy insofar as (a) its form of ruling can be in contradiction with its function of reproducing the economy, and either (b) this economic functioning plays a part in shaping the form of ruling or (c) the economy is the framework for shaping the form of ruling. Here (b) gives the internal and (c) gives the external perspective for judging incomplete autonomy. Outside the framework model, (b) alone would serve as a necessary restriction on autonomy for incompleteness, and conversely the failure of (b) would suffice as a restriction on autonomy for completeness. Thus, outside the framework model, it is only from the internal perspective that the state lacks or has complete autonomy. Yet, in the framework model, if (b) fails while (c) holds, autonomy becomes incomplete due to the role of the economic framework; likewise, if (b) holds but something other than the economy is the framework, autonomy also becomes incomplete. Thus, within the framework model, it is both the external and the internal perspectives that are relevant for judging incomplete autonomy. For nonatomist materialism, (c) holds as a matter of course and the state has incomplete or relative autonomy. (Henceforth, when I speak of autonomy, I shall mean not the neutral kind but incomplete or relative autonomy instead.)

4. Is incomplete autonomy reductionist?

Does making autonomy relative raise again the problem of reductionism? In fact, the form of ruling remains unreduced to the state's economic function despite the mere relative autonomy of the state. On the one hand, the state's economic function plays a part in shaping the form of the state. The state's justice carries traces of the struggles to try to avoid this justice and, through this, of the state's functioning for the economy. Though the form of ruling of the state is partly shaped by the state's economic functioning, plenty of room is left for the needs of ruling itself in fixing its form.[9] On the other hand, the economy is the framework for shaping the form of rule. It is the background that gives intelligibility to the narrative of struggles and negotiations leading to patterns of justice. In this role, though, it is no substitute for the varied elements in those struggles and negotiations.

What is it that makes this antireductionist view possible? The following analogy points in the direction of an answer. Imagine that you are seeking shelter on a planet where the only available building material is stone that contains dangerously large amounts of radioactive substances. You make your shelter but fail to protect yourself from radioactive damage to cells in the bone marrow, which leads to a lethal leukemia. The demands of seeking shelter lead to using

57

materials that defeat the aim of seeking shelter in the first place. The demand for shelter might explain your building a shelter, but it is not the direct explanation of the radioactive building material that kills you.

Analogously, the demands of reproducing the economy explain the fact that we have a state, but the only form of rule we can imagine is one that involves some conception of a just distribution. This general requirement that there be some pattern of justice derives from the need for legitimate rule if there is to be stability. But this need for legitimacy assumes something about the subjects who are ruled. They are assumed to have a potential for mobilization around their interests as members of dominated groups. This potential will be more or less latent according to the situation of the subjects. Thus differences in regard to ruled subjects, specifically differences in regard to their willingness to struggle for interests shared with other members of their groups, will be important in understanding differences in patterns of justice. Neither the economy itself nor the state as protector of the economy puts predetermined limits on how far this potential for mobilization can lead ruled subjects while they are advancing their interests. There is then no guarantee of the compatibility of justice with the economy. Just as we cannot explain the harmful character of the building stone by going back to the aim of shelter, so too we cannot explain the potentially dysfunctional character of the form of ruling by going back to the aim of economic reproduction.

On some other planet it will be possible to build shelters out of harmless rocks, and with some strain of humans, other than those we have encountered, it will be possible for a minority to enjoy economic dominance without the obstacle of justice. As it is, the majority must be promised something; not all promises can be broken; and a visible effort must be made to limit the well-off. How much they have to be promised for legitimate rule to be possible is fixed not by the needs of reproducing the economy but by the class struggle. The promises may then conflict with the economy.

It is ironic that Nicos Poulantzas, whose 1968 book on the state stimulated the subsequent debate on state autonomy, wanted to insist that the autonomy of the state was only relative or incomplete but was incapable in this early work of articulating this restriction without falling into economic reductionism. In this regard the view I am advancing has the advantage of not requiring a retreat to complete autonomy, as made by Bowles and Gintis, in order to avoid economic reductionism. Poulantzas held that in its basic form the autonomy of the state was the state's ability to transform an economically dominant class into a politically dominant class.[10] An economically dominant class will not find within itself the resources for displacing other groups from political dominance or for unifying its own factions. To compensate for this inadequacy, he held that the state itself acts as the political organizer of the economically dominant class.

In what way is autonomy involved here? The state does something a class and hence the economy cannot do. For it is only by participation in the state that the economically dominant class overcomes its internal divisions and adopts a unified perspective. Moreover, through the state, it learns to present its class interests as universal interests, as the interests of all. Also, through political power it comes to accept the compromises with dominated classes needed for continuing its economic dominance. So the state helps to organize a dominant class, a feat this class could not achieve on its own.

What constraints does Poulantzas put on the state in this activity? Could it just as easily organize a dominated class for political power? Clearly not, since Poulantzas says the state prevents dominated classes from developing a unified perspective by disorganizing them. Where, though, does this asymmetry have its roots? He finds them in a correspondence between the state and the economically dominant class. In that 1968 book, *Political Power and Social Classes*, he says, "Underlying Marx's analyses is the representation of the correspondence between the state and the *specific interests* of the hegemonic class or fraction." This correspondence is what, for Poulantzas, makes autonomy only relative autonomy.

This restriction, though, undercuts autonomy and leaves us with an economic reduction. This is not difficult to show. The state would not conform to the specific interests of the dominant class, without deviations that take account of the interests of other classes and groups, unless it owed its existence to the economic structure in which that class is dominant. From this it would follow that, though the dominant class cannot organize itself politically, its political organization is determined, through the state, by the economic structure in which that class is dominant. In short, the state's activity in organizing the dominant class for political power is only made to seem autonomous by considering it in isolation from the rigid claim that the state, at least in the last instance, must reproduce the economy.

To save autonomy here would require abandoning the view that the state conforms to the interests of the leading class and hence will not allow the economy to go under.[11] But the needed lack of correspondence between the state and the economy can't simply be asserted; there must be some reason for it. Would the state's organization of the leading class for political power provide such a reason? It would only point in the direction of the more fundamental reason. If ruling can call for compromises with the ruled that threaten the economy, then we have a reason. If ruling calls for compromises with the ruled, then the state's organizing of the economically dominant class for political power would force that class to make compromises with the ruled. The interests of that dominant class could no longer be treated as universal. It would have to accept other interests than its own as goals of the state. But these other interests may be at odds with the economic interests of this leading class.[12] Focusing on the requirements of ruling rather than, as Poulantzas does, on the mere fact that political power is different from economic power is then the key to a conception of state autonomy that discourages the effort to reduce it to the economy. Poulantzas was closer to our formulation when he used as an example of state autonomy the welfare measures "*imposed* on the dominant classes by the state, through the pressure of the dominated classes." Politics is *not* then a matter of presenting the interests of the economically dominant class as universal interests but is in part a matter of limiting those interests by a pattern of justice.

5. Materialism and autonomy

How, though, is autonomy in my sense compatible with materialist methods? Mustn't there be correspondence in the long run between patterns of justice and promoting the economy, if materialism is to hold? Instead, autonomy raises the possibility that in a given period a new element of justice will weaken the very economy the state is to promote. In some periods, the pattern of justice might even pose a direct threat to the system's survival. I indicated in Section 2 how the framework model helps assure us that autonomy is compatible with materialist method. Now that a fuller picture of autonomy has been drawn, I want to elaborate further on the role of the framework model in achieving this compatibility.

Consider, first, instances of dysfunctionality. I shall try to show that any such specific cases are best accounted for in the context of an economic structure cause, rather than denied outright on *a priori* grounds. A democratic militia, an equalizing welfare state, or a court that allows a transfer of management rights to workers might conflict with the capitalist economic system. In many circumstances such a conflict could be rendered less threatening by minor adjustments either in these institutions or in the capitalist economy itself. But these institutions might seriously imperil the capitalist economic system as a whole in the presence of crisis-inducing circumstances. Whatever the origins of these dysfunctional institutions, it is not an *a priori* fact about the capitalist state that the harm they might do will be stopped in time. The most we can say is that in some cases where institutions of the state seemed particularly auspicious for setting in train a revolutionary process the economy healed itself and those institutions were isolated and made ineffective.

The *sexenio* of President Lázaro Cárdenas of Mexico from 1934 to 1940 was suggestive in this regard. There was an incompatibility between the thrust of the Mexican state of that period and the capitalist economy of Mexico. In the right circumstances, this incompatibility would have led to a form of state socialism. Yet, in the actual circumstances, the effect was to strengthen capitalism in Mexico. Intensified land reform, experiments in worker control in nationalized industries, and expropriation of oil from foreign corporations were an auspicious institutional setting. Yet their revolutionary potential was counteracted through the state's using reformist leaders as a means to get control of Mexican peasant and worker unions.[13] Such an outcome is, though, a foregone conclusion for those who see the capitalist state as necessarily reproducing capitalism. A state that allowed capitalism to fail would simply not be considered a capitalist state. A capitalist state would by definition successfully support capitalism; but political theory is not simply a matter of definitions.

Can materialism allow that a state could fail to reproduce the economy? The capitalist state is, to be sure, not a neutral arbiter between classes; one of its functions is to reproduce capitalism. In some circumstances, nonetheless, it may not execute this function well enough actually to reproduce capitalism. The important thing for the materialist is not to insist, in the manner of the atomist materialist, that the state can never fail to be an adequate reflection of the demands of the economy. It is rather to insist that, if and when the state should fail to reproduce the economy, the causal sequence involved in this failure belongs to the framework of the economy that is failing. It is this framework that makes for the possibility of such a sequence. The stimulus cause for the failure of the economy might even be identified as the form of ruling, that is, as the requirement that state rule respect the limits of justice. Still, this cause would be a cause only because of the context of the economy, which it is the state's function to reproduce. Appealing to the form of ruling, as the source of autonomy, does not escape the materialist net.[14]

Consider, second, the origins of the general conflict between justice and the economy. I shall try to show that the conflict is rooted in class conflict and ultimately in the economic structure cause. Thus, whether we ask how a specific case of dysfunctionality arises or how in general the state can be a site of dysfunctionality, we are led back to the materialist structure cause of the framework model.

Let us then ask whether the conflict in the state between form and function is simply a feature of the state itself in isolation from society. Were this the case the form of ruling, institutionalized in a pattern of justice, would have to be derived in a formal fashion from the idea of ruling. Clearly, though, the form of ruling has social roots in that it responds to the need to promote social cohesion by satisfying the expectation that there be limits on benefits and losses. The form of ruling has these social roots since a need to promote cohesion will, in societies that have states, come from the division of roles within the economic framework into surplus taking and surplus making. In its economic function the state tries to insure that surplus taking will continue. To perform this function in the face of the division of roles requires a form of rule that gives consideration to surplus makers through a scheme of justice. There is, though, no guarantee that a scheme of justice sufficient for cohesion will be compatible with continuing surplus taking. We can then say that a contradiction between the form and function of the state will be rooted in the economic framework, where we find the division between surplus takers and surplus makers. (The need for cohesion will come from other divisions – ethnic and gender – as well, since they too can threaten the economy. But here we need only show that the class division is sufficient for the conflict between form and function.)

Within the economic framework we have, then, the basis for a battle between form and function. Who are the partisans of the two sides? In the simplest case, surplus takers will, at crucial junctures, try to push back the boundaries of justice for the sake of economic reproduction. Surplus makers, however, will either defend the boundaries of justice against such an offensive or, in auspicious times, take the offensive themselves to push justice forward, even if this means economic reproduction is imperiled. In any actual case, such as the struggle over the organization of the military, the class allegiances will not be so neatly defined. The old boundaries of justice may also be defended by a declining fraction of the surplus takers who are being marginalized. Also, some surplus takers are willing to push justice forward if the gains in stability are greater than the sacrifices they must make.

This is our first brush with divisions internal to the economic framework. Yet such conflict-generating features are essential to an adequate structure cause. We need, then, to make explicit that the economic framework contains opposed features which are needed for making sense of conflicting tendencies at the level of the state.[15] Without these opposed features – such as surplus taking and surplus making – it would be absurd to suppose that an institution like the state, which exists because of its function, could ever fail in its function of economic reproduction.

Part Two

An assessment of the place
of justice in the state

This part deals with justice as the form of ruling, and the next deals with the economic function of ruling. There will be considerable overlap since justice affects the way the state functions for the economy and hence affects the economy itself. Conversely, the economy and the state's functioning for it partly shape the struggles that eventuate in a pattern of justice.

This part has two major goals. The first is to state and defend a materialist conception of justice, which is part of a broader materialist conception of morality worked out earlier in my *Ethics and Society*. The second is to illustrate the effect of state justice on economic factors.

In addition to state justice, there is also the radical justice of opposition groups. State justice comes from the interest of rulers in continued rule. That interest leads them to adjust the demands of groups in the divided society they rule by the imposition of limits on benefits and losses. Yet a typical opposition group within a divided society will not view the justice of its state as valid from the perspective of that group's best interests. An ascendant opposition group will go further and project a new set of limits on benefits and losses against the state's official pattern of justice. This new set of limits is a radical justice. It has to satisfy two requirements: It must be more favorable than state justice to the interests of the opposition group, and it must be a basis for ruling, giving some weight to the interests of other groups through putting limits on the realization of its own interests.

Both state and radical justice are then grounded in group interests – those of classes, nationalities, and so on, as well as those of ruling elites – rather than in ideals such as the general improvement of society. Such ideals ignore the conflicts of interest in a divided society in order to project a conception of social improvement compatible with all groups. They are to that extent not

65

rooted in a materialist method that attends to social conflicts. Materialism, however, does not retreat to an acceptance of the status quo by rejecting such ideals. It makes room for the duality between state justice, which seeks cohesion by oppressing the majority, and radical justice, which splits society by denying privileges to elites.

The second task is to show how state justice changes economic factors. Though it does not end oppression, it conflicts with the unfettered development of the economy. I illustrate this in regard to property, to inequality, and to class. Property, for example, functions to reproduce the economy through controls over labor, plant, and profit. Despite this, these controls have been modified in numerous ways in the process of placing limits on benefits and losses. Justice, as a symptom of state autonomy, changes property but somehow leaves it the same.

5

Ideal justice

What do we do with the Nazi state? It seems to fit with one of our key claims, the claim about the state functioning to perpetuate the economy. But it is the other claim, the one about justice being a necessity for ruling, that gives us trouble when we come to Hitler and his twelve-year empire. He destroyed civil and political liberties in instituting a reign of terror designed to stamp out all resistance. The independence of the courts was subverted, making criminal courts instruments of arbitrary state violence and civil courts instruments for aggrandizing the cartels. The universality of the law was abrogated through allowing the SS and the Gestapo to make charges and execute punishment as they chose.[1] Shouldn't such a despotism have collapsed of its own weight rather than have waited to fall in a war that mobilized the human and industrial power of the Allies?

1. General social improvement

The conclusion derived from the Nazi state would seem to be that justice is not essential to the state. There are just and unjust states, and to deny this is to display an unhealthy moral sense. The Third Reich was an unjust state if there ever was one, whereas to import the idea of justice into the state is an implicit apology for despotism. The alternative suggested by this criticism moves in the direction of an ideal conception of political justice. I call it ideal since it is dictated not by demands of the state but by more general matters. There are two forms of ideal justice.

Ideal justice of the first form is not called for by governability but is anchored to general social improvement, taken in the following sense. When individuals are advanced toward their realizations there is general social improvement. If what individual realization is depends on group affiliation, then general social improvement will also imply an advance in the realization of group interests. Ideal justice will thus become practical where social conflicts stand-

67

ing in the way of general social improvement are reconciled. The official justice of the state sets limits on benefits and losses in a way that allows for governability. It can do this without advancing individual realization in all groups; it may only establish a line limiting the degree to which one group subordinates another. It would then fail to be ideal justice. The root of the difference is that the interests of the state in governability are not directly the interests of everyone, and hence official state justice, which serves governability, need not serve general social improvement.

Ideal justice of the second form sets limits on benefits and losses on a basis other than advancing social improvement. Those who promote this second form of ideal justice divide into two camps. On the one hand, there are those who are concerned with the impact of their view of justice on the good life, even while emphasizing that their view of justice has another basis. Plato finds the ultimate basis for his view of justice in connections between forms; still, he tries to show that injustice leads to social chaos.[2] Rawls starts with the argument that his view of justice is upheld in an ideal decision-making situation; still, he ends by showing that justice leads to the good life. In contrast with this camp, the typical Aristotelian finds no better basis for justice than its reinforcing the common good. On the other hand, a few moralists feel that the impact of justice on social improvement could be neutral or negative without undercutting the duty to be just. The Kantian view that if justice is not to be violated the last murderer lying in the prison of an island community ought to be executed before the community disperses deliberately ignores the social impact of justice.[3]

I shall concentrate on the first form of ideal justice, which is ideal only because it is anchored to general social improvement. Where ideality derives, as it does for Plato and Kant, from a more radical form of transcendence, it is in direct conflict with my materialist method. Thus little will be said about this second form of ideal justice. The requirement of social improvement would appear to give the first form of ideal justice better materialist credentials. Yet in the end it too is at odds with materialist method since it relies on an assumption about humans at odds with existing divided society.

2. Justice in an oppressive state

It is safe to assume that the Nazi attempt to achieve governability by brutal repression violated all of the familiar forms of ideal justice. If, then, ideal justice is the only relevant kind of justice, it was terror rather than justice that made Germany governable during the Third Reich. Our thesis that justice is necessary for governability seems refuted. But before abandoning the importance of official state justice in regard to governability more needs to be said.

There is another side to the Nazi case that offers us a different impression. The vast pool of six million officially unemployed in Germany in 1932 was almost dried up under Hitler even prior to his big push for military production. Those who had experienced layoffs during the depression viewed the active role of the state in stimulating the economy as a turn toward justice. This involved public credit, public investment, tax write-offs for investments, and credits and subsidies for homeowners. Wages, it is true, were held in line as an additional incentive for investors, but skilled workers were getting more and a piece rate seemed in keeping with the effort to revitalize the economy through achievement. Widening differences between worker incomes could be justified by merit and at the same time serve to keep the class internally divided. Moreover, the social security system of the Weimar Republic was funded and extended: There was unemployment assistance, a pension system, and health and accident insurance. The basic economic needs of German workers were being met as the Nazi state got monopoly capitalism back on its feet.[4]

At the economic level the rationality characteristic of capitalism was still a driving force in Nazi Germany, whereas at the political level all rationality had been destroyed. It was not of course that German capitalism had nothing to do with this political irrationality, for capitalism has both a side that promotes stable industrial relations and a side that, in the monopoly period, promotes instability in international relations.[5] This instability originates in the expansion of national capitals, which thrives on racial myths and anticommunism. In extreme cases, like Nazi Germany, this instability generates political oppression and hence marked unevenness as regards justice. Full employment and social entitlements showed that the aspect of justice having to do with the limits on economic losses had been redrawn for the benefit of the working class. By contrast, the liberty of the working class to realize its will through its old parties was at an end. The old limits on the losses of the lower classes politically and of racial monorities as regards equality were not redrawn at a lower level; they were simply removed. Yet even in this extreme case of Nazi despotism it is true that there were certain limits. There were limits to the poverty of the working class, which had been redrawn through the goals of full employment and social security so as to compensate for the removal of limits to political oppression.

The official justice of the Nazi state was of course challenged. The challenge came from two sources. One source was the proponents of ideal justice – there could be no general improvement, they argued, when, for example, working-class parties were destroyed and Jews were expelled from the civil services. The other source was the proponents of radical justice – the interests of workers and Jews were, they held, the basis for an alternative pattern of justice that promoted civil and human rights. So admitting that the oppressive state has a pattern of justice does not close the possibility of rejecting it, even when ideal justice is ignored.

Philosophers have, though, been reluctant to admit that ruling involves justice even where the rule is oppressive. The realistic Aristotle is no exception; he wavers on the point and finally settles for ideal justice.[6] State justice was for him a matter of the distribution of offices. Even in oligarchy and democracy he finds principles for distributing offices; in an oligarchy the rich get office, whereas in a democracy the rich are excluded. So he is willing to allow that there is a semijustice even in these perverse kinds of rule. Yet he points out that these kinds of rule do not take account of the interests of all, since they take account of exclusively either the rich or the poor, and are hence unstable. They do not set limits on benefits and losses for everyone, and thus they lack patterns of justice in my sense. Aristotle could have ended the matter by noting that stable rule requires justice in the sense of limits for everyone. But no; he jumped immediately to an ideal form of justice. Justice, he claims, derives not from requirements of stable rule but from the goal of every true ruler, which is the improvement of social life. Justice, as the distribution of offices, is decided on the basis of the degree of contribution of individuals to the goal of social improvement. The more you contribute, the better your chances for office. This distribution recommends itself since, inductively, it should enhance or at least continue the pace of social improvement. This does not answer the question of the nature of social improvement. We know that it cannot one-sidedly favor one class to the exclusion of the rest. But if the classes are in conflict, how can there be any improvement that does not hurt some of them?

Before dealing with this question, it will be well to compare briefly the sorts of political justice so far enumerated. *Ideal justice* in this chapter is a form of state justice; it is not, then, a more general form of ideal justice that would apply to all spheres of activity. Moreover, it is limited here to justice as based on general social improvement rather than transcendent forms or pure practical reason. It contrasts with *official state justice*, which may or may not advance general social improvement. (When I speak of state justice without further qualification I shall henceforth mean not ideal state justice but official state justice.) Official state justice does not mean the justice the state merely tells its citizens and the world it is practicing; it means the set of limits on benefits and losses that for reasons of governability are to a significant degree actually enforced by the state. So it is official in that it is a pattern of justice enforced by the state. Official state justice does not get its content just from the need to rule. It depends for its content, to varying degrees, on a mixture of the moral values present in the society. This mixture will include both values promoted as common to the whole society and values derived from the interests of specific groups. It is such a mixture that motivates the social pressures on the state that yield a pattern of justice. Beyond this official justice is *radical justice*, which is likewise a form of political justice. But it is not the actual justice of the state. Radical justice is a set of limits an oppositionist group would be likely to use were it to achieve state power. A materialist interpretation of radical justice makes it a compromise between the interests of an oppositionist group or alliance of groups and the requirements such a group or alliance must face in ruling.

3. True legitimacy

So far the motivation for allowing ideal justice is the reluctance to admit that in an extreme case such as Nazism there is justice merely because there is governance. Connected with this reluctance is the desire to be able to distinguish state power that has "true" legitimacy from state power without it. Those states that realize, or at least tend toward, justice are, in this view, the ones that are legitimate. Legitimacy here goes beyond mere governability. This is because ideal justice is involved and not just the minimal set of limits that allow governance. Ideal justice is then the touchstone of legitimacy. There is legitimacy where conflicts are settled not arbitrarily but by an appeal to ideal justice.

As an indication that there is no arbitrariness, ideal justice provides a way of settling conflicts that is connected with an important goal, the goal of improving the social order. Since the social

71

order is not separate from individuals, we realize this goal by increasing the degree to which everyone can realize his or her capacities. Here we go beyond the bare ability to govern on the basis of the imposition of certain minimal limits. Mere acceptance provides governability, but we are looking, according to the advocate of ideal justice, for rational acceptance of the state by its subjects. The difference between governability and legitimacy is that in the latter case there is a rational basis for acceptance. This basis is a link between the state's form of rule and the good life.[7] The link exists when the form of rule of the legitimate state is a pattern of ideal justice.

This attempt to distinguish true legitimacy from mere acceptance is not part of my program since I attempt to get along without introducing ideal justice. This does not mean, however, that in my view every state is acceptable that is in fact accepted enough to allow for governance. To make room for the acceptable/accepted distinction, I need only appeal to the interests of groups. It is in relation to these interests that the accepted state can be criticized. A state that is accepted enough to allow for governance may not be acceptable in relation to the interests of a group that, by and large, actually accepts it. But another group may find it acceptable in relation to its interests without there being a rational standard for settling this disagreement.[8] The accepted/acceptable dialectic works itself out within the bounds of competing interests, and independently of ideal justice.

4. The compatibility assumption

Behind the notion of true legitimacy is a general difficulty with ideal justice that I wish now to explore. It has to do with the connection between justice and social improvement, and hence the widest possible human realization. What I want to show is that a connection between justice of any sort and the general good requires an extremely strong assumption. This is the assumption that the capacities characteristic of humans in different groups are complementary rather than conflictive. I call this the *compatibility assumption*. Capacities, in the intended sense, include not only features such as the ability to write plays or to join communal decision making, which are only latent in most of us, but also features such as an interest in job security and in human support, which are quite alive in most of us. In face of conflicting interests – say, in oppressing and in overcoming oppression – attempts to satisfy

72

both sides exacerbate tensions and impede social improvement. Yet to satisfy only one side does not provide general social improvement. Because the needed compatibility assumption is doubtful, the conception of true legitimacy proves ineffective, and in turn the motivation for ideal justice disappears.

Beyond a divided society there is no need for the compatibility assumption. The problem for which this assumption provides a resolution exists only when there are antagonistic groups. Perhaps we have here an easy solution to the difficulty I am raising about ideal justice. If the specific social improvement resulting from a form of justice were the change to full socialism, then that form of justice leads us beyond antagonistic groups. It was precisely these antagonistic groups that led to the worry that people from such groups might have conflicting interests. And with conflicting interests any social improvement is not general but one-sided. So a form of justice that leads to full socialism can dispense with the compatibility assumption as a vehicle for getting to this type of good life.

The compatibility assumption is still needed. To see this one must look at socialism not abstractly but as coming out of an earlier society. Workers project a paradise without bosses in order to have a final solution to the exploitation problem. Yet bosses will surely object to this solution – before it is implemented, of course – by pointing out that it is one-sided since their interest in survival as a class is not realized by the socialist project. Socialism involves, then, a retreat from general social improvement. Only if we say the bosses' "genuine interests" are compatible with those of their workers could we say that socialism is a general social improvement. But here the compatibility assumption has come to the rescue. The problem with using the assumption is that it sets us off in a direction of thinking about humans that is not in any way controlled by considerations about their social context. In a society of antagonistic groups, our materialist method would indicate that the characteristic capacities of these groups are conflictive, as will be shown in Section 5 in connection with education.

We can see the need for the compatibility assumption in regard to ideal justice by examining Ernest Barker's theory of the state, which gave us an appealing update of Aristotelian political theory. For Barker the state exists not to centralize force or to protect the economy but to promote the good life. He understands the good life in terms of the capacities of citizens of the state. The state exists to facilitate the fullest realization of the capacities of all citizens. Justice plays a role in this process since the state applies principles of justice in order to resolve conflicts that would otherwise be an obstacle to full realization. Barker notes that the Latin etymology of our word *justice* gives it a root meaning of joining or fitting together. Justice joins or fits together the persons, groups, or principles that stand in opposition in a conflict situation. However, I would claim that justice can do this only if the compatibility assumption that conflict is eliminable is accepted.

On this assumption, justice will be able to deal with the often noted conflict between liberty and equality. Where there is an opposition between a principle of liberty that calls for freedom of enterprise and a principle of equality that calls for wider control of the means of production it is, Barker notes, justice that fits these principles together through putting limits both on free enterprise and on collective ownership.[9] If this fitting together is properly done, human realization will be advanced. If, though, the compatibility assumption is wrong, such liberty and equality may represent opposed tendencies basic to people in opposed groups. Fitting them together by putting limits on free enterprise and on collective ownership would then merely impede the realization of people in each group.

5. Education and the compatibility assumption

This difficulty with ideal justice can be illustrated by considering the specific case of state-supported primary and secondary education. Education puts the compatibility assumption that the characteristic capacities of people in different groups are not conflictive to a severe test. According to Barker, the state supports schools and makes attendance compulsory as part of its task of facilitating human realization. The schools are supposed to prepare people for the realization of their capacities through the appropriate skills, knowledge, and attitudes. Is this a goal the state can reach?

We know of course that the schools fall woefully short of preparation for fullest realization of human potential, thereby leading to a crisis of public confidence once every twenty years over whether the schools are doing what they should. Part of this failure derives from the fact that state-supported schools were and still are a response to the need to integrate people into their careers.[10] Since careers are not homogeneous, the educational system develops polar tendencies. Some students are on their way to jobs calling for, among other things, only the most elementary calculative and verbal skills. They are either shunted into a lower track or left to fall behind in an umbrella program. They end up with little stimulus either for intellectual and cultural development or even for basic skills of literacy. Other students are on their way to jobs calling for literacy, nonrepetitive action, and organizational skills. Their schools will encourage these traits if they happen to be the majority group in their neighborhoods. Otherwise, they can hope for special programs in more heterogeneous schools. Overall, the school system disables some for highly technical, nonrepetitive, and organizational work, whereas those trained for such work become disabled for satisfying work of other kinds. The educational system thus fails to prepare for human realization. It succeeds only in reproducing a rift in the work force, which is customarily labeled the division between the mental and the manual but which in actuality is a matter more of a division between greater and lesser authority than of the dualism of mind and body.[11] Does this failure to prepare for human realization reflect a failure of the compatibility assumption that human capacities are not conflictive? Or can a reform of education lay the basis for ideal justice?

There are several reforms that might be suggested in order to bring the schools into line with the state's alleged goal of human realization. The problem is that none of them is acceptable. First, there is the *discriminatory solution:* Some people deserve more and better education than others. People in different sections of the work force are, it is assumed, where they are because of greater or lesser ability. What is needed is an even greater polarization of the education system than exists now. Otherwise, we make the mistake of trying to elevate the intellectual level of the less capable beyond their capacities. At present the separation of the two groups is not rigorous enough; hence, those with genuine ability have their program diluted due to the effort to deal with those less capable. The assumption here of a correspondence between jobs and ability has not been shown to have a basis in fact, making this reform gratuitous.

Second, there is the *egalitarian solution:* People should not be treated as fodder for jobs; they should be educated as human beings. This requires, except for remedial work, a common curriculum for wealthy suburbanites, for future professional and technical workers, and for future unskilled and semiskilled workers. This reform proposal runs against the inability of the schools to transcend social differences; so long as the society reproduces sizable income and authority differentials, the reform of education for the full realization of capacities by a common curriculum is a will-o'-

75

the-wisp. This is not merely because the state must reproduce the divisions of the society through the schools. More basically, it is because in a divided society a common curriculum for all social classes and fractions of classes does not answer to the internal interests of all of them at once. Full realization for the members of any one group includes the realization of capacities characteristic of that group, and thus it cannot be promoted by a training common to all.

Third, there is the *pluralist solution:* As just suggested, people need to be educated for the realization of the capacities they are most likely to have, given the groups they are destined to live in. Since there are different groups, there will be different educational tracks but without the invidious distinctions inherent in a discriminatory solution. Each group will be trained in methods for realizing its interests. A proper implementation of this reform will have to put the force of the state behind education in methods of class struggle, in the liberation of the oppressed, and in the unwritten histories of the lower classes and the oppressed. At the same time the force of the state will back up a very different education for those in the wealthy suburban schools. In effect, one and the same state would, for the sake of a program of human realization that respects differences between people, underwrite a system of education that intensifies the divisions in the society and ultimately promotes revolution. Examples of such a pluralist reform are, naturally, few and ephemeral.[12] Its intensification of divisions is clearly at odds with a justice that is supposed to resolve conflict. Moreover, by educating classes for combating one another, the outcome would not be human realization all around, since there would be losers in the combat. Thus such a reform is not only at odds with a view of the state that gives it the task of reproducing the economy but also with one that gives it the task of human realization.

We reach the libertarian-sounding conclusion that in a divided society the state, at least through education and perhaps in other areas as well, cannot promote human realization all around and hence cannot promote social betterment. Appealing to ideal justice will not help the state in this task since our materialist approach points to conflicting interests.

6. Can the compatibility assumption be avoided?

I wish to end by showing that the problem raised by the pluralist solution to educational reform has wider implications for ideal justice. The compatibility assumption is needed to solve this problem, but the only proof of it reverts to an appeal to state justice.

Barker would respond to the seemingly libertarian conclusion with the claim that there is hope for the third type of reform, the pluralist reform, provided we reject the view founded on the materialist approach that promoting capacities in different groups in society stirs up conflict between those groups. There are indeed genuine differences, he would say, between people in different groups, but these differences are complementary rather than conflictive. If we have a good idea as to what justice is, then justice can serve as the touchstone for finding the genuine differences. How can this be done? In using the apparatus of justice to resolve conflicts over who gets what benefits or burdens, we peel away the adventitious differences associated with such conflicts. The difference between owners and workers based on the tendencies toward free enterprise and collective ownership is adventitious since justice resolves the conflict between these tendencies by placing limits on both of them. Only the remaining nonconflictive differences between humans in different groups are genuine. They can be reflected in a pluralist system of education that promotes human fulfillment.

It is vitally important that this conciliation by justice eliminate only adventitious differences; otherwise, the realization of some fundamental human capacities is being neglected. The difficulty is that our sole basis for designating differences as adventitious is that justice sidetracks them in the process of conflict avoidance. Why, though, must they be adventitious if justice eliminates them? Perhaps justice thwarts the realization of fundamental features. It will not do to respond that, since justice leads to a fuller realization of human nature, any restrictions imposed by justice affect only accidental aspects of humans. For what is in question is precisely whether some capacities are being denied realization simply for justice to advance conflict resolution. To save Barker's position, we are forced, then, to retreat to the strong but unproven compatibility assumption that human capacities, at least the fundamental ones, are not conflictive.[13] Only on this assumption is the conciliation of differences by justice compatible with full human realization.

If the assumption about the compatibility of capacities across groups has any plausibility at all, it comes from a quarter that undermines the whole spirit of the tradition that appeals to ideal justice. The justice that ends conflict does not do so by deliberately picking out and then eliminating adventitious differences between groups that spark conflict. Rather, it ends conflict by looking to see what differences jeopardize a form of rule that promotes a certain kind of economy. The judgment that these differences are adventitious is *post hoc* in relation to the determination that they must be curbed to provide for governability. So governability rather than maximum human realization is, after all, the root of justice.

One can actually read Barker's example of the fitting together of liberty and equality in this way. The fitting together meant that both the capacity for the unbridled accumulation of wealth and the capacity for posing worker control as an alternative to private ownership had to be modified and thus, in their pure form, eliminated. Otherwise, the state, in the name of full human fulfillment, would contradictorily not only advance capitalism but also become an enthusiastic booster of socialism. It is clear that Barker had no such thing in mind. Capitalism was the preferred form of economy for him. He worried that the attack on private property begun by the British Labour Party after World War II might end the private ownership of the means of production. So justice for him meant a fitting together of capacities that resulted in their being different from what they had been, provided the modification insured that the state would still reproduce the economy. Calling the differences due to the capacities in unmodified form adventitious to humans ceases to be a point about human nature and becomes a point about what is needed to reduce conflict in order to make rule possible. To that extent, ideal justice has been domesticated as justice necessary for governance.

How general, though, is the problem raised by the compatibility assumption? Does it affect theories other than those of the Aristotelian sort adopted by Barker? It is worth noting that Rawls's position in *A Theory of Justice* does not avoid this problem. He too holds that his conception of justice has a positive social impact by enabling people "to express their nature as free and equal moral persons."[14] His general principle of justice is that equality is to be pursued in the distribution of basic social goods so long as it tends to everyone's advantage. What counts here as an advantage is determined by what counts as a primary social good, a good that can be useful no matter what the differences in people's capacities and aims. He includes as primary social goods "rights and liberties, powers and opportunities, income and wealth." Advantaging people in any group in regard to rights, power, and income can, though, make them better able to exercise capacities that are at odds with the exercise of capacities of people in another group.

78

Thus a distribution that is to everyone's advantage would fan the flames of class hostility, thereby creating a socially chaotic situation in which people set up obstacles to the realization of one another's nature.

This runs against our intuitions since we normally suppose that advantaging everyone will satisfy everyone and reduce social conflict. But we suppose this in a context where capacities leading to conflict have been effectively controlled and only nonconflicting capacities benefit from advantaging everyone. Rawls himself supposes such a context. He supposes that where justice has become operative – "a well-ordered society" – any conflicting capacities would be reined in, since realizing them would doubtless rupture the social union that is supposed to result from justice. But it needs to be assumed that these conflicting capacities can be reined in without trampling on what is important about individual persons with these capacities. Thus the same strong assumption of the compatibility of capacities needed by Barker is needed by Rawls.

6

Property and justice

Sometimes classical debates help us with the formulation of contemporary problems. They can have a relevance that transcends the circumstances in which they were initiated. This is certainly true of the debate between Hobbes and Locke on the nature of property. It helps set the problem of how and to what extent state justice can modify the nature of property in the economy the state itself is supposed to perpetuate.

1. Hobbes and Locke on property

Hobbes takes the view that property is a creation of the state and thus has no place in a period of anarchy.[1] Locke, however, insists that property is at root a private right resulting from the interchange between a private individual and nature.[2] The Lockean view recurs today in libertarian defenses of property against the encroachments of the state. Following in Hobbes' footsteps are social democratic views of property that make it dependent on the state.

The political motivations of these views of property are an integral part of their justification. If indeed property is a private right, then it makes sense to say that the role of the state is the protection of property, along with other private rights such as the right to personal security. Property on this Lockean view is a given that the state accepts and supports; there is no justification for an interventionist state that would subvert these antecedent private rights. The consistent Lockean will object to taxation without unanimous support for it as vigorously as to compulsory draft registration since both infringe upon private rights, whereas the state should be limited to the protection of private rights.

If, on the contrary, property is not a private right, state interference with personal property is not a violation of private rights. Indeed, if it is a right created by the state, the state can interfere with it so long as this interference serves the aims of the state,

whatever they may be. There is no appeal to anything more fundamental than the state that would guarantee property rights that the
state could not interfere with. On this view, with its roots in
Hobbes, the state is regarded as an institution of positive reform,
and one of the things it can legitimately reform is the property
system. One cannot say that the state in its reforming zeal is interfering with property rights, since there are no property rights apart
from the state. So the Lockean and the Hobbesian views of property
reflect the divergent political views of libertarian suspicion of state
activity and social democratic encouragement of state reforms.

The actual relation of the state to property is more complicated
than is suggested by either view. In the end, what I want to say is
that neither view takes into account both the element of justice,
which limits the economy, and the element of economics, which
limits the state. The Lockean view does seem to contain an element
of justice that limits the economy. For Locke at first limits the
acquisition of property to leaving "enough and as good" for others
and to no more than one could use "before it spoils." But later in his
Treatise he sees that with the introduction of money into the economy such limits are unnecessary. An adequate subsistence, even for
the landless worker, will follow upon the productivity increases
encouraged by a money economy. Locke is then free to emphasize
how the state serves the economy without being forced to give
systematic recognition to the need the state has to limit property
for the sake of governability. But the Hobbesian view emphasizes
the limits imposed on property by the state without explicitly recognizing that the state operates in the service of the economy. For
now, though, I wish to point out the weakness in the justifications
given by Hobbe and Locke for their views.

The basic argument of the Hobbesians is that in a "state of nature" people cannot enjoy what might be called their property
rights with any degree of assurance. In the absence of a sovereign
over them all, people invade one another's domains with impunity.
But if people cannot have the assurance that they will get the
benefit of what is called theirs, then there is really no distinction
between "mine" and "thine" and hence no property. Thus, at its
origin, the state faces no preexisting property. It is, then, free to
distribute wealth and organize trade as it will, provided only that
it does not lose legitimacy in the process.

Hobbes was well aware of the active role the state had in fact
played in regard to property. He seemed to want to deduce from
this active role that the state was the source of property. Was he,

81

though, warranted in claiming more than that the state was active in changing a preexisting system of property that was in shambles? The state had intervened in important ways that Hobbes had witnessed. In 1646, during the Puritan Revolution and five years before the appearance of *Leviathan*, Parliament abolished feudal tenures, and the sequestered estates of royalists and bishops were to be sold. The movement against monopolistic trading companies, which had been able to keep their charters through bribes and winning favor at court, was far from a movement against state control of trade. The movement wanted an end to the exclusion of new enterprises from the privileges enjoyed by the 200 monopolies. To achieve this it moved against the royal prerogative that kept the control of trade and finance out of the hands of Parliament.[3] So to Hobbes it was clear that trade, whether in the hands of a monarch or a sovereign assembly, was a state matter – "to assign in what places, and for what commodities, the subject shall traffic abroad, belongeth to the sovereign."

Nonetheless, the visible hand of the state in matters of property in no way indicated that the state was the foundation of property. The state in England in the middle of the seventeenth century was at the intersection of conflicting property systems. But it was working out a transformation from one of them to the other rather than creating a system of property from whole cloth. The development of merchant capital depended on further expansion of the market, which in turn required the development of capitalist agriculture. This development in its turn was furthered by purchases by the new bourgeoisie of the sequestered estates made available by the state. Also, the movement against the trade monopolies came from the pressure of merchant capital. The state showed its cognizance of this movement through granting broader economic rights. Clearly, the older feudal forms of property were already present. There was no question of the state needing to create property. The question was what role the state would play in the combat between forces leading to capitalist agriculture and an expanded market and forces supporting feudal landed property and the monopolies sanctioned by the monarchy. The state regulated, reformed, and compromised property rights without being the source of property rights.

The basic argument of Locke is that it is sufficient in order to own something to mix one's own labor with it. Were this indeed true, then the state would not enter into the basis of property, though it might of course enter into its subsequent regulation.

82

Locke seems largely oblivious to considerations about the community of labor: How are we to assign property when most products are the result not of a single individual's labor but of the labor of a community? Even if there were not a division of labor in the production of individual things, there is an obvious division of labor in the production of the labor power that produces them. Thus something like the modern economic doctrine of reward according to the contribution of each factor of production to the final product seems a necessary emendation to the Lockean view of property as a private right.[4] But it is well known that there is no satisfactory way of judging the contribution of any factor of production, other than to assume that the market reward to that factor is a correct assessment of its contribution. Hence it is the social forces determining the distribution of the product and not private acts of labor that are at the root of property.

Apart from this difficulty of justifying property as a private right, there is the added difficulty of reconciling property in this sense with governance by the state. The state becomes ungovernable if property is a private right. Locke seems to recognize this, but his effort to deal with the problem leads him into inconsistency. Since for him the state exists to protect property, it would be absurd for the state to attack the property of its citizens without their full consent. It is possible to forego a private right by consent, but the consent would have to be individual consent. I cannot consent to your giving up property since you, not I, hold that property by a private right. That at least is what a consistent Locke would have us say. He tells us, though, that it is sufficient for the majority to decide for everyone in the matter of taxation.[5] This quite clearly violates the private nature of the right, but as he tells us earlier on, if the consent of every individual were necessary in order to decide any matter, the mighty leviathan would not "outlast the day it was born in." The nature of property is crucial here because governance "cannot be supported without great charge."

There is a possible escape that would make governability compatible with the inviolability of property rights. Locke was, after all, thinking primarily of a citizenry composed of holders of tangible property and of the possibility of taxing their property while protecting it. Instead, the great expense of government could be clapped onto those who lack tangible property as a tax on wages. They would own only their labor power and thus be beholden to the state for intervening to insure the conditions for their livelihood. Though this avoids the problem of majority rule among owners of tangible property, it creates serious stresses between the classes and thus raises the issue of governability from a different direction. In any event, property rights that cannot be violated by the state, apart from full consent, are a serious obstacle to governability.

2. The state's modification of natural rights

I turn now to the development of a middle position between the Hobbesian statist and the Lockean economist extremes. For our purposes, the Lockean notion of a natural right to what one has mixed one's labor with is not very useful. The controversy between Locke and Hobbes over property can, though, be carried forward to the present. Instead of speaking of natural entitlements, I shall introduce the interests of social groups. These interests lie behind the rights of those groups. The contrast between nature and state becomes that between group and state. When the rights of groups clash, the state interferes to put limits on their pursuit of their interests. It thereby contrives a pattern of justice for limiting the "natural" thrust of group interest. If the rights of groups are modified by the state, the narrowness of Lockean economism is avoided. But Hobbesian statism is also avoided since the justice the state contrives is imposed on pregiven group rights.

Consider the case of management rights, which are one aspect of the institution of property. The interests of surplus takers are behind a widely held conception of management rights in the modern corporation. Those rights inform us about the limits of worker control over the means of production. Thus management may determine when to lay workers off and when to shut the plant down; it may decide when it is time to start a product change; it may fire probationary workers. Lacking these management rights, workers are denied property in the means of production.

Management rights are not the only property rights making up the ownership of the means of production, but they, like other property rights, distribute control in regard to production differentially so that surplus makers have less of it. Those who have management rights may delegate them to others, who are then not owners but only their agents. The view that managers have taken control from owners – the managerial revolution – either mistakenly equates those who are mere agents of owners with managers in their own right or else mistakenly distinguishes those who have the underived right to manage from owners.

The matter does not end here. The state may be destabilized by the distribution of control contained in the surplus takers' conception of management rights. It is conceivable that the state could work for changes in this conception on several grounds. On the one hand, it could object to the conception as not providing enough control to surplus takers and their agents to assuredly reproduce the economy. On the other hand, it can object to the conception of management rights as providing so much control to surplus takers and their agents that surplus makers are encouraged to rebellion. In the first case, it is the state's role as protector of the economy and in the second case it is the state's impulse to self-preservation that leads it to change the surplus takers' conception of management rights. Yet the two cases are not thoroughly distinct since the state plays its role as protector of the economy partly because "it cannot be supported without great charge." Conceptually at least, there remains the distinction between the primary end of the state and its survival.

Those changes in management rights and other rights pertaining to property that are needed to maintain enough legitimacy for effective governance are the ones that lead to a conception of property that from the perspective of the state is just. I speak of justice in connection with this conception of property since it puts limits on the distribution of controls in a way that advances governability. This changed conception of property has two sides to it. It reflects both the antecedent surplus takers' conception of property that comes from considerations of economic self-interest and the need the state has for a legitimacy it can get only by curbing self-interest for the general benefit. The result is a just conception of property in a sense of justice that implies it is for the good of all concerned and not just those in a more powerful position in the economy. Both the Lockean emphasis on economic interest and the Hobbesian emphasis on governability are combined in this just conception of property.

For the above distinction between rights based on groups and state justice to be useful, it is helpful to view justice as modifying rights rather than denying the existence of the unmodified rights. Otherwise, it would seem that those privileges we call property rights but that in fact come to be compromised for the sake of governability are simply not rights at all but only presumptive rights. Yet making them merely presumptive suggests that groups cannot be a genuine basis for rights. I cannot accept this suggestion without being shown that reasons of state are higher than group interests. One might show this by showing that the state stands for

85

ideal justice. Having rejected ideal justice in the last chapter, I will treat the rights modified by state justice as genuine.

3. Property rights as controls for the economy

I turn now to a more detailed discussion, with the above as background. What is a property right? At the general level, a property right is a right to control something. We are primarily concerned here with rights of "productive" as opposed to "user" property. When you own productive property you have control over facets of the process of production, whereas when you own user property you have control over things you can consume for direct satisfaction. Within the category of productive property there is a distinction between "private" and "communal" property. It is the nature of the agency of control that is the basis for this distinction. Private property is controlled by one or more individuals. They may form an *ad hoc* association – called a corporation – to conduct their affairs, but private property is not controlled by anything with the established structure of a community. Members of a community are not free to divide communal property in order to exchange their shares for control over other things.[6] Since private property is controlled by one or more individuals, it can be either "individual" or "corporate" private property. Communal property, on the other hand, is sometimes the property of the state, but there are communities without states that are nonetheless not corporations, since they are not *ad hoc* associations for the realization of limited economic goals.

When considering private productive property within the capitalist system, we find several things to beware of. We cannot approach the matter with any hope of success if we insist on thinking of property as material things to which persons have some special relationship. It is common enough to speak this way, but for analytical purposes it is best to think not of things but of processes and not of a special relation but of several different forms of control. The relevant facets of the capitalist production process are labor, plant and material, and product. It is not material things that reveal the structure of capitalist ownership but the processes of using labor, using plant and material, and using the product for investment.

Control over any one of these processes is a property right.[7] First, control over labor is an ownership right exercised for owners usually by agents ranging from general managers to shop-floor supervisors. These agents control the application of labor to fixed capital through hiring, firing, work schedules, and work pace. Second, control over the use of plant and material involves determining the quantity, quality, and mix of products. Third, control over the product is an ownership right with several dimensions. On the one hand, there is the right of owners to make investment decisions; this gives owners or their agents the right to determine how much and where to borrow and whether to acquire existing facilities through purchase or merger or to expand by building new facilities. On the other hand, the right to make investment decisions implies the right to make distributional decisions. Ownership involves the control of distribution since it involves deciding on wages, deciding on the division of the surplus product between the shareholders and recapitalization, and deciding on redistributional schemes such as pension plans, profit sharing, and public service foundations. These investment and direct distributional decisions control the fate of the product.

Whereas control over any one of the facets of production is a property right, this control can vary considerably without destroying that right. Our account is not complete until we have found the basis for the variation. The control exercised by owners in any one of these three facets will vary from time to time and place to place. Control over labor, for example, is different in the *maquiladoras* on the Mexico–United States border, where workers have few rights, from what it is in a unionized auto plant in central Indiana, where workers have more rights. And control over investment is different when there are enterprise zones with their low taxes and favorable "labor climate" than when such opportunities are unavailable for the profit-hungry entrepreneur.

Normally, capitalist property would involve some control over each of the three facets of production. It is conceivable, though, that capitalist property could continue as an institution even if it lost control in one of the three facets of production. Capitalist property would not then involve property rights in all three areas. Keynes recommended a "socialization of investment" that would have given the state the right to determine the aggregate amount to be invested and the rate of return to shareholders.[8] The further step of allowing the state to determine what new facilities will be made and what mix of capital and labor will be used in them would not have pleased Keynes. Indeed, the property right to control investment would be effectively destroyed by these steps. Still, this might yet be consistent with capitalism's reproduction.

Here we arrive at the heart of the matter. The basis for this variation is that property is a support for the reigning economic system. As conditions change under which the economy must survive, the property system responds with changes that tend to promote survival.[9] Those forms of control that cease to be useful for the economy can be relaxed. It then becomes inappropriate to speak of those forms of control as being rights of property. This leads us to a positive formulation. *Those forms of control over facets of production that are useful for the economy's survival and that, when added to other such controls, make up an adequate set of controls for the economy's survival can appropriately be considered property rights.* In terms of the framework model, changes in property rights are stimulated by changing conditions, and this connection takes place within the framework of the existing economy.

Since the economic framework underlies property relations, the economic framework must be described independently of property. (This description will be carried out in Chapter 10.) The motivation here is that the pattern of activity characteristic of an economy is one thing whereas the system of controls that helps to get people to limit themselves to such a pattern is quite another. We do not know *a priori* the kinds of controls that will help to implement a pattern of economic activity. To find that out calls for looking at the historical situation into which the pattern of economic activity is being inserted. In many patterns of economic activity there is surplus making and surplus taking. Considered abstractly as economic activity, surplus taking does not force surplus from surplus makers, and thus it calls for no controls of the kind that make up property. Dropping the abstraction, we find that in most historical situations surplus takers bolster their position with socially sanctioned controls over the facets of production.[10]

Within the historical situations that have accompanied most economies, property has developed in such a way that those who have property rights are the surplus takers and their agents. They are the ones who exercise control in at least some of the forms we have been talking about. That these surplus takers have a right to exercise these forms of control depends on whether their exercising them tends to reproduce the given economic system. This of course goes around the Lockean view that property rights are prior even to economic systems by relativizing property rights to economic systems. If this relativization is correct, then there is no transcendent justification of property since every justification sets out from a given economic system.[11] The question-begging character of all the attempts at transcendent justifications of property I have seen reassures me that some form of relativization is correct.

88

4. How justice modifies property rights

On to justice! These property rights insofar as they arise out of the economy will be compatible with the state only in its role as a bulwark of the economy. But we need to consider, in addition to the function of the state, its form. The state is a ruling body, and it must secure its rule. One of the requirements of ruling is that the state be perceived as standing for everyone's interests. And it attempts to stand for everyone's interests by putting limits on benefits and losses. One way of putting limits on benefits and losses is by modifying property rights. The property rights that get modified are those that have arisen as jointly adequate controls for reproducing the economy. I shall call these the *initial* property rights. Of course, since the state is always active, initial property rights are an abstraction useful only for explaining the role of the state. If the state leaves the initial property rights unmodified, it may appear to have sided too closely with the surplus takers, who benefit by having surplus taking reproduced. Initial property rights cannot be modified drastically without putting the state in conflict with its own economic function. Governability may, on occasion, call for modifications so drastic that owners have too little control to assuredly reproduce the economy.

There are, to be sure, modifications of initial property that do stay within the limits of functionality. Initial property tends to promote economic reproduction. Still, this leaves considerable room for flexibility in changing property without undermining the economy. Taxation, for example, modifies the private right to invest the product, and in a context of a state that wastes its revenue taxation might weaken the economy sufficiently so that its replacement would be feasible. The context might, though, be changed in such a way that the state uses its revenue to overcome economic sluggishness and thus to promote investment. The initial right to invest was, along with other controls, adequate for the survival of the economy. Still, it was not necessary for survival since in its modified form it remained, together with other controls, adequate for the survival of the economy in the new context of an interventionist state.

In sum, the change of initial property by the state may give rise to challenges to the economy of two sorts. First, there is the *moderate* challenge that occurs when an adequate set of controls is modified to yield what, as a result of accompanying changes, is also an adequate set of controls for economic reproduction. Surplus makers may still see such a change as an improvement, at least as regards some controls. Second, there is the *extreme* challenge that occurs when property controls are so drastically modified that, without a change of circumstances that makes it politically feasible to reintroduce strong property controls, the economic system is so weakened that political events could easily precipitate its demise.

The challenge to the economy posed by the state's modification of property is not a challenge that comes in an abstract way. Property rights are not, that is, modified simply to suit the demands of an ideal justice. The challenge comes through the state from those who do not have production property and who are asserting rights that come under the general rubric of democratic control of facets of production. As a justice maker, the state must fit the rights of different groups together, but it may find that it is impossible to fit these democratic rights together with property rights without a restriction on property rights that threatens the reproduction of the economy. The goal of the fitting together is governability rather than an ideal such as the realization of the capacities of all. A challenge to capitalism introduces a tricornered struggle, with the state, the burgeoisie, and the nonowners as the contestants.

The recent history of welfare rights shows how the state's change of property creates the potential for conflict between the state and the economy. In the United States in the 1960s and 1970s income-maintenance programs were expanded as never before.[12] In those twenty years the numbers of people in the Aid to Families with Dependent Children rolls quadrupled. There was a sharp rise in the disability compensation rolls. The Comprehensive Employment and Training Act provided job training and public service jobs in an effort to attack chronic unemployment. An optimistic activism during this period coupled with a pessimistic foreboding that prosperity would wane before most people could share in it helped to promote the expansion of income maintenance.

Property rights were modified at that time by taking the funds for income maintenance out of the social product. There was a growing feeling on the part of the business community, articulated by conservative intellectuals, that this erosion of property was undermining capitalism. What was the state to do, reeling from lower-class pressure for a share in the waning prosperity and smarting from the delegitimation resulting from the Vietnam debacle and the Watergate scandal? Control over part of the product of enterprise – the part that would pay for welfare programs – was taken out of the hands of owners. Moreover, with income mainte-

90

nance for the unemployed, there was less possibility of disciplining the employed by reducing wages in a period of mild stagnation. All of these "attacks" on property set limits on losses and benefits that would let the state appear to act for all and not just for surplus takers.

We do not know whether another decade of income-maintenance expansion would have done the economy in, as the critics maintained. We do know that enough owners saw a serious threat and were more than willing to mount a counteroffensive, which culminated in the Reagan administration's welfare cuts in the heart of the 1981–2 recession. Hence, in the United States between 1979 and 1982 there was a 47 percent increase in poverty, and three million of the eight million added to the poverty lists got there as a result of federal budget cuts. The counteroffensive was well timed because the militancy that would have been a threat to governability in the wake of such cuts had they occurred in 1970 had completely dissipated by 1980. There was a double movement. The recession called for stronger controls to realize profitability. Thus there was an economic basis for stopping the erosion of property relations. Also, the broad movement for democratic controls of the 1960s and 1970s was dead. Thus there was also a political basis for stopping the erosion of property.

We have said that state justice adjusts initial property rights, but the just property rights resulting from this have a new basis. They are no longer a mere requirement of the economy for certain forms of control; they are now those forms of control by owners that are compatible with governability. That the state can adjust property rights, up to and including an extreme challenge, is a clear sign of its autonomy – of the way its form can conflict with its functional role.

This is very different from the view, common among Christian Democrats, that justice calls for a restriction of the unjustified claims of property.[13] They assume that the justified claims of capital and the restrictions of justice are compatible, and so there is no need to worry that justice will conflict with the viability of capitalism. Such a view starts with an assumption of harmony in order never to have to challenge capital. My view is that there can be no presumption of harmony between forms of property adequate for capitalism and the requirements of state justice.

91

7

Repression and radical justice

"I've been a hundred percent American all my life, but now I feel the justice system needs some help." This is how a strike leader summed up his experiences with the state toward the end of a seven-month-long strike by the Brotherhood of Railway Carmen against the Railcar Company in Washington, Indiana, in 1980. Police harassed strikers not just on the picket line but throughout the town; 30 of the 362 strikers were arrested. Another striker described the southern Indiana town of twelve thousand as "nothing but a kangaroo court aimed at the strikers." An administrative law judge for the National Labor Relations Board listened to the company's charges about union violence, but there was no place for responses from the union. In addition, strikers were outraged at the money the city was spending to protect and deliver scabs to the plant, scabs who proved unable to build the freight cars the company made. The strike was about the differential between the carmen's five-dollar-an-hour wage in Washington and their nine-dollar-an-hour national average. With the aid of the state the Railcar Company forced the union to accept its derisory wage offer and then shortly thereafter closed its Washington plant down anyhow. "Labor trouble" was the reason Mayor Leo Sullivan gave for the fact that three major manufacturers left Washington in a decade.[1]

From the perspective of the ruler, justice is a necessity; but from that of the ruled, it is rarely sufficient. It is to the perspective of the ruled that we now turn. In numerous situations, such as the Washington strike, repression is left to quash grievances that state justice fails to settle. Hence, people become morally outraged at the state. The set of limits imposed by the state on losses and benefits is inadequate protection for the realization of the interests of various groups of the ruled. In Chapter 6, I pointed out that in regulating property state justice may be in conflict with the interests of owners, that is, with the interests of those whose control over the facets of production permits the economy to persist. Now we see

92

that the justice of the state conflicts with the interests of many who are excluded from that control.

1. Outrage as the origin of justice

The state's role in bringing such diverse groups as owners and workers together to be ruled makes it inevitable that its justice will outrage each of these groups, though perhaps not to the same degree. State justice will, in any event, disappoint people like the Washington strikers since this same justice must also serve to legitimate the state for those who control Evans Products, the billion-dollar conglomerate that owns Railcar Company. Because ruling is supposed to encompass class, race, gender, and nationality differences, it is not surprising that the pattern of justice it adopts for legitimacy does not always guarantee universal acceptance. There is no reason to believe that there is a system of limits on benefits and losses that would guarantee acceptance in every corner. The state must nonetheless continue to act as spokesperson for the whole and to tout its justice as in everyone's best interest, even when it comes into collision with the central interests of some of the groups under its rule. Otherwise, it would provoke too much opposition to win it the widespread if not universal acceptance needed to govern.

The outrage is far from equally shared between dominant and dominated groups. The state is, after all, not playing umpire according to some ideal justice. It adopts measures of justice under the stimulus of circumstances in order to be able to rule, but these causal relations between circumstances and measures of justice are formed within the framework of the economy. That framework allows those circumstances to give rise to a wide range of possible measures of justice. But this range is narrower than it would be without the economic framework. As a result, measures of justice are quite likely to be half-measures or worse as judged from the perspective of a dominated class, whereas this is less likely to be true from the perspective of the dominant economic class. In particular, where the circumstances that act as stimuli for measures of justice are merely separate movements with sporadic activity, the economic framework will limit those measures to moderate challenges to the economic system. Where, though, the stimuli are broader, more insistent movements, it is still possible that within the economic framework the resulting measures of justice will be in conflict with the class interests of the dominant class. An economic framework is predisposed to connections with results that reinforce that framework, but this is the most we can say. The framework favors measures of justice that reproduce it, without guaranteeing, in extreme circumstances, measures that will not outrage the dominant group.

State justice has gone some way toward limiting property. But has it gone far enough to get regular support from workers? In the United States the employer must make a contribution to social insurance; the employer is expected to comply with health and safety standards; the employer is required to recognize a duly elected union as the agent of the workers. Still, a lot is left to the employer, as the Washington strikers found out. The employer can replace strikers after a certain period simply by refusing to budge on the strikers' demands; the employer can easily obtain an injunction against mass picketing; there is no expectation that strikers' complaints against plant security personnel or hired goons will be acted upon by the police or the courts. All of this falls under that aspect of property which concerns the control of labor. When there is no labor conflict, workers respect this state justice on the grounds that the boss has rights too. Yet, in periods of conflict with the intensity of a strike, the willingness to accept the imposed limits on benefits and losses for the sake of the whole society wears thin and finally frays out. The sacrifices required become too great and the benefits derived too few. Then, as the Railcar striker said, "the justice system needs some help." Dominated groups discover their outrage at the pattern of state justice when its inadequacy to protect their interests becomes clear in conflicts where their interests are openly challenged.

Here is the origin of various alternative conceptions of justice that attempts either to patch up or to overturn the justice of the state. The origin is the moral outrage that confrontations with the state occasion. This outrage identifies the system of state justice as itself a mechanism whereby the state controls groups within society.[2] In turn, it identifies this system of control as one that is at the expense of interests that cannot be neglected if there is to be a genuine unity of the groups of the society, as opposed to a forced truce between them.

The outrage itself does not then identify a new conception of justice but only rejects the adequacy of the existing system of state justice. It is, though, a first step toward a new conception. Its radicalizing potential can be wasted through the acceptance of myths of national and racial grandeur that are incompatible with the fundamental interests of the groups that were thwarted by the existing system of state justice. Nazi myths and attempts to act on them provided only a surrogate for, rather than a satisfaction of, the fundamental interests blocked by the Weimar Republic. My concern here is only with those rejections of state systems of justice that are built upon by an alternative conception of justice reflecting the fundamental interests of the groups rejecting state justice. I assume without argument that within historical materialism the economic framework plus the interacting roles of the various groups provide a basis for picking out the fundamental interests of those groups without recourse to an *a priori* humanism.

Radical justice is not identical with the rights of dominated groups. We have already seen that rights express group interests whereas justice, whether of an existing regime or of a group aspiring to state power, tends to take a view of the whole. Radical justice takes a view of the whole with a different bias. While reflecting the fundamental interests of those calling for a radical alternative, it cannot, since it must appeal to all, unfailingly support those interests. Both radical justice and state justice claim to fit different interests together so that no one's interests are totally neglected, but they fit them together with a different bias. Thus radical justice becomes a condition for undermining a preexisting economic framework and hence the dominance of the groups benefiting most from it.

2. Repression: a device for power, not justice

So far I have neglected explicit consideration of repression. Here I take repression in the sense of the use or threat of physical force by the state that interferes with the pursuit of interests blocked by state justice. Repression may then be either a response to a social movement or a response to an individual offender. Moreover, according to this definition, the use of force in repression need not conform to legality. Interests blocked by state justice are ones that cannot be satisfied because the limits on benefits and losses imposed by justice are either too narrow or too broad. Thus the limits on benefits would be too narrow – from the perspective of workers – if the right to strike was a benefit outside – prohibited by – those limits. But the limits on losses would be too broad for them if dying due to the inability to pay for health care were a loss within – permitted by – those limits. Repression of nonphysical sorts such as a denial of

95

access to information relevant to important decisions can be as significant as physical repression, but our focus will be sharper if limited to physical repression. It is not always repression that sparks moral outrage at the state, but repression lies in the wings in every case where confrontations with the state generate outrage. Repression is in this way associated with outrage at the state and hence with radical justice.

Why should there be repression? It is tempting to look for its basis in the fact that, since any system of justice, whether state justice or not, is more than a set of beliefs or documents, it must be backed by sanctions. If the setting of limits to benefits and losses either by the state or apart from the state is to have a practical significance, there must be a state empowered with the use of physical force. Otherwise, efforts to go beyond narrow limits on benefits or broad limits on losses would go unchecked and justice would be flouted. Moreover, to be effective in enforcing justice the state must aspire to a monopoly of this force.[3] Can we, though, be satisifed with this account of repression and the state monopoly of force? Do limits on benefits and losses of themselves bring people of goodwill to construct a state force as a sanction for those limits? This account – familiar since Hobbes among liberal theorists[4] – is designed more to avoid a materialist conception of the state than to meet the facts, as is clear from the following considerations.

Systems of justice existed in pre-state societies where no common authority was empowered to use physical force as a sanction. Among the Nuer of Sudan, a "leopard-skin chief" could attempt to reconcile feuding parties but had no authority to force a reconciliation.[5] He could recommend to the kin of a murdered man that they accept compensation in cattle, but they could nonetheless insist on their right of vengeance. It is when one crosses the divide to the state that a clear connection is forged between justice and official force. One cannot base this connection on the existence of warfare between states, since warfare exists also in pre-state societies. So the internal use of official force is not simply an offshoot of the use of physical force in warfare.

The critical factor is that state justice has a different function from justice in pre-state societies. In pre-state societies, the Hobbesian goal of peace and security may well have been the goal of justice. But when it comes to the state, the goal of justice is not peace and security but the ability to rule. Only insofar as peace and security are necessary for ruling will provision be made for them in state justice. What, though, does this have to do with the use of force? If pre-state justice does not call for official force as a sanction, perhaps it is the function of justice in state societies that is the clue to the use of official force as a sanction. My hypothesis is, then, that official force – repression – functions to strengthen state rule rather than being a demand of limits on benefits and losses just by themselves.

It is significant that in pre-state societies there was nothing corresponding to the idea of criminal justice, though there was an analogue of civil justice.[6] In pre-state societies the injured party could seek compensation from an injurer, as in a civil action, before an arbiter. But with the state came the idea that certain acts were crimes. Proceedings are brought against criminals by the state. Their crimes are punishable – through death, imprisonment, fines – by the state as an authority separate from the society. By allegedly harming the whole society, crimes call not for compensation to the injured but for punishment administered by the state acting for the society.

Without the state's ability to use force to deal with offenders there would have been justice, but it is unlikely that state rule could have been consolidated. Through the authority to accuse of offenses and to administer punishment for offenses the state keeps people in awe of it and gets to consolidate its power. In both pre-state and state societies there are various forms of unofficial retribution. One family avenges itself on another, or a village avenges itself on one of its members whose behavior is objectionable, as in the practice known as charivari.[7] But in all these cases those who regard themselves as offended administer the punishment. With criminal justice, though, the state inserts itself in place of the offended as both accuser and punisher. In doing so it drops the role of an arbiter between parties. Moreover, a growing list of crimes – understood as harms to the whole society – includes acts that are blows to the state's own ability to rule. Repression then works with state justice to reinforce the state's power to rule.

The connection between repression and justice can be formulated more fully as follows. We have seen that, to be effective, justice need not require repression. One aspect of the state that is important here is what in Chapter 12 shall be called sovereignty. Sovereignty is the ability or power the state has for taking care of itself. A genuinely sovereign state runs into no insuperable obstacles, from within or without, when it is trying to do what it normally does. In particular, sovereignty aids the state in regard to both form and function. The sovereign state has the power to overcome obstacles to its functioning to reproduce the economy. And it has the power to overcome obstacles to its getting the requisite legitimacy for governing through setting limits on benefits and losses.

Repression is an instrument of sovereignty. It is designed to insure that the state has the ability to overcome obstacles to its functioning and to its ruling through justice. The main role of repression is not to restore the acceptance of justice as a mere set of limits but to preserve sovereignty; for if the limits set by justice can be transgressed with impunity the state that sets those limits lacks the power to insure its own legitimacy. Repression against transgressors bolsters the state's power to attain that legitimacy by insuring that the limits the state sets are respected. But insuring that these limits are respected is only instrumental to repression's main role of bolstering sovereignty.

Repression and justice parallel the Machiavellian themes of coercion and consent, which Gramsci updated in "The Modern Prince."[8] In a class-divided society – one thus distinct from the pre-state societies where justice has no official sanction – ruling requires an effort at unification based on universally required limits. But this unity is never quite achieved due to the inability of any conception of justice to resolve grievances felt among the dominated. State justice leaves a deficit of consent.[9] Repression is needed to deal with the consequences of this deficit of consent. Through it the state hopes to enhance its power – its sovereign power – to insure that there are few obstacles to its rule through justice. Many times, in using repression to establish sovereignty, the state restores justice, but not because justice itself must be restored. Undercutting its sovereignty makes room for its replacement with another state. So the governability the state cannot achieve with consent it hopes to achieve with coercion, and the governability it cannot achieve with coercion it hopes to achieve with consent.

3. Just repression

Repression too is limited by state justice, excluding thereby a despotic rule in which the ruler can decide at whim what behavior is to be a crime and what punishment it is to receive. Yet, just as the state's function may be undercut by state justice due to stringent requirements for ruling, so too the state's justice may be transgressed by state repression due to stringent requirements of overall sovereignty. The phenomenon of the approved police riot is one example of repression transgressing state justice.

98

In 1982 in Boston the appearance of twenty-three hooded Ku Klux Klan members sparked a large protest, leading the police to put the Klanspeople in vans and rush them from their attackers. After this, waves of horse- and motorcycle-mounted police came through the crowd of protesters; as a result, thirteen of the protesters were treated at a nearby hospital for injuries. Though the presence of the police was ostensibly to protect the civil liberties of the Klanspeople, their brutality occurred after the Klanspeople had been removed. They acted with the approval of the authorities, who said they "responded appropriately to the volatile nature of the crowd." The police superintendent said, "I would call it a riot."[10] And it was indeed an approved police riot, which dispersed the protesters not to protect anyone's rights but to demonstrate state sovereignty against a dissident crowd. So not only is repression underived from the need to restore justice by a physical sanction, but also repression that is approved to insure sovereignty may transgress even that aspect of state justice that limits its own repression to a reasonable use of force.

Let us turn from transgressions of limits on repression to those limits themselves. Justice includes not only limits on ordinary behavior but also limits on adjustments and penalties for violating the limits on ordinary behavior. With these limits we move away from distributive justice, which sets limits on benefits and losses but does not categorize the types of offenses involved in transgressing them or specify the consequences for the transgressor. Limits of this new kind fall within the general area of corrective justice, which in turn covers both compensatory and criminal justice. Thus there is not only a limit on what you can do with your neighbor's reputation but also upper and lower limits on the compensation you must pay for damaging it. Also, there are not only limits on what you can do before doing it becomes a crime but also limits on the kind and degree of punishment to be administered to you if you transgress the original set of limits and commit a crime.

Corrective justice poses a problem for my view that repression is to enhance state power rather than to serve justice. For here punishing the criminal is the just course, so repression does serve justice, where corrective justice is in question. Only if the punishment were not in accord with corrective justice could we say that it does not serve justice but instead enhances state power. We are then forced to the conclusion that, where the demands of sovereignty do not push the state to illegal repression, repression and justice are one and the same.

This challenge can be met as follows. Even when we assume that repression stays within the bounds of corrective justice the distinction between the two remains. Just repression has two sides to it. Insofar as it is just it tends to promote acceptance of the state among those who oppose tyranny. Insofar as it is repression it makes up for the deficit of acceptance of the state among those who might transgress state justice. It is as repression and not as justice that just repression is effective in stopping acts against the state by those who do not accept it due to a deficit of consent.[11] There is an obvious qualification to this; a person who takes actions against the state solely because the state has no limits on repression will be deterred, even without being repressed, if the state reforms itself by putting significant limits on repression. With this exception in mind, we can say that generally repression is useful for the state because it is repression, not because it is just. Thus repression remains distinct from justice.

4. Genealogy of political morality

Repression becomes a major stimulus to radical justice, because it often creates moral outrage when people are punished for pursuing group interests that are blocked by state justice. This outrage provides a context for an alternative justice based on those interests. The justice of the existing state fails to protect the fundamental interests of a ruled group when protecting those interests is not necessary for ruling. Radical justice, however, supports the fundamental interests of the dominated, provided supporting those interests is consistent with taking the perspective of the whole.

Patterns of radical justice may and often do reflect the interests of more than one dominated group. They reflect the interests of workers and peasants, or of workers and national minorities, or of women and blacks. Such patterns of radical justice treat the fundamental interests of the relevant groups as reconcilable through the interest in overcoming domination. Still, mutual support between these groups for overcoming domination may conceal fundamental differences that will break up the alliance later on. Even where the fundamental interests prove reconcilable, this is not something that exists from the outset as an already given fact. It is something that emerges as the groups work together.

Radical justice has its ultimate roots in the basic structures of morality. The outrage generated in confrontations with the state is

100

a moral outrage. And it is this moral outrage that opens the door to a radical justice. The outrage is moral since it comes from the underlying dimension of moral awareness, which tells us that social existence imposes some restraints on those within it.[12] This awareness includes the understanding that these restraints should not compromise the basic interests of those in a given group. This underlying dimension of moral awareness is in some cases contradicted by the state. For the state, while professing to rule for everyone and hence to impose restraints compatible with one's own group, actually sets restraints counter to the basic interests of one's own group. Moreover, protesting this fact meets with repression. With the underlying dimension contradicted, the outrage one feels has the status of a moral outrage, which then provides the motive for a group morality that does aim at protecting the interests of one's group. Moreover, when such a group morality is modified by the requirements generated by the aim of ruling later on, the result is a radical justice. This radical justice is an alternative "general will" since the modifications called for by the requirements of ruling result from considering the interests of everyone. Thus, under the stimulus of moral outrage in the face of the state, a radical political morality is formed.[13]

Even the official "general will" of the state has its roots in the same basic moral structures. In order to govern, the state accepts the underlying dimension of moral awareness that social existence requires restraints that do not impede people's basic interests. In elaborating these restraints, it forms an official political morality. This morality gets its content both from the need to govern and from the moralities of the groups pressuring it to impose restraints. Some of these restraints make up state justice. Thus group moralities play a role, directly or indirectly, in the formation of both an alternative and an official general will.

Neither radical nor state justice is ever simply an application of a pure morality to politics. Abstract moral principles are conceptually incapable of antecedently determining the content of political morality, even when we add in facts about existing conditions. It is only after the fact of the formation of a political morality that conceptual connections are drawn with abstract principles. But then those principles are already filled with new content. This *post hoc* subsumption of a political morality under a pure morality has, since Plato, been thought to justify the political morality. Prior to such an after-the-fact extension of an abstract moral paradigm to a political morality there is, though, a conceptual gap between the abstract and political moral ideas. The justification of political by pure morality fails then to validate the political morality.

5. Radical justice and social change

There is, in addition to the tension between state justice and the economy, a tension between state justice and radical justice. The state will defend itself on both of these fronts.[14] Repression is, though, not the only means the state has for dealing with radical justice. The tension between state and radical justice can lead to reform. In a reform effort, the state can modify its justice and hope thereby to meet radical justice halfway. The reform effort changes the allowable limits on benefits and losses in some dimensions, thereby establishing a new conception of state justice. This does not eliminate reliance upon the strategy of repression; it at best changes the level at which repression enters in. Reform provides flexibility by giving the state access not just to coercion but also to consent.[15]

Though radical justice stimulates reforms, it is not their only basis. It is currently fashionable to treat reforms as victories of the dominated rather than as functional necessities of the state and the economically dominant class. But this is a spurious opposition. Reforms can be both victories for the dominated and functional for the dominant. And they usually need to be both in order to exist at all. Revolts sparked by moral outrage are the stimulus cause for most reforms, whereas the goal of widening acceptance of state justice is often a condition for such a stimulus to be effective. Emphasizing revolt as the only source of reform serves the view that continued reforms must ultimately break the back of the economic system and provide a new economy appropriate for realizing radical justice. But if the goal that makes the stimulus of revolt effective is that of widening acceptance of state justice, then, far from breaking the back of the system, reform merely gives it a new lease on life.

Changes in the state are not always motivated by radical justice. Many times they result from the need to reproduce the economy. In order to win acceptance for them, these reforms are called progressive, with the implication that the opposed reforms of radical justice are schemes whereby sectional interests would hold society back. The idea of progress was used by the U.S. government and by Brazilian generals to set a course for Brazil from 1964 through

102

1984. The democratically elected Goulart had strengthened labor and peasant organizations as a counterweight to both the United States and the military. This was seen as a threat to capitalism in Brazil. He was overthrown in 1964, with Central Intelligence Agency help, on the basis of the hope that progress was to be found not by fighting imperialism but by joining it as a junior partner. As Nelson Rockefeller put it in his 1969 report to President Nixon on Latin America, the military is "the essential force of constructive social change." The generals projected development based on privileges for multinational corporations and on a denial of rights to Brazilian labor and peasants.[16]

It is not to be assumed, moreover, that a vigorous reform movement stops or even slows down repression. In the first two decades of the twentieth century, progressive movement reforms in the United States were regulating business, strengthening the franchise, and expanding workers' rights. At the same time state repression was unabated. As a result of the reforms, a Federal Trade Commission was to regulate the growth of monopolies, the Interstate Commerce Commission was to set maximum freight rates, and the Federal Reserve Act was to insure a flow of credit. Cities called for a direct primary, and the Seventeenth Amendment to the Constitution took the election of senators away from the state legislatures and gave it to the people. States passed laws for the safety inspection of factories, for limiting the workday, and for the provision of compensation for injured workers. Toledo, Cleveland, New York, and Chicago experienced agitation for municipal ownership of utilities and for inexpensive street transportation.[17] Despite the depth and breadth of the reforming spirit, workers were killed during the Lawrence woolen mills strike in 1912; the lynching of southern blacks reached an all-time high with the implicit approval of successive administrations in Washington; the killing of women and children at Ludlow by state troops in a strike against Rockefeller in 1914 was an inevitable outcome of widespread antiunionism; and during World War I Woodrow Wilson's Espionage Act, after being upheld as constitutional under the "clear and present danger" doctrine, was used to imprison 900 people, including Eugene Debs. Reform in a divided society is then best seen not as an alternative to repression but as a product of the dialectic between radical justice, state justice, and repression.

8

Justice and materialism

We may seem to have given away too much in our discussion of state justice. How can state justice liberate people from the worst effects of the economy but at the same time fit within the canons of a materialist political theory? Our account seems to tie the state at one end to the economy, but at the other end, where justice is concerned, the state does not seem restricted by the economy. Don't we have to face a hard choice here? Either we return to the atomist materialism that allows no autonomy to the state, in which case justice as a form of ruling reflects the economy; or we resort to imposing ideal justice on the operation of the state from totally outside the economy. This is a choice that many have felt they could not escape. The framework model, however, allowed us to escape from this choice by supporting a contextual materialism adequate for state justice.

1. Weak and strong limits

As I have formulated the thesis of state autonomy, it does not imply independence from the economy. It is the rather different thesis that the form and the function of the state may be in conflict. This conflict is quite compatible with the view that not only the function but also the form of ruling are derived from the economy, in a sense of derivation that fits with the idea of structure cause in the framework model. What the thesis of autonomy says is that state justice, as a form of ruling, cannot always be equated with a set of limits on losses and benefits that would guarantee the reproduction of the economy. There are several ways sets of limits on losses and benefits might be related to the economy.

Let us speak of *a weak set of limits* on losses and benefits as a set that, in relation to the given circumstances and others rather similar to them, poses no threat whatsoever to the reproduction of the economy. The losses that workers might suffer that are allowed by these limits, especially in times of economic downturn, would be

104

considerable. The welfare safety net would be very porous. Yet the benefits owners might gain that are allowed by these limits, during both downswings and upswings in the business cycle, would also be considerable. Low rates of taxation on high incomes, token health and safety regulations, and a favorable balance of management over union rights would be compatible with the limits on benefits from a quite weak set of limits. In addition, when it comes to civil liberties, the losses that workers might incur would again be considerable. Under certain weak sets of limits, economic development could be pushed through by censoring the press, restricting the democratic right to political participation, and denying the right to assembly.

In contrast, *a strong set of limits* on losses and benefits is one that, in relation to the given circumstances or ones similar to them, poses a threat to the reproduction of the economy. The debate in neoliberal circles over whether democracies are any longer governable is precisely a debate over whether a strong set of limits on losses and benefits shouldn't be replaced by a weak set in the interests of economic recovery from long-term stagnation.[1] A pattern of radical justice is often a quite strong set of limits, whereas a pattern of state justice is a strong set of limits only when the state is under extreme pressure. A strong set, like a weak set, is relativized to circumstances. One and the same set of limits might be weak in circumstances of prosperity and political stability but strong in circumstances of underdevelopment and regular coups d'état. For there to be a strong set, the threat to the economy need not come in the given circumstances but must come in circumstances to which the given ones can lead with minor changes.

In determining what sets of limits are weak and what sets are strong, there are two well-known problems that have to be faced. First, we are dealing with benefits and losses in many different dimensions. Strong limits in one dimension, that is, limits that of themselves would threaten the reproduction of the economy, might be paired in the same system of justice with weak limits in another dimension, that is, with limits that of themselves would pose no threat whatsoever to the economy. A welfare state that of itself would be a drag on the economy might, for example, be combined with a despotic state that by effectively destroying all civil liberties offsets the drag on the economy by welfare measures. Thus the strength or weakness of a set of limits cannot be assessed by considering only one or two prominent dimensions of benefits and losses. A composite picture is needed.

105

Second, in making the composite picture the relative weights of the different dimensions of benefits and losses must be settled. Is the state that combines despotism with welfare a state with an overall strong or weak set of limits on benefits and losses? Is the drag created by welfare more important for the reproduction of the economy than the flexibility created by despotism? I assume some reasonable empirical conjectures can be made toward deciding questions of these kinds.

2. Least weak limits

I want to focus on certain patterns of state justice that are weak. Specifically, I want to focus on those patterns of state justice that are only barely compatible with reproduction; if they were any less weak or, equivalently, if they were any stronger, they would, in relation to the given circumstances or ones similar to them, threaten the reproduction of the economy. I shall call any such pattern of justice *a least weak set of limits* on losses and benefits. Because there are several dimensions of benefits and losses, there will doubtless not be a unique least weak pattern of state justice.

This enables us to give a new formulation to the thesis of state autonomy. The thesis of state autonomy becomes the thesis that state justice, as a form of ruling, may be stronger than any of the least weak sets of limits on benefits and losses, in relation to the given circumstances or ones similar to them. It is possible that state justice, because of the demands of ruling, is a strong set of limits on benefits and losses. Thus state justice might, because of the demands of ruling, threaten the reproduction of the economy.

The notion of a least weak set of limits is also important in relation to conflict in society. State justice tends toward a least weak set of limits, when we ignore the possibility of a strong set allowed by autonomy. But why are all weak sets of limits not possibilities? The reason for focusing on the least weak sets is that in a divided society the remaining weak sets are impractical. The state must face the problem of ruling in a divided society, a problem that can be solved only by achieving wide consent on the fairness of benefits and losses. This problem could not be solved by a very weak or moderately weak system of justice. There are two reasons for this failure. First, such a system would appear gratuitously to run counter to the fundamental interests of dominated groups. Stronger limits would not threaten the economy. Second, the state

106

would have difficulty mobilizing against attempts to alter such a gratuitous system. After all, such an alteration would leave the existing system of domination intact. There would, in short, be no equilibrium in the social struggle around weak sets of limits that are not yet least weak sets.

The difference between those advocating state autonomy and those denying it is over whether equilibrium in the social struggle must be reached with the least weak sets. The advocates of lack of autonomy want to say that equilibrium is achieved with the adoption of a least weak set of limits. Neither side holds that limits weaker than the weakest sets are feasible. The advocates of autonomy – myself included – say that in some circumstances ruling may require moving over from the weak sets altogether to one of the strong sets of limits, that is, to a set that threatens the reproduction of the economy. To say it threatens the economy's reproduction is of course to retreat a bit from saying it destroys the economy so a new form of economy can replace it. There are numerous eventualities that could save the day for the economy. Circumstances beyond anyone's control could change drastically in favor of the economy, or repression might be substituted for consent as the axis of ruling. There was nonetheless a threat since only such eventualities prevented an end to the economic system.

3. Economism and justice

A rather rigid version of the view that the state cannot set justice autonomously comes from the Soviet legal theorist Pashukanis. Property, law, and justice were for him all isomorphic reflections of commodity relations under capitalism. Though notions of property, law, and justice may outlast the capitalist market and remain important during a transition period, they would have no place in a genuine communism. The juridical subject is, for him, fashioned on the agent who engages in commodity exchanges in a capitalist market. Thus this subject has as inherent rights those corresponding to the rights an agent in a free market must possess. The juridical subjects must be equal and must never be faced with force except as the instrument of an impersonal law rather than of a personal will. Pashukanis, then, accepts the economist view that "the concept of justice is itself inferred from the exchange relation and has no significance beyond this."[2] A natural extension of his view would be that state justice will follow closely the requirements of reproducing exchange relations; it will have to be a least

107

weak set of limits, since as an exact reflection it is just what is required by the market and nothing more.

If we let ourselves think in the way Pashukanis did, we must exclude all those influences on state justice that have a potential for preventing it from being a least weak set and for making it a stronger set. Not only that, but even if those influences do not push state justice toward being a stronger set of limits, we miss the fact that in being a least weak set of limits state justice is already a product of struggle that has prevented it from being a far weaker set of limits. Pashukanis failed, then, to treat the economy as a framework within which classes and the state would work out a pattern of justice. Instead, he made the mistake of atomist materialists by insisting that economic factors generated patterns of justice in the manner of stimulus causes. If his view is rejected under the assumption that it is the only form of materialism, then, as we shall see, a switch to ideal justice is inevitable.

One might defend the unfortunate Pashukanis – even after "correcting his errors" he was liquidated as a "wrecker" in 1937 – by saying his account was purposely abstract, showing only what property, law and justice would be like if the system of capitalist exchange were abstracted from the class struggle. What on earth, though, could the point of such an abstraction be, since state justice is precisely a requirement of rule in a divided society? It is not intelligible at all apart from its role in winning consent, reducing the burden of economic growth for the dominated, and preventing a shift to total repression. I have nothing against reliance on abstractions, as the discussion of the revolt against theory in Chapter 3 made plain, but abstractions that leave out the root purpose of an institution are unilluminating.

The mistake of economism is of course not just a bad abstraction but also bad politics. It leaves out the struggle necessary for getting even a least weak set of limits. The least weak set of limits – however much it might have cost in sacrifices by the dominated and however much protection it affords the dominated beyond the weaker protection of a very weak set of limits – is then treated derisorily as "bourgeois justice" and nothing more.[3] By calling state justice bourgeois justice one implies that (a) it is determined – in the last instance at least – by the demands of a bourgeois economy and (b) it is formally in the interest of all though actually in the interest of the bourgeoisie alone. There ends up being a close parallel between economist account of the law with radical intent, such as Pashukanis's, and economist accounts with conservative intent, such as the recent one of Posner.[4]

Those who denigrate a least weak set as mere bourgeois justice catch themselves in a practical contradiction. When reforms are possible and militancy is running high, they urge abstention from efforts to win the measures that together make up the least weak set of limits on the grounds that the real task is to get beyond the justice allowed by the bourgeoisie rather than to help the bourgeoisie establish its own justice. Yet, when the tide turns and a reinvigorated right wing attacks these limits, the advocates of abstention are transformed into defenders of bourgeois justice by calling for an end to attacks on the working class.

There may, though, be a way out of this contradiction. The least weak set of limits may have become, without changing content, a strong set of limits due to a change of circumstances. What was bourgeois justice has ceased to be bourgeois justice, and it is then no longer inconsistent to abstain from supporting what was bourgeois justice while defending what is no longer bourgeois justice from conservative attacks. Still, this doesn't help those who accept the Pashukanis view. For them, justice must reflect the economy, and hence justice will stay in correspondence with the economy – at least to the extent of not threatening the economy – despite wide changes in the circumstances surrounding the economy. From this perspective, allegations that a least weak set of limits has become a strong set of limits without changing content are merely part of a right-wing scare campaign; all that has happened is that the restrictions contained in even a least weak set of limits have become a burden to the bourgeoisie. Thus it remains inconsistent, for the advocate of this economist view, to abstain from supporting the introduction of a least weak set of limits, on the grounds that it is only bourgeois justice, while defending that same set of limits when it comes under attack by conservatives in a period of slump.

Economism accounts for its seemingly contradictory behavior by an appeal to irrationality. On the one hand, redrawing the limits of benefits and losses to the advantage of the working class is seen as something that will happen or fail to happen depending solely on the economy. On the other hand, trying to do away with advantages enjoyed by the working class is seen as an attempt to eliminate something that has become a natural outcome of the economy. Thus this attempt is a perversion of bourgeois justice itself representing the irrationality of the bourgeois state. There is then room to fight against such irrationality because it blocks the natural logic of the economy. That logic will move toward reestablishing a justice accurately reflecting the economy if the forces of irrationality are countered. So irrationality warrants struggle as a response. However, though needed to account for that seemingly inconsistent behavior, irrationality itself has no explanation within economism.

This denigration of state justice as mere bourgeois justice has the further political consequence that it alienates liberals, who smell in it an attack on civil liberties, in the broad sense that also includes political liberties. Within the theory of autonomy, though, alienating liberals is avoidable and hence silly. For in this theory state justice is conceptually distinct from bourgeois justice. This was clear in regard to property: Purely bourgeois limits on property were defined by controls that adequately insured the reproduction of the bourgeois economy, whereas state limits on property were defined in a radically different way as the control of the means of production and related factors necessary to allow the bourgeois state to rule. This type of distinction spreads through every area touched by justice, making it simply misleading to think of state justice in a bourgeois society as mere bourgeois justice.

In application to civil liberties, it is theoretically and politically important to see the difference between the liberties that the dominant economic class would grant compatibly with the reproduction of its dominance and the liberties the state is forced to grant so that it can realistically claim to act for the whole society.[5] The bourgeoisie is never comfortable with extensive civil liberties for those beyond its own ranks, and so a purely bourgeois pattern of civil liberties for the whole society would have to be a narrow notion indeed. The state pattern of civil liberties is, at least potentially, a challenge – moderate or extreme – to the dominance of the bourgeoisie. This is because it is not a "reflection" of the economy, which would then automatically reproduce the economy. It is, rather, a compromise worked out in the struggle-*cum*-debate that is the process of the formation of the "general will."

The economist view is a poor guide to the history of state justice in general and of civil liberties in particular. Among the stimulus causes of winning civil liberties were always noneconomic causes. The British working class won its civil rights beginning in the late eighteenth century by building on the Whig libertarian tradition that began in the previous century. Ideas and attitudes were crucial stimulus causes of their gains. In Thompson's pithy formulation, "The insurgent British working-class movement took over for its

110

own the old Whiggish bloody-mindedness of the citizen in the face of pretentions of power."[6]

Similarly, the U.S. working class insisted on its freedom from interference by a centralized army and its freedom to organize unions as part of the republican tradition that began with the War of Independence from the English monarchy. In the aftermath of the 1877 rail strike a Pittsburgh brakeman blamed the violence on a general manager who treated the railway workers as "no better than the serfs of Great Britain." Gutman attributes the strong sense of rights among the U.S. workers in the last part of the nineteenth century to the double source of that original American republicanism and the Protestant perfectionism of the off–Main Street churches.[7] Of course, winning these rights was, whatever their political or religious ideological stimulus, based solidly in the economic framework of industrializing Britain or the United States.

The framework model keeps the economic structure cause in its proper role. The influence of the struggles of the Whiggish British working class and of the republican and millenarian U.S. working class on subsequent formulations of state justice makes it impossible to treat justice as a reflection of the economy. This makes it inappropriate to label such justice as merely bourgeois. Instead of alienating liberals with slogans that reduce civil liberties to the level of a sham, it is important to share with them the historical record of the crucial role of the working class, of minorities, and of women, through their struggles in one revolt after another, in fashioning state justice to secure civil liberties.

4. Noneconomist materialism

Enough of being nice to liberals; let me now be critical of them. The liberal or the liberalizing social democrat will conclude from this that any attempt to tie state justice to the economy is doomed to failure and that hence justice must in one fashion or another drop from a higher level of human activity onto humans in their everyday lives. Materialism is then rejected within this perspective for ideal justice.

At the one extreme within this perspective is the view of the state as the moral liberator. For Durkheim the state brought the individual to the level of moral existence and out of the particularism of special interests.[8] Through redistributive policies it could overcome class divisions.

111

At the other extreme within this perspective of ideal justice is the more critical view that the state, with the complex administrative tasks given it by postmodern society, needs to be legitimated by a moral conception of which it cannot itself be the origin. According to Habermas, the moral conception of individualism that until recently the state relied on for its legitimation had come from the religious tradition of Protestant secular asceticism. But today, for various reasons, this conception is being undermined. There is then a crisis in the legitimation of the state because the older moral conception is being weakened. The state cannot replace this moral conception since such conceptions cannot be hothoused administratively but must be grown within a cultural tradition.[9]

The feature that unites these very different views is their willingness to consider moral forces – and hence justice – in separation not only from the economy as an abstract structure but also from the class struggle. Neither of these antimaterialist views can, though, provide a credible account of the facts.

On the one hand, Durkheim overemphasizes the role of the state as liberator. There is, to be sure, the fact that state justice puts restrictions on what can be done to reproduce the economy. Beyond that the state's record for moral progressivism will not stand up. After all, it appeals to its sovereignty in order to justify doing what would be a crime for other groups to do. Moreover, it is false that particularism is incompatible with moral existence. Rather, the particularist movements of workers, women, and minorities have demonstrated the vitality of their moral conceptions as opposed to the formally universal morality of the state.

On the other hand, Habermas underestimates the potential of the state for developing the elements of a moral code that can support its own legitimation.[10] The independence he attributes to the cultural in respect to both the state and the economy ignores the political and economic factors needed in understanding the cultural. The norm of the depoliticized professional, for example, has been one of the notable achievements of state policy. The bureaucratic revolution in the state that began in 1877 in the United States made professionalism a norm and politics a dirty word; it displaced political power from the parties to the executive of the state. This is not to say that the state by itself created this norm. Other influences, though, will not be ideal but will have a group origin.

Today much of the Left has beaten a retreat from materialism and promotes some form of ideal justice. I have no illusions about stopping this retreat with abstract arguments, since it is linked to a political strategy that minimizes the role of class in social change.[11] Still, it needs to be pointed out at the abstract level that the failure of an atomist materialism, like that of Pashukanis, gives no theoretical warrant to this retreat from materialism. Yet the antimaterialists try to justify themselves by such a failure.[12]

Within the framework model, however, the failure of the economist view that justice mirrors the economy is no surprise. Instead, the economic dependence of the form of ruling allows considerable flexibility in ruling. Most importantly, justice can be a strong set rather than a weak set of limits. The economic dependence of the form of ruling allows for a variety of factors that stimulate changes in state justice. Those factors have the effects they do on state justice not in isolation but in terms of what is made possible for them by their being embedded in the given economy. This raises two kinds of questions. First, what sorts of factors are allowable in stimulating changes in state justice? Second, in what way does embedding these factors in the given economy constrain the effects they can have?

As regards the first question, all of the factors we have mentioned – moral outrage, a republican political tradition, a perfectionist Protestant tradition – can come into play. Letting them be stimuli for change in the pattern of justice is in no way to say how these factors themselves have originated; in particular, it is not to suppose that they belong to an isolated cultural realm. What we must say is that the materialist framework model is to be used in accounting for the origin of these stimuli. This restricts the additional stimuli appealed to in explaining their origins only by saying that they do not exist in isolation from an economic framework.

As regards the second question, we cannot say *a priori* that the framework constrains the stimulus causes to have effects compatible with promoting that framework. All we can say is that having the economy as a framework acts as a balance wheel countering the most destabilizing effects of some of the stimuli. The Jacobin and populist tradition that values a democracy of small producers will attempt to put restrictions on the big industrialists and the big banks. But these restrictions, though a nuisance to the monopolists, never succeed in returning an economy like that of the United States to an economy of small property owners. This failure has to do with the fact that the monopolist framework, within which the Jacobin and populist efforts take place, acts as a balance wheel.

In sum, it is possible to say both that the form of the state's

113

rule – state justice – cannot be derived from the function it has of reproducing the economy (this is the thesis of autonomy) and that the form of the state's rule is something that does not come from a separate cultural level (this is the thesis of the framework model of materialism). So, in saying that it is not enough to consider the state as an institution functioning for the economy, I am not committed to saying that state justice, as its form of rule, has an origin in a separate realm, isolated from the economy. For atomist materialism, the distinction between form and function must effectively collapse since the form of ruling is always adequate to its function; it must be adequate because the form of ruling is no more than a reflection of the economy. On the framework model of materialism, though, the economic framework allows for a form of ruling that might be an obstacle to the reproduction of the economy.[13] This form of ruling is, nonetheless, materialistically based in that framework.

9

Equality and liberty

Equality and liberty have been variable conceptions in the modern period. There is not, then, one conception of equality and liberty that usefully sums up what struggles for equality and liberty since the seventeenth century have been about. One of the factors behind these changes is the state itself. The demands of ruling have required that the state extend equality and liberty beyond what would be demanded by the role they play in reproducing the economy.

1. Equality and liberty in the French Revolution

During the French Revolution vast changes in equality and liberty were compressed into five short years. Despite the reversals during the counterrevolution that began in 1794, these changes impressed themselves on subsequent generations either as a model to be emulated or as a tragedy to be avoided. In January of 1794, three deputies from the colony of San Domingo were given seats in the National Convention in Paris. One was a black who had been a slave, and another was a mulatto. On the day after they were seated, the ex-slave pledged blacks to the revolutionary cause and called for the abolition of slavery. Moved by his speech, the National Convention declared slavery abolished in all the colonies. The slaves on San Domingo had been in revolt since 1791, and they had already overthrown slavery there by 1794. The action of the Convention reflected not only that revolt but also the greater involvement of the Parisian masses in the Revolution after their mobilization for national defense against the forces of monarchy, within and without, in 1792.[1]

This momentous step could not have been anticipated by concentrating on the principles of the Declaration of the Rights of Man of 1789. These principles enshrined little more than those rights claimed by a property owner in a market system. Robespierre himself was opposed to abolition and was not present at the Convention

115

when it was adopted. After all, Article 16 of the 1793 Constitution contained a statement on the right to property, proposed by Robespierre, that left the owner free to dispose of his possessions at will. This freedom was at odds with abolition. Slavery had indeed been abolished in France itself in 1791, but the Assembly had then been too timid to cross the maritime bourgeoisie of Bordeaux and Nantes by abolishing slavery in the colonies. These centers processed the sugar, cotton, coffee, hides, and cocoa emanating from the West Indies, and the larger part of the finished product was in turn sold outside France. In addition, Marseilles, Bordeaux, and Nantes profited from the export of French wines, meats, and flour to the West Indies. When in 1794 slavery was abolished in the colonies, the maritime bourgeoisie instructed its deputies in the Convention to retort that this concern for human rights had stopped shipbuilding in their ports and that three thousand workers had been idled. Their oppposition was in fact consistent with the Declaration of the Rights of Man, which in Article 2 had defined property as an inalienable natural right and hence as a basic liberty. The Declaration of 1789 expounded equality so as to make everyone equal before the law, without giving everyone the right to vote on what the law would be. Later this restriction would be made precise with a property qualification for the franchise.

We fail to capture the changes that were taking place if we try to explain them in terms of a gradually more consistent application of the same concepts of equality and liberty. The concepts of 1789, which emphasized the sacredness and inviolability of property, were not the same as those of 1794, which emphasized the ending of oppression. The difference was the shift from the motivation of ending monarchy and feudal dues in 1789 to the quite different motivation of fraternity in 1794. The Declaration of Rights that precedes the text of the Constitution voted on in June 1793 went beyond the Declaration of 1789 by proclaiming that "the aim of society is the happiness of all." People were to have the right to public assistance as a "sacred debt." Education was to be brought within "the reach of all citizens." Jacques Roux, who spoke for the masses against those like Robespierre who were content to use them, challenged the proposed Constitution on the grounds that it did not guarantee the rights proclaimed in the Declaration of Rights and hence could not "ensure the happiness of the people."[2] It guaranteed only a liberty and an equality that were vain shadows of their real selves. There was no real liberty or equality when one class could with impunity starve another by the manipulation

116

of food prices. From the perspective of fraternity, the bourgeois conceptions of liberty for the owner and of equality before the law were simply not the right conceptions.

The perspective of fraternity, which was that of "the happiness of all," required social security, education, price controls, the abolition of slavery, none of which automatically fell out of calculations based on bourgeois liberty and equality. Popular pressure forced the legislation of price controls in September 1793, the adoption by the Convention in December 1793 of a program of compulsory, free, and secular primary education, which was not implemented, and the passage of a social security program, with annual pensions for the indigent and free medical care, in May 1794.

Why, though, did the state go beyond the conceptions of equality and liberty of the Constitution? It adopted the more radical conceptions of the Declaration of Rights to control the masses in the process of building a bourgeois society. However radical, these conceptions were viewed as protecting people from the market rather than making a clean break with it. There is no doubt that the maritime bourgeoisie, which opposed the abolition of slavery in the colonies in 1794, was satisfied with the conception of rights in the Constitution and saw no need to advance the radical conception of rights in the period of the Terror. Nonetheless, the radical conception of equality and liberty of those like Jacques Roux went from a popular slogan to an ingredient in state policy in 1793–4.

The conflict between moderate and radical – between Robespierre and Roux – over equality and liberty has not ended. It goes on in the dispute between a conception of justice based exclusively on the market and one based on fraternity or solidarity. The state has been unable to rule by relying on the market conception precisely because, as during the French Revolution, people have demanded a conception based on solidarity. No state condemns all its citizens to accept the fate the market determines for them. Those states tempered by democracy provide for the popular participation that can be effective in countering the damage done by the market. This participation is realized not because of anything about the market itself but because of the mutual consideration and respect that bonds together those disadvantaged by the market.

2. Universality and liberal equality and liberty

Moderates like Robespierre held conceptions of equality and liberty that were part of a developing liberal ideology. This ideology developed to support private property, free market exchanges, and the irrelevance of personal status in public transactions. The idea of universality was behind these conceptions of liberty and equality that became part of liberal ideology.

Consider liberal equality first. When there are principles that apply to some but not to others, then some admit of different treatment, and hence there is inequality. However, when principles are taken to be universal, they do not distinguish one group from another but treat everyone as equal.

The revival of Roman law in the late feudal period, the period of absolute monarchy, brought to the fore the spirit of universalism of parts of the Roman law. The part called *jus gentium*, the law of nations, had developed alongside *jus civile*, which applied only to Romans and to those admitted to the status of Romans. The requirements of empire were not met with *jus civile* alone, and thus a more universal law that embodied elements of the traditions of non-Romans, including the commercial law of the Greek city-states, was developed to govern dealings with foreigners. As Rome's economy became a universal economy, through the spread of its empire, its law became a univeral law, embracing Roman and non-Roman alike.[3] With the revival of Roman law, *jus gentium* became the basis for the commercial law of modern legal systems.

The growth of trade through both geographical expansion and the development of capitalist agriculture made the universalism of *jus gentium* highly relevant again. In the evolving market all agents sought through their dealings to improve their position, and all were subject to the consequences of scarcity or glut. These uniform principles gave all market agents the same standing. The market, then, called for a legal universalism, modeled on *jus gentium*, that would be consistent with its economic universalism. This legal universalism protected the equal standing of market agents.

Liberty in the liberal ideology is also tied to universality. If one group is subject to another, then there is a failure of liberty since the subjected group is dependent on the will of a dominant group in regard to what it can and cannot do. The ideal of liberty depends on that of universality since it is not realized when some are free and others are not.

This does not yet capture the liberal idea of liberty since this idea had to be compatible with the subjection of a large section of humanity to drudgery and hunger. Efforts to get a shorter working day even during periods of high unemployment and efforts to develop agriculture in a way that ends peasant poverty have been

118

actively opposed by the wealthy. The defender of the liberal idea of liberty will, however, contend that those who do drudgery and those who are hungry have in general not been interfered with by the wealthy in their efforts for a better station but have simply failed to achieve a better station. If their efforts to obtain relief are based upon the claim that the rest of the world should do better by them, it is justifiable that those efforts should be opposed. What should not be opposed are their efforts by skill and honest toil to improve their station.

So liberal liberty means not freedom from domination but freedom to try to overcome domination while not interfering with others. In practice, most efforts to realize freedom from undesirable stations involve interfering with the freedom others have to achieve even more desirable stations. But in theory the universal noninterference of liberal liberty is solidly based in the market. Any tampering with the market upsets an order that entrepreneurs have already taken their chances on. These entrepreneurs would be denied their well-deserved benefits and losses if interference were made for the sake of improving the lot of those who work or those who hunger. The most natural place to find the universality behind liberty is, then, the universality of the principles of the market; as a workable system the market requires that there be no interference with any economic agents as they make their way within the system.[4]

The universality on which liberal equality and liberty were based had nothing to do with solidarity. Whereas universality is realized in instances that need not be connected except as instances of the same universal, solidarity is realized only in communities, whose members are socially bonded. From the point of view of universality – whether it is used to back up equal standing or noninterference – persons are considered only as so many isolated instances on which a general system is imposed. They are regulated by a system of positive law that is impersonal, and they are governed by a system of market relations that supposes they make their decisions independently of one another and that they act for their own advantage. To argue against what Tawney called the "tranquil inhumanity" of such a view of equality and liberty involves abandoning the point of view of universality, which makes people into disconnected instances. Within the perspective of universality, there is no patching up of the liberal view sufficient to deal with the objections to it. The alternative is the perspective of solidarity, within which consideration and respect for others become the driving force behind the struggle for equality and liberty.[5] It is from within this perspective

119

and not that of universality that we have to understand the thrust toward the abolition of slavery, price control, free education, and public assistance in 1793–4 in France.

3. Can solidarity be derived from universality?

Rawls has tried to derive solidarity within the classical liberal perspective of universality. His argument is not that the market left to itself will guarantee an end to misery and political powerlessness. He has no truck with the invisible hand. Rather, he claims that agents who are self-interested rather than motivated by solidarity and who abstract from their personal situation as regards wealth and power would choose a conception of justice that involves full democratic political participation and restrictions on enterprise necessary to promote a high degree of economic equality.

This is a drastic break with the classical liberal ideas of liberty and equality. On the one hand, the classical liberal idea of liberty as the freedom not to be interfered with in no way guarantees full democratic political participation. First, political participation was seen as something only some had striven for and hence deserved whereas others were implicitly viewed as incapable of achieving it. And, second, some were denied political participation on the ground that they could not be trusted to use it without denying it to others. The propertyless, women, Catholics, blacks, and Communists have thus had limited political rights in various liberal regimes. On the other hand, the classical liberal idea of equality as equal standing under universal principles – ultimately market principles – in no way guarantees a high degree of economic equality. Laudably enough, Rawls, while staying within the confines of the market, wants his "postliberal" conceptions of liberty and equality to mean more for humanity. But can he reach this goal within the perspective of universality?

There are two sides to Rawls's argument, one dealing with what seems fair in the setup he calls the initial position, which results from abstracting from personal situations as regards wealth and power, and the other dealing with what promotes stability in the political situation in the actual world. In regard to the first, once we rule out personal preferences for continuing to hold power and wealth, there is no reason to favor anyone over anyone else. In the distribution of power and wealth there is no reason to depart from general political participation and a high degree of economic equality. This is Rawls's idea of justice as fairness.[6]

It will be objected that Rawls can indeed give a positive reason for equality. He can rely on the desire to avoid large disadvantages – the desire to maximize the minimum. Greater equality raises the floor under those at the bottom, reducing the disadvantages of ending up at the bottom. However, this desire to maximize the minimum may not be universal, since some people in Rawls's initial position may be willing to risk larger disadvantages, either because doing so makes larger advantages possible or because of a personal preference for greater inequality irrespective of the personal sacrifices made as a result of inequality. Faced with these conflicting motives, we are warranted in saying that Rawls's argument for more equality is that, in the initial position, there is no reason for inequality based on personal status.

There is, though, an important difference between there being no moral reason for an unequal distribution and there being a moral reason against it. To deny this difference would be to assert a moral analogue of the strong principle of sufficient reason. According to the latter, if there is no reason something does not exist, there is a reason it does exist. Unless a basis could be concocted for this principle and its moral analogue, it seems correct to say that, even without any reason for a disparity of power and wealth, there need not be anything unfair about such a disparity. Rawls's initial position, which abstracts from reasons for inequality based on personal status, fails to provide a reason against inequality.

What's missing then? The perspective of universality, which is that of the initial position, does not yield a restriction on subordination and inequality. To get such a restriction it is necessary to move from universality to community. It is only from the perspective of consideration and respect, which characterize a community, that subordination and inequality become unfair.[7] If the abstraction from wealth and power that reuslts in the initial position also involves an abstraction from community in even the most general sense, then there will not be that consideration and respect flowing from community that would lead to a sense of liberty and equality that goes beyond the liberal one.

The second side of Rawls's argument – the one dealing with stability – also takes him beyond the perspective of universality. Stable rule, he thinks, depends on a form of justice that involves the postliberal extensions of liberty and equality. Without fuller political participation and distributional mechanisms the state, at least in developed bourgeois societies, does not maximize its acceptability. I can certainly agree to this, but the difficulty for Rawls is that a government that depends for its credibility on these postliberal rights will be one that must interfere with normal social processes to protect these rights. The stable rule that we argue from in order to derive these postliberal rights is, then, not the rule of the classical noninterventionist liberal state. It is the rule of a state that is forced to reckon with the mutual consideration and respect among the less advantaged in ways that commit it to interfere with others on their behalf. So the derivation of postliberal liberty and equality does not take place within the perspective of universality, since within that perspective there is universal noninterference. It takes place within the perspective of community.

It is, though, not the whole society but subcommunities within it that demand liberty and equality. The demand emerges from the solidarity within these communities, but in a divided society, at least, this solidarity within subcommunities will not account for the realization of the demand. The demand will be opposed by other communities, who see in it a threat to their own position. The sansculottes of Paris demanded going beyond the Declaration of the Rights of Man, and their demand was promoted by the Montagnard leaders of the revolutionary government of France in 1793–4. The state's need for governability leads it to support the demands of groups that would be incapable of forcing those demands through on their own.

The view the state itself promotes of all this is quite different. The state sees the solidarity that pressures it to adopt postliberal equality and liberty in a classless way. The state can then portray itself as the defender of the interests of humans generally, not of the interests of only one class or group. The state hopes in this way to avoid the taint of class partisanship. In fact, though, postliberal extensions of equality and liberty are based not on a generalized and classless solidarity among citizens but on a solidarity within just those groups pressing for those postliberal extensions, such as the sansculottes of Paris. The intellectual justification for such extensions must, despite Rawls, appeal to solidarity, but the state due to its task cannot let it appear that the justification is the solidarity of a partial community. The extensions of equality and liberty foreshadowed by the Declaration of Rights of 1793 had to be justified by the aim of "the happiness of all," not the happiness of the disadvantaged. So we have the paradox that the state extends equality and liberty on the real basis of class, race, gender, or national solidarity while justifying itself on the unreal basis of universal solidarity. Despite this paradox, the point remains that the evolution of equality and liberty from the liberal to the postliberal phase has been characterized by a shift from considering individuals as instances under universals to members of communities bearing consideration and respect for one another.

4. Is there a correct conception of equality and liberty?

I want now to go beyond considerations arising out of liberal equality and liberty to some general issues. There are many conceptions of equality and liberty, and many of these conceptions conflict with one another. One of these conceptions may be right for a given community or may be the least weak set of limits for a given state. Beyond that it is difficult to claim that any one conception of liberty and equality is absolutely right. One could claim this if one were willing to appeal to the compatibility assumption, thereby abandoning materialism for ideal justice.

Consider, first, conflicting conceptions of freedom. The freedom to run an enterprise for the profit of a relatively small number of nonworking owners conflicts with the freedom to run an enterprise on the basis of the decisions of and for the benefit of its workers.[8] One might want to deny the validity of one or the other of these freedoms. But in doing so one inevitably runs the risk of appearing to neglect the fundamental interests of that class whose freedom is denied. Even without appealing to the freedoms of conflicting classes, we find conflicting freedoms between society and the state. I pointed out that property is a right that derives from the needs of reproducing a given economic system. Hence, freedoms associated with the use of property are bound up with the reproduction of a given economic system. The state, though, will not fully accept these merely economic freedoms but will modify them to promote governance. Here, then, freedom as unmodified property conflicts with freedom as state-modified property. In addition, there will be a third set of freedoms – radical freedoms – that can be justified only on the basis of the revolutionary rights of groups that are not locked into the reproduction of the economic system. Such revolutionary freedom conflicts with the freedom to act in accord with a given social system. This sequence from class-based freedoms to state freedoms to radical freedoms is not a smooth progression toward a universally valid conception of liberty and equality. Even to characterize this sequence as an advance will depend on the social perspective one takes.[9]

123

Equality is also beset with contradictions. For example, there is, on the one hand, the ideal of *social equality* that is operative in the struggle against all forms of discrimination within the market system. The assumption behind this social equality is that all are to be allowed to use their abilities, precisely as their situations allow them to develop these abilities, in order to get their reward within the market. Religion, class, race, sex, and deformity are not of themselves to be obstacles to succeeding in the competitive struggle.

On the other hand, there is the ideal of *effective equal opportunity* that is operative in efforts to compensate those who, through no fault of their own, would start the competitive struggle with fewer advantages than others. It is recognized that even in the absence of individual discrimination some young people have their later opportunities restricted by inferior schooling and inferior health care. So social equality as described here removes an obstacle to equal market chances, whereas effective equal opportunity calls for a form of market interference. This interference is in the name of making the market serve fairness. Once slavery had been ended, consistent champions of free enterprise tended at once to support social equality but still to harbor reservations about effective equal opportunity. A state that puts effective equal opportunity in its pattern of justice thereby modifies, for the sake of governability, the principle of social equality that comes directly from considerations of the market. Effective equal opportunity will be judged an advance on social equality by those who recognize that without it they must start their competitive struggle at a handicap. Yet it will not be judged an advance by those who recognize that without it they will instead start their competitive struggle at an advantage.

In relation to the liberal state, social equality and effective equal opportunity are no longer a part of radical justice. Among the various radical conceptions of equality is the ideal of *equal well-being*, which is behind the Marxist slogan, "From each according to his or her abilities, to each according to his or her needs." This ideal requires not that people be given the same resources but only that they be given the resources called for to generate a comparable level of well-being.[10] Unlike the previous forms of equality mentioned in this section, this form goes well beyond the market setting. The attraction of the market is its ability to increase initial advantages. Under the principle of equal well-being, one's well-being is, though, not dependent on one's luck at increasing one's advantage in a competitive struggle. In fact, a state of any class-divided society that adopted the principle of equal well-being

124

would clearly go beyond the least weak set of limits on benefits and losses to a strong set of limits, one that poses a threat to the reproduction of its economy, whatever it might be. This follows since there can be equal well-being only in a classless society.

5. Justice without liberty

It needs noting that equality and liberty are not necessarily prominent features of all patterns of justice. Historical factors play a large part in determining what goes into a pattern of justice. It is no accident that equality and liberty were integral parts of state justice where both the struggle against absolutism and the rise of the market were important. The progression that began with liberal justice and developed into postliberal justice was not then repeated universally.

In other places the state has been able to rule with patterns of justice that are rooted in different circumstances and that emphasize different values.[11] Countries like South Africa and South Korea developed market systems and integrated themselves into the world market more through actions of the state than through actions of an ascendant national bourgeoisie. In these cases the liberal sense of liberty and equality had a narrow foothold, and hence by the 1980s there had been only a restricted evolution toward the postliberal sense of liberty and equality that involves both political participation and welfare measures.

In some of these cases, and in the case of postcapitalist states like the Soviet Union and China, a conception of equality, disassociated from that of liberty, became a component of a stable state. Thus the pairing of liberty and equality in the liberal and postliberal conceptions was ruptured. The equalizing state, as the modern counterpart of the headman distributor, provides education, social security, employment, and a moderating influence on income inequality. Thus, in the early 1970s, Taiwan and Sri Lanka had a greater degree of income equality than did the United States; South Korea had about the same degree of income equality as the United States.[12] But neither Taiwan, Sri Lanka, nor South Korea was notable then for its tolerance for dissent.

In regard to the Soviet Union of the 1970s, Roy Medvedev could say, "We still do not possess the freedoms our socialist society deserves."[13] The courts, for example, are severely limited in the kinds of cases involving abuses by state authorities they can handle; citizens must complain through administrative channels. (Gorba-

125

chev's *glasnost* touches only a part of the issue of freedom.) Still, sizable gains were made, many of them during the 1970s, in regard to economic opportunity and security since the 1917 revolution. These gains point toward an equality that is quite different from even postliberal equality. Postliberal equality makes adjustments against the current of the market economy. But in a postcapitalist economy, equality is a tendency against which forces of political power act to create inequality.

Can one anticipate a historical convergence within this wide diversity of conceptions of liberty and equality? Patterns of justice in states that are not liberal democracies are changing in response to mass protest or economic failure. The survivors of the Stalin Terror – seven million were released after his death – provided a formidable basis for the short-lived Khrushchev reforms, which still have supporters. Though Gorbachev has taken up some of these reforms again, there is no indication of a convergence toward liberty and equality with a liberal or even a postliberal tilt. The question should not be whether, out of the diversity, there will be a convergence on a liberty and an equality that belongs to the broad liberal tradition. It should rather be whether opposition currents, in both liberal democracies and states that play a more central role in their economies, will precipitate a new form of radical justice, a form that supports workers' freedom in regard to the facets of production and also equality of well-being. The ascendancy of such a conception of radical justice to the level of state justice would take us beyond both the liberal and the Soviet-style tradition in regard to equality and liberty.

10

Class and the limits of control

Class itself is an issue of justice. It suggests inequality in several dimensions, and putting limits on this inequality impacts on the class structure. Control is the most important of these dimensions of inequality. Upper classes have the balance of control over lower classes. This is not to deny that economic relations are at the root of class. Still, a complete understanding of class involves three levels of consideration: the level of economic relations, that of control relations, and finally that of the modification of control by state justice. The theory of class that then emerges is integrated into the theory of the state.

1. The economic and the political

There is an old debate about the relation of the state to the economy. The debate turns on what we are going to mean by *distinctness*. Is the economy distinct from the state? The economy in the period just preceding monopoly capitalism is often seen as having operated autonomously from political influences. There was a free play of market forces without political constraints. In contrast, it is held that there was no economy distinct from the political sphere in the feudal period and that the same has become true once again in the recent period of what is sometimes called state monopoly capitalism. Of course, if not being distinct means inextricably held together, then it is true enough that in the contemporary as well as the feudal period there is no distinct economy. Under this interpretation, though, there was also no Garden of Eden period for the capitalist economy just prior to its monopoly phase. There was never, that is, a time when market forces worked without political constraints.

Though politics and economics are intertwined, there is still a sense in which a line exists between them. Otherwise, how do we account for the fact that we make quite good sense when we talk about economic forces on some occasions and about forces of the

127

state on other occasions? Let me then grant that the economic and the political cannot stand on their own apart from one another and are hence not really distinct in the above sense. I would still insist that they are quite "different" aspects of a society.[1]

As we shall see, the phenomenon of class is best analyzed by relying on an analogous difference in nondistinctness. Class, it turns out, is the intersection of both the economic and the political. On the one hand, class would not be intelligible unless, by means of a legitimate abstraction, we could formulate the idea of a pure economic system; yet, on the other hand, its intelligibility also requires the idea of control, which cannot be explicated economically. Control in the capitalist economy implicates the idea of the state and for that reason is a political rather than a purely economic fact.

In summing up his excellent discussion of the late feudal period, Perry Anderson nonetheless cannot resist the myth of a Garden of Eden capitalism in order to have a contrast for feudalism, which for him admits of no economic characterization.[2] "Capitalism is the first mode of production in history in which the means whereby the surplus is pumped out of the direct producer is 'purely' economic in form – the wage contract: the equal exchange between free agents which reproduces, hourly and daily, inequality and oppression." But the wage contract – the mere sale of labor power – cannot be the means of pumping out surplus without controls – extra economic sanctions.

From the start the state surrounded the wage relation with controls through the legal system. In the sixteenth century, the wage relation was already treated as defined within property law. We saw that property involves controls, so in this case the wage relation is surrounded by employers' controls backed by the state. Though the modern concept of the contract in property law comes from sixteenth-century England – the point of origin of modern wage labor – it was only toward the middle of the nineteenth century that the wage relation was subsumed under contract law.[3] Before this subsumption, the wage relation was backed by the threat of state repression. Thus, in the eighteenth and early nineteenth centuries, labor disputes were handled under the law of master and servant,[4] which granted the employer proprietary rights to the employees' services; sanctions against labor were at that time criminal rather than civil. But even when they became civil after the subsumption under contract law, the wage relation existed only with the control over labor inherent in the ownership

128

of productive property. Moreover, beginning with the Statute of Labourers of 1349, there were legislative efforts in England to lengthen the working day, and then beginning with the Factory Act of 1833 there were legislative efforts to shorten the working day.[5] Either way, the wage relation acted as a pump for surplus in conjunction with state control of working time. Finally, English poor law and its significant nineteenth-century reforms had the effect of regulating the labor market, thereby insuring that the wage relation did not operate to pump surplus apart from state control of the labor market through handling the poor.

Anderson goes on to claim that "all other previous modes of exploitation operate through *extra-economic* sanctions – kin, customary, religious, legal or political. It is therefore on principle always impossible to read them off from economic relations as such." As a matter of fact, it is always impossible to read off any mode of exploitation, that is, any mode of production, from economic relations as such since the very idea of a mode of exploitation or production includes the idea of control. But why can't the control needed for some modes of exploitation be purely economic?

The exploiter does not get control over the exploited just by the fact of being a surplus taker. The exploited can and do challenge surplus taking, thereby making control necessary to shore up surplus taking. This control is no part of the bare economic fact that surplus is transferred from some individuals to others. Nor does it come from ownership since it simply *is* what we call ownership. Our problem is then equivalently posed as the question whether ownership is purely economic. One has to appeal to extraeconomic factors included among those Anderson mentions – the state, tradition, religion – to understand control even in the capitalist period. The surplus taker controls surplus making and the surplus itself by mechanisms developed during periods of challenge to surplus takers. The surplus taker relies on law, force, social norms, education, and myth to build controls. Thus the forms of control useful in allowing economic exploitation are not themselves economic in content. Behind these forms of control there is no primordial economic control. Class can then be viewed as the intersection of extraeconomic controls with purely economic relations.

Anderson says that "pre-capitalist modes of production cannot be defined except via their political, legal and ideological superstructures, since these are what determine the type of extra-economic coercion that specifies them." Again, this is perfectly true, but it is equally true of the capitalist mode of production. I

129

have been arguing that there is no form of control constituted economically. The notion of control – and hence that of class – built into the notion of a mode of production unfolds to reveal a cluster of extraeconomic notions.[6] The purely economic relations we abstract from such a full-bodied mode of production exclude control, class struggle, and the state. Within feudalism and within monopoly capitalism it is possible to extricate the economic relations that serve to distinguish these systems from others. Yet this process of extrication is in principle no different from that needed to uncover the economic relations of nineteenth-century capitalism. That century was not a Garden of Eden period in which the economic relations constituted a *sui generis* form of control, free of political and ideological content.

Since politics and economics are intertwined though different, I am not claiming there is an economic stage without control. It would be absurd to suggest that humans could fill the slots called for by a set of economic relations that involve the appropriation by the few of the surplus produced by others without the existence of control, subordination, and domination. Surplus makers would not continue their task in the absence of control by surplus takers. This, though, is a fact about how a set of economic relations becomes actual, and of course there are factors beyond control itself that will also be needed to make those relations actual. Still, whatever conditions are needed, it is worth asking what the relations are that are made actual, and it is worth keeping these relations in a separate mental compartment from the needed conditions. As pointed out in Chapter 3, it is an elementary mistake, resulting from an antitheoretical bias, to argue that since the economic relations cannot exist without their conditions for actuality there is no significant difference to be drawn between these two. Unless we insist on this difference, we will have to beat a retreat in which difference after difference collapses until there is – as in Hegel's dark night in which all cows are black – only the undifferentiated unity of the whole, which is then worthless for explanation.

2. Economic productive relations and control

It is helpful to look at a specific set of economic relations in order to understand how these relations differ from control relations. There is no undisputed view about what set of economic relations – or, as I shall call them, economic productive relations, to distinguish them from a mode of production that includes as well control

130

relations – adequately describes capitalism. I shall list here the set of relations characteristic of the Marxist description of capitalism. The point is not to defend the adequacy of this set as the framework of capitalism. I happen to believe that the simple counterexamples adduced against it by neo-Marxists today are not decisive. But that is a matter for an economic discussion and not for the present political one. The so-called relations in the economic productive relations are in reality tendencies that, if they happen to be those of capitalism, can be actualized in the different periods of capitalism only with the help of different supporting controls over labor. So the point is not to defend a particular set of these tendencies as those of capitalism but to show that any such set will need to be backed up by controls over labor. The tendencies making up the economic productive relations are then listed in abstraction from the controls that accompany them.[7] There are five tendencies in the economic productive relations of capitalism listed below. Ownership does not appear in this set since it involves controls.

(1) *Wage labor.* The first tendency underlies the others. It is the tendency for there to be a rough division of the population in a market setting into those who sell their labor power and those who do not sell it. This tendency provides the different kinds of agents needed to implement the realization of the other tendencies.

(2) *Accumulation.* The second tendency introduces a basic asymmetry. It is the tendency toward an increasing accumulation of value by some individuals among those who do not sell their labor power.[8] This accumulation of wealth is one of the things – in the broadest sense – with value. It is not a collective but a private accumulation. Moreover, things with value have the power to command given amounts of other things in economic exchanges. Since we are abstracting here from control, accumulation does not imply control that prevents intrusion but only possession and use as dictated by the economic system.

(3) *Exploitation.* The third tendency is another aspect of this basic asymmetry. It is the tendency for the wealth produced to come not from those who accumulate it but from the productive activity of some of those who sell their labor power. All who sell their labor power work during a period of surplus labor time, a period that goes beyond what is necessary in order to produce what is needed for labor to produce itself. But the accumulation of wealth requires that there be some labor that not only works during surplus labor time but also produces surplus value. This surplus value is the basis for the wealth of those who do not sell their labor.

131

(4) *Value.* The fourth tendency concerns the accumulation process itself. In the accumulation process, there is an allocation of value for the purchase of various factors in the process, some to cover labor costs and some to cover costs of materials and equipment. There is a tendency for the allocation of value to follow the so-called law of value. The law of value tells us that value is allocated to production in accord with a proportionality between value and labor time.[9] Suppose you are directing the production of product *A* and you find that it is taking more labor time to make a unit of *A* that will exchange for a certain number of units of a product *B* than it takes to make those units of *B*. You will not allocate more value to the purchase of labor power to make even more units of *A*, but you may well allocate more value to the purchase of labor power for a new product that will exchange more favorably with *B*. So value is allocated to factors of production in a way that tends to make quantities of products that are equivalent in exchange, and hence in value, also equivalent in the labor time of their production.

(5) *Crises.* The last tendency concerns the evolution of capitalism as a whole. There is a tendency for the ratio of overall capital to overall labor to rise over time. Here the measure of aggregate capital is its value, and the measure of aggregate labor is the aggregate wage, that is, the value of labor power. This rising capital intensity of production is ultimately tied to the rising productivity of labor. Among its consequences will be chronic unemployment and a tendency for the rate of profit to fall. Why is there a tendency for an increase in capital intensity rather than a decrease in capital intensity? At any given time, when there is sufficient disposable capital for innovation, it is easier to find a method for cutting costs of future production that is more capital-intensive than to find a method of cutting costs that decreases capital intensity.[10]

The element of control comes not from these five tendencies – or whatever alternative there might be to them – that make up the economic productive relations of capitalism but from efforts to insure the continued realization of this set of tendencies. Opposition on the part of those who sell their labor power is not built into these five tendencies. If it were, then there would be a universal human nature which is incompatible with capitalist economic relations. It is more illuminating to try to understand the opposition to these relations by reference to specific historical circumstances. It is only when historical circumstances generate opposition forces that control and the institutions of control come about.

If we abstract from these specific opposition forces and the controls responding to them, we are left with an inertial drift that favors the capitalist economic productive relations. This inertial drift comes from the tendency of a system that is in place to repeat its characteristic activity when there is no opposition. With capitalism in place, activity conforming to its economic productive relations is, in the absence of opposition forces, simply *the way things work*. This inertia might be overcome by any opposition, however rudimentary, however economist, that poses a threat to the system. Controls are the devices that restore the system when an opposition has upset it. The way things work is thus a hypothetical background against which we can appreciate the interaction of opposition and control.

Influences that upset this inertial drift are the stimulus causes of control and ultimately of class. Workers coming into early American and British industry from the rural areas had been accustomed to regulating their own pace of work. Absenteeism for planting, hunting, harvesting, and weddings had to be met with plant discipline. Also, skilled workers viewed the demands of their craft as having priority over the demands of the workplace. In an industrial setting a redivision of labor would be necessary to overcome the opposition of skilled workers. Moreover, workers who experienced the ravages of the early years of the U.S. depression without unions or with only paper unions came back in the better circumstances of 1934–8 to demand union recognition in the face of the goons the companies had hired to stop unionization and of the police and militias of the New Deal mayors and governors. Later on in the United States, Vietnam veterans returned to factories with their heels dug in against the way things worked, and they were met with newly organized systems of management that were designed to be tough. In each case, a system of control is designed to stem a specific form of opposition to the way things work, that is, to the economic relations of production.[11]

How, though, are forms of control related to class? Workplace opposition, which generates workplace controls, is not the only form of opposition. Other forms of worker opposition generate controls over the means of production and over the investment of surplus. All of these forms of control over workers are part of the characterization of the working class. The control characteristic of class is, then, formed against the background of economic relations by stimulus causes that represent various historical sources of opposition to these economic relations.

133

3. Definition of class

I proceed now to enumerate the general elements in the conception of any class in capitalism. First, a class is a division of the population. The first tendency in our list of economic productive relations indicates what the basic division in capitalism is. There will be those who derive their income from selling their labor power and those whose income is not derived from selling their labor power. The actual division to be used in defining class will be narrower than this division. Among those who sell their labor power are those who are exploited – those whose work period includes surplus labor time. And among those who do not sell their labor power are those who live from the surplus product and accumulate individual wealth. In the broader division we will be concerned with only the exploited and the accumulators.

Second, the way each of these groups derives its income will be in accord with tendencies (2)–(5) of the capitalist economic productive relations. Labor power is also sold in noncapitalist planned economies, but not in accord with (2)–(5). Moreover, in feudalism landholders can aquire larger holdings, but this is not accumulation in accord with (2)–(5).

Third, there is an asymmetry in the control that insures that all five tendencies are realized. The group that sells its labor power is controlled, in a manner adequate to continue the realization of all five tendencies, by some among those outside this group. It is this element of control that is crucial for the existence of class and that goes beyond the economic productive relations. (Some analogue of these three elements – a division of the population, the economic structure, and control – will make up definitions of classes for noncapitalist societies as well.)

The two basic classes of capitalist society are both defined by different specifications of these three general elements:

The *working class* is (a) that division in the population that for income sells its labor power for a period that includes surplus labor time (b) on conditions that accord with the capitalist economic tendencies (c) as those tendencies are supported by control over this division by some among those who do not belong to it.

The *capitalist class* is (a) that division in the population that accumulates individual wealth and for income distributes some of the surplus product among itself (b) on conditions that accord with the capitalist economic tendencies (c) as those tendencies are supported by control exercised by members of this division or their agents over those whose labor power they buy.

It needs emphasizing that the control referred to in these formulations is control of a kind that is adequate to reproduce the economic productive relations. This allows for the same variability in regard to specific types of control as in the case of property. For example, control at the workplace may be weak at a given time if control that excludes labor from investment decisions is strong enough so that overall there is adequate control to reproduce the economy. It is, then, wrong to say that the working class can be defined as the group that has *no* control in any of the three key dimensions of production: the labor process, the means of production, and investment.[12] The working class may have a foothold that enables it to exercise some degree of control in each of these dimensions. What is required is only that, on balance, this allows capitalists to have enough control over labor in these and possibly other dimensions to stay in business.

The old formula that capitalists are owners of the means of production needs reinterpretation in light of our flexible view of ownership. Ownership can no longer imply a form of total control that excludes labor from a role in workplace decisions, from a role in decisions regarding the use of the means of production, and from a role in investment decision. This helps to avoid the objection that a capitalist social order no longer existed after the managers allegedly won out over those who control investable capital. This does not end the existence of the capitalist class, and hence of capitalism, for a change from the dominance of those who control investable capital to the dominance of those who control the means of production does not lead outside the capitalist class. In both cases the working class is controlled in a way that reproduces capitalist economic relations.[13]

There will be a number of groups different from both the working class and the capitalist class. It is not to the point here to indicate how they all fit within our class picture. I wish, though, to discuss one such group, the ruling class. There are people who are not only concerned with exercising control over limited segments of the work force but also concerned with control over the work force as a whole. Unlike individual capitalists, they are active as well in controlling labor as a class. Here we are talking about judges, generals, and top members in the executive of national and

135

other divisions of government and their advisors, who together make up a ruling class.

On the one hand, members of the ruling class disqualify themselves for membership in the working class since they are not controlled by members of another group. Thus condition (c) of the definition of the working class fails. Otherwise, the ruling class would not rule and the state would fail to have autonomy. It is also clear that the ruling class does not actually sell its labor power – condition (a) – since positions in it are remunerated on nonmarket criteria. However, lower-level public employees do qualify as members of the working class since not only do they sell their labor power but they also are controlled ultimately by the ruling class. On the other hand, members of the ruling class are not capitalists just because they control the working class.[14] Capitalists accumulate individual wealth in accord with capitalist productive relations. The ruling class as such, if it accumulates at all, accumulates not through production but through some form of plunder. Thus conditions (a) and (b) of the definition of the capitalist class determine its difference from the ruling class. This is not to deny an overlap in membership between the capitalist and the ruling class.

4. Limiting class control by state justice

The state has a dual role in regard to class. On the one hand, its general function leads it to back the efforts to control labor, whether these efforts are undertaken by capitalists or, in the case of public employees, by heads of bureaus. This support has a classwide thrust since it is not limited to support for individual capitalists in their efforts to control labor or for individual heads of bureaus. On the other hand, state justice restricts the control inherent in class. In order to rule, the state needs to put limits on the control the capitalist class and heads of state bureaus exercise over the working class. The imposition of these limits affects the ongoing relations between classes without, as is clear from their definitions, changing what the working and capitalist classes are.

It is the second of these roles that points to my general theme about state justice. The right to strike, the outlawing of the yellow-dog contract, plant-closing legislation, and the power of eminent domain are some of the ways in which limits are put on capitalist control over labor. In each of these ways state justice is involved.

The right to strike, whether over violations of an existing contract or over getting a new contract, is rooted in the right to unco-erced consent to terms and conditions of work. When the state denies workers the right to withhold their labor, in either case, it substitutes coerced for uncoerced consent as the acceptable norm for the labor contract. In contrast, the right to strike is a restriction on the control of the employer over the labor process.

Freedom, and hence control, was also the issue in doing away with the yellow-dog contract. Justice Brandeis had appealed to the liberty of contract in his dissent from the majority of the U.S. Supreme Court in the Hitchman Coal and Coke Company case in 1917.[15] The case concerned the yellow-dog contract used by Hitch-man; not joining a union was a contractual condition for staying in Hitchman's employ. A United Mine Workers organizer had, ac-cording to the majority of the Supreme Court, unlawfully and maliciously attempted to have workers break their contract with Hitchman. Brandeis complained that Hitchman's use of superior bargaining power in getting miners to sign a yellow-dog contract created a situation of inequality that obstructed the miners' freedom. It was only in 1937 that the National Labor Relations Board, by appealing to the Wagner Act's prohibition against dis-crimination in hiring, made the yellow-dog contract unenforce-able, thereby limiting the control employers had.

The sale of labor power entered our economic productive rela-tions, in tendency (1) of Section 2, in an antediluvian form; in the context of our abstraction, the sale of labor was not the focus of a power struggle and certainly not the creature of a state. Once we added control relations to the abstract economic productive rela-tions, the labor contract came to be determined by a three-cornered struggle among workers, capitalists, and the state. The state can limit the control of capitalists over labor resulting from the sale of labor by imposing its pattern of justice on that sale.

The state also puts limits on the attempt of employers to exclude workers from decisions regarding the use of the means of produc-tion. The pattern of the capitalist use of the means of production is like the pattern left by the flight of locusts; living material is con-sumed, and skeletal plant structures are deserted for another feed-ing area. In some U.S. states workers and community activists have won legislation that restricts to a modest extent this destruc-tive pattern. In some countries, like West Germany, there are stronger restrictions on plant closings. Plant-closing legislation can restrict control by employers through requiring public hearings on a plant closing, a period of notice before closing, relocation of affected workers, and funds to help the community adjust to the closing.

Finally, as regards investment, workers in various countries have had some success in having capital diverted to fund certain public facilities. But in regard to the private investment of the remaining capital, the control exerted by capitalists has kept workers from having an effective say. In the recent past a number of unions in the United States have attempted to use laws of eminent domain – hitherto used by divisions of government for wartime production, for public utilities, and for highway construction – to have cities or counties take over investments that corporations are decapitalizing prior to closing and selling them. In 1984 in the United States the United Electrical Workers were attempting to municipalize a Gulf-Western machine tool plant and the United Steel Workers were attempting to form a steel authority through use of eminent domain in the depressed Homestead area of Pennsylvania.

The role of the state in limiting the control that forms classes is generally not a serious threat to the existing class system. We should not, then, become optimistic about the possibility that state justice will, by continuing to restrict control by employers, eliminate the control needed for reproducing capitalism through numerous small steps. It has to be kept in mind that limits are imposed on capitalist control so the state can enjoy stable rule. And it rules in order to perpetuate the dominant economic order, one that needs class control to exist. Yet the limits to capitalist control are desirable obstacles to certain aspects of class oppression, even if they fail to prevent other aspects of it. They have been won by the working class at considerable expense.

Part Three

A functional view of political institutions

We often resort to exaggeration to get a neglected point across. Frequently, though, it leads to misunderstanding. I have been emphasizing the role of justice in state rule because it is often neglected in materialist political theory. Thus I have been at pains to call attention to the liberatory, unconditional, restraining, and noninstrumental side of the state. The king's peace is not only upheld by the the king's magistrate but is an embodiment of fairness not to be reduced to sectoral needs. Matters cannot be left there, since there is also an instrumental aspect to ruling. By appearing to give primacy of place to justice rather than to this instrumental aspect of ruling, my position is easily misunderstood as a version of the view that the state is a *Rechtsstaat*, that is, a legal association, an association for the protection of rights, an association in which no person or group is exempt from publicized limits of action. However, justice is not more important than the state's functioning to reproduce the economy.

I shall examine in this part a variety of state institutions that contribute to the reproduction of the economy. Some of them will be economic institutions, specifically those connected with welfare and subsidies. Others will be political institutions, specifically those connected with democracy and political parties. I shall raise the question whether these institutions can be accounted for by their functioning for the economy, once certain other requirements are satisfied. They do indeed function for the economy as well as contribute to the state's pattern of justice. Welfare spending, for example, not only provides the economy with a floor under demand but also guarantees that a subsistence level will be a limit below which people cannot fall. It turns out that this guarantee of a certain level of justice is important if there is to be a functional explanation based on the usefulness of welfare spending to the economy. It is not just this abstract usefulness but also a degree of active support that is needed to have a genuine functional explanation. Support must come both from those who see a chance to entrench the economy and from those who see a chance to get justice. These two kinds of support come together to provide a stimulus cause for welfare spending or any other of the above institutions. In a functional explanation, this complex stimulus cause must supplement considerations of functionality. Many of the familiar objections to functional explanation can be met by noting that it has these two sides; it is at once structural and voluntarist. It relies on structure by depending on the functional fact that a certain institution helps reproduce the economy. Yet it also relies on will by depending on choices that generate movement toward the functional entity.

11

On functional explanation

In accounting for political institutions, functional explanation is often relied on, yet it is just as often rejected because of unanswered objections to it. Instead of rejecting functional explanation, I shall try to make it less vulnerable by placing a number of restrictions on it. We end up with a more complex but a more credible form of functional explanation.

1. State institutions

To prepare the ground for a discussion of the state's functioning and for explaining it through its functioning, I shall start with comments on the institutional nature of the state. The state appears as an ensemble of institutions in the sense of established associations with limited aims. Apart from these institutions the state has neither an economic function nor a form of justice. We never want to be so caught up in the relations of the state to the economy and its responses to popular opposition that we begin to ignore the fact that through its institutions the state is something in itself. The underlying subject that functions to reproduce the economy and whose behavior is restricted by justice is an ensemble of authoritative institutions. Yet even materialist political theory has of late been corrupted by the strong idealist currents that dissolve everything in meanings, purposes, and forms. These currents ignore the central fact that institutions make up the state and that institutions are more substantial than the relational realities of the idealist.

The importance of state institutions at this point is that they combine the potentially conflicting form and function of the state. The form of justice and the function of preserving the economy are not disembodied features existing in separation from one another. They are embodied together in state institutions, thereby introducing conflict within those institutions. The design and behavior of those institutions are rarely a pure expression of either form or

141

function but are often a mix, not necessarily equal, of both of these features.

Moreover, since these are institutions of political rule, they will have authority. They will, that is, speak, order, act in the name of the society as a whole rather than simply for a dominant group. This authority of state institutions is not just an institutional embodiment of the authority of classes, for the state can have authority when no class is recognized as a representative of the whole society. Nor is the authority of state institutions a transformation through those institutions of the power of classes, since the state can retain its authority even during periods when there is no class with an assured dominance, economically, politically, or ideologically.[1] The most we can say is that state authority would not survive an extended and systematic absence of the dominance of some class. The form of justice and the function of preserving the economy are then aspects of authoritative, concrete state institutions.

Hobbes's definition of the state unites a number of these features in a way that is worth recalling. For him "the essence of the commonwealth" is summed up in terms of (1) institution, (2) authority, and (3) function. The commonwealth is "one person, of whose acts a great multitude, by mutual convenants one with another, have made themselves every one the author, to the end he may use the strength and means of them all, as he shall think expedient, for their peace and common defense."[2] The "one person" is the institution of the sovereign, whether it be a single natural person or an assembly. This institution is authoritative since it speaks and acts for all the people. And, finally, this authoritative institution exists so that by being able to govern the actions of the people it can realize the end of peace and defense. We might have major differences with Hobbes over the nature of the institution of the sovereign, over his view that mutual covenants are the origin of authority, and over the goal he sets of peace and common defense. We have, though, no difference with him over the general requirement that a state involves institutions, authority, and teleology.

Engels gives us a more differentiated account of state institutions than Hobbes while at the same time emphasizing authority and functionality.[3] Perhaps all who have studied pre-state society, as Engels did at second hand, are impressed with the absence in pre-state society of institutions commonly associated with the state. The contrast serves to emphasize the institutional makeup of the state, without implying that pre-state societies have no institutions. He identifies three institutional features of state societies

142

that are not to be found in a clear form in societies held together by kinship. First, there is territorial administration. The state is extended through a given territory and its rule applied to everyone there irrespective of difference in clan membership. There will in general be subunits of administration that cover different regions of the territory. When the king appointed a chief to rule a certain region, the chief was often empowered to determine how land was to be divided, and his determination could conflict with the claims of kinship groups.[4] Second, there is the institution of a public force, which differs from the armed people of a kinship society and entails institutions such as prisons and the courts. Third, there is the institution of public financing, involving tax collecting and state borrowing, needed for administration in general and repression in particular. In elementary stages of the evolution of the state, territorial chiefs were responsible for the state's collection of grain from the harvest, tusks from the elephant hunt, and labor for public works, including the maintenance of the chief's and the king's compounds. In advanced stages of the evolution of the state, a more complex institutional structure has become necessary. In particular, there has been a rapid differentiation of institutions within the capitalist state.

2. Institutionalism

Institutions are important for keeping form and function anchored in the concrete. But saying this does not commit me to an "institutionalist" interpretation of the state. The institutionalist takes the institution itself as the grid on which all else is built; everything – classes, the economy, and war – springs out of that grid as a result of the internal demands of the institution.[5] In contrast, the approach here is to consider institutions within the framework of the economy and hence, while affirming their importance as concrete carriers of form and function, to understand their changes against the background of the economy. The economy and not the institution is the theoretical grid. (The economy is not itself an institution since it is a structure rather than an association and its goals are broad rather than limited.)

This approach keeps us from making the institutionalist mistake that Lindblom made. In an effort to relate the state to the economy, he identified as the fundamental link the dependence of the state for the revenue that maintains it on the smooth running of the economy.[6] Thus, because of this need for revenue, the state will do

143

what it can to promote the economy. The imperatives of the state institution of public financing are what lead it to support what Lindblom delicately calls "business." For him this restricts the possibility of the state becoming fully democratic. Institutions of the state become the grid for explanation.

It becomes a mystery on this institutionalist view why it is there is a state at all. All we can find out is that once the state exists, as just another set of institutions, it has its distinctive institutional imperatives, one of which is its need to be fed large quantities of money from a prospering economy. If we accept Hobbes's linkage between institution and function, we will ask first what it is the state does that leads it to need to be fed this money. How does it function? But, once this question begins to occupy us, the state's need for revenue begins to look like a matter that, far from being primary, is actually secondary in relation to others. The state needs revenue from the economy for, among other things, carrying out its function of supporting the economy. We must grant with Lindbolm that the behavior of the state is in fact subject to this internal imperative to protect its source of financial support. But we must reject the implication of his view that this internal imperative has no wider context within which it is to be understood.

I could also be accused of institutionalism if I were to emphasize the role of justice in the state to the exclusion of the state's functioning for the economy. Just as the need for revenue is internal to state rule, so too the need for justice is internal to state rule. State justice is an institutional imperative. To emphasize the need for justice, to the exclusion of the state's functioning for the economy, would leave it unclear why the state normally adopts only a minimal justice. Why does it adopt only a least weak set of limits when a strong set would make ruling easier for it? To understand why, it suffices to reflect that the internal need for justice comes not from ruling in the abstract but from ruling to reproduce an economy. Thus popular demands for a more radical justice run up against this goal of ruling, showing thereby that ruling is no more solely a matter of applying justice than it is solely a matter of encouraging high state revenues. The state, in short, is not a *Rechtsstaat*.[7]

3. Tendencies plus agents

I turn now to functional explanation. Part Three will be primarily about how state institutions function for the economy. Saying they function for it is not, though, saying that those institutions are

144

accounted for by it. Only a secondary task of this part will be to ask whether functional explanation can be relied on, even if only in certain cases, to account for state institutions. But to do this I must in this chapter develop a plausible notion of functional explanation. I shall begin by answering some common objections to it.

Functional explanation is suspect because things explained by their ability to perform a certain function often fail to perform that function. It is supposed that functional entities must infallibly serve their purpose. The confusion behind this suspicion is a confusion of a tendential form of explanation with a determinist form of explanation. Functional explanation is not intended to be determinist; it is not intended to tell us that if an institution exists because it is needed to perform a certain function it will infallibly perform that function once it exists. Infallible performance is out of the question. The most required is that the functional institution be endowed with a tendency that left to itself would perform appropriately. Of course nothing is left to itself, and the tendency that would make the system perform appropriately is surrounded with other tendencies that either provide no support or if left to themselves would develop in a contrary direction.

The issue behind the suspicion boils down to this. On the one hand, a need for a system that behaves in a given way is held to be an explanatory basis for the emergence of a new system or of a radical change in an old one. On the other hand, the new system thus explained may in fact not behave in the way required to satisfy the initial need. We seem to have here an obvious case of an ambiguous middle term in the explanatory argument. In the first premise it is claimed that a system will exist which behaves in a way that actually satisfies a given need, but in the second premise the system actually identified as the one satisfying this need possesses at best only a tendency that left to itself would satisfy this need. From these premises it is deduced that the system thus identified must exist due to that need. This deadly ambiguity is, however, easily avoided without destroying the argument. It can be avoided by revising the first premise to say that a system will exist which has a tendency that left to itself would satisfy the given need. It makes little sense to say that a system is called for that most likely could not exist anyway, which is what a system infallibly satisfying the need would be. To require in advance that systems performing infallibly in an appropriate way are the ones called for in a functional explanation is, then, to reject the project of functional explanation in an *a priori* way.

From here it is an easy step to clarify what is meant by a "capitalist state." We have noted much earlier that a capitalist state will not be an infallible performer; it may run the economy down and ultimately prove incapable of preventing its replacement with a novel form of economy. Just what kind of functionality must a state have to warrant calling it a capitalist state? Here I am not asking if the capitalist state can be explained functionally by the reproduction of the economy. Only in subsequent chapters will I try to show that some of its institutions may admit of functional explanation.

Suppose that functioning for the economy implies infallible appropriate performance. Then we get the unwelcome conclusion that *either* the capitalist state does not function for the capitalist economy and we are left wondering why the state is capitalist, *or* there is no such thing as a capitalist state and we are left wondering what the state in capitalist society is. There is a mass of experience shared by millions of working people that seems most easily articulated by saying that state institutions are functioning to perpetuate the economy. We need a notion of functionality that does not dismiss this experience as class envy, vengefulness, paranoia, or conspiracy mongering. What is wrong is not the experience but the rigid and self-defeating notion of functionality that theoreticians bring to it.

Using a tendential notion of functionality, we can say that a capitalist state neither guarantees the reproduction of the capitalist economy nor takes a stance of neutrality in respect to the capitalist economy. Rather, the capitalist state has within its institutional ensemble tendencies favoring the reproduction of capitalism. The resulting behavior of the state is not a result of these tendencies in isolation, and thus this behavior may not always favor the reproduction of capitalism. There are other tendencies within the state that are in conflict with the tendency to reproduce the economy in the sense that their realization might weaken the tendency to reproduce the economy. For example, if state justice should be stronger than the least weak limits in relation to the reproduction of the economy, state justice would weaken the tendency to reproduce the economy. In addition, there may be tendencies in the wider society, not to be found in the state, that pose obstacles to the tendency to reproduction.

Tendential functioning, as opposed to determinist functioning, is an outcropping of contradictions within the total social formation.[8] These contradictions wreck plans to build perfect tools for reproducing the economy. The existence of tendency and countertendency becomes the norm. This does not imply an effective neutralization of all state institutions. There can, of course, be countertendencies that in certain circumstances do neutralize the state as an instrument of reproduction. But more frequently the dominance of the capitalist class is manifest in the weakness of the countertendencies. The claim that there are tendency and countertendency arises from our general theme that the form of ruling requires, through setting limits on benefits and losses, an amelioration of what would be justified merely in the name of the reproduction of the economy. This conflict between legitimacy and accumulation is rooted, in its turn, in the fact that the population is divided into surplus makers and surplus takers. This division is the basis for class conflict, which calls for ruling in a form that involves justice.

Another reason for being suspicious of functional explanation is that it seems to pull new systems out of the blue in the absence of any catalyzing occasion. If wishes were horses, then beggars would ride; but, sadly, beggars never got themselves together into a strong enough pressure group to bring about a redistribution of horses in their favor. So needs without action go unsatisfied, but needs with action can bring about systems that help satisfy those needs. The suspicion then rests on the assumption that functional explanation is to proceed without reliance on human effort. But there is no trouble incorporating agency into functional explanations, once we recognize that a multiplicity of basic categories of cause is involved in most relatively complete explanations. We have already insisted on the need for structure causes alongside stimulus causes in familiar explanations by agency. Now all that is needed is the recognition that in functional explanations needs are to be supplemented by both stimulus causes and structure causes. A government regulatory agency may be needed by the economy, but it will not come into being without the stimulus of negotiations at a variety of political levels.

4. Functional explanation without paradox

Some sense of the full complexity of a functional explanation in political thought is given by the following highly schematized account. First, we start with the basic fact that a state institution serves or tends to serve the goal of economic reproduction. This will be called a functional fact and it can be presented as follows:

147

(1) State → Reproduction,

where the arrow can be read "brings about or tends to bring about." Second, we want to say on the basis of (1) that the state agency will exist. This is the place where tending to satisfy a need is used as a basis for claiming existence. It is then the place in the argument where we find the nub of the functional explanation. One can represent it as follows:

(2) (State → Reproduction) → State,

where the second arrow is no longer a causal arrow but can be read as a logical connection of relative sufficiency.[9]

Third, the explanation is still incomplete without bringing in the catalyzing occasion or agency that is the stimulus for the existence of the state institution. This stimulus acts to bring the state institution about but only on the condition that the state institution serves economic reproduction. Thus,

(3) Stimulus → ((State → Reproduction) → State),

which might be read to say that the stimulus – perhaps in the form of a series of popular protests coupled with protracted negotiations within elites leading up to legislation – brings about a state institution on condition that it serves the reproduction of the economy. So a functional explanation can be viewed as a conditional form of stimulus explanation.

A bit more needs to be said about the stimulus cause in (3). In cases of functional explanation in political thought the stimulus includes choice. Specifically, if a state agency is functional for economic reproduction, then a functional explanation of that institution requires, as part of the stimulus, activity chosen on the assumption that the agency functions to reproduce the economy. Choice gets a place alongside impersonal economic structures with the introduction of the stimulus cause.[10]

Suppose a state institution is in fact functional for the economy. A variety of groups with different intentions may together generate the stimulus cause for that institution. One group might try to create the agency in hopes of using it to plunder state revenue. Another group might try to create it in hopes that it will provide justice for itself. Finally, a third group might try to create it in the belief that it is beneficial for maintaining the economy. If we had only the first two groups, there would be no functional explanation

148

in relation to the functional fact stated in (1). There are other functional facts – connecting the state institution to plunder or to justice – in relation to which it might be possible to construct a functional explanation with a stimulus cause that involves only the first two groups. But only when the stimulus cause involves as a dominant element the activity of the third group is there a functional explanation in relation to the functional fact that the state institution is beneficial to the economy. In short, the stimulus cause must involve as a dominant element a choice based on acceptance of the functional fact in relation to which the functional explanation is made. Otherwise, in relation to that functional fact it is an accident that the state institution emerges.

It might still be argued that functional explanation should not be based on antecedent stimuli, as in (3). It should rest on a quite different mechanism, a feedback mechanism. A functional entity such as our state institution will generate benefits that will motivate agents to support the continued existence of that entity. Only then, it will be claimed, can we say this entity is explained by its having those beneficial consequences. A feedback loop is a sequence that begins with the functional entity and proceeds through the benefits it brings about to the motivation based on these benefits and finally back to support for the functional entity.[11] If there is a feedback loop, there is a mechanism for the functional explanation of the state agency, a mechanism consisting of a chain of antecedent causation.

But is a feedback loop necessary for a satisfactory functional explanation? I think not for the following reasons. On the one hand, a feedback loop is supposed to insure that the functional entity is explained because of its beneficial effects rather than by some antecedent cause that is only accidentally related to these benefits. This demand is met just as well by the requirement of a stimulus cause, as in (3). This stimulus cause is not any antecedent that might produce the functional entity but one that involves as a dominant element choices based on the acceptance of the relevant functional fact, such as (1). These choices could be made prior to experiencing the beneficial effects of the functional entity. On the other hand, the tendential nature of functional facts allows that there should be no beneficial effects of the functional entity. The tendency could be blocked without destroying the functional explanation. The state institution may be unable to produce the effects needed to reproduce the economy because its justice is a strong set

149

of limits on benefits and losses. Still, the state institution is an entity that tends to reproduce the economy, and its existence can be pinned to this functional fact.

Fourth, to complete the schematic picture one more thing is necessary. The causal connections that are the main connections of (1) and (3) hold only in relation to a certain system of an encompassing sort, in this case a society. This is the general thesis of the theory of the framework model of explanation. The operative feature of the social whole for a causal connection is its essence or structure.[12] The five tendencies listed in Chapter 10 as making up the economic productive relations may be considered as one hypothesis about the makeup of the structure of capitalist society. They may then provide a structure cause in explanations involving capitalist society. The complete schematic picture is

(4) [Society] (Structure → (Stimulus → ((State → Reproduction) → State))),

where we can read through the first arrow, "for this specific society, its structure supports the complex connection." If we stay aware of the range of ambiguity involved, we can for convenience read each of the arrows in (4) as "determines." (In all rigor, (1) itself should be embedded inside a structural determination since the state agency does not reproduce the economy except as part of a society with that economy as a structure cause. As so embedded it would show up in (4).) In line with our tendential reading of (1), we are assuming that within the structure of the society there are contradictions which are the basis for conflicting tendencies that rule out guaranteed reproduction of the economy by any state institution.

There is a final objection to consider. Functional explanation is supposed to be objective, whereas explanation by intentions imports subjective factors. So, by relying on intentional agents in functional explanation, an important distinction has been ignored. My response to this objection is that I am purposely rejecting rather than ignoring the distinction.

My reason for rejecting it is that, if we reject the idea of unconscious goal seeking, things happening without forethought do not happen in order to serve some end. There is, though, still a place for functional explanation, after purging political thought of the animistic idea of unconscious goal seeking, only if the intentional element is allowed into functional explanation. There is indeed a place for functional explanation, for there is a difference worth noting between two types of explanation. On the one hand, we

150

might explain an institution on the ground that people chose to construct it because it would actually serve a certain purpose. On the other hand, we might explain an institution on the ground that people chose to construct it because they thought falsely it would serve a certain purpose. The former is the functional explanation, and it calls for a functional fact like (1). The latter is not a functional explanation; though there is an intentional agent as stimulus as in (3), there is a lack of correspondence between the intentional belief that the institution chosen serves a certain purpose and any true functional fact about it. I am then recognizing the fact that, once functional explanation was abandoned in regard to physical nature, there was no reason to retain impersonal teleology in regard to social matters. Functional explanation still has a place only if it calls for intentional activity backed by functional facts.

5. Second-order functionality

The above schema can be applied as well to state justice. The difference is that the goal becomes the reproduction of state power rather than the reproduction of the economy – as in (1)–(4). Thus, in place of (1) and (2), we have

(1′) Justice → Power,

which is to read "state justice serves or tends to serve the perpetuation of the power of the state to rule," and

(2′) (Justice → Power) → Justice,

which tells us that state justice will exist on the condition that it serves state power. The full picture of how state justice is explained is then filled out by providing a stimulus and a structure cause, in the manner of (3) and (4). Thus agency supplements teleology in

(3′) Stimulus → ((Justice → Power) → Justice).

The stimulus for justice as greater equality, in 1793–4 in France, was both the movement of the sansculottes and the agitation of those in the Convention who wanted a stable state based on small ownership. And the underlying structure cause appears in

(4′) [Society](Structure →̇ (Stimulus → ((Justice → Power) → Justice))).

A movement like that of the sansculottes together with that agitation in the Convention could well have been ineffective in bringing

151

about such a postliberal equality where the structure was not that of a society in transition to capitalism.

In this sequence for explaining justice the state, or state power, is assumed, whereas in the previous sequence, (1)–(4), it was explained. Since justice is assumed in neither but only explained, we can say that justice is a functional requirement of the state, which is already a functional requirement of the economy, and hence that the justice of the state is a second-order functional requirement. In contrast, the state's promoting the economy is a first-order functional requirement. Thus the needs behind these functional requirements can themselves be ordered; the reproduction of the economy is a primary need in respect to the reproduction of state power, which is then a secondary need. Far from being a primary need, justice is not a need that state power serves; instead, justice serves state power.[13] But primacy here is not identical with the primacy of the economic as a structure cause, though it is connected with it. The economic structure cause supports connections between stimulus causes and justice *on condition that* this justice serves state power. Yet the economic structure cause does not support connections between stimulus causes and justice *on condition that* this justice serves economic reproduction directly. Rather, justice functions at one remove from the economy by supporting state power.

We have then answered one of the major questions facing us from the beginning. The view of state justice of Part Two was intended to show that justice is not directly derivable from the need to reproduce the economy. Is justice then ungrounded in the need to reproduce the economy, and if so how is this squared with historical materialism? What we have done here is to admit openly that justice may admit of a functional explanation. Yet in doing so the point that state justice gives the state autonomy in respect to the economy is not abandoned. This is possible because justice emerges here as a second-order, not a first-order, functional requirement. Justice serves the power of the state to rule, which in turn serves the economy. It does not follow that justice itself serves the economy, since in fact it may be incompatible with the economy due to state autonomy. The functional character of state justice relates it only indirectly to the economy.

6. Structuralism and multicausalism

The account of functional explanation in this chapter relies not just on structures but also on agents. Traditional views of social science tend to try to operate with one or the other but not both. It is worth emphasizing just how mistaken this is.

On the one hand, there is the structuralist opposition. Poulantzas quite rightly attacks Lukács for treating class agency as sufficient for all the results of history.[14] We have already seen that class agency is itself built up in specific historical circumstances against the background of an economic structure. It is hardly sufficient as a dynamic of history, as leftist voluntarism of Lukács's sort would like it to be. But this is no reason to reject class agency. Incredibly, though, Poulantzas throws agency out on the ground that it is not sufficient for history. Appeals to agency in explanation are branded by him as "historicist" whereas structures are erected as all-sufficient. As a result, causal agency is eliminated from functional explanations. Moreover, if causes are limited to structures, then effects themselves will only be structures. The class struggle becomes a mere appearance resulting from structures reflecting one another. Despite these inadequacies of structuralism, there is surely a need for structures, as I have indicated in Chapter 2. But structures must be part of a broader *historical structuralism* that incorporates agency and needs, without which we have no functional explanation.

On the other hand, there is the Weberian opposition. Since Weberians champion multicausalism against vulgar Marxist monocausalism, one would think that this open-mindedness would extend to championing a multiplicity of different levels of cause as well. However, the Weberian Giddens rejects functional explanation on the grounds that it leaves out agency. He says, "Not even the most deeply sedimented institutional features of societies come about, persist, or disappear because those societies need them to do so. They come about *historically*, as a result of concrete conditions that have in every case to be directly analysed; the same holds for their persistence or dissolution."[15] Exactly! Needs are never sufficient without concrete causal agency. So why not recognize that functional explanation is a complex affair, as set out in (4) above? Because multicausalism means for Giddens not multiple levels of different kinds of causation but rather a multiplicity of individual stimuli, a chaos of atoms in the void. The structuralist point is that behind these individual stimuli there are tendencies for which the stimuli alone cannot be the ground. That much of the structuralist view is valid against the Weberian attempt at atomization of causation.

153

12

Power and function

State power conjures up images of riot police, tanks, and missiles. Yet this is only one dimension of state power. For a fuller understanding of state power I shall relate it to state functions. So far I have discussed the economic and legitimating functions of the state. A third function – associated with sovereignty – will be introduced here. State power will then be treated as the ability to exercise these three functions.

1. PATCO and state power

On August 3, 1981, twelve thousand air traffic controllers walked off their jobs across the United States.[1] A week later ten thousand dismissal notices were in the mail to the strikers. Transportation secretary Drew Lewis had fired the strikers on the ground that it is illegal for federal employees to strike. In due course, the government officially dissolved their union, the Professional Air Traffic Controllers Organization (PATCO). Unions bargaining with the private airlines, whose operations were subsidized by the government through the services of the controllers, did not go out with the controllers in order to help them save their jobs and their union. The public largely bought the argument that legality had to be defended, an argument it forgot when the same administration, two years later, invaded the island of Grenada in violation of international agreements. The defeat of the PATCO strike had a cooling effect on an already demoralized labor movement, thereby making possible lower inflation and higher profits through labor austerity. The strike took place at the beginning of a period of contract concessions to the U.S. corporations on wages, benefits, and work rules. The defeat of the strike by the Reagan administration helped create a concessive attitude on the part of labor that aided the corporations in coping with the 1981–2 recession and gave them a running start on the recovery of 1983–4.

When we speak about power we are always speaking about the power to accomplish something, and state power is no exception. Did the smashing of PATCO manifest state power or not? If what the U.S. government wanted was to smash some labor organizations in a fierce enough way that other labor organizations were deterred from solidarity, then we can say that smashing PATCO was indeed a manifestation of state power. Suppose, though, that the pressing issue of the day was not defeating labor but controlling civil strife in the form of racial violence and that the federal government found itself incapable of reducing violence, just as it was incapable of preventing the spread of rioting from one city to another in the 1960s. In a desperate effort to assert its authority, the government, nonetheless, focused its might on a federal employees' strike. Though it crushed the strike and the strikers' union, doing so was, in this context, a sign of its weakness, not of its power. Power here has to be judged in relation to quelling civil strife. Crushing the strike does not change the fact that the state is unable to stop racial violence. State power is, then, never a direct reflection of the state's physical might to shackle, to bloody, or to poison with chemicals or radiation. This might becomes state power only when it can serve the goals of the state.

In 1981 the might of the state to keep PATCO members from control towers did serve the goal of economic reproduction, which is not a remote function of ruling but a first-order function of ruling. The state had not been frustrated over lack of recognition for its authority in some other area, such as racial violence. So the attack on PATCO was far from a move of desperation or a sign of a power vacuum at the political level. The lightning-like blow to PATCO was a clear demonstration of the power of the state; it illustrated the state's ability to carry out its function. What was needed was an ability to prevent labor militancy and to increase labor austerity through unemployment, a reduction of social security, and lower earned income. A victory for PATCO or even a standoff would have crippled the state's efforts to carry out its function.

2. Power and its sources

We are now in a position to give a general formulation of this concept of state power. *State power is the ability of state institutions*

155

to pursue state goals successfully. This general formulation would be acceptable to those who differ on what the goals of the state are. It could even be accepted by Weberians, who deny that the state has any fixed goals but say it has different goals at different times. If the aim of the state is order and tranquillity within the populace, then its power is its ability to avoid civil strife and external aggression. In the special case of the view adopted here that the fundamental aim of the state is the reproduction of the economy, state power is first and foremost the ability of its institutions to reproduce the economy successfully. The mechanisms of state power are left indeterminate by this formulation; physical might of the kind involved in shackling, bloodying, and poisoning might or might not be necessary, and might or might not be sufficient, for the ability to pursue goals of the state successfully.

Moreover, the PATCO example tells us only about one kind of ability that goes to make up state power. That is the ability to pursue state goals through the successful execution of decisions about appropriate means for realizing state goals. Crushing the strike was a means of reproducing the economy that the administration decided on and then executed through various branches of the state: the Department of Transportation, the courts, and the Federal Bureau of Investigation.

Not all power involves the ability to have decisions executed. State bodies themselves, in the absence of active decision making on their part, can be the source of a capacity to thwart actions incompatible with state goals. The long, involved, and expensive process of defending one's rights in the courts acts as a deterrent to defending one's rights and encourages passivity. The resulting passivity in the face of violators of rights is, insofar as it facilitates realizing state goals, a manifestation of state power, even though the state has not had to lift a finger to get this passivity.

Finally, there is power based on consent. In this case the state's ability to reach its goals is facilitated by the fact that there is implicit agreement that these are appropriate goals. On the basis of this consent it is easier to obtain the people's collaboration in state projects designed to secure those goals. The projects for which consent is important may be inspired by broad policy statements. The decisions about means for realizing broader policies might then be taken collaboratively in the context of consent. Thus the ability to reach goals with consent and collaboration is not reducible to the ability to have decisions about means executed.[2]

3. Functional and hegemonic state power

There is a more specific division of power on the basis of different kinds of goals. The division in Section 2 had to do with the source of power, not the goals it helps to realize.

A state that, abstractly considered, has the ability to support the economy may lack the ability to dictate effective limits to benefits and losses and may thus be regarded as a one-sided class state. Without this ability it eventually undermines its own ability to rule and hence its ability to support the economy. Any state must have the ability to curb the excesses of one class or group in order for its rule to be regarded as legitimate by all classes and groups. A state is weak that lacks the ability to get acceptance of its rule through its justice. State power facilitates both the economy and the state's own legitimacy. We can ask not only whether a state has the ability to support the economy but also whether it has the ability to achieve legitimacy through a conception of state justice. I shall now consider these two forms of state power more closely.

Was the American state up to 1877 a weak state? The institutional ensemble was simple and decentralized. The organization of the territory was effected through land offices, post offices, customhouses, and the small regular army. These institutions provided federal revenue, laid the basis for population expansion across the continent, and, through the army engineers, aided economic development. Economic regulation was left to the courts in their capacity as interpreters of public interest.[3] The corporate charter, a holdover from mercantilism, was granted by government to private companies in order to serve the public interest. The individual states competed with one another for wealth by making charters easily available. Free enterprise eviscerated effective state control of corporations, but the courts did retain the right to determine that a corporation violated its charter by acting against the public interest. For example, in the first half of the nineteenth century, the courts found labor organizations to be conspiracies to restrain trade and hence to be against the public interest. The simple administrative structure did not prevent the Congress and the president from giving over 100 million acres of land to the railroads during the Civil War. The mercantilist system of state involvement in enterprise was still alive, but now as a means of promoting private wealth rather than public interest. How can we rank the American state in relation to the first form of state power, the form related to the goal of supporting the economy? If

157

we consider whether the American state was a weak state in relation to the goal of capital accumulation, the verdict has to be that despite its streamlined nature it had considerable ability to promote this goal and was thus strong in relation to this goal. As Franz Neuman put it, "No greater disservice has ever been rendered political science than the statement that the liberal state was a "weak" state. It was precisely as strong as it needed to be in the circumstances."[4]

It must not be overlooked, though, that the American state up to 1877 imposed few limits on the gains of capital and on the losses of workers, women, Native Americans, and blacks. This situation provoked an undercurrent of opposition that for its slogans harked back to the revolutionary tradition. Attempts at political stability were clumsy and ineffective; they relied heavily on the use of military force. There were sporadic protests against property, such as the Flour Riot of 1837 in New York where a third of the work force had been idled and the Dorr Rebellion of the 1840s when freshly urbanized Rhode Island workers opposed the property franchise. The Lynn shoemakers struck for union recognition in 1860 in the largest strike before the Civil War, and antidraft rioters in New York in 1863 both attacked the homes of the wealthy and murdered blacks.[5] There was neither a credible ideology to cushion the effects of urban crowding, low wages, and ethnic antagonisms nor a program of reform that could have engendered hope. Self-interest was an excuse but not a justification, and the state was little more than an instrument for promoting the self-interest of the mill owners who wanted cheap and disciplined labor, the rail owners who wanted free land, and the cotton planters who wanted to expand into lands occupied by the Native Americans. There was a deficit of state power, the symptom of which was the chronic threat of political instability due to an undeveloped pattern of justice. As this instability intensified in the 1870s, due to both the depression of 1873 and the maturing of the industrial corporation, this deficit of power had to be made up. The task of winning governmental reform was thus set for the next half-century. The Molly Maguires, the Knights of Labor, the Socialist Labor Party, the Greenback Party signified the formation of an opposition that had to be cajoled back into the political mainstream.[6]

There is, then, a second form of state power, a form related to the goal of having state rule accepted. This second form of state power is the ability of institutions of the state to win acceptance of state rule through an effective pattern of state justice. The laissez-faire period in the United States illustrates the possibility of an inverse relation between the first and the second form of power; a high level of ability to promote accumulation can be accompanied by a low level of ability to achieve stability through justice. In the long run, though, the two forms of power are more equally related; it is hard to conceive of instability lasting indefinitely without actually undermining the economic ability to promote accumulation. True as this may be, it is still useful to maintain that there is a difference between these two forms of power in order to handle such periods as that up to 1877 in the United States, the year the Great Rail Strike demonstrated the need to redo government.

The difference between the first and the second form of state power corresponds in part to that between an irreflexive and a reflexive power. An irreflexive power is possessed by a system when it has the ability to support some system other than itself, but this ability does not allow it to support itself directly. The power of the state to support a capitalist economy is an irreflexive state power. In contrast, a reflexive power is possessed by a system when it has the ability to support itself directly. The power of the state to support itself through an effective pattern of state justice is a reflexive power of the state.

However, the distinction between the first and second forms of state power does not fully coincide with that between irreflexive and reflexive state power. It is perfectly possible that the goal of a state is the reproduction of an economy the state itself runs. This would be true both for a simple agricultural economy run by a king in conjunction with his chieftains and for a complex industrial economy run by a modern nation-state. The power of the state to reproduce an economy it directs itself is clearly a reflexive state power, like the power of the state to win consent to its rule.

There is a potential problem of circularity here. Consider a state that is a reflexive power in that it can reproduce an economy it directs itself. Imagine now that this state is so undifferentiated that it exists only in the form of reproducing this economy, which of course it directs. The circularity enters when we try to say what such a state is. If we say it is simply a state that reproduces an economy, we run into trouble since, on inquiring what this economy is, we find it is an economy this state runs. So to know what the economy is we must already know what the state is. Reviewing the supposition that this state is undifferentiated makes clear, though, that it is not a realistic case. In reality, any state is always sufficiently differentiated so that it is made up as well of institu-

159

tions other than its economic ones. There are, for example, the war-making abilities of the state and the rituals and the ideology of the state. Thus, though the state's support for the economy is in these cases support for itself, it clarifies matters to qualify this by claiming that this is never more than support for an institutional part of itself. There are other parts of the state to which we can refer in identifying the state.

Because there is a difficulty with drawing the line between the first and second forms of state power in terms of the distinction between the irreflexive and the reflexive, I shall distinguish them instead as *functional state power* and *hegemonic state power*. Power of the first form is the state's ability to carry out its first-order function. That function could be any number of things, but when its function is to reproduce the economy, I shall call power of the first form economic functional state power. Power of the second form is the state's ability to gain acceptance of its rule through state justice. Since an institution that gains acceptance for its rule is hegemonic,[7] I call this hegemonic state power. We saw that state justice is a second-order functional requirement of the state, so hegemonic power is also an ability to carry out a function but not a first-order function. We still have another important form of state power to mention, one that is also clearly reflexive like hegemonic state power.

4. Sovereign state power

This third form of state power originates from the fact that the state has its own power to defend. In other words, it must defend its functional and hegemonic powers against attacks on them. A state that can defend itself in these ways will not be subject to subversion of its economy and of its justice either from within or from without. It thus has freedom from damaging interference, and this freedom to pursue its goals is what we call state sovereignty. A state with sovereignty has *sovereign state power* – the ability to protect its functional and hegemonic powers against external and internal interference.

What is the basis for sovereign state power? Though there is no single basis for sovereign state power, one indispensable basis for it is force. Ideas are certainly another basis for sovereign state power, since internal oppositions can be weakened through ideas. The mystique of state power, for example, provides an ideological basis for sovereign state power. It casts state leaders as demigods and the state repressive apparatus as a faithful instrument of the collective will.[8] Statesmanship can also be a bulwark against the erosion of functional and hegemonic power, and it is thus another basis for sovereign state power.

A distinction needs to be drawn between sovereignty as a feature of the state as a whole and sovereignty as a feature of one aspect of the state. I am concerned here only with the first kind of sovereignty. The second kind of sovereignty would be ascribed to an aspect of the state that had ultimate authority in respect to the other aspects of the state. There are well-known differences over whether the constitution, the people, the generals, or the parliament is sovereign in the sense of having ultimate authority.[9] It is perfectly conceivable that there is no ultimate authority within the state; different state institutions might have ultimate authority on different matters, or there may be a constant struggle for ultimate authority without resolution. Sovereign state power can be weakened by confusion regarding authority inside the state but is clearly different from ultimate internal authority.

Leaving ideas and statesmanship aside, let us ask what kind of force sovereign state power calls for. To defend itself the state will attempt to acquire a monopoly of the major means of violence within its jurisdiction. Without such a monopoly the state is faced with the possibility of losing its functional and hegemonic power either through the challenge of an internal force directly or through the challenge of an external force in league with internal forces opposed to it.[10]

It might be objected that the state's defensive role is primarily for protecting the lives and possessions of its citizens, rather than itself. I think, though, that this ignores the noninstrumental aspect of the state, which in turn is connected with its autonomy. In the first place, protecting lives and possessions cannot be regarded as a universal state function. In Guatemala, for example, the destruction of Indian lives and communities has, since the overthrow of Arbenz in 1954, been taken as a precondition for defending capitalist relations of production and a system of justice sanctioning high levels of inequality and poverty. Violence against the Indians is a way in which the state protects its own functional and hegemonic power.

In the second place, even where the state is committed to protect lives and possessions, this activity is derivative from the state's defense of itself. It is committed to protect them only when this serves its goals. The reproduction of the economy and also the

161

legitimation of governance would, in such cases, be undermined without a defense of the lives and possessions of citizens. Neither the economy nor justice could survive the unlimited invasion of persons by others. How then is a defense of lives and possessions carried through? With the state monopolizing force, citizens will not be self-sufficient in their defense. They will rely on the state, which will defend their lives and possessions in its efforts to defend its power to reproduce the economy and to achieve legitimacy through justice. This represents an important shift from pre-state societies where socially organized physical force is used to defend social order directly. But in a state society such force is used primarily to defend the state itself and secondarily to defend the social order.

A state that is not sovereign would have difficulty performing its function of reproducing the economy. Either its power to reproduce the economy would be directly undermined, or this power would be indirectly undermined when its power to win acceptance is undermined. Thus sovereignty is not an ornament superadded to functional and hegemonic state power but a necessary condition for these basic forms of state power. The Sandinistas, both before and after their 1979 revolution, insisted on sovereignty for Nicaragua in order to counter the tradition of U.S. interference in the economy and justice of the country. In contrast, Nicaraguan employers have appealed to the United States, in both periods, to put them in power, thereby ignoring the requirement of sovereignty. It is not accidental that in our theory, which puts functional and hegemonic state powers in the front row, we also find sovereign state power in a supportive role right behind them. It is significant here that sovereign power is the ability to defend state power and not just territory or some national belief about territorial rights. The Thatcher government was not securing several South Atlantic rocks when it retook the Malvinas from Argentina, but it was securing its power as a state, specifically its power to obtain access to the southern cap of the globe for supporting its economy.[11]

How does sovereign state power fall within our general formulation of state power in Section 2? Sovereign state power is an ability of the state to pursue one of its goals, the goal of defending its functional and hegemonic power. This goal is not, of course, a primary one. The primary goal is the reproduction of the economy, which is a first-order function of the state. In fact, the goal of sovereign power is a tertiary goal of the state, made necessary by the primary goal of reproduction and the secondary goal of govern-

162

ability. Treating sovereign state power as something to be glorified in itself, as various forms of statolatry require, ignores not only the functional character of power – its relativity to a goal – but also the derivative character of the actual goal of state sovereignty – its status as a tertiary goal. Still, sovereign state power falls within our general formulation of state power as the state's ability to pursue one of its goals.

5. Class, state, and power

A reductive version of Marxism will find all of this unsettling. I am attributing power to the state, along several dimensions, without yet indicating how state power is related to class power. Isn't state power simply a special way of organizing the power of an economically dominant class?[12] The sentiment behind this question is that the state should be superstructural; it is derived either from the economic productive relations or from associated control relations. Perhaps we are supposed to think that power, like water, is a substance with different phases; power changes from a class to a state phase in the way water changes from a liquid to a gaseous phase. The metaphor is hopeless; there is no alternative to granting that the state has a power of its own. The power of the state is to a considerable extent a matter of the cohesiveness and determination of the institutions it develops over time. An economic crisis that weakens a dominant class may still leave the state with ample power to counter the crisis.

This is not to deny a materialist foundation for state power; the framework model provides what is needed. For it is against the background of a set of economic tendencies, such as the five of Chapter 10, that historical circumstances stimulate new dimensions of power and changes in old ones. The connection that exists between state and class power is not described by the crude physicalist phase-change analogy. It is described by noting that within the economic framework systematic changes in class power will, in a variety of complex ways that depend on important nonclass variables as well, change the various dimensions of state power.

In fact, as noted earlier, a class of great power can weaken the state, just as a supremacist racial group or an intolerant religious group can weaken it. A capitalist class powerful enough to get the state to accept the ideology that what is good for the owners is good for the community and to get its own members into key positions at all political levels can weaken the state in a number of ways. The

163

capitalist class was in this position in the mid-nineteenth-century United States and Great Britain. A philosophy of laissez-faire was propounded in a way that, on the one hand, rejected the income tax as class legislation – taking from the rich and distributing to the poor – but on the other hand, accepted subsidies for canals and railroads as in the interest of all.[13] Given the transparent double standard of this ideology of laissez-faire, the state lost its ability to propound a credible sense of justice. Its power to function for the economy would soon be threatened by its growing inability to rule. Corruption in the United States made it even more difficult to achieve wide acceptance of state rule on the basis of the belief that the state was designed to serve the common good through promoting laissez-faire. Yet corruption in politics was a logical consequence of the view of the state as a mere instrument of a single class. It would seem, then, that maximum state power, however we might go about getting a measure of the composite of the three forms of state power, would require a limitation of the power of a dominant economic class.

It is instructive that the development of the modern conception of a secular state was due in part to the recognition that state power would be weakened by intolerant but dominant religious groups. In France in the mid sixteenth century, the state's persecution of the Huguenots followed from a conception of the state that gives it the duty to defend a religion. But politicians and philosophers were willing to compromise this position in the interest of ending the civil strife that was undermining the power of the state.[14] In 1560 the chancellor, Michael de l'Hôpital, argued that the state's duty to maintain peace was greater than its duty to defend the Catholic faith. Nonetheless, civil strife intensified, and Catherine de' Medici sanctioned the massacre of over ten thousand Huguenots on Saint Bartholomew's Eve in 1572. Perhaps because of this national disgrace, Jean Bodin in 1576 reaffirmed the pragmatic position that a sect is to be tolerated if its suppression would threaten the destruction of the state. (He also argued for toleration on the more principled ground that religious beliefs were not certain.)

Both laissez-faire and religious intolerance suggest a more sweeping hypothesis: The requirement that ruling be represented as in the interest of all makes state power dependent on curbing the power of any dominant group within society. In Chapter 11 we spoke of authority as the ability to speak for all, relating it to the idea of being a representative of the people. If my hypothesis is plausible, it rests in part on the claim that, in the case of the state, power depends on authority. State power is the power to rule, and in order to rule the state must be able to speak for all. The state loses its ability to speak for all when, by not curbing the power of dominant groups, it seems to favor them and thus to speak for them rather than for the populace. The chief means of curbing this power is by imposing limits to benefits and losses. Thus justice is necessary for state power.

13

Democracy, its bright and its dark sides

In talking about democracy we sometimes talk about a goal of participation in governance, whereas on other occasions we speak about institutions that are more or less adequate for such a goal. In this chapter the focus will be on democratic institutions in modern societies. So the dark side of democracy exposed here is not that of the goal of participation in governance but that of modern democratic institutions. In fact, it is vital for the interests of the dominated that the goal of participation in governance continue to be pursued, even if this means changing democratic institutions as we know them.

In a democracy of the kind found in our period, there is a system of representing citizens. Specifically, a democracy is a system of representation that gives citizens a right to participate in governance through their selection of those who will exercise state power by an established form of voting. The selection of some state leaders may not be made directly by the vote, but it must at least be made by other state leaders who are themselves selected directly by the vote. However, the degree of participation in governance guaranteed by democratic institutions varies considerably.

The democratic goal of participation can be realized by current democratic institutions only through the selection of representatives. To realize it more fully would require, in addition, independent popular bodies whose decisions are not ignored by representatives. The fuller realization of the democratic goal is taken up in Chapters 23 and 24.

1. The functions of democracy

It is clear that democracy embodies a pattern of justice; it limits the power of the wealthy and hence of the state itself to exclude the average citizen from political participation. This is indeed the bright side of democracy. Nonetheless, it is necessary to affirm the

166

critical perspective that democracy functions to channel all forms of opposition into a form of participation that accepts the underlying economic framework of the society. Thus conflict is displaced into an institutional setting. This function is what I call the dark side of democracy.

The bright side of democracy has been appealed to both by conservatives who want support for "the free world" against "communist slavery" to be intense enough to get large military budgets passed and by social democrats who find it ungrateful to reveal the dark side of democracy when in fact democracy is an achievement of the working class that even its critics benefit from. One who advocates a form of radical justice cannot, however, be an uncritical cheerleader for modern democratic institutions in view of their dark side. Yet, in view of their bright side, those who suffer from lack of economic or political power can find democratic institutions useful both immediately and in the long run. Just how useful democracy can be to the exploited and oppressed depends on its role in channeling opposition into participation. It is, then, only with an awareness of the dark side of democracy that the bright side can be evaluated.

It is not the channeling of opposition into an electoral system that by itself undermines the struggles of the dominated. Such a system cannot provide effective governance unless there are limits on the debate among representatives. The debate must be contained within the basic social framework, which includes the economic framework. It is this condition of effectiveness that undermines those struggles. Thus it is that democracy, as we know it, functions to limit participation in governance within the economic framework.

The dark side of democracy expresses how it functions for reproducing the economy; its bright side expresses how it functions in overcoming powerlessness. Yet the mere existence of these functions is insufficient to imply that democracy has a functional explanation. For that, a stimulus cause is needed as well. Whichever functional relation we start with, the stimulus cause will likely be a mixture of pressures for limiting power with pressures for channeling all forms of opposition into a form of participation that accepts the existing economy. Without both pressures there would be an insufficient basis for democracy. As noted in Chapter 11, there will be no functional explanation unless within this mixture there is a dominant element; for otherwise there is simply no dominant goal that explains democracy. If pressure for limiting power and pressure for channeling opposition converged on an equal footing to give rise to democracy, then democracy could not be explained functionally either by its providing limits on power or by its channeling the opposition.

Suppose we want to construct a functional explanation on an economic basis. If the pressure to limit power is integrated with and becomes directed by the pressure to channel the opposition, then the latter becomes the dominant element in respect to the former in the overall stimulus cause. This dominant element contains the motivation to choose democracy due to its ability to safeguard the economy. Even though pressure for limiting power is part of the stimulus cause, democracy can then be explained by its ability to channel the opposition rather than by its ability to limit power. It is explained by its dark rather than its bright side. Still, the struggle of the lower classes for democracy may have been essential for obtaining it, even though that struggle is not the dominant element within the stimulus cause.

Democracy might instead admit of an explanation by a functionality involving justice. If this were the case, then not only would there be the functional fact that democracy limits power but also, within the stimulus cause, the dominant element would be the pressure for limiting power. However, on the basis of the following account, it seems like a safe hypothesis that democracy is better explained functionally by appeal to its economic usefulness rather than to its serving justice.

Though justice and stable rule are linked, people who intend to realize one of these need not intend to realize the other. Members of an oppressed group might want to limit the powerful without wanting stable government, which could have the opposite effect of consolidating the power of the ruling class. Thus a third possibility for explanation opens up. Democracy might be explained functionally by appeal to its making governance possible. If this were the case, then democracy would promote the state's stability, and the dominant element in the stimulus cause would be pressure to promote democracy for its stabilizing effects. Indeed, democracy would promote stable rule through the fact that by limiting power a democratic state would be seen to be ruling in the interests of all. Despite democracy's advantages for ruling, I do not think the dominant element in the stimulus cause for democracy is pressure to promote stability through democracy.

2. The economic basis for U.S. democracy

It will be well now to consider an illustration. The framework for the origins of democracy in the United States was that the interests of large landholders, slave owners, and rich merchants had primacy over the interests of tenant farmers, blacks, and poor white workers. Nonetheless, the American Revolution was successful only as a result of the ability of the well-to-do revolutionaries to get the support of many sections of the lower classes. The widespread conflict that existed at the time between the poor and the wealthy was temporarily hidden behind a united front against the oppressive English monarchy. The populace still remained as capable of venting its anger against the tyranny of local wealth as against the tyranny of the foreign monarch. The postcolonial order would, then, have to take account of the growing sentiment both that the revolution was not fought to replace the tyranny of the monarch with the tyranny of wealth and that the soldiers who defeated the British could rule themselves. There was great concern within the revolutionary elite over how to control this sentiment. The democracy allowed by the new states and the Articles of Confederation added to the worries of the revolutionary elite since the earlier colonial charters had not been as democratic. These were not idle worries. Shays' Rebellion in western Massachusetts in 1786 was interpreted as a symptom of a democratic distemper. Debt-ridden farmers refused to pay their debts, and the state legislature refused to issue paper money, which would have made the payment easier. The farmers organized resistance to the courts, only to be put down by the army.

A system of representation would have to be shaped that could contain the passion behind such rebellions. It would have the potential of institutionalizing the protests of those who felt aggrieved. And so James Madison wrote in 1787, in supporting the ratification of a constitution sanctioning a centralized form of government, that "Those who hold and those who are without property have ever formed distinct interests in society. . . . The regulation of these various and interfering interests forms the principal task of modern legislation, and involves the spirit of party and faction in the necessary and ordinary operations of government."[1] Entwining the spirit of party and faction in the operations of government is the mechanism by which challenges to the system responsible for exploitation and oppression can be transformed into discussion of how to operate that system more effectively.

169

Madison worked out a means whereby the majority, who are not wealthy, would be prevented from taking control from the wealthy minority in an institution that remained democratic.[2] Democracy would be an institutionalization of the struggle of the majority against the dominant minority only if it maintained the *status quo* in the struggle, thereby preventing the majority from winning. The point, then, was not just to stop tumults but to prevent a decisive victory against property by the majority. Madison recommended diluting constituencies so that it would be difficult for a majority faction to form within them. "Extend the sphere, and you take in a greater variety of parties and interests; you make it less probable that a majority of the whole will have a common motive to invade the rights of other citizens." A working-class neighborhood would be too cohesive a constituency; expand it, then, so that some of the members of that neighborhood share religious interests with nonworkers outside that neighborhood in the new constituency. It becomes possible to split off some of the working-class vote on a religious issue that unites them with some non-working-class voters. Even if the working class is still a majority in the extended constituency, the cohesiveness of the smaller constituency is shattered. The sharing of interests with non-working-class voters erodes the possibility of the working-class members of the larger constituency becoming a majority faction.

Madison also suggested that a strong central government could keep local agitations from spreading. With the central government secured against a national majority faction by crisscrossing interests, it would be willing to suppress a local majority faction that threatens property. "A rage for paper money, for an abolition of debts, for an equal division of property, or for any other improper or wicked project, will be less apt to pervade the whole body of the Union than a particular member of it." The wicked projects listed are precisely those that a wealthy minority of landholders, slave owners, and merchants would want suppressed. The ratification of the constitution Madison was supporting did give rise to a democracy that institutionalized conflict within the state by giving it the form of the vote, thereby preventing the rise of a majority that might block the accumulation of wealth.

The important functional fact in the process of ratification was the ability of democracy, as so described, to channel conflict within the economic framework and hence to reproduce the economy. The resistance to the privileges of property expressed in Shays' Rebellion played a role, to be sure. But the forces sympathetic with that

170

rebellion and with a more radical form of democracy were unorganized. They played the role of the symptom of the problem to be solved by the conservative forces that agreed with Madison. These conservative forces made the motive of protecting property the dominant element in the stimulus cause for the new democracy. Similarly, stable governance was a concern, but this concern was not the dominant element in the stimulus cause. Had the motive of stability been the dominant element, a more radical democracy could have been the outcome; for once the motive of protecting property loses its strength, the desire to achieve a stable government could lead the economically dominant class to make compromises with the propertyless and the small owners. One of these compromises might be to support a form of democracy in which popular bodies independent of the state were a central feature. In fact, the concern with stability was not dominant, and it appeared only as a concern for a kind of stability that protected property.

There is no simple formula for deciding which element is dominant in a stimulus cause for functional explanation. An important factor in this regard is the economic framework itself. As we noted, a framework does not contribute antecedent causes, but it does determine what kinds of effects those causes can have. In the same way, the framework determines within a complex stimulus cause which element will integrate and direct the others. In this way, being a dominant element will be relative to the economic context. The context of early capitalism enabled the conservative forces that support this form of economy to integrate and direct the lower classes more easily than these conservative forces could have been integrated and directed by the lower classes. This is a sign of what may be called the "inertial tendency" of frameworks: A framework will tend to favor causal connections that will help reproduce it. One way of showing such favor is to promote the dominance in the stimulus cause of the motivation to reproduce the economic framework. Of course, there will be occasions on which such elements are outweighed by elements disruptive of the economy.

3. Limiting debate in democracies

Let us turn now to the way democracy serves its purpose. Democracy institutionalizes conflict in a way that sets limits on debate. Involving the spirit of faction in government, as Madison put it, amounts to involving factions in debating the burning questions concerning effective rule in the framework of the given economy.

171

These burning questions will not be the "improper or wicked" projects of certain factions. Political debate is in actuality quite useful in respect to the aims of the state. The major factions within the dominant economic group can use the parliamentary system to air their differences and to gain acceptance for the resulting parliamentary compromises. Also, factions outside the dominant economic group can use the system to air their grievances and to seek remedies typically compatible with state goals. In the absence of such a debate, the state would be less flexible in response to the circumstances that bring sections of a dominant class into conflict and that generate new sources of conflict with the exploited and oppressed. Aristotle's praise of the debates in a representative body, in contrast to the dictates of an autocrat, would be merited by modern parliamentary government.[3] But it is praise for a method of solving the problems of governability where the underlying goal is economic reproduction.

What is the mechanism for limiting debate? There is of course no single mechanism, but the discussion of any one of them would be incomplete without mentioning the power of the economically dominant class. We could talk about the power of the executive to set the agenda, the power of committee chairs to suppress bills, the power of lobbyists and campaign contributors. But the ways these mechanisms limit debate is indeterminate apart from the power of the economically dominant class.

The power of this class is not simply *economic power* – the ability to control the factors of production in a way that will reproduce the economy. This class is economically dominant simply because it can reproduce the economy against initiatives of other classes that would undermine it. Yet this economic power is too narrow a base on which to build power in other areas. It does not guarantee, for example, that people will accept the view that the dominant economic class is progressive, that surplus extraction is fair, or that equality is the slogan of those who would enslave the lower classes. Thus it does not guarantee the *ideological power* of the economically dominant class – the ability to have the reproduction of the economy and all it depends on evaluated positively.

Finally, economic power does not guarantee *political power* – the ability of a group to get the backing of the state for its basic interests. A group's having political power will imply that normally those selected for top positions in the state will support that group's interests. When a group gets state backing for its basic interests to the exclusion of other groups, it is politically dominant.

172

This still allows a distinction between a dominant political group and a group that has attained the status of a ruling group. For a ruling group, as distinct from a politically dominant group, presents itself as pursuing the interests of the entire society and also actually selects those who are to get the top positions in the state. How, though, does a group get the backing of the state, so that policies and personnel accord with its interests? This will require political organization, whether in the form of special bodies, such as institutes, or in the form of parties.[4] Clearly, political power, along with ideological power, will play an essential role in the efforts of an economically dominant group to limit debate in a democratic society.[5]

There is, though, a countervailing influence resulting from state autonomy. The state is limited by its pattern of justice in the degree to which it can back the interests of an economically dominant class. If opposition struggle has become fully institutionalized within the state, then there will be no pressure on the state from opposition groups against the interests of the dominant class. If, as is actually the case, the process is incomplete and there is still independent opposition, pressure will be brought to bear on the state against the dominant class, and hence the limits on debate in representative bodies will not be as strict. Despite this, debate will typically be limited.

In the late nineteenth century, the industrial city of Paterson, New Jersey, illustrated the differences between these forms of class power. Paterson manufactured a quarter of the nation's locomotives and was preeminent as a silk manufacturer. Yet, between the 1870s and 1890s, the industrialists did not have their way with the city administration and with its courts.[6] Their economic power did not translate into either ideological or political power in Paterson. The industrialists proved unable to defeat two major strikes during the end of the depression of the 1870s, and they proved unable to get rid of the Irish editor, Joseph McDonnell, of a socialist newspaper that had attacked the "scabs."

The industrialists' weakness had several roots. The city officials, though men of property, had started as workers and still sympathized with them as opposed to the industrialists, many of whom had brought their mills into Paterson from the outside. These officials did not adopt the laissez-faire ideology of the day and instead agreed that the industrialists should "put conscience as well as capital" into their enterprises. Since the industrialists couldn't get what they wanted by demanding that city hall crush

173

the despotic mob, one newspaper suggested that they take the step of getting into local politics. Instead, they subscribed funds for a private militia. They had power at the statehouse in New Jersey and at the Capitol in Washington, but in Paterson their power was less than that of the working class. To reverse this power relation, the national bourgeois ideology would have to triumph over the ethnic and petty-bourgeois ideologies of Paterson, and the Paterson industrialists would have to organize to engage in local politics. Until then the Paterson industrialists lacked the power to limit the debate to how to crush strikes and to how to crush socialist editors who had a working-class readership. Until then it was possible to debate whether strikes and socialist editors should be crushed at all.

It would be as wrongheaded to say that ideological and political powers simply flow out of economic power as it would be to say that they are independent of economic power. The Paterson case is decisive here. There was a need to wean the officialdom and the small merchants away from precorporate ideology. There was an equal need for a capitalist political organization that could appeal to the electorate of Paterson. A class that exercises control only over the factors of production will soon lose that control.

The Lindblom thesis that economic power is enough to limit debate within democracy is too crude.[7] The state may need the revenue it gets from a booming economy, and capitalists may have the power to strike in order to stop that revenue. But the state must already be influenced by the power of capitalist ideology and by the power of capitalist political organization in order to be influenced by such pressure. Otherwise, those running the state might find no point to keeping the capitalist state alive. A strike of capital against the capitalist state brings about a change in the policies of the state through strengthening those elements in the state most committed to its aim of reproducing the economy. It is these elements that have been successfully won to capitalist ideology and capitalist political organization. It is not, then, the economic power of the capitalist class that is a direct agency of limiting debate within democracy.

4. Limiting political power

So much for the dark side of democracy; we turn now to the bright side that necessitates the imposition of some limits on benefits and losses. The power of dominant groups, which is one of their advan-

174

tages, is limited by democracy, and the powerlessness of dominated groups, which is one of their disadvantages, is also limited by it. Democracy is an actualization of justice since it promotes a redistribution of power. Civil rights associated with democracy – the right to free speech, the right to personal security, freedom of mobility, and freedom of association – receive part of their support from their vital role in promoting a redistribution of power. It is of course political power that is being restricted or expanded by democracy; this is the immediate effect of democracy, though the change in a group's political power inevitably has an effect on its ideological and its economic power as well.

The dark and the bright sides of democracy are not two separate things admitting of different explanations. The democracy that admits of a functional explanation on the basis of its supporting the economy is also a democracy that limits power and powerlessness. However, if there is to be such an explanation, there will in general have to be a stimulus cause with at least two elements. First, there will be a dominant element. In this case it will be an economic motivation. There will be forces promoting democracy for its ability to limit debate within the economy. And their motivation will be dominant. Second, there will be the motivation of the dissident forces who want an escape from powerlessness. This motivation will not be a dominant cause within the stimulus for democracy. Nonetheless, the dominant element will need reinforcement by the secondary one. Though democracy might be explained by its functioning for the economy, it may have needed the support of the aspirations of the lower classes. This seeming paradox[8] makes sense within my understanding of functional explanation.

It is not part of my claim that democracy in all its historical manifestations is explained functionally by the economy. It could be that in some cases it either has no functional explanation or has a functional explanation based on either justice or stable rule. The direct democracy of ancient Athens was a response to the landed aristocracy's monopoly of political power. But it was not the wealthy merchants of the ascendant economic order based on trade who were active in placing power in a popular assembly in which every freeman could sit. The pressure of the artisans, small tradesmen, maritime workers, indigent peasants, miners, and shepherds was crucial for direct democracy in Athens during the two centuries beginning with the Cleisthenes reform of 509 B.C.[9] It seems plausible to say that the dominant element in the stimulus cause of Athenian democracy was pressure from these lower classes and that their motivation for pursuing democracy was the functional fact that it would lead to a redistribution of political power. Here the bright side motivates the dominant element.

So far I have talked only about the origins of democratic institutions. What about a functional explanation of, say, U.S. democracy throughout its history? The claim that there is such an explanation is an extremely strong claim. An institution like democracy comes about and then endures either because there is no major challenge to it or because on the occasions it is challenged forces motivated by its functionality rally to save it. Thus, to say that democracy in the United States has through its history a functional explanation based on its usefulness to the economy is to say (a) that it is functionally explained at its origin on the basis of the economy and (b) that when there was a challenge to it at a subsequent time there was an appropriate stimulus cause at that time – one in which the dominant element was the motivation for upholding democracy due to its usefulness for the economy – for a functional explanation of its continued existence. Condition (a) may be satisfied without condition (b), since after its origin challenges to U.S. democracy may have been overcome through stimulus causes in which the dominant element was a motivation based on justice rather than the economy.

How, though, can democracy consistently contain bright and dark aspects? On the dark side, democracy institutionalizes conflict, thereby reducing the chance that a majority group will gain political dominance through independent struggle. On the bright side, democracy limits the power of a dominant minority group. So each side seems both to lose and to win. Abstractly speaking, there is no incompatibility here. In the first place, the power of the dominant minority can be limited without losing its dominance; Madison's tactics saw to that. And in the second place, when the power of an ascendant majority is institutionalized it loses power in one form but gains it in another. The power of independent struggle is traded for the power of the ballot and of making deals in the corridors of the state. Thus, limiting the power of a dominant minority and limiting the power of an ascendant majority are perfectly compatible at this abstract level. We shall soon see that practically speaking they are at odds.

The idea of limiting power is broader than that of democracy. Democracy in our sense functions to limit the power of interacting social groups. It is concerned only secondarily with limiting the power of the state in its relation to social groups. However, in

176

feudalism the nobility tried to restrict the power of the sovereign through one form of medieval constitution. This was not a direct attempt to limit the power of groups but an attempt to change the power relation between, on the one side, a social group and, on the other side, the sovereign him- or herself.[10] The roots of modern democracy are, rather, to be located in another form of medieval constitutionalism, a form that gave commoners representation and limited the power of both the nobles and the sovereign. For example, the efforts of the Third Estate of Paris in 1358 to limit the power of Charles also put it at odds with the nobility and the clergy. Those efforts resulted in a constitution that gave commoners a voice in taxation and that initiated a short-lived experiment of a democratic character.[11]

It is, then, mistaken to insist that modern democracy is fundamentally a barrier against the arbitrariness of the state. The aim of the lower classes participating in a struggle for democracy is certainly not to keep the state from interfering with the upper classes. It is, rather, to limit the power of the upper classes and, in so doing, limit the power of the state to interfere with the lower classes. Of course, the power of the state is not just a reflection of the political power of the upper classes. But, over time, limiting the political power of those upper classes will soften the effect of the state on the lower classes. Sometimes, though, the upper classes look to democracy not just as a way of institutionalizing conflict but also as a barrier against state power. For instance, the Nicaraguan bourgeoisie looked to democracy as a way of throwing off the restrictions imposed on them by the Somoza clique; they were tyrannized by a section of their own class that was using state power for its advantage. From the perspective of the urban poor, workers, and peasants in Nicaragua, democracy was not, though, a matter of the bourgeoisie settling its accounts with Somoza but a matter of limiting their own powerlessness in a class society.

5. Independent political activity and democracy

It is the bright side of democracy that, unfortunately, makes it unstable. The reason for this is that political power is a cherished possession of any class that has it.[12] When a class sees its political power ebbing, it is likely to crush the democratic restrictions on that power. Earlier I spoke about advancing justice to a point beyond which it conflicts with the reproduction of the economy; justice at this point is a least weak set of limits, since any stronger

177

limits would erode the reproduction of the economy. If a democratic institution weakens the political power of an economically dominant class, the democratic state may still be able to reproduce the economy. Though weakened, that class may still be able to use what political power it has left to keep measures that threaten the reproduction of the economy off the legislative agenda. However, in some circumstances a democratic institution may weaken the political power of an economically dominant class so severely that it cannot prevent the adoption of measures that undermine economic reproduction. In such a situation, the class whose political power is being weakened may respond with force to prevent a further erosion of its political power. In Germany after the elections of March 1933 and in Brazil during the Goulart administration in 1964 democracy was smashed on the assumption that it posed a political obstacle to the reproduction of the economy. These eventualities are compatible with a functional explanation of democracy since democracy's functioning to limit debate is at best only a tendency that in extreme cases will not be realized. In those extreme cases the bright side of democracy comes into conflict with the actualization of its dark side.

This instability of democracy, which we have witnessed time and again in capitalist countries, teaches dominated groups to maintain their independence within the democratic trade-off. Self-organization and civil strife are traded for the ballot in order to gain wider participation and limit the power of dominant groups. But a working class, an oppressed race, or an oppressed gender that makes the trade-off in a complete and final way weakens its position immensely; it is absorbed into the state and cannot defend democracy on an independent footing. This is the old difference between absolutism and natural rights in a new form. For the absolutist, individuals give themselves to the prince by a thoroughgoing alienation of their rights. In contrast, for the advocate of natural rights, they are never more than temporarily delegated to the prince. The analogue of the absolute prince is the absolute democracy, which tolerates no independent political action outside the parliament. In dedicating himself to a pure parliamentarism, Tawney says that people must adhere to democracy "when it is not to their advantage as well as when it is. In this matter neither an individual nor a party can ride two horses."[13]

Yet the democratic institution owes its bright side precisely to an incomplete institutionalization of the struggle of the dominated. Only if there is a continuation of politics by extraparliament-

178

ary means will democracy be able to establish limits to the power of a dominant class. Work stoppages, resistance to court orders, demonstrations against officials all have their place as expressions of independent organization in insuring that the democratic process is not destroyed by the political power of one class. Once the tradition of self-organization outside the institutions of the state is suppressed, only the formal mechanism of democracy will remain. Totalitarian rule will then have triumphed within a democratic form.

The bright side of democracy – a just limiting of political power – is at odds with its dark side, the channeling of conflict into the state. For the limiting of the political power of a dominant class is effective only when the channeling of conflict into the state is incomplete and there is still struggle independent of the state. And conversely, the channeling of conflict is complete only when the pressure for a just limiting of power has vanished. There is then a contradiction between the form of justice and economic functioning at the heart of democracy in a class society. We see now why this contradiction is ineliminable; for there to be democracy in such a society there must be a stimulus cause that contains two elements, one pushing for limiting political power and the other pushing for channeling conflict into the state. In sum, the contradictory character of democracy in a class society is a basis for neither an outright rejection of it as one avenue of struggle nor an enthusiastic acceptance of it as the only avenue of struggle.

14

Welfare capitalism

The welfare state serves several functions. On the one hand, it promotes the economy by generating economic demand. On the other hand, it promotes stable rule by compensating for losses associated with the economy. The possibility of constructing a functional explanation of the welfare state on the basis of these functions is discussed here only briefly. The main emphasis will be on the conflicting tendencies created by the welfare state and their impact on the capitalist economy.

1. The welfare boom

Even after concerted attacks on it, welfare spending remains a significant part of the United States economy. President Carter's last budget, the one for 1981, made income maintenance 43 percent of the federal budget. President Reagan's budget for 1985 set aside $374 billion for income-maintenance programs. This was 42 percent of a total outlay of $926 billion. Income maintenance is made up of direct payments for benefits to individuals and does not then include budgeted purchases by the government itself of goods and services for the welfare areas of education and health. This sum for income maintenance was 10.5 percent of the roughly $3.5 trillion gross national product (GNP) of 1985. Reagan's cuts in housing, food stamps, family aid, and job training had been offset by the absence of cuts in the basic retirement program.

Nonetheless it is undeniable that, beginning in the late 1970s in the United States, the share of welfare spending in the economy stagnated. What makes this stagnation so striking is its contrast with the brisk rise in the share of welfare spending in the preceding decade and a half. New programs were enacted, such as Medicare, the food stamps program, and the Comprehensive Employment and Training Act. Moreover, earlier programs, including rent assistance and Aid to Families with Dependent Children, were vastly expanded. Along with the shrinking military budget of the post–

180

Tet-offensive period of the Vietnam War went a rapid increase in the part of the federal budget devoted to income maintenance.[1] While the military share dropped from 45 percent in 1967–70 to 26 percent in 1975–80, the income-maintenance share of the federal budget rose from 29 percent in 1965–70 to 48 percent in 1975–80. The political reaction of the 1980s did not lead back to the 1965–70 percentages; military spending in 1985 was 29 percent of federal outlays, and welfare transfers to individuals in 1985 were 42 percent of federal outlays.

The boom in welfare spending was international in scope and coincided with a boom in overall public spending. Public expenditures as a percentage of GNP grew between 1960 and 1982 in the United States from 28 percent to 38 percent, in Germany from 31 percent to 49 percent, in France from 34 percent to 52 percent, and in Japan from 17 percent to 33 percent. Welfare expenditures as a percentage of GNP rose as part of this expansion of government. By 1980 income-maintenance programs in advanced capitalist countries were providing households with from one-eighth – in Japan and the United States – to one-fourth – in France and the Netherlands – of their incomes, and these are shares close to those provided by property income.[2]

This "quiet revolution" in welfare spending was not just a response to the winding down of the Vietnam War; it began before the war and caught up countries uninvolved in the war. It was not a result of leftist government; France had conservative governments during the quiet revolution, and the Swedish welfare state continued to grow after the socialist government was voted out in 1976. In the United States the boom was during the Republican Nixon–Ford decade. Nor was it the result of a period of sizable growth on the part of the trade union movement; in the United States union membership was becoming as small a part of the labor force as it had been in 1920; in France and Germany unions grew slightly, and only in Belgium, Britain, and Sweden was there marked growth.

There have been many discussions of the origin of the welfare state, which here means a state that makes payments to and provides services for individuals that typically satisfy basic needs. Those discussions make us conscious of the variety of forces that joined together to form the welfare state. In the case of Germany, Bismarck promoted social insurance for health (1883), accidents (1884), and old age (1889) in order to defuse the growing social democratic and trade union movements. Later, in England, the Liberal Party, which had been the party of laissez-faire, pushed for

181

a program of social reform and received the temporary support of Tories like Winston Churchill, who joined Lloyd George's Liberal cabinet. With the backing of the new Labour Party, which reflected the growing strength of the union movement, the Liberal government put through a scheme for old-age pensions in 1909, an act to set a minimum wage and to stop sweated labor in 1910, and an insurance act in 1911 designed both to raise the national standard of health and to avoid the hardships of unemployment with contributory unemployment benefits. To finance these welfare measures, the budget of 1907 taxed unearned incomes more heavily than earned incomes, and by 1909 there was a supertax on high incomes, increased death duties, and a capital gains tax on land.[3] So the pattern was set early on of a combination of lower-class and upper-class pressures for welfare legislation and the matching taxation. The political initiative for welfare was, though, in the hands of an upper class which felt the pressure of a trade union and a socialist insurgency.

2. The functions of welfare

Intriguing as the stories of the origin of the welfare state are, it is equally important to learn something about the long-term functioning of the welfare state. I shall consider here two functions of the welfare state. The first of these roles came to be doubted along with the shift in state economic orthodoxy that took place with the opening of the Thatcher–Reagan era.

The earlier neo-Keynesian orthodoxy had given the welfare state an intellectual basis that was not available at its inception, when laissez-faire was still the soul of economic science. In the 1930s Roosevelt's secretary of labor, Frances Perkins, justified social security on the grounds that in England it had proved able to "to maintain necessary purchasing power."[4] But the turn in the late 1970s to supply-side economics, which coincided with the deceleration of income maintenance, involved an emphasis on capital investment rather than consumer demand. Welfare spending came to be seen as reducing capital investment and hence employment. Along with welfare cuts came a more regressive taxation, leading to the poor in the United States paying a sixth more of their income in taxes in 1988 than in 1977 and the rich paying a twelfth less. All of this was to support capital formation. As one banker put it, "Nothing could be more salutary for the prospect of long-term productive investment and indeed the global financial system than the news that

these grotesquely large obligations to pay public retirement benefits were being reduced and brought under control."[5] In short,
supply-side economics, while agreeing that welfare spending puts
a floor under demand, attacks it for undermining capitalism by
undermining economic growth.

This attack on the economic functionality of the welfare state is,
we shall see, largely unwarranted. True, the welfare states does
tend to undermine capitalism, but not for the reason given here by
supply-side economics. Furthermore, within my tendential view of
functionality, it is perfectly consistent to say both that the welfare
state functions for the economy by putting a floor under demand
and that it has other effects that undermine the capitalist economy.

So I shall begin with a hypothesis that in no way commits us to a
neo-Keynesian optimism about the welfare state. It is that *the welfare institutions of the state function to reproduce capitalism through
the mechanism of maintaining a high floor for demand.* This function is important in a period when capitalism is less and less capable of insuring that what is supplied out of the production process
will confront a demand fully able to absorb it. Marx and Keynes
had, for different reasons, begun their macroeconomic considerations with a critique of Say's law, according to which there was no
possibility of an imbalance between what is supplied through an
investment in capital and labor and what is realized in the form of
economic value through purchases based on demand.[6]

For Marx the problem has its source in the tendency within
capitalism for there to be increasing capital intensiveness in relation to labor in the production process. (This was the fifth tendency
making up the capitalist economic relations of production in Chapter 10.) Increased capital intensiveness leaves less room for labor to
add value – in particular surplus value, which is the source of
profit – to the unit product. Under certain conditions, this tendency is, then, associated with a tendency for the rate of profit to
decline. To counteract this tendency there is an overall slackening
of investment in capital goods until places for investment that are
competitively advantageous can be found. This slackening leads to
a failure of demand to meet supply and hence to economic crisis.

For Keynes the problem stems from what he saw as the techno-
logically inevitable fact of diminishing returns to investment. Following Ricardo, he thought that as resources get scarcer and as
improvements in equipment both become more expensive and
yield ever smaller gains the rate of return on capital would approach zero. Entrepreneurs become correspondingly more reluc-

183

tant to sink their liquid capital into productive investments. Capitalism slinks toward its grave, the process being slowed only by the action of government, which has the power to pry investable funds out of capitalists in order to rejuvenate demand.

It does not matter here whether we accept the Marxian or the Keynesian diagnosis of the failure of Say's law. In each case it is the development of capitalism itself that makes it harder to obtain a balance of supply with demand and thereby avoid overproduction. Both view direct measures to increase demand as little more than palliatives. Neo-Keynesians nonetheless ignored Keynes's gloomy predictions about capitalism; in the 1950s and 1960s they argued that "Modern democracies have the fiscal and monetary tools, and the political will to use them, to end chronic slumps and galloping inflation."[7] In the context of the stagflation of the 1970s, the fatuousness of such a claim contributed to the rise of supply-side economics, which fails to be more tenable because of this.

The second thing that welfare spending does is to head off insurgencies that might undermine the state. If the capitalist state makes no effort to reduce poverty, unemployment, and the dearth of vital services for the lower classes, then it will be blamed for favoring the upper classes, for class rule. *Welfare spending functions to legitimate the state through the mechanism of compensating for the ills of capitalism.* After unemployment compensation was legislated in 1938 in the United States the mass movements of the unemployed of the 1930s were never repeated. Old-age benefits were legislated in 1935 more on the basis of elite pressure to give the capitalist state a human face than on the basis of the movement of the elderly for the unsuccessful Townsend Plan of 1933.[8] The black movement of the 1960s started as a political and civil rights movement but quickly dramatized the problems of U.S. poverty.[9] The U.S. welfare system's greatest growth began as a response to the black movement but was sustained through the 1970s in the absence of any related insurgency. Establishment pressure to sustain an acceptance by blacks of the capitalist state had outlived the black movement.

There are, then, at least two important mechanisms whereby welfare spending functions: maintaining economic demand and compensating for economically induced ills. Large increases in welfare spending in the United States, and elsewhere, began as the high point of the post–World War II economic boom was reached in 1966, at which time profit rates in the United States began to tumble. Government transfer payments to individuals increased from around 5 percent of the U.S. GNP in the late 1960s to around 10 percent of the GNP in the late 1970s. The recessions of 1974–5 and of 1981–2 would have been deeper, longer, and socially more explosive without this large increase in welfare spending.

Each of the mechanisms is, though, connected with a different function. Through increasing demand the welfare state maintains the economy, whereas through compensating for ills it maintains state legitimacy. The possibility then exists of combining both functions into a single functional explanation of the welfare state. Its continuation would then be grounded in the fact that it promotes both the economy and legitimacy. With such a range of consequences beneficial to the powerful in and out of the state, there would be a strong motive to sustain the welfare state. What is required to espouse such an explanation is the empirical assurance that a dominant aspect of the stimulus cause is in fact the motive to promote the economy and legitimacy together. It is plausible to think that this requirement has in fact frequently been met when the welfare state has faced challenges. The coalition sustaining the welfare state in the United States was for a long period united by a mixture of neo-Keynesianism and concern for the image of government. More recently, of course, the emergence of supply-side economics has meant that the welfare state has come to be sustained primarily by the motive of legitimating rule. In both cases pressures from below have been part of the stimulus cause, but the dominant motive in organizing the efforts for welfare has come from elites. Similarly, the welfare bureaucracy itself is part of the stimulus for sustaining welfare, but, I would suggest, its self-serving motive has likewise not been the dominant one.

3. Subsistence justice

Welfare spending limits the losses of the less advantaged by compensating for the ills of capitalism and is thus part of the state's pattern of justice. As such, welfare spending functions to make the state's rule stable. A virtual consensus has emerged that a person's fate should not be decided by laissez-faire and hence that the invisible hand of the economy needs guidance by the quite visible hand of the state. Even as staunch a supporter of laissez-faire as Milton Friedman would not go so far as to unravel the "safety net" for the less well-off. He would propose in place of the current welfare system a negative income tax for those with low income.[10] Low-income people could buy pension plans and health care insurance from private firms with the money they receive from the negative income tax. Whether even the most provident among the low-income group could afford pensions and health care insurance if wages could not be regulated is another question. The important thing is that even a Friedman puts himself within the welfare consensus by calling for a state that helps the less well-off. A state that ignored such a broad consensus would have difficulty winning acceptance. Anticipating such difficulties, elites have pieced together the welfare state. The form of the state that functions to reproduce late capitalism will be a welfare state.

It is a mistake to suppose that the welfare state aims at greater equality. Thus the justice of the welfare state does not tend toward more equality. The important index for realizing the goal of greater equality is not the change in the difference in income between those who are better off and those who are worse off. Rather, it is the change in the *proportional* difference between the income levels of those who are better off and those who are worse off. (Here income includes the value of welfare benefits.) Progress is made toward equality when a difference between twenty dollars for the better-off and ten dollars for the worse-off, making a proportional difference of 1 – twenty dollars minus ten dollars divided by ten dollars – yields later on to a difference between sixty and forty dollars, making a proportional difference of 0.5 – sixty dollars minus forty dollars divided by forty dollars. There is then progress toward the goal of equality when the proportional difference between the better- and worse-off decreases, even though the absolute difference increases. (In this case the absolute difference increases from ten dollars to twenty dollars.) Some would say such progress toward equality is the aim of the welfare state. For them the capitalist state can transform itself into an egalitarian state through its pattern of welfare justice.[11] Perhaps some reformers are motivated by greater equality when they advocate welfare measures and progressive taxation. But egalitarian justice does not fit the pattern of the welfare state's justice.

As far as the state is concerned, justice is done when there is freedom from hunger, joblessness, ignorance, and avoidable illness. *The justice of the welfare state is justice as subsistence rather than justice as greater equality.* Its realization requires maintaining a certain minimal level for the less well-off, and of course this maintenance need not require a narrowing of the proportional gap between them and the most well-off.[12]. In the actual situation since

186

World War II in the United States and France, this gap – defined for family income – has not narrowed as a result of welfare spending increases. In Britain and Sweden it has narrowed somewhat. Since the gap is defined for family income, part of this narrowing may have resulted not from welfare but from the fact that, by entering the work force in large numbers, lower-class women have increased their family incomes.

The welfare state works through redistribution. But the connection between redistribution and progress toward equality is not a simple one. There is a distinction between reducing inequality at a given time by a redistributive measure and reducing inequality continually over a period of years by continually strengthening such a measure. Suppose we reduce inequality at a given time in order to realize subsistence justice. Maintaining this reduction of inequality by continuing the redistributive measure, if this is what is necessary to continue to realize subsistence justice, will not in general tend to reduce inequality any further. This will be true even though the norm for subsistence rises as productivity increases, for as productivity increases the structures in the society promoting inequality will tend to maintain or even increase the proportional difference between the better- and the worse-off.

Even in the context of a tax structure that has become more regressive, the welfare state has some redistributive effect. Though it is not strongly redistributive, it serves to realize some of the demands of subsistence justice. Still, it cannot be said that this redistribution is reducing inequality step by step over time. The most that can be said for the welfare state in the United States is that the redistributive measure supporting it makes possible a partial realization of subsistence justice and may prevent an even greater inequality than already exists.[13] In Britain too there has been redistribution, but once the initial effect was absorbed, there was no ongoing reduction of inequality.[14] Up to the 1970s at least, Sweden could claim to be the exception with a steady reduction of inequality through strengthened redistributive measures.

Rulers run a risk by neglecting subsistence justice. The 1974 famine of Bangladesh, resulting from the flooding of the Brahmaputra River which created unemployment among rice workers, is a case in point. The famine was not the result of less food in the new country; food availability was not seriously affected by the flooding. But the lack of employment and the skyrocketing rice prices, partly due to hoarding by wealthy merchants, left the rice workers

187

without subsistence.[15] In China, by contrast, famine had come under control through public guarantees of subsistence. The rice workers would also have survived in Sri Lanka with its relatively advanced welfare system. In the absence of these guarantees of subsistence in Bangladesh, the regime of Sheikh Mujibur Rahman was shaken as a result of the flooding. After losing his charismatic hold on the Bengalis due to famine, the disintegrating economy, and corruption, he was killed by the military in 1975. Stability was not established until General Ziaur Rahman introduced martial law in late 1976. Part of his program was to promote Islamic social justice and equality. To deal with the eight million unemployed agricultural workers, he established an arduous food-for-work program. But his regime was unable to reduce the misery created by the drought of 1978–9 and the flooding of 1980, which left five million homeless. And so he too was assassinated in 1981. The logic of the erosion of Sheikh Mujibur's rule is the logic that kept a President Reagan from cutting farther than he did into benefits programs.

It is, then, true to say that welfare spending serves to legitimate the state. It is best, though, not to leave this matter with the suggestion that legitimation is but another commodity, having a higher or a lower price as the times require. To see why legitimation is not a commodity, it needs to be pointed out that it is not achieved until a pattern of justice is actual, or at least promised. Actual or promised limits on losses and benefits are a prerequisite for legitimacy. This pattern of justice mediates the link between legitimation and state spending; the spending must satisfy the requirements of justice in order to legitimate the state. Legitimation is not an immediate consequence of state spending. This is what is right about Habermas's insistence that a crisis of legitimation is based on moral values.[16] When the values are more demanding, it will be difficult to legitimate the rule of the state with spending that falls in the range of what is politically feasible. (O'Connor, though, speaks of social expenses as part of legitimation with no hint that more is involved than a trade-off between misery and money.)[17] A pattern of justice that the populace expects the state to uphold is the norm for legitimation; if there is a change in the pattern of state justice the same level of spending will not necessarily yield the same degree of legitimacy. If in Sweden state justice is no longer subsistence justice but has become justice as greater equality, then legitimacy will not be possible with spending at the level needed to realize subsistence justice.

188

4. How the welfare state threatens capitalism

A conflict usually emerges between the form of justice and the function of reproduction. Yet subsistence justice that compensates for the ills of capitalism and the maintenance of effective demand by welfare budgets seem harmoniously linked. Maintaining effective demand is not, though, the only task involved in reproducing the capitalist economy. Subsistence justice reduces the severity of recessions, but there is a way it undercuts capitalism. Thus the welfare state has contradictory tendencies. The reason for this is that the capitalist state cannot reproduce capitalism if it does not reproduce the boundary between the private and the public. A state that allows the public sector to push the private sector into economic insignificance may be a capitalist state in the sense that its role is to promote capitalism, but it is operating in the presence of obstacles that do not allow it to perform its role. Subsistence justice pushes the public/private boundary in a direction that favors the public sector. State institutions – schools, hospitals, welfare offices – have become a larger presence in the society. And income-maintenance programs contribute what is in effect capital – variable capital, which is capital devoted to wages – to make up a part of the wages of workers in the private sector. This part is often called the social wage, and it is a part of wages over which capitalists have no direct control. It is not the size of these institutions and programs by itself that is important but something more basic that it signifies: the increased control of investable capital by the state.

When the state taxes corporations and the wealthy and borrows money from banks and the wealthy, it puts under its control the decisions as to how that capital is to be spent. This is not the nationalization of individual capital enterprises, but it is the nationalization of a chunk of investable capital. Ownership, we recall, is control over labor, plant, and investment. What welfare spending by the state does, as already noted in Chapter 6, is to reduce the control owners have over both investment and wages. It is then an attack on property and is understood as such by capitalists. This specific attack on property shifts the public/private boundary in favor of the public sector. Yet capitalists are faced with a dilemma: Unless they relinquish some control over investment and wages, they lose not only a mechanism for generating demand – a mechanism that increases growth in good times and puts a floor under employment in bad times – but also a mechanism for stabilizing the capitalist state through its legitimation.

189

The reason state control over investable capital is so pernicious takes us to the heart of capitalism itself. For centuries capitalism was successful in bringing more and more resources – labor, materials, machines, land – under its control. Its strength would be greatest when all noncapitalist competitors for control of these resources were defeated. It could then use those resources solely to serve its aims of accumulation. But once feudal and other precapitalist competitors were reduced to insignificance, another obstacle appeared – the welfare state. Powerful state agencies then developed to allocate resources, not directly for the accumulation of capital, but for generating demand and legitimating the state.

Supply-side theorists raise a different problem, that of economic growth. They allege that the remedy for slow growth is more investable capital. And for them one of the reasons there is too little investable capital is that too much capital is going into state welfare programs. The inverse connection between welfare spending and economic growth seems, though, less compelling when there is a boom period that generates enough capital for consistent growth and welfare too. So it is reasonable to conjecture that the slow growth bothering supply-side theorists is less a problem of available capital than one of rates of return. When rates of return on investment are higher, there tends to be a pickup in the investment of capital in productive enterprises. The onus for slow growth thus gets shifted away from welfare spending by such considerations.

In contrast, I am raising a problem not about growth but about control. Whether or not there is slow growth, the welfare state restricts the control of capitalists to a more limited field of capital. Their power as a group is tied to their monopoly control of capital. Yet the state appears here as a competitor siphoning off investable capital into noncapitalist uses. Chances are that as the norm for subsistence justice changes there will be a further increase in the amount of investable capital to which the state will lay claim, giving its institutions even more economic power. Supply-side economics is thus only a distorted reflection of the uneasiness felt within the capitalist class as the public/private boundary shifts against it. In periods such as the 1980s when labor and other groups are weak, the capitalists have fought to reverse this movement of the boundary.

To appreciate the significance of this loss of control, it is well to make a distinction. On the one hand, loss of control of investable capital means that the capitalist does not decide how it is to be

190

used; other criteria than those used by the capitalists, such as the criterion of justice, become relevant to its use. On the other hand, loss of control by the capitalist is to be distinguished from a disappearance of these resources from the capitalist system altogether; one way or another, welfare spending contributes to economic growth and cannot then be viewed as a dead weight pulling the system down. All the evidence points to the fact that welfare spending tends, in periods that include both recession and prosperity, to promote economic growth and hence capital formation. Sweden, Belgium, and the Netherlands spend more on welfare in relation to their national product than does the United States. Has this pulled their economies down? Quite the contrary, for between 1960 and 1980 not only have their per capita national products grown faster than those of the United States but also their per capita national products matched or surpassed those of the United States. Clearly, then, loss of control over investment by the capitalist class in a welfare state may mean greater rather than less prosperity. It is regarded as pernicious by capitalists only because, if the loss is carried far enough, capitalists cease to exist as a class.

Another way of looking at compensating the ills of capitalism leaves the state out except as an enforcer. Workers would then have to win subsistence justice from their employers, with the state merely insisting that the employers provide it. In this case, capitalism would also suffer a loss of control in regard to variable capital, since workers would have to be paid enough to buy private education, private insurance for health, unemployment, and disability, and private pension plans.[18] So, even without a welfare state, it is pernicious from the capitalist perspective to lose control over variable capital by not being able to cut corners on wages.

The capitalist wants to avoid the loss of traditional capitalist controls even if this means a rejection of subsistence justice. The rejection of subsistence justice increases exploitation and allows the capitalist to employ more labor and to buy more materials and machines. It is precisely to allow the capitalist this control that is the root motivation of the criticism that welfare spending slows production. Milton Friedman makes this criticism when he calls for "a higher rate of capital formation" by ending the welfare state.[19] This criticism of the welfare state is, as I noted above, not justified by an actual slowing of production by the welfare state. It is not about production and prosperity at all but about the loss of traditional capitalist controls. Increasing exploitation by ignoring

191

subsistence justice is justified not by gains in production but by preserving traditional controls for capitalists. The best defense of subsistence justice is, then, to go beyond it with a radical conception of justice that directly challenges all the traditional capitalist controls of production.

15

The new mercantilism

Welfare spending is not the only way the state intervenes in the economy. Income maintenance has an impact on consumer demand that is functional for an economy that generates its own unfavorable conditions for investment. The state has other, more direct ways of supporting the accumulation of capital, ranging from subsidies for private production to helping negotiate the conditons for private investment abroad. Direct support to capital is won in the political process through the formation of a political alliance that often includes organized labor. This direct support is a key factor in the ability of capitalists to organize their economy. The period of state intervention called mercantilism that lasted from the sixteenth through the eighteenth centuries was followed by laissez-faire, but now the extent of direct state support for capital accumulation has become so great that we are warranted in speaking about a new mercantilism.[1]

1. Thinking about functions

This area of state activity displays the functional character of the state if any area does. Unfortunately, the fad that has made functional thinking unpopular has blinkered people to the patent functionality of direct state support for capital accumulation.[2] This fad is based on a mistake that can be cleared up on the basis of what was said in Chapter 11. The fad emphasizes concrete social and political situations, called historical conjunctures, rather than functional links. The mistake is to make this an either–or matter, thereby requiring the rejection of the functional element if any play is to be given to the conjunctural one. But it is obvious that both elements have a role to play.

Both the institutions of intervention and specific interventions themselves are the outcome of struggles within and outside the state. These struggles make up the conjunctural factor, or what I call the factor of stimulus causation. There is, though, a selection of

193

the kinds of institutions and the kinds of specific interventions that can be brought about by these concrete struggles. They are only stimuli, unable of themselves to determine outcomes in isolation. The selection of outcomes is at two levels, the level of functionality and the level of framework. At the level of functionality, social and political struggles have as outcomes those institutions or interventions that tend to support the economy. (See (3) in Section 4, Chapter 11.) The support is not infallible but only tendential. At the framework level, this functionally mediated connection between struggles and both institutions and interventions is one that is possible only because the struggles take place in the presence of the basic tendencies of capitalism. (See (4) in Section 4, Chapter 11.) This double selection gives a role to both struggle in its concreteness and structure – at the level of function and at that of framework – in its abstractness. To appeal to the former without the latter is an atomistic form of empiricism that makes any connections magical; to appeal to the latter without the former is a Platonic form of idealism that makes change a mystery. With this mistake out of the way, let us return to state intervention.

2. Justice as mutuality

If it is to be politically feasible, direct state support for private capital accumulation needs to be widely accepted. Acceptance comes from showing that direct support tends to improve everyone's chances of economic well-being. The basic way of improving these chances, at least where workers get work through a labor market, is to encourage the growth of employment. On the face of it, direct support for capital favors only capitalists. But the state wants to avoid the appearance of ruling for merely a few. By averting the common ill of unemployment, direct support for capital favors not just capitalists but also those who depend on employment.[3] The positive effect on employment makes direct support for capital fully compatible with acting in the interest of all. In the United States, the Full Employment Act of 1946 committed the federal government to creating and maintaining useful employment opportunities. That act set up the Council of Economic Advisors to promote economic growth in order to stimulate full employment.

The pattern of justice involved here is that of class mutuality. Justice does not impose a limit on the amount of direct support by the state for capital. Instead, the limit is imposed in a conditional manner: If there is direct state support for capital, justice demands

194

that this support contribute to, or have a high likelihood of contributing to, the growth of employment. The imperative of justice is not that employment grow; the growth of employment by itself might be at the expense of profits and thus might be interpreted as unfair. The imperative of justice is, rather, that employment should grow if capital is benefited by the state. We have then an imperative of class mutuality that is a special case of Rawl's difference principle, according to which the prospects of the better-off are to be improved only when the prospects of those less fortunate are also improved. Justice as subsistence was quite different from this justice as mutuality since justice as subsistence put a limit on the losses of the less fortunate in an unconditional fashion. True, limiting their losses created demand, which benefited owners, but the justice itself of limiting their losses was not conditional upon creating benefits for the more fortunate. Justice as mutual benefit implies that any skewing of direct state support to capital that thwarts employment growth will undermine popular acceptance of the interventionist state.

3. Forms of state support for capital

We have yet to look into the forms that direct state support for private capital take. An important factor in shaping any form of support is the national identity of capital. So it is appropriate to begin this section with comments on the relation of nationality to the economy.

The state supports capital that pertains to the national economy. There is then a nation on which the state's support for accumulation focuses. Insofar as foreign capital invested within the nation and domestic capital invested outside the nation both pertain to the national economy, they are both possible recipients of direct state support for accumulation. The basic system of support is, then, national in character; to deal with it requires an addition to the basic concepts of abstract economics.[4] The problems that emerge within the economy are first identified as national problems; it is the nation's unemployment, the nation's inflation, its weakness in international competition, and its inability to concentrate capital for growth that are perceived as the problems to be solved. An internationalist perspective is either lacking altogether or a weak component in the debates over how to handle these problems. The problems are not treated as those of an international system of capitalism.[5]

195

Economic problems are solved within the bounds of capitalism, not because of support for international capitalism but because the nation is capitalist. In this way the element of nationality must play an indispensable role in thinking about the functions of agencies of the capitalist state. The mere existence of a capitalist framework is ineffective in originating such agencies. The class struggle is also insufficient since it swings back and forth, whereas state agencies are stable. The injection of the factor of nationality is just what is needed to derive that stability. When a national unemployment problem is to be solved, the debate over how to solve it is limited by the identification of the nation with a given economic system. The solution then takes on the stability this identification has acquired. Where, however, national unity is threatened by class strife, the identification of the nation with a given kind of economy has less power to limit solutions. There may then be attempts to solve problems by means of state agencies that aim at a new kind of economy.

Direct state support for capital accumulation responds to a general problem that capitalism cannot handle on its own. Capital itself is the prime scarce commodity of capitalism. The state is the supplier of last resort to capitalists of this commodity. The scarcity has different roots at different times and places, but the common theme is that capitalism would have starved itself for lack of capital had it not been for the state. Because of this, agencies of the state that support private investment directly can be said to function for the reproduction of capitalism. (This functional element could perhaps be the basis for functional explanations of these agencies, though I shall not pursue the matter further here.)

Two kinds of capital scarcity are relevant here, and to each corresponds a different form of state support. First, a nation sometimes has a need for a *large-scale expansion* of invested capital. Extending its internal market might call for highways, and staying competitive internationally might call for cheaper energy. Capitalists may have to turn to the state to fund highway construction and new power plants. This capital scarcity is relative to the need for large-scale expansion.[6] The rate of profit may be perfectly healthy, and the growth of investment from year to year may be fairly brisk. Even so, individual corporations and cartels may not be able or willing to raise the sums needed for the desired expansion.

The state can provide the capital in several ways. On the one hand, land was handed over to the U.S. railways in the nineteenth

196

century, and plants, built by the U.S. government for war production, were handed over to manufacturers at the end of World War II. On the other hand, the state can itself make the needed investment and operate it as a subsidy for corporations. Thus the Panama Canal was built and operated by the United States as a subsidy for U.S. shipping, and the U.S. air traffic control system is outfitted and staffed by the government as a subsidy for the airlines. These large-scale expansions include both a constant and a variable capital component. When, for example, the state underwrites research and development for technology in agriculture it saves agribusiness enormous sums for both laboratories and salaries – for both constant and variable capital.

The second kind of capital scarcity leads to a form of direct support for capital accumulation to be called here *growth maintenance*. Economic growth is threatened by recurrent problems with the rate of profit. Reducing the severity of crises of profitability calls for growth maintenance. But how are profit rates connected to capital scarcity?

When the overall rate of profit decreases, there tends to be an eventual decline in the rate of increase of investment. With a lower profit rate there will be a relative scarcity of capital available from profits with which to increase investment. This in turn will slow down the rate of growth of the entire economy. A slowdown in the rate of growth may lead to a rate of growth so low that unemployment is generated. A decrease in the rate of profit, though, may not lead to such an unacceptably low rate of growth. If, for example, the decrease in the rate of profit is quite small, there may still be an increase in the amount invested. This could be because the constant capital on which the profit is made will be larger than it was in the previous period of investment. Even at a lower rate of return, a large capital may yield more to invest. But with a sizable decrease in the rate of profit, profits may well not provide as much to invest as was provided by them in the previous period. The decrease in investment will most likely lead to a negative growth rate. Demand for production goods and labor is reduced, pushing the rate of profit down still further.[7] This ignores the possibility of counteracting the ill effects of the failure of profitability with borrowing. Investment could continue to rise on the basis of borrowed capital. But if this fails to induce a higher profit rate, investment will inevitably decline. Even if the downward spiral of the rate of profit can be stopped, it may be several years after it is stopped before the effects of renewed growth of investment will show up in a return to the level of employment reached when the rate of profit first began its drop.

I have examined the effects of a fall in the rate of profit apart from considerations about what happens to the incentive to invest. Suppose that at a lower rate of profit a smaller fraction of overall profits is invested, due to a decreased incentive to invest. The effects on investment will then be even more profound than just indicated. Or suppose the same fraction of overall profits is invested but there is a shift of investment from less to relatively more profitable enterprises, where the incentive to invest is greater. Investments might, for example, move out of basic industry to speculative enterprises or move from a high-wage to a relatively low-wage section of the nation. The resulting imbalances could well continue the depression of the economy as a whole. The state attempts to overcome the scarcity of capital that initiates these lapses of growth by using its ability to concentrate capital through taxation and borrowing.

State funding for large-scale expansion and for growth maintenance plays a role in making capitalism viable in the form of national units. In particular, the state can help lay the base for a nation's competitive position in the world economy. But it also helps in the development of the internal economy of a nation. Without these connections between enterprise and nationality, state support for capital accumulation anywhere would be a mystery.

The importance of nationality for direct state support for capital is evident from the workings of several state agencies. For example, the Export–Import Bank increases exports from the United States by making purchase money available to foreign buyers. The bank attempts to maintain the profits of U.S. exporters through generating demand for their products rather than those of their foreign competitors.[8] State export credit accounted in 1980 for 39 percent of Japanese exports, 35 percent of British exports, and 18 percent of U.S. exports. Moreover, by tolerating tax inequities favoring large corporations, the state provides them with additional capital. In the United States in 1978, Chase Manhattan Bank paid no taxes, Exxon paid only 8 percent of its world income in taxes, and A.T.&T. paid 9.5 percent. Also, the individual U.S. states provide capital to attract corporations. In 1984 Indiana used a package of concessions that included $30 million for roads and sewers to lure a General Motors truck plant from Flint, Michigan, to Fort Wayne. Michigan would lose from 3,500 to 4,000 jobs and Indiana would

198

gain 3,000 jobs, but the purpose of reproducing capitalism in Indiana was served. The competition between nations thus develops an analogue at the subnational level.

The economic crisis of the early 1980s gave us striking examples of funding for the maintenance of growth rather than for large-scale expansion. The United States loaned Chrysler $1.2 billion in 1980; a smaller Chrysler employing fewer workers survived the crisis. The government bought fourteen million shares of Chrysler in 1980 and sold them in 1983 at a profit of $122 million. Direct support by the state is even good business for the state. The Federal Deposit Insurance Corporation (FDIC) rescued Continental Illinois Bank, the United States' eighth largest, in 1984 with a $4.5 billion bailout. In the process the FDIC bought most of Continental's problem loans, which had precipitated the depositors' run on the bank. (But the FDIC did not buy Continental's $2 billion in problem loans to Latin American for fear this would make trouble for other banks with shaky foreign loans.) The FDIC became 80 percent owner of the bank as a result of the rescue. In the 1970s, Continental had only been doing what a bank should by making low-interest capital available. But in the 1980s many of these loans became problematic because of economic pressures on the borrowers. To get new capital the bank had to attract deposits by awarding premium rates. The rates it had to pay on deposits were higher than the rates paid to it on those earlier loans. The burden of all this on the bank was great enough to move depositors to make massive withdrawals. The state let smaller corporations and banks sink in the early 1980s; but letting Chrysler and Continental sink would have been system-threatening.

4. Assumptions about profits and markets

There are far-reaching economic assumptions behind my interpretation of state support for accumulation. One assumption worth noting is that the state intervenes because capitalism is unable to overcome the scarcity of capital by itself. Opposed to this assumption is the view that capitalists have plenty of capital available but do not invest in productive enterprise because demand cannot keep up with increasing capacity to produce.[9]

Surely, though, in regard to large-scale expansion there is scarcity throughout the world. Individual capitalists must appeal to the state to raise the capital for such expansion. The state uses its power to raise capital by austerity, by unequal terms of trade, by excessive taxation of the working class, by borrowing, and by deficit spending. But the debate over capital scarcity has most often centered on the maintenance of growth to counteract crises. And on this issue the position I am taking is that the primary cause of the decline in growth during crises is not insufficient demand but insufficient profits. That there is a connection between profitability and economic growth is suggested by trends in twentieth-century U.S. capitalism.

A decline in the rate of profit preceded periods of economic sluggishness and unemployment in twentieth-century United States. The rate of profit dropped by nearly half in the decade prior to the 1920s and recovered only slightly in the 1920s.[10] Similarly, the rate of profit dropped 40 percent between 1966 and 1970, before leveling off in the 1970s.[11] These periods of declining rates of profit set the stage for periods of sluggishness and unemployment, first in the 1930s and then in the 1970s and early 1980s. The weakening of demand in these subsequent periods reflected a slowdown in the rate of increase of investment that was connected with scarcity of capital brought on by the dramatic reductions in rates of return.

As already noted, a lower rate of profit will not necessarily decrease the absolute amount of capital invested in durable producers' goods, but it will eventually tend to slow down the rate of increase in such investment. In the years 1966 to 1973, 73 percent more was being invested annually in durable producers' goods than in the years 1958 to 1965 in the United States; but from 1974 to 1979, 38 percent more was being invested annually than from 1966 to 1973; and between 1980 and 1982 only 19 percent more was being invested annually than between 1974 and 1979. When an economy has come to rely on large increases in durable producers' goods in order to keep capacity utilized and to avoid high levels of unemployment, such a trend toward slowing down the rate of increase in investment produces economic crises. In sum, in the cycles that characterize capitalism, a falling rate of profit precedes a failure of demand and also explains slowdowns in the rate of increase in investment that generate unemployment. Direct state support for capital accumulation can be used to offset slowdowns in the rate of increase in investment.

Second, it is assumed that the capitalist economy continues to exist despite direct state support. The goal of the economy remains private accumulation, and the medium of its realization is still the market, however skewed it might be by state intervention. Thus it remains true to say that the state functions to support the capitalist economy. Opposed to this assumption is the view that politics has replaced the economy as a result of state intervention. It would then no longer make sense to speak of the state as relatively autonomous from the economy since the economy would have been fully absorbed by the state. Under such circumstances there would be no economy for which the state functions.

Behind this opposed view is the conviction that only market factors can determine investment in a capitalist system. But do capitalists invest precisely as the market instructs them to? Instructions from the market are never perfectly clear, leaving the investor uncertain whether there will be enough demand for a new product line. With other entrepreneurs acting independently, as the free market requires, the investor cannot be sure about wages, prices, or the mix of products on the future market he or she is aiming at. Those market factors that happen to be fully known fail to determine the investment decision, leaving ample room for discretion that is conditioned by nonmarket factors. When the state enters the picture and influences the investor's decision by providing capital, the situation is not drastically changed. The investment decision is still in a market context, but not all the important factors contributing to it are market factors.[12] The state is an added factor conditioning the discretion of investors, not a factor that eliminates the market and thus reduces the economy to the state.

5. Does state intervention promote justice?

Having looked at the forms of state intervention in Section 3, I turn now to consider whether state intervention in these forms can satisfy justice as mutuality. How in fact does direct state support for capital affect employment? A state policy of support for accumulation that had no significant payoff for employment would be seen as one-sided and would undermine the state's ability to rule.[13] Is it obvious that the largess of the state will satisfy justice as mutuality?

There are two ways state support for the economy by injections of capital tends to undermine the state's own policy of promoting employment.[14] As a result, we get the widespread impression that the state is committed to capital without the balancing factor of class mutuality. Yet so far this impression exists without a serious impairment of the state's power to carry out its function of reproduction. How can this be? A transition may be in progress away from justice as mutuality between classes to some other not as yet fully definite pattern of justice. Examining the two ways state sup-

201

port undermines national employment provides a clue about this transition.

First, state support has been decisive in the movement of corporations beyond their national homes to other countries. The state performs invaluable tasks and makes important concessions to promote the location of corporate activity abroad. In the United States twenty government agencies promote international business. The state checks for favorable investment climates through an organization such as the Overseas Private Investment Corporation; the Agency for International Development provides loans to strengthen third world capitalism, which then becomes a favorable context for multinational expansion; through the Economic Cooperation Act of 1948 firms can get state guarantees of their investments in certain countries; immunity from antitrust legislation and bank regulations also facilitates international activity. But the flight of capital to other nations is a drag on employment growth at home. For example, U.S. multinational corporations account for almost half of all imports into the United States, and a growing portion of their imports comes from their majority-owned foreign affiliates – this portion doubled from 16 percent in 1970 to 32 percent in 1982. This is part of the reason there has been no growth in manufacturing employment. Because support for national capital has led to jobs abroad but unemployment in manufacturing at home, mutality, at least on a national basis, has failed.[15]

Second, the state supports financial institutions, whose activities have a more and more tenuous relation to stimulating national employment. State-guaranteed loans, state support for loans through the International Monetary Fund, and state rescue operations for giants like Continential contribute to the growth of the financial sector. Yet in recent years this growth parallels the decline of the productive sector. Large corporate mergers and speculation in securities, real estate, and commodities involve capital circulating within the financial sector that rarely breaks out in the form of productive investment.[16] Admittedly, a collapse of the financial sector would precipitate a general economic crisis, but state support is encouraging a growth of the financial sector that if continued will strangle productive investment and employment growth.

What then are the limits on direct state support for accumulation? Is the matter beyond justice altogether so that capital enjoys unlimited sway? The difficulty facing us stems from trying to define state justice within national bounds whereas capital in the major areas of manufacturing, finance, and service is now international. The trade-off for state support of capital accumulation can no longer be a benefit, such as employment, for the nation's working class. It is a trade-off that enhances the standing of the nation in the community of nations. Mutuality between capitalists and workers is replaced by mutuality between capitalists and the nation. The trade-off for state support of capital is greater stature for the nation in the community of nations. The new mercantilism, like the old, promotes the interests of the nation. The state will prove able to rule while ignoring the requirement of class mutuality only if this other requirement takes its place. In discussing the community of nations in Part Four, we shall see how a powerful state's effort to promote global peace and prosperity enhances national stature. The state can claim to act evenhandedly when, in return for aiding capitalism, it brings the populace together in national pride.

16

Organized labor and the state

This chapter turns to two institutions – parties and unions – given little attention earlier. Parties function as parts of the state, and through them unions are incorporated into the state. This incorporation is political, in that through it the unions acquiesce in the state's goal of economic reproduction. In many countries unions retain economic independence, through which a form of workplace justice is still realized.

1. Economic, political, and ideological state activity

State activity that ultimately serves the reproduction of the economy falls into several distinct categories. Sometimes that activity is primarily political, as when the state channels dissent into the parliamentary process. Sometimes state activity is primarily economic, as when it puts a floor under demand with welfare spending and when it makes capital outlays to promote growth. The activity is judged political or economic by its direct results; the integration of dissent is a political whereas the floor under demand is an economic result. The results of state activity become means toward the goal of economic reproduction. Since all state activity is inherently political, we must go to its results to distinguish these kinds of activity within it. These kinds of activity correspond to the variety of conditions needed for economic reproduction. Both favorable political and favorable economic conditions are needed for economic reproduction. In addition, there is also need for favorable ideological conditions, and if these are lacking the state can attempt to supply them too. For example, in the mid 1960s it was discovered that the Central Intelligence Agency had played a role in developing a favorable ideological context for capitalist reproduction in the United States by funding the National Students Association and the Congress for Cultural Freedom.[1]

Paralleling this varied activity on behalf of economic reproduction is the effort to enable the state to rule. Setting up a pattern of

204

justice is one way of giving the state the ability to rule. It is a second-order functional requirement of the state since, by making governance possible, justice contributes indirectly to the ability of the state to reproduce the economy, which is a first-order functional requirement of the state. The activity that makes ruling possible is not to be explained by concentrating on what serves the reproduction of the economy. There will be overlap between activity that serves economic reproduction and activity that serves the ability to rule. We saw, for example, that welfare spending both keeps demand high and legitimates the state. But a state activity that serves economic reproduction does not, just by that fact, serve the ability to rule.

Paralleling the economic, political, and ideological activity that serves economic reproduction will be economic, political, and ideological activity that serves the ability to rule. Though justice is only one facet of the state that serves its ability to rule, it too will have economic, political, and ideological dimensions. Take, for example, justice as mutuality. Where it is part of the state's pattern of justice, the state is forced to support capital accumulation in directions that significantly increase the growth of employment. So being committed to justice as mutuality leads the state to take economic measures. Nonetheless, the state's pattern of justice will also involve it in political and ideological activity that serves its ability to rule. Consider in this regard democratic justice. Where it is part of the state's pattern of justice, the state puts a floor under the political power of the people. By insuring that political power is shared, the state engages in political activity on behalf of justice. Finally, there is the state's ideological activity, which is inseparable from its pattern of justice. The state needs ways to establish its justice as the norm of reasonable people; otherwise, radical justice would form a pole of attraction. It becomes the norm of reasonable people more easily if the state represents its justice as conforming to the nature of its citizens.

Economic, political, and ideological activities are then indeterminate in regard to the purpose they serve. They can serve the state either in its role of reproducing the economy or in its role of keeping the power to rule. The conflict between function and form within the state has to be seen in light of this. The activity chosen to serve either economic reproduction or governability may become an obstacle to realizing the other of these two goals. Thus democracy as a means to governability may come into conflict with the reproductive function of the state. Or, conversely, state

205

support for accumulation as a means to reproducing the economy may conflict with the goal of governability.

2. Political parties and the state

The primary purpose of Part Three has been to study state activities that serve economic reproduction. I have suggested ways these activities can be explained by the state's economic function. Many of the activities we have examined in this part were also seen to promote governability, but this was not our main focus.

The state has various relations to organized labor, but in view of the plan of Part Three, my focus will be on the state's use of organized labor for economic reproduction. It is certainly true that by allowing unions to exist the state adopts a measure of justice, since unions limit both the control of the bosses and the powerlessness of their employees. Though I will discuss this aspect of state justice, my focus will be on the economic function, not the form, of the state. Moreover, within this focus I shall give special attention to the state's political activity. By means of this political activity the state coopts the unions so that they do not become a source of independent political activity that could threaten the economy. To be sure, the state takes economic measures in regard to the unions, as when it prohibits a secondary boycott. But I shall look at the way the state incorporates the unions within political parties committed to the status quo, that is, to economic reproduction and to continuity of the state. This is part of the more general activity of institutionalizing dissent within democracy, with the new element being the use of political parties as instruments.

The channeling of dissent into parliamentary democracy opens up the possibility that mass parties of dissent will contend for power with parties of the status quo in the parliamentary arena. To head off this alarming prospect, an additional effort is needed, which will take different forms in different contexts. First, where mass parties of dissent have already formed, either they are crushed by repression or, to stay alive, they compromise their position and openly endorse the aims of economic reproduction and of continuity of the state. Second, where mass parties of dissent do not yet exist but conditions may seem ripe for them, an effort is made to draw their potential constituencies into existing mainstream parties, ones not just committed to the status quo but also enjoying broad electoral support. My focus will be on this second case, which fits the United

States where union leaders cooperated with the Democratic Party to thwart the development of a labor or socialist party. More writing has been done on the first case, which instead fits the evolution of leftist European parties into parties defending their nations' economies and capitalist states.

Parties do not have to be ruling parties to be part of the democratic state. A party that is "out of office" will nonetheless occupy offices at lower levels and will continue to have legislative, judicial, and administrative functions. Still, the reason-for-being of a mainstream party is to contest and win a ruling position. A mainstream party will get state power by, among other things, using positions that are not outside the state itself. Thus the state's complexity goes beyond the multiplicity of its administrative units, its representative bodies, and its courts. It includes as well the mainstream parties. This incorporation of political parties within the state does not imply that they lose their identity by collapsing into other state units. Like other units of the state they remain centers of action, but they gain state support through adopting its goal of economic reproduction. The mainstream parties organize pressure on the state from inside it.[2]

How does a party benefit from its position within the state? Typically, a mainstream party uses the fact that it is within the state, and even a potential ruling party within the state, to encourage groups outside the state to pursue their interests through the party. The party can credibly promise to mobilize state power someday on behalf of the interests of outside groups. These groups are led to accept the state's function of reproducing the economy in order to get a party to intercede with the state on their behalf. If some of the interests of an outside group are incompatible with the reproductive function of the state, then the cooperation of a party will require the group to compromise those interests.[3] Parties that are not mainstream parties, because they control only an insignificant number of offices and no major offices, cannot offer the same enticement a major party does. However, being outside the state, minor parties are not fettered with a commitment to the state's reproductive function and its continuity. Parties may of course gain broad electoral support for a period without being committed, in principle or in practice, to the reproduction of the economy. But the state's ability to reproduce the economy would be threatened by the long-term presence of such a party within the state; if there is not a revolutionary showdown, such a party must be repressed

207

or incorporated. In the United States, though, things are more straightforward since the two major parties accept the reproductive function of the state.

3. The origins of unity between U.S. labor and the Democratic Party

My theme is that, where no mass party of dissent has emerged, at least one mainstream party has as one of its functions incorporating the political force of the working class, preventing it thereby from forming parties not committed to reproducing the economy. A complementary theme is that, in these circumstances, the leaders of organized labor have as one of their functions channeling labor's political activity into a mainstream party. Consider the case of U.S. labor.

In the United States it seemed at first as though no mainstream party had the function of incorporating labor's political force. And Samuel Gompers, the American Federation of Labor's first president, was against aligning the unions with any party. His tactic for labor was for it to vote for its friends and defeat its enemies, whatever their party affiliations. There were, however, efforts in numerous cities to form labor parties, and many workers voted a Socialist ticket. The AFL secretary, P. J. McGuire, urged Gompers not to endorse Democratic presidential nominee Bryan in 1896, claiming, "That is a trap, for if you declare for Bryan or anyone else it will be a pretext for the Socialists to drag in their politics."[4] The nonpartisan approach of the AFL was, then, a way of keeping the politics of labor from finding its natural expression in a party committed to the working class. This tactic was not without advantage to the leaders of the AFL. The Knights of Labor, with their call for undermining the wage system, were declining as the AFL grew. It seemed that the survival of a labor organization and hence the legitimacy of its leaders depended on not taking a political stance at odds with the function of the state. Gompers made this principle of survival the key to his success.

Yet the nonpartisan approach to taking this political stance was doomed, since the call for effective political action within the ranks of the AFL became irresistible. The right of workers to unionize was being denied by court injunctions based on the Sherman Anti-Trust Act. A capitalist state was acting true to kind in undermining the existence of the independent organization of labor and in the process undermining the legitimacy of the labor officialdom. In

208

defiance of the Gompers leadership, central labor bodies wanted political action against the antilabor injunction. The San Francisco central labor body endorsed the formation of a local labor party, which in 1901 won control of the mayor's office. In response to such defiance, Gompers resorted to the political smear; he claimed, for example, that Debs's new Socialist Party was backed by money from the National Association of Manufacturers. And so in 1908, in response to the insurgency for labor political action, the AFL gave the Democratic slates its backing after the Democrats adopted an antiinjunction plank. The Democrats were, though, warned by Gompers in 1911 that if they did not deliver for labor he could not stop a third-party revolt.

The nonpartisan approach was dead after 1908, and the unbroken marriage of labor officials to the Democrats began. The labor leadership had been determined enough to insure that, when it was forced to become partisan, it would choose a mainstream party rather than a party that rejected capitalism. Of course, the marriage was one-sided from the start; the Democrats did not deliver. Despite the Clayton Act of 1914, there was to be no relief from the antilabor injunction before the Norris–La Guardia Act of 1932. Gompers's thunder aside, this failure to deliver was a secondary matter; the important thing was that the politics of organized labor had been domesticated.[5] After the nonpartisan transition period, Democrats and labor officials worked together, and continue to do so, to neutralize labor politically. The exceptions – Meany's balking at Democratic Party reforms in 1972 and the defection of the Teamster tops to the Republican Party – do not alter the overall picture.

4. The trade-off of political dependence for workplace justice

The right of labor to have unions, a major part of which is the right to bargain collectively, is a matter of state justice. Collective bargaining puts limits on power and powerlessness; it redresses the powerlessness of the individual employee in relation to the power of the employer. Party politics enters as a determinant of this aspect of state justice because it is through party politics that the state comes to commit itself to workplace fairness. However, in the United States it is mainly through only one party – the Democratic Party – that the state commits itself to collective bargaining as a normal procedure in labor/capital interaction. When that party is

209

not in power, collective bargaining as an instrument of labor is usually weakened.

The party that supports collective bargaining gets something in return. Union leaders act as brokers who deliver the reward from the ranks to the party. The reward is the vote of labor for that party. Union members still give Democractic presidential candidates more than half of their votes. In Senate and House races, Democratic candidates get up to two-thirds of the union vote. Still, efforts by union leaders to get their members to vote have run up against a national trend toward abstentionism. Despite some success in competition for workers' votes, the Republican Party seems willing to let the logic of capitalist hostility to orgnized labor work its course. The dog days of labor during the 1920s and the 1980s in the United States were associated with the rule of the Republican Party. The state's commitment to workplace justice varies in its worth with the party in power.

There is a risk for capitalism when the state grants the right to collective bargaining. To minimize this risk the state will try to channel the politics of the working class into a mainstream party. The risk arises from the need working-class organizations that bargain collectively will have for political action. To be effective at the bargaining table they have to provide themselves with a favorable context through political action. Yet a genuinely favorable context for collective bargaining would be one in which many capitalist prerogatives disappear. A favorable context would not include the ability of the capitalists to use troops as strikebreakers or the ability to use the lockout to extract bargaining concessions. Political action eliminating such prerogatives would threaten economic reproduction. The granting of workplace justice through the right to bargain collectively must, then, be countered with the withholding of independent working-class political action by means of channeling labor politics into a mainstream party. Otherwise, workplace justice would be not a least weak set of limits on capitalist control, but a strong set of limits, a set undermining the reproduction of the economy.

There is, then, a trade-off. In order to maintain its function the state demands in exchange for workplace justice that labor forfeit its political independence. As a consequence, labor leaders can preserve their jobs in the labor movement only by attempting to deliver the labor movement to a mainstream party. The role these leaders played was a crucial one in channeling labor into a mainstream party. To be sure, factors beyond the leadership also played a sizable role, such as the fateful divisions of the U.S. working class into native and foreign-born, black and white. But the political acquiescence of labor did not result simply from a pregiven disunity.[6] Encouragement of the third-party insurgencies by that leadership could have created a new pole of unity. Instead, the labor leaders were active agents of the acquiescence. When faced from within labor with pressure for independent labor politics, they assumed that, if the taste for independent politics were to be gratified, then without militancy of a kind that would undermine their own power, the labor movement would be smashed and they would no longer lead anyone. They had to agree with Gompers when he said to the Socialists, "Morally you are unsound, socially you are unsafe, and industrially you are an impossibility." They then acted to channel labor into a mainstream party out of the belief that this would serve capitalism and in turn make it tolerate unions.

5. Labor politics in Mexico, Britain, and the USSR

Even where the organizational relations among unions, parties, and the state are different than in the United States, we find a similar political pattern. The condition for the right to organize independently and for the state's recognition of trade union leaders is that trade unions channel the political aspirations of the working class within a party committed to the state's reproductive function.

In Mexico, where despite sizable opposition from the Left in the 1988 elections there is still only one major party, the dominant union federation, the Confederation of Mexican Workers, is, along with peasant and other groups, an offical part of that party, the Institutional Revolutionary Party (PRI). Top union leaders are, then, institutionally part of the ruling group of the state. Dissident unions and dissident political movements are at a disadvantage since they compete with an official union movement having the power of the state at its disposal. Through this incorporation the official union movement commits itself to keeping the working class within the bounds of capitalist ends. In exchange for this political acquiescence, the state agrees to uphold the right to organize, to strike, and to boycott, and it also respects the legitimacy of the union officials. So despite the political acquiescence there is economic independence in relation to employers.

The similarities with the situation in the United States outweigh the differences. In both cases labor is incorporated politically into

211

the state in the sense that for the most part it acts in step with a party that has committed itself to the state's goal of economic reproduction. Moreover, in both cases the integration into a party, which is itself part of the state, is the means whereby labor is incorporated politically into the state. Unions end up as part of the state in both the United States and Mexico, even though the institutionalization has gone farther in Mexico. State justice as the right to organize is just as fickle in Mexico, where there is only one major party, as in the United States, where only one of the major parties is made the guardian of that right. The PRI looks the other way when strikers are beaten and condones antiunion practices in the border industries.

The differences between Mexico and the United States largely reflect their different histories of union incorporation into the state. The origin of incorporation in Mexico dates from 1915 during the Mexican Revolution. At that time one of the victorious revolutionary generals, Alvaro Obregón, was turning his Constitutionalist forces against the peasant armies of Zapata and Villa. To split the small urban working class from the radical forces of Zapata and Villa, Obregón promised support for organized labor in return for Red Brigades of workers taking the field against Pancho Villa's army.[7] The House of the World Worker, the existing labor central, produced a majority in favor of the deal, thus positioning labor within a state that aimed at building a capitalist society.

Twenty years later, in the 1930s, President Lázaro Cárdenas helped to strengthen organized labor in Mexico by supporting its demands against the intransigence of domestic and foreign owners. Once he had strengthened it, he proceeded to restructure the ruling party along corporatist lines, giving the major worker and peasant centrals, whose formation he had also urged, an official place within this party. A politically independent labor movement could be the context at some future time for anger that would result in a massive attack on the fragile shoot of Mexican capitalism.[8] But a labor movement incorporated within the major party would be a pillar of the capitalist state.

Is the common political pattern broken when labor does form its own party and gives it a nominal socialist purpose? Consider the case of the British Labour Party. At first the Labour Party was a loyal partner of the Liberal Party; that partnership required Labour's commitment to an emphasis on constitutional action as opposed to direct action by the rank and file through political strikes. The militancy of the working class at the end of World War

I created tensions within the Lib–Lab partnership, so the Labour Party stood on its own in the 1918 election, but not without leaders committed to constitutionalism and against the spirit of bolshevism. These leaders wanted to show that "Labour is fit to govern"; that is, it is able to end strike waves and defend the empire.[9] The Labour Party has from its inception restrained the Labour Left that would have turned the Labour Party toward a rejection of the state's role of reproducing capitalism. But for years it successfully defended the right to independent union organization in an enviably strong form. So the political pattern of trading labor's political independence for its right to organize economically is repeated again in the British case.

Even in the case of the USSR the pattern holds true, at least indirectly. There the incorporation of the unions into the state is not just political but also economic, with the result that the unions, even as economic agencies, have no independent existence.[10] In the previous cases, the political neutralization of the unions by means of mainstream parties was matched by a guarantee of their economic independence. This independence took the form of their being able to recruit, bargain, and strike, and it was required by state justice.

Unless, though, the state guarantees rights to economic organization while it denies political independence, the state restricts its ability to rule. This is becoming more and more obvious in the case of the USSR, and thus the USSR is indirectly a confirmation of the common political pattern. Instead of using economically independent unions to moderate exploitation, workers in the USSR reduce the surplus available to the state's ruling group in unorganized ways: resistance to full utilization of plant capacity, high job turnover, absenteeism, drinking on the job. A Communist Party study in the early 1980s showed that in two hundred Moscow factories only 10 percent of the work force was at the workplace by the end of the day.[11] The goal of the ruling group to encourage economic growth is thwarted by the difficulty of increasing labor productivity under these conditions. Even without economically independent unions and without worker control over positive decision making, workers exert a negative control that thwarts state goals. The ability of the state to rule, with the goals of raising the standard of living and staying militarily strong in a hostile world, is threatened by this negative control. A possible trade-off for getting increased productivity under *perestroika* may have to be granting economic independence to the unions.

213

6. Limiting justice to independent organization

Where unions have economic independence, doesn't state justice go beyond the mere right to this independence? After all, this independence is nothing more than the union's right to recruit, bargain, and strike. In return for playing the capitalist game, unions surely get more than their bare existence and the plum of legitimacy for their leaders. State justice should, one might think, also remove obstacles in the way of their strengthening themselves in confrontation with employers.

We must be careful here not to confuse the ideal with the real. It is all too easy to substitute ideal social democratic or even Christian democratic conceptions of justice for an operative pattern of state justice. If we read only the history of periods of labor strength, we are apt to conclude that even for the capitalist state the necessity of ruling for everyone leads to a pattern of justice that makes real an ideal harmony based on rough equality between organized labor and the employing class. We need, though, to read the history of periods of labor defeat as well. Then we see that overall the least common denominator of state justice is no ideal harmony but a grudging recognition of the existence of organized labor.[12]

This pessimistic view of state justice in regard to labor is confirmed by the U.S. record. It is true that Roosevelt approved of the Wagner Act of 1935, which formalized organized labor's right to existence. But after labor officials John L. Lewis and Sidney Hillman expended great effort to deliver the labor vote for Roosevelt in 1936, he did not lift a finger to prevent his New Deal governors from using federally trained National Guardsmen to break the Congress of Industrial Organizations (CIO) organizing drive in Little Steel in 1937. Even the right to exist seemed too much. Ten years on, Truman broke strikes by seizing mines and railroads, and he called for an antilabor revision of the Wagner Act that would include making the secondary boycott illegal. He thus laid the basis for the Taft–Hartley Act, which for the sake of labor support he vetoed, knowing that Congress would override his veto. Nonetheless, labor officials viewed their legitimacy as tied to Truman's reelection in 1948. To prevent the ranks from drawing votes from Truman by going into Henry Wallace's Progressive Party, the CIO leadership required each state and city CIO council to "express opposition to any third party in 1948 and . . . support for the Marshall Plan."[13] This established a political orthodoxy

214

within the more militant CIO unions; the CIO unions that rejected it were raided and purged. By the late 1970s the promise of organizational strength found in the Wagner Act had turned into defeat. At that time, another Democratic president, Jimmy Carter, was unwilling to push labor-law reform through a Democratic Congress. Nonetheless, there was a need – demonstrated by the J. P. Stevens case – for overcoming both employers' opposition to organizing and their refusal to recognize the will of workers in elections for union representation.

We can now summarize the forms of justice linked to economic functions of the state. As in the case of subsistence justice and justice as mutuality, justice as the recognition of independent economic organization is, in its sphere, a minimum needed to preserve the ability to rule. Collectively, these aspects of state justice appear impressive: There is welfare, employment, and independent economic organization. Each separately is in reality less than the slogans used by the state would imply. They are the modest price the state pays for its continued ability to rule. The price is indeed modest since each of these kinds of justice is associated with institutions that also function to promote the state's goal. Subsistence justice is realized through welfare spending, which is functional since it puts a floor under demand. Justice as mutuality is realized through state support for corporations, which is functional since it overcomes capital scarcity. Justice for the workplace is realized through the political acquiescence of unions, which is functional since it avoids a political challenge to capitalism. There is no guarantee that justice will be realized through these functional measures; subsistence may require more than what is required for demand, employment need not be generated by favoring corporations, and economic independence may be endangered by political acquiescence. The potential then remains for a conflict between the form and the function of the state. But in many circumstances justice of these three kinds is indeed promoted by institutions that are explained by their functioning to reproduce the economy.

There is, nonetheless, a more positive side to state justice in regard to labor. Granted, labor does not guarantee greater organizational strength for itself by fitting its political program into that of a party committed to the reproduction of capitalism. Still, its political voice gets heard, which was not true under early Gompers economism. The debate within the capitalist state includes a suitably modulated voice of labor speaking on behalf of free health

215

care for the elderly, civil rights, raising the minimum wage, and health and safety in the workplace.[14] The need to contain organized labor politically within the framework of private property and imperialism has led the state to incorporate a mainstream party that supports reforms which organized labor either comes around to backing or takes the initiative in backing. It is, though, only because of its independent economic organization that the voice of labor is not totally silenced as a result of its political dependence and that it can win the support of a party for certain reforms. These are not reforms that all sectors of the capitalist class will initially support, though so-called progressive sectors of that class often conceive of and organize for these reforms. By containing organized labor politically the state, through its parties, introduces programs of reform that split the capitalist class politically.

Labor's independent voice within political dependence makes it appropriate to speak here of a *liberal corporate state*.[15] Labor is incorporated by accepting the goals of the state, but it remains economically independent. As an economic organization, it is not the creature of the state. With this independent base, it can raise issues within the state that are only reluctantly taken up by many sectors of the capitalist class. By contrast, in an *authoritarian corporate state*, labor organization is in no sense independent – either politically or economically. As authoritarian, the state would mete out repression to those who would attempt to organize an independent union. Without an independent economic base, such a labor organization would be incapable of being a voice for reform in a debate within the state.

Liberal corporatism is as far as union officals think. Their instinct for survival tells them that there is no other course. The unions that in the late 1940s in the United States had doubts about the orthodoxy of private property and imperialism were either raided – the United Electrical Workers – or crushed – the Mine, Mill, and Smelter Workers. Working-class organizations that are only economically but not politically independent will, though, continually fight defensive battles for even their economic existence. Moreover, their economic interests, when consistently pursued, will lead them into collision with the goal of reproducing the economy. They must then decide to become politically independent against great odds, or else to accept the fact that even their economic independence is quite limited. Political independence for trade unions in a capitalist country will lead to the formation of a party that is earnest about its opposition to a state that is commit-

216

ted to the reproduction of capitalism. Such a party can participate in a capitalist state if it is not repressed, but the result of its participation will be a debate on the function of the state. With the opening of this debate, the capitalist class will unite in its effort to keep the state functioning for the reproduction of capitalism.

Part Four

An account of the community of states

A state's pattern of justice need not stop at its boundaries. Dominant states consolidate their influence by establishing a global justice. This theme conflicts with the view that behavior in the international arena is unrestricted by normative principles. I will be arguing that, just as a state gains legitimacy domestically by accepting limits on losses groups suffer, so too it gains the legitimacy to extend its rule internationally only by putting limits on losses states under its rule suffer. The full picture of state justice requires both domestic and international justice.

To carry through this expansion of the idea of state justice we must first be willing to challenge views that picture states as though they existed in isolation from one another. On these views interconnections between states become accidental features of them. It is an unfortunate fact that much political theory not only has been but still is written in this vein. I shall counter with the view that a global framework enters into what individual states are. States are brought together by the framework not as identical units but as uneven economic powers. This view represents a middle road between two extremes. On the one hand, it does not reduce states to the status of emanations from a global social unity. On the other hand, it gives them autonomy without thereby making their interrelations irrelevant to what they are. A central task will be to show how both capitalist and noncapitalist states, both the United States and the USSR, fit into one global economic framework.

Within this framework of uneven power, the dominant states promote a pattern of justice whose main features are peace and prosperity. They can legitimate their imperial rule by providing security from hostile incursions as well as prosperity. Peace as an aspect of global justice is allegedly promoted through the current conventional and nuclear arms race. An arms buildup is, though, also an instrument used by an imperial power to prevent its rivals from interfering when it makes an aggressive move to control a

219

lesser state. This behavior at the periphery clearly comes into conflict with the efforts called for by global justice to secure peace for ruled states. Similarly, promoting prosperity within ruled states has its contradictions. Although economic growth certainly does occur within less developed nations, it is a growth that in most nations has done little to alleviate grinding poverty.

The promise of global justice is, then, blocked by other aspects of the imperial state. The contradiction between the form of justice and the economic function of the state reemerges at the more extended level of global justice. The consequence is that global justice is not sufficiently realized through the efforts of the imperial powers to insure a stable community of states. This instability has been manifested since World War II in an unprecedented number of wars and revolutions.

17

Global justice

A speculative effort is called for to discuss international relations. The atomistic philosophy of current political theory has led nowhere. There is, then, some excuse for taking a daring step that adopts a holistic approach. The relations of state will be viewed from within the framework of the international economy. From this perspective, it is easier to see how justice, rather than force alone, can play an important role among states.

1. The international essence of the state

The modern analytical approach in philosophy is summed up by its emphasis on the part rather than the whole. When this approach is brought to bear on the state, the goal of political theory becomes knowledge of the state taken in isolation. To advance to international relations, it should suffice to make deductions from this knowledge of the state in isolation. That in any event would be to follow the advice of Descartes, one of the founders of the analytical approach. He urged that we first reduce complex propositions to simple ones and then by an inspection of the simple ones advance to a genuine knowledge of the complex ones.[1]

It is remarkable that so many political theorists treat the state as an island, assuming that its relations to economies, nations, and states somewhere offshore will be external to its insular essence. This approach is adopted by those theorists who, like Ernest Barker, treat the state as a legal association that functions to promote the national common good.[2] Whatever is outside the nation makes an impact on the state through impinging on the legal order; its status is thus no different than an internal opposition. Similarly, Rawls sees the state as a legal association committed to assuring individuals that others in their nation are upholding their commitment to a just order. Warfare between nations is recognized by him as a possi-

221

bility that is to be allowed when needed to defend a just national order.[3]

The liberal tradition is not alone in this one-sidedness. Neither a traditional Marxist emphasis on the state as the guardian of the national economy nor a neo-Marxist emphasis, of a Gramsci or a Poulantzas, on the state as a principle of national cohesion avoids this one-sidedness. It is assumed that relations with other nations and states will become clear on the basis of a Cartesian inspection of all the simples, that is, on the basis of an inspection of states understood in terms of themselves.

To all this I wish to counterpose a holistic approach, one whose consequence will be that the state reflects a context that extends beyond itself. There are several different holistic approaches, and not all of them resolve the problem of isolation created by the analytical approach. On one view of the holistic sort, the individual state is an emanation of some more basic ontological background. There is on this view a world economy that condenses into state formations at various places throughout its extension in order to resolve problems for the reproduction of this world economy.[4] These singularities in the economic field can claim little in the way of autonomy. There was an affinity for this kind of holism during the early years of the Third International when national peculiarities were viewed as natural features of a world capitalist process.[5]

This reductivist holism can be avoided without retreating to the view that states have only external relations to one another. The reductivist holism that sees states as singularities in a world economy is indeed too cosmopolitan since it fails to give to national pecularities the autonomy they actually have. In Chapter 15, I emphasized that direct state support to capital is primarily about the reproduction of a national economy and cannot be understood in any other way. However, it is equally undeniable that the national economy operates within a framework of an international economy. Neither the national nor the international can be ignored in constructing a view of the community of states. On the one hand, the community of states is not formed on the basis of the separate and independent dynamics of the individual states in the way the analytical approach treats wholes as formed by atomistic processes. On the other hand, the community of states is not formed on the basis of a single world economy which condenses into national state singularities in the mysterious way that idealist philosophers have always claimed unities emanate multiplicities.

222

2. The international economic framework

The framework model of Chapter 2 provides a way of formulating a holism that avoids emanationism. I shall call this a pluralist holism to distinguish it from the reductivist holism that relies on emanation. The multiple states are no longer to be derived as singularities within a world economy but are to be assigned a role coequal with that of the world economy; neither is to be derivative from the other. But at the same time the behavior of the states, both internally and in relation to one another, is made possible by a framework that includes the international economy as a whole and the positions of the national economies within it. This framework does not provide a stimulus to change but makes it possible for a given stimulus to act as it does. A purely internal dynamic for change is an impossibility since internal factors act in the context of a broader framework. The internal features of a state realize their potential for both change within the state and interaction with other states only through the global framework. Conversely, the existing framework does not of itself suffice to account for the external thrust of states, since it only limits how other factors – stimuli – lead to certain external thrusts.

Here is an illustration of the way the international framework operates. The threat of internal overproduction may lead to military adventures for the sake of opening up external markets. There are, though, several imaginable world economic circumstances in which this threat would not lead to such a military outcome. Those external markets may already be open as a result of struggles that ended colonialist restrictions on trade; in that case peaceful penetration of those markets in competition with other developed nations might be the answer. Or, if the markets are closed, they may be so well defended by superior military power that political negotiations aimed at prizing them open, rather than military adventures, might be the answer. State action in response to internal overproduction is then indeterminate in the absence of determinate international circumstances. Our way so far of thinking about the economic function of the state must be changed in view of this. The state functions to reproduce a national economy *within an international economy*. What it does to reproduce the national economy is made possible by this international framework.

The international framework will lack a tidy uniformity. In the first place, there is a division within it between dominating and dominated nations. This is to be an exclusively economic division that abstracts from domination taking political and military forms. (The nature of the domination in question will be explored in Chapter 18.) The division is not a static one since there are possibilities for development that allow an initially dominated nation to become a regional economic power or even to advance to the top range of dominating nations. This division itself is also not an absolute one; it does not allow us to say that if a nation is dominant it cannot also be dominated. It can at once dominate some nations and be dominated by others. Though standing in a secondary position in respect to the United States and certain European nations, South Africa dominates some of the nations of southern Africa. Moreover, the division is not a determinate one; it does not allow us to say of every pair of nations whether one in that pair is dominant and the other dominated. Singapore and Hong Kong have emerged as powerful trading centers with considerable autonomy in respect to the major capitalist nations, but neither dominates the other. The division I am talking about respects the complexity of relations of domination in the global economy, without trying to describe it as a clear separation of imperialist centers from the nations of a third-world periphery.[6] I want to stress only that the dominant/dominated polarity between certain economies is a crucial part of the global framework that lies behind relations of all other kinds between states.

(Earlier, when I spoke about economic productive relations, I made an abstraction from relations of control and domination and I looked at the way the latter relations developed within the purely economic framework. Here we could base ourselves on the same distinction, but that would entail a discussion of how the domination of nations emerges within a purely economic international framework. Since such a discussion would distract us from the central point here, relations of domination are directly incorporated in the international framework.)

In the second place, a tidy uniformity is subverted by a division within the framework between market and planned economies. This division seems at odds with the idea that there is a single world economy, and thus it seems to favor a return to the atomistic viewpoint of the analysts. An easy way with this problem is to stretch the idea of a capitalist economy far enough so that it includes the planned economies of the Eastern bloc. But no more than metaphorical sense has ever been made of the idea that these planned economies obey the law of value, listed in Chapter 10 as one of the tendencies of capitalism.[7] A more fruitful attack on this problem involves the recognition that today's planned economies

224

are not independent of their market counterparts. Indeed, such planned economies are reflections that internalize their market counterparts. They do this not by eventually converging with capitalism but by internalizing the market economies in their own goal. Their goal is to preserve themselves in face of the challenge posed by the tendency of the market economies to expand.

More will be said about this internalization of "the other" in Chapter 20, but this much suffices to suggest that there can at present be a single world system that provides the framework for the interaction of states. It is not a uniform system but one characterized by both market and plan. Thus the system has within it a contradiction between the goal of the accumulation of capital measured in terms of market value and the goal of production for security against being swallowed by capitalist production. The contradiction allows for unity since the elements of the contradiction are internally related. Ultimately, state action on behalf of a national economy is determined by stimuli that act within the framework of an international economy with this contradictory content. Neglecting this contradictory framework and treating state action only within the framework of, say, the capitalist economy make it impossible to understand the interaction of the United States and the USSR on a materialist basis. Cold wars and arms races would then become the outcroppings of ideologies deprived of an economic framework.

3. The market model of the community of states

Pluralist holism not only gives individual states their due in a way that is impossible for the reductive holist but also gives the connecting medium between states its due in a way that is impossible for those who view states as islands with only external relations to one another. Nonetheless, liberal theory thinks it can account for the connecting medium. It uses a market model of how states treated as islands come to be related.[8]

States, like individual buyers and sellers in a market, are defined by their self-interest. Since there is no higher power than the states themselves, any relations among themselves must result from the pursuit of their own judgments as to how best they can pursue their self-interest. When an equilibrium in the form of a balance of power does result, it results from the pursuit of individual interest. As one state tries to gain superiority over another, the response of the latter will be to take whatever action – whether it be engaging in an arms race or seeking alliances – will prevent the former from actually becoming superior. Moreover, just as the market is supposed to evolve from pure anarchy to an admixture of anarchy with central direction, so too the community of states is supposed to evolve from a pure anarchy within which equilibrium is reached in a haphazard way to an admixture of anarchy with a form of cooperation that can organize and sustain a balance of power. But the market model remains basic.

To use this market model for the community of states is to carry over the limitations of the market in explaining relations even among individuals. In a class society individuals are not definable in terms of a self-interest that is independent of all connecting contexts among them. The equality called for by the market requires, though, an absence of combination. Yet a combination exists when individuals express not only themselves in their self-interest but also the class to which they belong. As a result, when individuals cooperate in collective action, this cooperation cannot in general be viewed as the outcome of the separate pursuit of self-interest by all the individuals involved. There is already a basis for the cooperation in a common class position. A market model with its reliance on individual self-interest cannot then explain such cooperation.[9]

In regard to states, the framework that the various states share places them in a more intimate connection than would be allowed by the market model. They are not simply self-sufficing units that happen across one another in the pursuit of their self-interest. They are units whose behavior is conditioned by their presence in an international economy. The kinds of relations states can establish among themselves are conditioned by the positions they occupy in this framework. Like individuals, states do not have the primordial equality required by the market. They do not exist without internalizing certain power relations to one another. Some will be states with dominated economies; others will have economies run for the purpose of *not* becoming capitalist. The play of self-interest is no longer random since conflicts and alignments are shaped by divisions in the framework.

A consequence of the market model of the community of states is the view that the pursuit of self-interest is of itself the source of war. Even if states can work out temporary accords, they are led by their self-interest to break these accords and resort to war. On this model war can be blamed only on the self-interestedness of the state; so lasting peace requires either total anarchism or a world state with no competitors. In either case the state as we have known it would vanish.

Our framework model, however, leaves more options open. It is not self-interest as such but ultimately the power relations within the international economy that bear the responsibility for war. Pursuing self-interest in a context of rough equality, rather than in one of domination, need not lead to war. The threat to peace could be considerably reduced even without the abolition of the state provided adjustments were made in the international economy. The structuring of the international economy by domination is certainly a more promising subject to consider in pursuit of the roots of war than is the abstract subject of the self-interested state.

4. The tricornered nature of state rivalries

The framework model of the community of states leads us to a broader view of state justice. A dominant state's pattern of justice will have to limit losses and benefits in dominated states; for its pattern of justice is needed for it in some sense to rule beyond its borders. Yet, to determine what the state needs to rule in this way, one must first have a look at the place it occupies in the global system. We shall find that its justice depends on the tricornered nature of its rivalries in that system.

But is justice really relevant to international relations? It might be thought that states are uninhibited by moral considerations in their foreign relations; here is a place where the play of sheer power determines outcomes.[10] This simplification rests on the assumption that rivalries are bipolar, but in their foreign relations states are often involved in triangular situations. This is certainly true of the rivalry between the superpowers, the United States and the USSR. Their conflicts have been focused on the in-between zones – as they were in the Berlin crises, the 1973 Arab–Israeli War, and the Cuban missile crisis. The subjection of a third state or region, a subjection that is not limited to the economic level, is at stake in the rivalry between dominant powers. I call this the Orwell thesis because he formulated it clearly in his *1984*.[11]

But why is it important as regards justice that rivalries be tricornered, involving the subjection of a third state or region? The point is that to be able to get power over and benefit from an alignment with a third state or region more than sheer force is involved. A pattern of justice in relation to other states or regions is of crucial importance. The subjection of other countries or regions

227

by a state leads to an extension of its rule. We are not talking here just about the limited economic domination of the framework but about the fully concrete domination between states that inevitably has various dimensions, including a political one that involves ruling. In comparison with domestic rule this is often but not always only one degree or another of partial rule. The rivalry between great powers for lesser powers is a rivalry over the extension of their rule in a variety of forms including colonial and noncolonial ones. It is, then, an imperial rivalry. A state rules its people and, in a somewhat analogous fashion, rules the peoples of other states, states that it has won in the international rivalry. There is thus not only a question about the pattern of justice needed to rule its people but also a question about the pattern of justice needed to rule others. In ruling the people of other states, an imperial state must recognize certain limits to losses and benefits. The Orwell thesis leads to the recognition that state justice includes a pattern of global justice as a component. (Global here need not mean universal in all strictness but only going beyond one state to embrace others.)

The market model of the community of states underplays triangular in favor of bipolar relationships. It sees a bipolar competition resulting from states' pursuing their separate interests. But with its conception of the equality of market agents, this competition is not for the sake of winning and preserving alignments with lesser powers. It ignores the background of inequality within the global economic framework. Yet this unevenness in economic power shapes competition so that it is not just between rivals wishing to subject one another but also between major rivals for the subjection of lesser powers. The market model misses all but the play of sheer power that one would expect between bipolar rivals. Thus it misses the element of justice that makes alignments between unequal powers possible and that is an important factor when a rival power attempts to challenge that alignment.

The market model provides no conception of justice that could cement a treaty between bipolar rivals; the sudden opportunity for superiority for one of the parties is sufficient to dissolve such a treaty. A Hobbesian compact between states seems, then, no more secure than one between individuals. How, though, could the pluralist holism of the framework model fare any better on the problem of the viability of treaties?

The division between economically dominant and dominated states within the framework model favors stability in the direct relations between major rival powers; for major rival powers will have to moderate their behavior in respect to one another in order not to upset the alignments of lesser powers with them. This can be seen as follows. Those major rivals are committed to patterns of justice that enable them to keep lesser powers subjected to them. But aggressive behavior directly between these rivals will have repercussions on their relations with these lesser powers. In particular, hostilities between the rival powers will often force them to suspend their commitment to justice for lesser powers within their orbits. There will then be a mutual acceptance between the rival powers of limits to benefits and losses that will not be upset by momentary advantage. This justice between major rivals is rooted in their need to preserve alignments with lesser powers. Whereas mere bipolar rivals interact through the play of force, the interaction of rivals for the allegiance of other powers is mediated by a global justice.

5. Peace and prosperity

So far nothing has been said about the content of justice between the dominant and the dominated. The content of this global justice falls under the general headings of peace and prosperity, though these headings will be interpreted differently by states like the United States and the USSR. A major power will cement the allegiance of states it exerts partial rule over by promising them peace with dreaded enemies and an end to economic stagnation. In turn, the state with less power gains acceptance among its people for its supine posture by proclaiming that this posture is the only avenue to peace and prosperity. A powerful state whose ability partially to rule a less powerful state depends on the promise of peace and prosperity will be willing to moderate its behavior toward rivals so as not to destroy the prospect of peace and prosperity for that less powerful state.

We must not, though, neglect the domestic impact of global justice. How does a state secure its rule over its own people when it is about the business of subjecting foreigners in competition with its rivals? It can do this by leading its citizens to believe it is bringing peace and prosperity to a significant part of the rest of the world. It is implicit in this that peace and prosperity for others may have to be won through certain hostilities and through certain domestic economic sacrifices. (But when they are won for others, peace and prosperity will return to the nation that has made these sacrifices.)

229

Citizens of dominant states can then feel pride in their nation for having played a decisive role in bringing about peace and prosperity elsewhere. This national pride is, as noted in Section 5 of Chapter 15, a benefit that makes up for the loss of domestic jobs resulting from economic development abroad. Allowing the nation this feeling of pride becomes part of the state's global justice.

The conception of global justice I have been outlining conflicts with the idea that between states there is only the play of force. Such an idea is part of the general conception of states as isolated entities. But the basis offered here for global justice is not an ill-founded idealism that looks for easy solutions to chronic strife among states. The basis for global justice is, rather, a consequence of the integration of states into a world economy. This integration means that governance will be affected by inequalities in the international economic framework. Specifically, the requirements of ruling imposed on states will go beyond those that would limit the losses of the citizens of an isolated state. The additional requirements limit the losses of citizens of other states as well. And these requirements are still for nation-states rather than for a yet-to-exist world state.

This global extension of the scope of justice has some unexpected implications. We have seen that in order to function for the economy, and hence for the class that is dominant in the economy, the state must show regard for all classes by setting up a pattern of justice. The form of the state is governance for all the people. Now we see that the state governs not just for all its citizens but for humanity generally. Through the state's being embedded in a world economy, the state transcends not just a narrow class rule but also a narrow nationalism. This leads to the conclusion that the state is not for a class or even for a nation; it is for humanity. This is clearly true for powerful states, but it is also true for lesser ones since, by collaborating in the global peace and prosperity that a powerful state establishes, those lesser states are doing their share to advance humanity.

Before enthusiastically embracing this conclusion as the end of a quest for the redemptive nature of the state, we should face up to the contradictions inherent in the state. While promoting global justice, the state is at the same time serving to reproduce the national economy, which will include domestically based multinational corporations. In fact, it is precisely in order to govern in a way that reproduces the national economy that the state is obliged to advance global security and development. There may be times

230

when there is no conflict between these two goals, but inevitably there are times when the demands of reproducing the national economy call for measures that do not promote peace and prosperity generally. In such bad times the reality of peace and prosperity is replaced with slogans. Poor terms of trade, low third world wages, a high ratio of payment on foreign debt to yield from exports, and repressive military regimes reflect a cheating on global justice in the interests of the national economies of the powerful states. Because of this, unstable situations bob up continually across the globe, making the international dimension of the state's task of reproducing the national economy an exceptionally difficult one.

Consider some of the ways global justice gets limited by these contradictions. First, limits on peace are inherent in unequal economic power. The economic domination found in the framework tends to favor restrictions on internal political and welfare rights. Democracy is at best only formal, trade unions are not economically independent, and misery abounds in the absence of a social safety net. The pattern of justice of a state whose economy is dominated is then likely to guarantee fewer limits on losses than are guaranteed by states whose economies are dominant. The equity aspect of the state – its protection of basic political and welfare rights – so familiar in the industrial states in the Northern Hemisphere remains underdeveloped in the most dominated states.[12] This leads to sharper class conflict within nations whose economies are dominated by stronger ones and thus places an obstacle in the way of realizing the peace promised by global justice. The authoritarian and repressive regimes that are introduced to deal with class conflict actually introduce a higher risk of civil war and, as a result, of war of intervention initiated or backed by a more powerful state.

Thus the peace of global justice can no longer mean the absence of hostilities; it comes to mean not being taken over by "the main enemy." Hostilities will be essential in thwarting the main enemy, whose sympathizers must be crushed. Thus global rule will have to get by on a limited pattern of global justice. Of course, for countries aligned with the United States this main enemy today is the so-called communist takeover. U.S. domination establishes a Pax Americana, not by avoiding hostilities altogether but by granting protection against communist takeovers. This limitation of the peace dimension of global justice is not without cost; it reduces the effectiveness of global justice in helping establish global rule.

231

Second, prosperity is hostage to the internal needs of the dominant economies. The flow of capital across the international economy to investments in economically dominated nations has a potential for leading to prosperity. And if there were a perpetual boom in the world economy, signs of that prosperity would multiply. For many nations, the reality has been a debt trap which retards the advent of prosperity by draining so much money out of these nations that growth stops. High interest rates accelerate this drain. Terms of trade that force a state with a dominated economy to buy dear and sell cheap bolster the profits of the corporations of a more powerful state but put prosperity off into a more distant future for that less powerful state. The prosperity promised by global justice comes to mean in many states not an elimination of poverty and hunger but greater wealth for an upper class that has promoted greater involvement in the world economy.[13] Again, the limitation on prosperity implied by these restrictions on global justice reduces the effectiveness of global justice as a means of establishing global rule.

18

The imperial state

The 1941 declaration of President Roosevelt and Prime Minister Churchill known as the Atlantic Charter announced the beginning of a new world order. The mantle of imperial world leadership passed from Britain to the United States with the Charter's recognition that nations had the right to self-governance, as they did not under colonial rule, and that nations would participate on an equal basis in free trade, as they did not under a system of colonial preferences. Most importantly, the new imperial leader, with the help of the old imperial leader, would establish a global order characterized by "freedom from fear and want."[1] A promising beginning would soon be made against fear with the Allied war effort to defeat fascism and had already been made against want with booming war economies that had ended the Great Depression. Earlier in the year, Roosevelt had justified the Lend-Lease Bill in his Four Freedoms speech by appeal to freedom from fear and want, in conjunction with freedom of speech and worship.

A lot remained to be determined; isolationism was dead, but what would be the mechanism for insuring peace and prosperity in the postwar world? Would this conception of global justice be effective in advancing the interests of U.S. capital, or would it place obstacles in the way of those interests? How has the U.S. state been altered by embodying this conception of global justice? In this chapter I shall look at prosperity as one aspect of global justice, and in Chapter 19 attention will shift to peace as the other aspect of global justice.

1. Combined and uneven development

A world economy, like a national one, is incapable of organizing itself automatically. The state is needed to organize a national economy, and an economically dominant state, or group of states, is needed to organize the world economy. The absence of leadership within the world economy during the Great Depression is even

233

thought to have led to its having been deeper than it would otherwise have been.[2] But the United States vigorously assumed the leadership it had declined in the 1930s once World War II was well under way. The task of that leadership was to obtain international agreements that would establish the ground rules for a stable global economy and to create international bodies for executing the intent of these agreements. The Bretton Woods discussion in 1944 led to the creation of the International Monetary Fund (IMF) and the World Bank, which were designed to avoid the breakdown of world trade that took place with the onset of the Great Depression.

On the one hand, the creation of these international bodies was recognition that the health of national economies depended on the health of the global economy. For the U.S. economy in particular, with its commanding position in the world economy, these international bodies were ways in which its interests could be promoted around the world. The state's responsibility for reproducing the U.S. national economy had come to include a responsibility for reproducing capitalism at an international level. It had, then, a responsibility to support and influence international bodies like the IMF and the World Bank, which are insurance against another worldwide collapse. Today the U.S. economy no longer enjoys the unique position of dominance it had after World War II; it has been challenged by the developed economies of Japan and West Germany and must share the world market with the developing economies of countries like South Korea and Brazil.

On the other hand, these same international bodies serve the goal of global justice, which is necessary for a state with imperial ambitions. The idea of development expresses the economic side of global justice. For our purposes, more or less development can be understood as measured by the level of productivity of an economy in relation to others. The partial rule appropriate to an imperial power can be made a stable relationship when the ruled state with its less developed economy can expect economic development as the reward for its subjection. The imperial state does not leave the development of the less developed state to the latter's own powers within a world of more powerful offsetting forces; it exercises its leadership by organizing international bodies that make development a multilateral effort.

If the goal of equal development were actually reached, then it seems that the imperial relation would end. So we are faced with the contradiction that, on the one hand, the imperial state is able to continue its partial rule over other states only through the carrot

234

of development but, on the other hand, development lays the basis for a self-reliance that is sufficient to do away with the stick of imperial rule.

How is this contradiction dealt with? In general, it is dealt with by means of the form of development promoted by the dominant national economies. It is a limited and distorted form of development that gets promoted. It is limited both by the necessity to which it gives rise to service debt owed foreign banks and by its emphasis on exports that leaves domestic markets small. It is a distorted development due to its channeling of investments into selected areas and its targeting benefits for the already affluent, thereby increasing inequality. In contrast, development that is balanced, that promotes the internal market through raising the standard of living of the majority, and that limits external dependency I shall call comprehensive development.

Despite the effort to limit the form of development, some less developed economies will be able to become regional financial, industrial, or trading powers. They change their position within the economic framework by coming to dominate certain lesser economies and to rival certain greater ones. In doing so they develop greater room for their own choice of the further course of their development. This occurs against the background of the majority of the less developed economies that advance more slowly because of the limited and distorted form of development. There are historical, demographic, political, and natural factors that determine which path a nation will take in the uneven pattern of economic development. Still, though their paces of development are uneven, individual nations are not developing in isolation from one another. They are tied together in the economic framework in a combined and uneven development.[3] Given the unevenness of development even among dominated economies, no example can be truly typical, including the following one.

2. Limited and distorted development in Jamaica

The effects of the limited and distorted form of development promoted by interests associated with imperial states can be illustrated in the recent history of Jamaica.[4] In the boom period of the 1950s and 1960s, the multinational aluminum companies poured capital into the bauxite-rich Jamaica. A third of domestic investment came from foreign capital. The economy was dominated by foreign trade, with three-quarters of the export sector coming from

235

sugar, bananas, bauxite, and alumina. The resulting development, though real enough, was limited and distorted, for, despite the robust growth of GNP, inequality increased, unemployment rose, and poverty deepened.

This was the context in which the reformist People's Nationalist Party (PNP) came to power in the elections of 1972. It projected development of a more comprehensive sort at odds with the limited development Jamaica had been following under the leadership of the multinationals. The new government of Michael Manley would attempt to develop the economy more comprehensively on the basis of greater national control. A production levy on the aluminum companies would increase government revenues dramatically. An alumina refinery was to be built in partnership with Mexico, Venezuela, and Hungary. But the mid-1970s were not auspicious times to defy imperialism. The aluminum companies were reducing their investments, the costs of imports soared, partly due to the oil crisis, and there was a decline in exports. With an adverse balance of payments, the economy was in serious trouble. International political reaction to Manley's assertion of economic sovereignty intensified the problem; a press campaign in the United States coupled with a wave of violence in Kingston aimed at destabilization cut the tourist trade in half.

With foreign banks refusing loans, a test of political will with the IMF was inevitable. In his defiance of the IMF up to 1976, Manley still had the backing of his lower-class base. This was demonstrated in his solid victory in the 1976 elections, despite Jamaica's growing balance-of-payments deficits. However, by 1977 he was willing to compromise with the IMF, which wanted wage reductions, devaluation, budget cuts, and an end to price controls, import controls, and state enterprises. If such an attack on labor and the public sector were allowed, "Jamaicanization" – national development – would be dead and political support for the PNP in the lower classes would be eroded. In the United States the Carter administration hid behind the IMF, offering assistance to Jamaica if it accepted the IMF's requirements.

Agreements were reached with the Fund in both 1977 and 1979. But in both cases the Fund suspended its program on the grounds that the Jamaican government was still spending too much. This charge of fiscal irresponsibility needed critical examination in light of several factors: On the one hand, revenues were chronically down as a result of the reaction of the aluminum companies to the production levy; and on the other hand, by 1978 a quarter of the government budget was going to service the external debt. By 1980 Manley recovered his resolve and refused to deal with the IMF. Politically it was too late; he lost the 1980 election to the Jamaica Labor Party, which had been given plenty of time to exploit his inconsistencies and to tout a policy of limited and distorted development approved by the IMF and the United States. Above all, he had alienated those who had most to gain from a defiance of imperialism – the Jamaican lower classes. In turn, the Labor Party's failed economic policy brought Manley back to power in 1989, but this is now a chastened Manley, willing to cooperate with imperalism.

3. The dialectic of imperial economics and justice

The point is not to insist that the global justice of the imperial countries is a sham. There is, after all, development within the dominated economies; it shows up clearly in the statistics. There is growth in the total output of the economies; this growth is often more rapid than it is in the dominant economies. In Jamaica in the boom years total output increased by 5 or 6 percent each year, whereas it increased by 3 or 4 percent in the United States. This growth in output in the dominated economies is not attributable simply to an increase in population; in many cases there has been a genuine surge in productivity. Per capita output has therefore increased in most of these countries, though in sub-Saharan Africa per capita output has almost stagnated.

It needs to be observed that, though aggregate output has been growing more rapidly in some dominated economies, the spread between living standards in the dominated and the dominant economies has, on the whole, been widening. This is because the growth rate for per capita output has been lower than that in the dominant economies. The spread is already enormous among capitalist countries: In 1980 in nineteen high-income countries average per capita income was $6,658 at 1975 constant values; in sixty-three middle-income countries average per capita income was $903; and in thirty-three low-income countries average per capita income was $168.[5] And this fortyfold difference between the top and the bottom is expected to become even greater.

Though development is not a sham, it has its limits. It is not necessary for an imperial state to encourage comprehensive economic development in the countries over which it has partial rule. If this were a necessity of the partial rule an imperial state exercises, then the economic dominance of imperial states would be

237

rapidly liquidated. But being economically dominant over the economies of other states had become a requirement for the reproduction of the national economies of the imperial states. A form of rule that liquidated this economic dominance would conflict with the economic function of those imperial states. Given the autonomy of the state, this possibility is not automatically excluded. An imperial state may go beyond a least weak system of state justice by systematically promoting the comprehensive development of all the states over which it holds sway. Its system of justice would be stronger than any that could be reconciled with the reproduction of the imperial state's national economy. In contrast, a limited and distorted development of the sort allowed by an IMF standby agreement is a least weak system of global state justice.

The view of economic development taken here involves, then, a dialectic between conflicting tendencies. Imperial rule promotes a certain degree of development in order to legitimate itself. Achieving such legitimacy was an element in both Kennedy's Alliance for Progress and the Trilateral Commission's reliance on the multinationals rather than larger military budgets for the United States' global presence. But imperial rule attempts to limit development in order to realize its national economic function. The first of these tendencies is at odds with the view of some dependency theorists that the economically dominant nations develop by promoting underdevelopment elsewhere.[6] The second tendency may, though, promote underdevelopment. However, it is not this second tendency alone that determines reality, even though an extreme dependency theory would claim that it does. The effect an imperial state has on the development of a dominated economy depends on both its promotion of development for global justice and its distortion of development for its national economic function. (The actual course of development will, of course, also depend on the political, natural, technical, and employment resources of the dominated economy.) Such a dependency theory ignores the degree to which the trend toward underdevelopment based on economic interests is counteracted by the trend toward development based on the interests an imperial state has in governability.

4. The basis for partial rule

We can now characterize the imperial state itself. It promotes among states it dominates levels of development consistent with its own economic well-being. What kind of rule is imperial rule?

238

There is a spectrum of types of imperial rule, running from partial to total rule. The ethnic and linguistic diversity of the nobility within the Habsburg Empire never allowed the Habsburg dynasty to exercise a total rule, whereas the sultan of the Ottoman Empire could exercise total rule by controlling all its land through a bureaucracy of warriors and slaves. The subject states within contemporary imperialism are sometimes under total rule – for example, the Baltic states in the USSR – but my focus here will be on the subject states under only partial rule.

States under partial rule combine both national sovereignty in regard to some matters and economic domination by a foreign state. A certain autonomy is then left for a ruling group within such a subject state; this ruling group will collaborate with the dominant state, with international finance, and with the multinationals, but despite this framework of collaboration it exercises a fair amount of discretion in handling many problems.[7] Because of this discretion, the collaborator group is not reduced to the status of being merely part of an imperialist bureaucracy. The rule of the dominant state is then not total.[8]

How does it come about that today some states exercise at least partial rule over others? There are clearly both historical and structural reasons for this; together, these reasons show us why it is implausible to adopt the market model view of states as equals.

(1) *Historically*, there is the fact that capitalism developed at first in only a few centers. In other areas there were precapitalist relations of production that developed the forces of production more slowly, if at all. Even the penetration into these precapitalist regions of markets that linked them with the capitalist centers did not have the effect of increasing productivity at the rate it increased in the capitalist centers. For that it was necessary to have not just market links with capitalist centers but also the capitalist system of wage labor. The result was then a division between the capitalist centers with their more developed forces of production and a periphery of areas where, since labor was still utilized in a precapitalist way, the forces of production were less developed. The bourgeoisie that did emerge in the periphery did not promote capitalist development since its fate was closely connected with the success of mining and agricultural production based on precapitalist labor. There were then lack of development at the periphery and development in the capitalist centers.[9] This early low productivity put many areas at a disadvantage later on in their efforts to catch up with the more developed capitalist economies.

(2) *Structurally*, a low level of productivity is the basis for being economically dominated. Thus differential productivity is the key element in the global economic framework with its network of domination relations.[10] Of course, these different levels of productivity are not taken as an unexplained given; they are, as we just saw, conditioned by the relations of production in the various nations. One should be careful, though, to avoid thinking that these different levels of productivity are generated in isolation purely on the basis of local relations of production. There is always a global background in which the relations of production and hence the class relations of a given nation are to be understood. Here one cannot ignore the dialectic between the local and the global. But the thing I wish to emphasize is that, whatever the origins of the productivity differences, these differences are an integral part of the global framework of economic domination.

In sum, to account for the partial rule of imperial states over others we can begin by referring historically to the origins of productivity differences and structurally to the link between low productivity and economic domination. But we still need to spell out exactly what this economic domination is and to show how it is a factor in partial rule. Whatever it is, though, economic domination is only one aspect of partial rule, which also includes political factors such as the attempt of any imperial state to legitimate itself through efforts at foreign development. Economic domination is then never itself sufficient for partial rule and hence for imperialism; a nation's economic power may put it ahead of its rivals before its imperial hegemony is developed.[11]

5. The link between economic domination and partial rule

Elaboration of the idea of economic domination will make clear how imperialism, in forms that involve partial rule, is nonetheless based on this economic form of domination. There are at least three forms of economic domination. There is domination in regard to market outlets, in regard to obtaining credit, and in regard to access to advanced technology.[12] These forms of domination are characterized here as they exist between economies that are capitalist in nature, though they could also hold between economies of different natures. It is to be kept in mind that behind each of these forms of economic domination are gaps in productivity between more and less developed nations. It is not assumed that these forms

240

of domination preclude narrowing the productivity gap between nations; development, of the limited and distorted kind, is indeed possible under economic domination. Being dominated as regards markets, credit, and technology opens up numerous ways that sovereignty itself is eroded. When this happens there is imperial control in the political, military, and ideological areas as well.

As regards economic domination, there is, first, *commerical domination*. This shows up in the fact that the less developed countries trade primarily with the more developed countries, whereas only a quarter of their trade is among themselves. Moreover, the less developed countries are dependent on the more developed ones in determining the character of both their imports and their exports. Despite the oil price increase of the 1970s, the value of exports from the more developed countries has gradually become an ever greater share of the value of total global exports. Terms of trade for less developed countries will be unfavorable simply on the basis of the productivity gap,[13] since commodities produced with more labor by less productive methods will trade on the world market for commodities produced with less labor by more productive methods, thereby limiting the buying power of workers from less developed countries. Commercial domination means, then, deprivation for the working class.

Second, there is *financial domination*. Foreign capital becomes necessary for development where the level of productivity is low. Priorities for its investment are often set to fit the needs of the more developed countries, thus leading to a distorted and limited development. This leads to a sharp contrast between areas of development and areas of underdevelopment even within the same less developed country. These injections of outside capital become addictive due to what is often a net outflow of capital from the less developed nation. The net outflow results from sending a fraction of profits, some depreciation funds, large private holdings, and debt service payments back to the nations that injected the capital in the first place. The phenomenon of debt peonage means that workers expend a significant portion of their labor not for national development but for the international banks.[14] In contrast, developed debtor nations, like the United States, with their large markets experience the reinvestment rather than the repatriation of foreign revenues.

Third, there is *technological domination*. To try to overcome the productivity gap the less developed country attempts to negotiate the transfer of advanced technology from the more developed coun-

241

tries. Often the technology remains in the hands of multinational companies setting up enterprises in the less developed countries. Only some less developed countries gain the capability of producing this technology on their own. Yet for comprehensive development a diversified capital goods production sector is indispensable. So a low level of development makes a nation vulnerable to technological domination that in turn is an obstacle to comprehensive development.

Political and military domination takes shape within the framework of these forms of economic domination, limiting the sovereignity of less developed countries and introducing partial rule by one or more developed countries. Through economic domination various levers of economic control are taken out of the hands of less developed countries. The developed countries, through international bodies like the IMF, are able to set economic conditions for advancing capital to less developed countries. They are able to destroy import controls, which may be essential to protect fledgling industries in less developed countries. They are able to demand the devaluation of the currency of a less developed country, thus reducing the standard of living of its working class. They can impose "fiscal responsibility," thereby initiating welfare cuts and an end to consumer goods' subsidies.

In order to win these economic changes, a political or, in extreme cases, a military struggle will ensue. To be assured of winning this struggle, the imperial powers often intervene directly or by proxy in the political or military affairs of a less developed nation. Thus economic domination shades imperceptibly into political and military domination, only of course in the appropriate political or military circumstances, because this is not a matter of an economic reduction. Examples of the connection between economic and political/military domination are abundant. The IMF in late 1977 demanded the dismissal of David Coore, the Jamaican finance minister and PNP chairman, in order to get its "standby" program reinstated. Pressure has been exerted by developed countries on their collaborator states to limit trade with and to form military alliances against states, like Castro's Cuba and the Sandinistas' Nicaragua, which opted out of the Western imperialist scheme of development. Notorious attempts have been made by the United States to split the labor movement of less developed countries by supporting the formation of proimperialist labor centrals and to encourage the electoral struggles in those countries of proimperialist political parties. In these and other ways national sovereignity is undercut, and the partial rule of an imperial state is asserted.

When a capitalist state is imperialist, its imperialism is not an accidental and optional side of it. Rather, an imperial state combines within itself both a national and an international function and a national and an international form.[15] After all, the national economy is not committed to limiting itself to operations within the territorial boundaries of the nation. It pursues the accumulation of capital wherever it can, yet it remains formally a national economy and continues to rely on the nation-state for the reproduction of its extended operations. The reproduction of a national economy becomes the reproduction of a global economy coordinated through a national base.

Though the national and international economic functions of the imperial state fuse in this way, there remains a duality between national and global justice. National justice in most dominant capitalist states includes political and civil rights, but these tend not to be promoted abroad by the global justice of imperial rule. This justice is shaped on the assumption that, since there will be ongoing resistance to economic domination, there must be a large element of repression. This repression will be a source of instability within dominated states. Yet, to guarantee governability, global justice would have to call for comprehensive development, which is not feasible. Why not?

Capitalists in the economically dominant countries have grounds for believing that a world of developed states would be a world of cutthroat competition, scarce resources, low commodity prices, and no more imperialist superprofits based on favorable terms of trade. They need only refer to the rapid rise of international competition in the 1970s and 1980s. Why should they encourage their own loss of domination by implementing on a world scale their own ideology of unrestrained exchange among equals? For, with limited and distorted development, profits can still be extracted from the less developed countries, sustaining the gap in productivity on which economic domination is based.

6. Does investment lead to development?

In conclusion, a word about the opposition to the view that economic domination perpetuates uneven development. For this opposition imperial states are economically self-destructive because their transfers of capital to dominated states will lead to equality

243

of comprehensive development. Thus economic domination does not thwart equal and comprehensive development.

This opposition harks back to Marx's 1853 articles on India in the *New York Daily Tribune* in which he claimed the British colonialists were unwittingly laying the basis for India'a development as a Western-style industrial nation. Marx, though, took a different view a decade later, when, in Volume 1 of *Capital*, he insisted that India had had its handicraft industry destroyed only in order to become a supplier of raw material to British industry.[16]

There is little evidence for the mechanistic thesis that, because of growing foreign investment in the less developed countries, quantity must someday turn into quality, thereby giving rise to comprehensively developed capitalist economies bargaining on a basis of equality with all other economies. The position adopted here is that there will be financial, technological, and commerical domination working against such an outcome wherever there are productivity differences. Sheer quantity of investment is of itself incapable of overcoming these obstacles and leading to full development with equality. There will, to be sure, be individual countries that, in view of their special origin and situation, will make great strides toward changing their status of being economically dominated. But this opportunity does not exist for the less developed countries collectively. This is true even after adding the fact that global justice requires that imperial states make some effort to promote development among economies they dominate, thereby counteracting certain tendencies to underdevelopment inherent in being economically dominated.

Moving to the stage of having an export-oriented industry is no guarantee of escape from economic domination. Consider the case of the Philippines. Since it ceased to be a U.S. colony, the Philippines has experienced economic growth while continuing to be economically dominated.[17] At the outset in 1946, the United States gained control over the exchange rate of Philippine currency. Nonetheless, between 1950 and 1962 an import substitution industry was able to grow up in the shelter of import controls. The IMF was enthusiastic when import controls ended, and the United States responded by loaning the Philippines money in the 1960s to increase imports. Wages decreased, and the external debt began an inevitable rise. In 1970 the IMF was demanding devaluation and imposing conditions on loans to service the large debt. The debt was behind Marcos's declaration of martial law in 1972.

The next step was for the international bodies to encourage investment in export industry. With its blackened name, the IMF passed the baton to the World Bank. Over the resistance of the Philippines Central Bank, which had an interest in national development, the World Bank got approval of a package that gave a spurt to export-oriented industries. Import liberalization and devaluation were conditions for this 1980 deal. As a result of this new turn, more domestic businesses folded, young women went to work in garment and electronic plants for derisory wages, and even the Marcos dictatorship could not prevent a mass walkout in 1982 of workers from the export industries.

There is little evidence that the Philippines is closer to assuming a place among the developed capitalist countries. Its political sovereignty is still being violated; the World Bank created a new unit within the Central Bank to get its way. When Marcos became a liability, the United States eventually, in 1986, encouraged his replacement with another regime loyal to it. The welfare, or lack of it, of the working class continues to be decided in part by international bodies. The Philippines has not moved closer to the possession of integrated industries but possesses only segments of the global production process for electronics and textiles. The investment of more capital has changed the production processes to allow for a limited and distorted development but has not moved the Philippines closer to overcoming its status of being economically, and hence politically, dominated.

19

Peace through strength

Since the Reagan–Gorbachev meeting in Reykjavik in October 1986, some steps have been taken toward arms reduction. It will, though, take more than this to end the forty-year military competition between their countries. Whether with more or with less arms, each country competes with the other for the edge in military strength it can then use to further its goals. An important aspect of the imperial state is revealed by this competition between the United States and the USSR. There have been many attempts to see the competition as grounded in the nature of the state.[1] But in fact it is within the context of the imperial state, rather than of the modern state in general, that the military competition has its roots.

The partial rule of an imperial state over the outposts of its empire requires imperial justice with its double aspect of prosperity and peace. In regard to prosperity, the benefits the imperial state gets from its empire are to be balanced with economic development in the states it dominates. In regard to peace, the imperial state's potential for protecting itself with unmatchable military might has as a complement a military umbrella that brings peace to the outposts of its empire. I am concerned in this chapter with this second aspect of imperial justice and how it is undercut by imperialist rivalries. I shall argue that the military competiton of the period after World War II is not a freak phenomenon since it flows from the interaction of imperial states.

1. Imperial state sovereignty

To develop this point it is useful to recall from Chapter 12 the notion of sovereign state power. A state has a certain ability to reproduce the national economy, and this ability I called functional state power. Also, a state has a certain ability to gain acceptance of its rule through its conception of justice, and this ability I called hegemonic state power. These abilities may be destroyed due to the internal

246

conflicts within and between them; we have, for example, emphasized the conflict between function and hegemony all along. But in addition there may be external attacks on the state institutions giving the state these abilities, attacks by either domestic or foreign challengers for state power. Such attacks may be infrequent, but they have a systematic basis in both the conflictive class structure within a country and the inequalities and rivalries within the community of states. Whatever their basis, the state needs the ability to defend itself from these attacks on its functional and hegemonic power. The state will get this ability by having, among other things, a military apparatus. Since this ability enables the state to pursue its goals of reproducing the economy and ruling without interference, it is what we called sovereign state power. This ability is weakened in a state that has its action controlled by a foreign imperial state.

Sovereign state power leads in turn to the monopolization of force by the state.[2] With alternative forces at large within the state's jurisdiction, its functional and hegemonic power can be diminished by disruptions that serve either the interest of an internal dissident group alone or the interests of an external enemy working through an internal group. To avoid the loss of these powers, the state cannot tolerate alternative forces within its jurisdiction. Sovereign power will then monopolize force, or at least be in the process of doing so. The right of citizens to bear arms is not itself a threat to the state's monopoly so long as their use is restricted by the state.

How is all of this changed by the fact that we are dealing with an imperial state? Certainly, functional and hegemonic state powers will have their scope expanded; they will have an international scope. Functional power will not deal narrowly with the reproduction of the national economy, but, as we saw in Chapter 18, it will deal with the reproduction of the national economy within a global economy. But then the reproduction of the national economy requires the reproduction of the global economy through a national base. Collaborator states will do their share alongside an imperial state to reproduce this global economy. Likewise, hegemonic power will not deal exclusively with ruling over the citizens of the imperial state itself but will deal as well with partial rule over the citizens of dominated states. Hegemonic power is then an ability to rule not just through an internal conception of justice but also through a global conception of justice.

We come finally to sovereignty and consider how it is changed. It is no longer an ability to defend a narrow national functional and hegemonic power. It is much more, since it is the sovereignty of an imperial state whose functional and hegemonic powers are themselves international in scope. Sovereignty for an imperial state calls for the power to defend institutions that reproduce an economy which, though coordinated through a single national base, is genuinely international. Sovereignty also calls for the power to defend institutions that rule over a home base and partially rule over the outposts of empire through both an internal conception of justice and a global conception of justice.

The monopoly of force undergoes a parallel change. Imperial sovereignty does not demand a monolithic control of the means of violence. The collaborator elites in partially ruled states are given a certain autonomy in military matters. But their allegiance is secured in a variety of ways: through a shared ideology of opposition to the top imperial rival, through military training provided by the imperial state, through corruption that the imperial state tolerates or is a party to, and through military supplies made available through loans or grants. This allegiance circumscribes their autonomy; in general, a partially ruled state will not use its military to pursue goals opposed by the imperial state. There may still be differences over the tactics used to realize these goals. Though supporting Israel militarily as a foil to Arab powers in the Middle East, the United States still objects to certain Israeli tactics in which it nonetheless acquiesces. In contrast, in the United States the gradual absorption of the state militias within the federal government strictly monopolized force, leaving individual states without military autonomy.[3] Thus the monopoly of force within the empire is, like rule within the empire, only partial.

2. The superiority principle and legitimacy

How in general does a state legitimate its monopoly of force? There is an understandable popular resistance to monopolizing force both within the imperial nation and within its empire. The monopoly, whether full or only partial, is needed to protect the state's interests in reproducing the economy and in ruling. Thus the monopoly of force is a direct consequence of state sovereignty. The most direct way for the state to legitimate its monopoly of force is for it to point to the fact that without the monopoly it could not be sovereign, that is could not pursue its goals without interference. But these goals must be presented not as arbitrary but as promoting the common good, whether of the nation or of the empire. Then the monopoly of force is legitimated as instrumental to the common good.

All does not end here, for though a monopoly of force may be a condition for realizing the goals of the state it may not be enough. In addition, the force that is monopolized must be adequate to its tasks. If the force were not adequate, what good would the monopoly be? Groups of subjects might as well retain full discretion over the use of arms when the state is ineffective in building on its monopoly to realize its goals. The French resistance of World War II arose in part as a challenge to the prewar order that was unable to defend France. It was left to Charles de Gaulle to crush the resistance as an alternative force when the war was ending and to establish again the state's monopoly of force. Once the Nazis retreated from France, the Communist Party leader Maurice Thorez helped to legitimate the Gaullist state's claim to a monopoly of force with the slogan "One state, one police force, one army."[4]

How much military strength will be needed to make it appear that the state's goals can be realized and hence to make the state's legitimation of its monopoly of force feasible? A certain amount of military might will be needed to deal with internal disruption, which is inevitable where there are dominated classes, races, or nationalities. And a certain amount is needed to deal with threats of external invasions. However, the resources needed for handling civil war and invasion appear very modest indeed when they are compared with the resources needed to defend an empire. After all, with only limited resources the Yugoslav partisans defeated the Nazis and the Vietnamese NLF defeated the United States.

But in all these cases a *principle of superiority* is at work, which is a consequence of sovereignty. The amount of military strength required by a state with a legitimate monopoly of force is the amount needed to make it superior to its current rivals. Superiority for the nonimperial state is superiority in dealing with the rebel and the invader, but for the imperial state it is also superiority in maintaining partial rule and in including new states under partial rule. The nonimperial state may acquire its superiority either through its own resources or through alliances with other states, including perhaps an imperial state that dominates it. An imperial state rarely generates enthusiasm for its rule at its periphery, but high morale makes up for the scant resources of a nonimperial state fighting for its liberation. Thus, when it is challenged at its periphery by an insurgency, the imperialist state turns to the show and

249

the use of extraordinary force either by itself or by a surrogate. Sometimes this is unnecessary if prior efforts to weaken the insurgency economically and politically have been successful. Furthermore, a way must be devised of dealing with an intervention of a rival imperial state at the periphery. A lack of military strength could tempt a rival to intervene on behalf of an insurgency in a dominated country. The only guarantee that this intervention will not happen is the possession of a superior force, with which the rival would be afraid to compete.

A competiton for getting the edge militarily follows upon a rivalry between imperial states. We are unlucky that the current imperial rivalry between the United States and the USSR had nuclear technology at hand from the time it began. Thus the present competition, unlike that between the British and German navies before World War I,[5] runs the gamut of conventional and nuclear weaponry. In this as in other competitions the principle of superiority cannot require that each power be superior to the other but only that, for the sake of legitimating its monopoly of force, each power be perceived by those ruled or partially ruled by it as endeavoring to become superior with some chance of success. The military competition is not merely about communism and capitalism; it is primarily about state sovereignty within rival imperial systems. Within the framework of state sovereignty, anticommunism on the one hand and anticapitalism on the other hand can function as vital stimulus causes for the appropriations of revenue that fuel the military competition. Also, within the framework of state sovereignty, the capitalist and noncapitalist character of the rivals accounts for the asymmetries in the military competition.

Once it is granted that the military competition is primarily about imperial state sovereignty, it becomes clear that efforts to stop it that do not call into question the continuation of sovereign imperial states are self-deluding. Recognizing this, many of those who oppose the competition without opposing the imperial state were, until recently, content to advance so-called arms control measures. These measures – like the SALT II agreements – have the effect of reducing the speed of the arms race and of channeling it into a less destabilizing path.[6] There are, however, those like George Kennan who, well before President Reagan's pursuit of strategic arms reduction (START), advocated going beyond arms control to disarmament without calling for dismantling imperial state sovereignty.[7] He called in 1981 for an across-the-board 50 percent reduction of nuclear arsenals, to be followed by a two-thirds reduction of what would be left. But the goal of a military competition is military superiority rather than superiority in the absolute number of weapons. This is why it is misleading to call this competition an arms race, though at times an arms race was its paramount feature. Even when arms are being dismantled, the jockeying for superiority continues. So arms reduction, of the Kennan sort, can be made consistent with a continuing imperial rivalry. Limited disarmament, followed by attempts to get superiority at a lower arms level, would be compatible with imperial state sovereignty. What is ruled out is the attempt to deprive an imperial state of the arms it needs to compete for superiority with its rivals.

Superiority means here more than an ability to win or, more modestly, to prevail. Each side might have the capacity to win provided it strikes first at the other. There must be an asymmetry in the situation before there is superiority. Only one side can win, or prevail, if there is to be superiority. So superiority is an unshared ability to win, or at least prevail. Thus, having the unshared ability to undermine with a first strike an opponent's capacity to fight would be a mark of superiority, even though that weaker opponent might, through a first strike of its own, be able to destroy its rival's superiority. The ability to win is not, though, important just to those who strike first. A surprise attack is never to be ruled out, and so winning even after being attacked is worth preparing for. The relevant factor then becomes the ability to survive a first strike and still retaliate with a second strike. A military power will, then, also be superior when it has a survivable military capacity that can destroy its opponent's ability to continue fighting. So there are a variety of things that make for superiority, even though superiority itself is always the unshared ability to win. It is worth noting that a system of defense against attacking nuclear weapons – realizing some aspects of Reagan's Strategic Defense Initiative – can both undermine the earlier superiority of an attacker's force and, by enhancing survivability of the defender's force, upgrade it to a superior force.

3. Does nuclear deterrence make superiority obsolete?

Has the advent of nuclear arms made the principle of superiority obsolete? The nuclear military competiton still seems to conform to the principle;[8] nonetheless, there is no necessity for it to conform to the principle, provided nuclear deterrence is a sufficient basis for legitimating the monopoly of force. Once rough equivalence is reached between nuclear rivals, a strategy of mutual assured destruction, on which deterrence since the 1960s is based, does not of itself call for a continuation of the effort to get superiority. Rough equivalence without superiority, then, satisfies state sovereignty. The reason is quite simple: Neither side can initiate large-scale hostilities, either conventional or nuclear, against the other, either at its center or at its imperial periphery, without a real threat of nuclear retaliation that could destroy a significant part of its population and of its industrial capacity. This military stalemate provides no incentive for continuing the arms race toward superiority. Nuclear weapons, which are otherwise so destructive, have then the constructive consequence that they have undermined the most threatening aspect of conflict between imperial states, the principle of superiority.

Why, then, has the nuclear and conventional competition continued in the precise manner predicted by the principle of superiority? The root of the paradox goes back to imperial sovereign power. The functional and the hegemonic powers of an imperial state are expansive and thus run into conflict with the functional and the hegemonic powers of a rival imperial state. This limits the basis for cooperation between the rival imperial powers; they pursue basic interests at one another's expense. In particular, since sovereign power is the reflexive power that protects functional and hegemonic powers and the interests embodied in them, there will be little basis for cooperation between the rivals' institutions of sovereign power. Neither rival will aid the other in protecting its state power. Cooperation at the level of sovereign power would imply that at the level of functional and hegemonic power there was no longer an imperial rivalry.

But don't imperialist powers transcend conflict in favor of cooperation when they form alliances and sign treaties? It is to be granted that, within the basic framework of noncooperation due to rivalry, there will be circumstances in which noncooperation fails to advance the rivals individually as much as cooperation. Specifically, there are times when restraint in the pursuit of imperialist goals is imposed on imperial powers because they face a common enemy. Metternich and Bismarck after him tried to maintain an equilibrium between the great powers of nineteenth-century Europe in order to thwart the forces of liberalism and nationalism, thereby giving absolutism one last gasp. After World War II, the North Atlantic Treaty Organization (NATO) was formed by the Atlantic powers to thwart a global victory by anticapitalist forces. When there is a common enemy, rivals can cooperate. This cooperation does not eliminate basic conflicts that would lead to noncooperation apart from the common enemy. It only restrains them on the basis of enlightened self-interest. A common enemy may someday emerge to provide a basis for significant U.S./USSR cooperation. A firmly antiimperialist and democratically socialist Latin America, for example, might be a sufficiently frightening model to inspire an unholy alliance between them. The record to date is that the only treaties the superpowers have signed leave conflict the dominant theme in their interaction.

Without the mutual commitment present in cooperation, there is no solid basis for trust. Without cooperation at the level of sovereign power, then, imperial rivals cannot trust one another. Specifically, they cannot trust one another to do what might lead to the best outcome for both. According to those who advocate nuclear deterrence as a solution to the endless military competition, the best outcome is a static deterrent force on each side that makes possible mutual assured destruction. But notice that this involves trust. If one of the rivals would agree to rest satisfied with its current deterrent force, it would trust the other rival not to start developing new weapons systems that would make its deterrent force vulnerable to a successful first strike by that rival or to start developing a defensive shield that would make its retaliation ineffective. There can be no such trust without a basis in cooperation. Since neither competitor wants to fall behind the other, neither will be content with a static deterrent force. Their military competition will continue in accord with the principle of superiority.

Continuing the military competition to achieve superiority is judged by each of the two rivals to be better than the situation of blackmail each would find itself in if a window of vulnerability should open on its static deterrent force. They find themselves in a true prisoners' dilemma situation.[9] Thus each side opts not for the best outcome – ending the military competition – but for the better of the two worse situations, either continuing the military competition or stopping while the rival continues. So the principle of superiority is still valid in the nuclear age. This conclusion follows not from the usual formal assumption that states, like individuals, act self-interestedly but from the substantive assumption that imperial states pursue interests that lead them into conflict rather than cooperation.

253

4. Extended deterrence

We are led to the same conclusion when we consider the more elaborate idea of "extended deterrence." Aggression is stopped all along the line, from skirmishes to firing off intercontinental ballistic missiles (ICBMs), by extended deterrence. This ability calls, though, for superiority all along the line.

The idea that it is important to be able to engage a rival or a rival's surrogate with a good prospect of success at various levels of combat fits nicely the need an imperial state has to be able to fight wars at its periphery, that is, where it exercises partial rule. Threatening global nuclear war is hollow bravado in quite limited engagements, and thus there must be military superiority adapted to such limited engagements.

If, however, there is at some rung on the ladder of escalation an absence of superiority on one side, that side must be willing to go to a higher rung on the ladder to win. But if that side is not superior at the top rung, where ICBMs would be used, then, even if it had military parity there with its rival, it would face two unacceptable alternatives. Either its rival, despite parity, could win or prevail over it with a first strike, or, assuming its rival lacked this first-strike capability, it would have little motive after an attack for retaliation.[10] There would be little motive since the attacker could answer a retaliatory strike with a third strike that would destroy a large part of the population of the country that retaliates. If the retaliatory strike were capable of making a third strike impossible, then the side that retaliates would be superior to, rather than at parity with, its rival, who is assumed, on this alternative, to be incapable of winning or prevailing. Conversely, if an attacker's defensive shield could make retaliation ineffective, then it would be able to prevail and hence be superior.

The alternative to extended deterrence is forbidding. Either an imperial state must escalate to dangerously high levels of force to fight the limited wars at its imperial periphery when it lacks superiority at lower levels. Or, if there is not superiority at the top of the ladder of escalation, the state must inhibit itself from fighting any war that might escalate to the top of the ladder, where its rival could win with a first strike or to retaliate would be suicidal.[11] Thus, far from having the constructive consequence of undermining the principle of superiority, the nuclear age has extended it to call for superiority at all major levels of engagement. It has this form in official U.S. military policy, outlined in the Single Inte-

254

grated Operational Plan–Six, adopted in 1983 but having earlier roots. The imperial rivals thereby commit themselves to exhaust their resources in pursuing superiority at every level.

5. The utility of nuclear weapons

There is still a third challenge to the principle of superiority. Much has been made of the alleged uselessness of nuclear weapons. They cannot further the goals of states, and thus there is no rational basis for the pursuit of superiority today, since it would have to be based on nuclear weapons. Accepting this view of nuclear weapons gets one off the hook of demanding fundamental changes in the imperial state. One can accept the imperial state and appeal merely to the irrationality in military establishments that call for more sophisticated weapon systems.[12] It is this irrationality and not imperialism that is to be expunged. Before resorting to this psychopolitical account of the arms race, we should first challenge the thesis of the uselessness of nuclear weapons.

There are two possibilities here. First, nuclear weapons may be useless because they are a means which by their very nature frustrates the realization of the end they were designed for. This would be the case if nuclear war were inevitably so intense that the human species would be destroyed by it as a result of radiation and a nuclear winter. Second, nuclear weapons may be useless because no one is willing to risk using them. Here it is granted that a nuclear war could in principle stop short of destroying the species. But because the risk of its escalating into a species-destroying war is significant, no one would be willing to take the responsibility for starting a nuclear war.[13]

Clearly, nuclear weapons are not useless for the first reason. They need not be used in a way that escalates into a global holocaust. Do they still remain useless for the second reason? Allowable risks are different for people in different positons. I do not have responsibility for the imperial state and would not risk the lives of others to save it. I am only a professor who likes thinking about the imperial state. It is different for those who are identified with the imperial state by having positions of power within it.

They have struggled for those positions, and the responsibilities they assume with those positions commit them to taking considerable risks for the sake of the imperial state. They have responsibility for protecting a system of international economic and political domination. Any hesitation on their part will be used to oust them

255

from the positions in the state they have struggled to occupy. Personal revulsion at the possible consequences of initiating a nuclear war is secondary. Those in power in the imperial state participate in a collective institutional resolve to save the empire when it seems endangered. This resolve extends to a willingness to use nuclear weapons, even if the risk of annihilation is significant. Unfortunately, then, nuclear weapons are not useless. There are those in the state willing to take the risk involved in using them since this risk falls short of the certainty of universal destruction. This willingness to risk annihilation establishes the thread of rationality that links the imperial state with the military competition and the struggle for superiority.

This willingness to use nuclear weapons is essential for their value as a threat in superpower conflicts at the periphery. The Yom Kippur War of October 1973 ended with a close encounter between the United States and the USSR.[14] Israel had surrounded Egypt's Third Army and continued the fighting despite a ceasefire agreement worked out by Henry Kissinger while shuttling between Moscow and Tel Aviv. The USSR readied forty thousand troops for intervention, and nuclear material of some kind was detected on a Soviet ship entering the Mediterranean. On October 24, Kissinger rejected Anwar Sadat's proposal for a joint U.S./USSR peacekeeping force to separate his army from the Israelis. The USSR then indicated it would proceed alone to establish peace. The next day, at 2:00 a.m. there was a U.S. military alert to the third-highest level. At 5:40 a.m., President Nixon gave the Soviet ambassador in Washington a letter pointing to the "incalculable consequences" of a unilateral Soviet action. At noon, Kissinger said the issues did not justify "the unparalleled catastrophe that a nuclear war would represent." With this the crisis ended. The United States had used the nuclear threat to keep the USSR from interfering with its periphery in the Middle East.

6. How superiority undermines global justice

What are the consequences of the principle of superiority for imperial peace and security? They are decisively more negative than they would have been in the prenuclear period. The military umbrella that is geared to insuring imperial peace becomes, as we shall see, the means of undermining it. Global justice fails to be realized, intensifying thereby the problem of the acceptance of

256

partial rule within the empire. Imperial state sovereignty undermines the power to rule it is supposed to protect.

Why, though, are the consequences for peace of the principle of superiority so negative? First, the threshold for starting wars in the periphery has been reduced by nuclear weapons. Conversely, the likelihood of involving the two superpowers directly in a ground war was reduced by nuclear weapons; each became more reluctant to enter hostilities directly with the other when an escalation to nuclear war loomed in the background. This reluctance, though, did not curb wars along the periphery. In fact, wars centering on lesser states became easier to begin since they were less likely to draw the imperialist rivals into conflict. Wars that in a prenuclear era would have provoked a direct conflict between major imperial powers could now be fought without serious risk of such a conflict. The nuclear and conventional military competition between the United States and the USSR has, then, had the effect of limiting rather than enhancing security for subject states. Whereas the nuclear arms competition raised the threshold for direct superpower conflict, it lowered the threshold for conflict centering on states subject to the partial rule of an imperial power.

Second, there is the risk of nuclear war itself. This impinges negatively on the security of subject nations, who had been promised global justice. There are many sources of the risk of nuclear war, but conflict centered on subject states is surely one of the most important. We have just seen that conflict centered on subject states is made more likely by the competition for superiority. Through this effect on subject states, the superpower competition actually makes the risk of widespread nuclear war greater. The U.S. doctrine of extended deterrence is addressed directly to the danger of nuclear war resulting from a conventional one centered on subject states. Since the imperial powers are rivals, they can, despite the high threshold for their involvement, be drawn into escalating wars centered on their subject states. If nuclear weapons are used by one of the imperialist rivals or one of their surrogates in such a war, what response can the other imperialist rival make? If it refuses to respond with nuclear weapons directly or through its surrogates, then it deserts the states relying on it for security and weakens its imperial rule. If it responds to the nuclear attack in kind, escalation to a broader nuclear conflict that undercuts the security of still other states it dominates becomes likely. The promise of peace and security, in exchange for imperial rule,

257

becomes harder and harder to believe whether in the third world or among NATO nations. This becomes a basis for the movement in Europe to abandon NATO for an independent European course, a course that would put an end to the various ways the United States limits the sovereignty of its NATO allies.

How might peace be brought to nations under imperial rule? On the one hand, imperial states might try to reform their militarist tendencies in order to avoid the erosion of their power to rule due to the insecurity created by militarism. If I am right, this effort would have to go beyond mere reform and reach the level of the abandonment of imperial status altogether. This is because the imperial state is constrained to attempt superiority in relation to its rivals. On the other hand, the erosion of imperial power to rule due to insecurity might lead to a coordinated rebellion by subject states against the dominant states. The goal of this rebellion would be the founding of a cooperative rather than an exploitative community of states. To realize this goal the rebellion would doubtless have to go deeper than changing relations between states. It would also have to transform class and other forms of domination within states. Still, in both the case of reform and that of rebellion, the condition for realizing the peace aspect of global justice is that the system of imperial states be ended. We arrive at the paradox that global justice as regards security can be achieved only when there is no longer an imperial state that needs it for its partial rule over other states.

The political pressure against imperialism within the United States, which shows itself in the form of solidarity with struggles for independence around the world, is a small but not insignificant part of the effort to end superpower status for the United States. The main force, though, is in the struggles in Europe against NATO, in Brazil against the international banks, in El Salvador against the U.S.-armed government. But what about the superpower status of the USSR? If a struggle against the superpower status of the United States were to succeed, would the USSR be left to dominate the world?

20

The Soviet Union as other

In discussing the community of states I am trying to counteract the familiar attempt to derive the nature of the state from dealing with states in isolation. This tendency leads in the direction either of the liberal market model of international relations or of the reductionist model that makes international relations a by-product of domestic production relations. If this atomist tendency has difficulty understanding the capitalist bloc, it has even more difficulty understanding the Soviet state and its foreign relations.

A clearer view of the USSR calls for taking two steps. First, the Soviet Union must be understood within the global economic framework, where states articulate their rivalries and their imperial ambitions. Second – and here I come to the step peculiar to the USSR – the Soviet Union must be seen to have an economy whose goals make reference to the encircling capitalist economy. Having such goals makes not just the Soviet economy but also the Soviet state different from capitalist economies and states. Their status is that of *an other* in relation to capitalism and its states.

1. Between socialism and capitalism

Before trying to show why I think the Soviet economy is internally related to capitalism, I shall explore some consequences of this view. It leads us to reject some rather familiar views of the Soviet system. On the one hand, it precludes our thinking of the system of the Soviet Union as a socialist system. Were it a socialist system it would make sense to speak of this system as spreading to become worldwide. This is the fear nourished by those who wish to picture the Soviet threat in its most awesome form.[1] They imagine that it would be possible for capitalism to be replaced by a global system in which the Soviet system is reproduced many times over at different places.

What, though, if capitalism is internalized in the goals of the Soviet system? Specifically, suppose the system aims not at a direct

259

goal, such as the equal satisfaction of human need, but at the goal of defending its institutions against their destruction by capitalism. In this case it would be impossible for the system to become worldwide, for then the system would lose its status as an other. It has this status so long as its goal can be defined as the defense of its institutions against capitalism. It clearly loses its status as an other when it has extirpated capitalism root and branch, but in losing the status of an other to capitalism it ceases to exist. The void it leaves will be filled by institutions differing from those of both capitalism and the Soviet system. This transition to new institutions – including possibly socialist institutions – will result not from the abstract fact that the other is ceasing to be but from the political untenability of a system that bases itself on opposition to something that by ceasing to be is no longer a threat. People will simply reject the rule of such a system and in the process create a replacement for it. This will be true whether the Soviet system begins to erode capitalism or capitalism destroys itself from within.

On the other hand, viewing the Soviet Union as an other precludes our thinking of its system as a variant of capitalism itself. Were it a variant of capitalism, the rivalry with the United States would not be fundamentally different from that between Britain and Germany before World War I; the current nuclear and conventional military competition between the superpowers would not be qualified by any important asymmetries between the behavior of the two sides; and the relations between collaborator and imperial states within the Soviet bloc would be perfectly congruent with the relations between collaborator and imperial states within the Western bloc. But as the other of capitalism, the Soviet system should manifest differences – to be confirmed in Section 6 – in respect to the United States when it comes to military competition and imperial relations. And should there be a convergence with capitalism,[2] it would not be a smooth process but one involving radical breaks.

The Hegelian metaphor of "the other" can be developed a bit further. Not only does it enable us to destroy the opposed myths of, on the one hand, the Soviet thrust toward total world domination and, on the other hand, the gradual convergence of the Soviet Union with the capitalist West. It also provides a hint about the transition to socialism. Marx would have had us believe that socialism was to be the immediate result of the negation of capitalism; it was to be the expropriation of the expropriators coming on the heels of the socialization of the workplace that took place in large-scale industry. Facts about the community of states have developed in a way that calls for a revision of this picture. Socialism is not the immediate but a mediated result of the negation of capitalism.

The expropriation of the expropriators has become infected with ambiguity. In addition to signifying a transition to socialism, it may also mean a transition to a Soviet-style economy. In the case of a nation dominated by capitalist imperialism, it would not be easy for the expropriation of the expropriators to lead to a socialist course through transcending the present division between capitalism and the Soviet system. To transcend that division, not only capitalism but also the Soviet system must be negated. There will be nothing approximating the workers' democracy essential to socialism without this double negation. It is not just capitalism that is surpassed by a transition to socialism but capitalism together with its other, the Soviet system. This does not call for supporting a capitalist war against the Soviet system, since the outcome of such a war, if it could be won by the West, would be a strengthened capitalism. Western social democratic support for a hard-line anti-Soviet foreign policy promotes such a tragic outcome.[3] Yet a resolution to the dialectic between capitalism and its negation – the Soviet other – requires that both be negated through socialism.[4]

2. The new mode of production

I want now to review briefly the history of how the Soviet system came to be the other of capitalism. There were two revolutions in Russia, the revolution of October 1917, which brought the Bolsheviks to power, and the revolutionary defeat of the peasant classes in the late 1920s. For the purpose of properly placing the Soviet Union inside the community of states today, the second is more important to us. The first revolution established the Bolsheviks as a ruling party without resolving the rivalry between various classes for political dominance. Thus there was a ruling group, but it was not settled what class would have its interests advanced within the limits of state justice. The Fourteenth Party Congress, of December 1925, took a major step toward resolving this rivalry by pointing the way toward rapid industrialization and an end to concessions to the peasants through the New Economic Policy (NEP), which had begun in 1921.[5] Since the market was the expression of the important role of the peasants in the economy, the showdown with the peasants that was looming would involve a conflict between the market and the centrally directed planning of the industrialization program.

The market was attacked in several ways.[6] Prices were reduced in 1926–7. This created shortages, which gave the state an excuse to centralize the control of distribution. Credit for industrialization was expanded beyond the growth of production, violating the financial policy of the NEP, which was premised on the stability of the currency. In March 1926 the ruble ceased to be convertible; the Treasury would no longer buy it for gold or foreign currency. Industrialization, where socialism in one country had been declared a possibility, was not to remain hostage to the stability of the currency on the world capitalist market. Finally, investment was detached from profitability and hence from the law of value. Nikolai Kondratiev of the Commissariat of Finance argued that investment should be in the more profitable agricultural sector, which could then become the basis for manufactured imports. Kondratiev was dropped from his position in 1928.

As the market declined, bureaucratic planning became the dominant mode of production in the Soviet Union. Its ascendancy involved the defeat of the peasants and the emergence of two other classes as the polar classes of the society, a new proletariat and a new bureaucratic class. The political dominance of the bureaucratic class, which had begun to emerge under Lenin and which contained personnel from upper levels of the Communist Party and the state, was achieved during the turn to industrialization. The revolutionary proletariat of 1917 had been decimated with the collapse of industry at the time of the 1918–20 civil war. Now there was a new proletariat, without a revolutionary tradition, which was subjugated during the rise of bureaucratic planning. First, workers' control had given way to one-man management in 1918; then wages were tied to productivity during NEP; and finally, since planning from the top was clearly incompatible with wage negotiations, the trade unions were reduced to mobilizers for plan fulfillment. A new class map emerged with full clarity in all details but one: What goal did production serve under its bureaucratic mode?

There were two parts to the goal of production, the first domestic and the second international. Stalin articulated them both.[7] In April 1929 he said it was not just any growth in productivity that was desired but a growth that "insured *the systematic preponderance of the socialist sector of the economy over the capitalist.*" The bureaucratic planner aimed at growth in order to insure the dominance of his position in the economy over that of the kulak (the well-to-do peasant) and the trader. This goal was realized when the kulaks were driven off their land to make way for collectivization. After that the international aspect of the goal became prominent. In February 1931, halfway through the first five-year plan, Stalin asked if the tempo could be slowed. "No, comrades, it is not possible. . . . On the contrary, we must increase it. . . . We are fifty or a hundred years behind the advanced countries. We must make good this distance in ten years. Either we do so, or we shall go under." Stalingrad was only a decade away. The goal here is not human needs as opposed to profits, which would have distinguished socialism from capitalism. It is not even the global triumph of socialism; it is the goal of a beleaguered garrison, which is simply to hold out. Polish economist Oskar Lange called Stalin's economy "a war economy *sui generis*," which could be interpreted to mean that it runs to prevent itself from being subverted by the encroaching capitalist market.

3. Defenses of bureaucratic planning

A number of important tendencies in the developed Soviet economic system are best interpreted as defenses against the subversion of bureaucratic planning. I shall consider here three such tendencies. They have to do with trade, with investment, and with the military.

In the discussion of these tendencies, it is important to take into account the fact that the system of bureaucratic planning has, like capitalism, undergone a variety of changes since its days of origin. So far these changes have not altered the basic economic framework and hence have not eliminated the goal of defense against capitalism. After becoming party secretary in 1985, Mikhail Gorbachev introduced a number of reforms that might be interpreted as leading toward a totally new mode of production. Though revolutionary change is never to be written off as a possibility, of themselves neither Gorbachev's intentions nor the changes he set in motion altered the framework from that of bureaucratic planning.[8] What he has changed are the details of how the framework is to work. The framework itself is compatible with certain market mechanisms in the way the capitalist framework is compatible with state intervention. New tensions are thereby created, but tensions don't make incompatibilities. Moreover, because the alteration in the class map of the USSR that took place in the late 1920s has yet to be subverted, there is still no class to play the role of the economically dominant one in a new mode of production based on the market in the way the kulaks played such a role during the NEP.

(1) In the case of trade, there is a tendency to limit exports and imports.[9] The Foreign Trade Ministry conceives of exports, on the whole, as a source of hard currency for imports required by the plan rather than as a direct response to foreign demand. However, circumstances have pushed the Soviets to make dramatic increases in foreign trade.

The capitalist recession of 1975 and 1981 decreased demand for many Soviet goods; to reduce the resulting foreign debt the Soviets increased their petroleum exports, which earn them over half of their hard currency. Poor harvests have required imports of grain that have caused adjustments in planned imports. And of course imports of technology have become necessary for military production, for competitive manufactured exports, and for improving the standard of living. Accordingly, the Soviet Union with its great natural wealth has increased exports of oil, gold, natural gas, timber, titanium, and chromium. In order to keep its military-industrial sector at work, the Soviet Union has increased arms exports to around $10 billion (American billion) each year, providing it with a convenient source for hard currency.

A significant part of production has thus become dependent on foreign demand with the result that the desired course of autonomous development becomes in fact a course of development closely tied to the world market. Zigzags in demand and prices on the world market undermine the power of the Soviet planner to set production goals, prices, and employment. Despite all this the planner's power is not ignored. Things were further complicated when Gorbachev ended the Ministry of Foreign Trade's monopoly, allowing enterprises and other ministries to deal with foreign exporters and importers directly. Though breaking a bottleneck, this liberalization could usher in large trade deficits that would have to be balanced through austerity measures. The political risks of austerity are still too great to let this process get completely out of the planners' hands. Even with these changes added to earlier ones, centralized restraint on imports and exports still protects bureaucratic planning from total collapse and thus serves the economy's goal of holding out against capitalism. The cumulative effect of such restraint is that Soviet foreign trade remains exceedingly small in relation to the size of its economy.

(2) In the case of investment, there is a tendency to set priorities politically rather than on a basis of profitability.[10] I am talking here

264

about prioritizing investment for an industrial sector with an output of a certain kind over a sector with a different output. I am, for the moment, ignoring the prioritizing of investment for one technology over another within a single industrial sector. The plan, since it sets priorities politically, need not call for investment in areas of production where there is an advantageous rate of return. For some time the rate of return in light industry has been higher than in producer goods production. Despite the relatively greater emphasis in the announced economic plans on consumer rather than producer goods in the 1970s and 1980s, the growth of investment in the two sectors has increased at about the same rate. The reason for this is embedded in the system's class structure. If investment priorities were to be set on a basis of profitability, economic power would pass from the planner to the enterprising firm manager.

The reason for making decisions on grounds other than profitability had nothing to do with the worry that, if profitability were the basis for investment decisions, then the Soviet economy would be led by an immanent logic to private ownership. It was, rather, that profitability ignored the goal of the system: Investment priorities needed to be set in a way that enabled the system to hold out against capitalism. This could not be guaranteed if they were to be set by profitability. If light industry were to be emphasized because of its profitability, then a one-sided development requiring that more producer goods be imported would make a balanced and autonomous development impossible. Thus the Soviet economy would risk being absorbed by capitalism, not directly through its immanent development but indirectly through the effect of capitalism on it.

Neither the Kosygin nor the Gorbachev reforms gave priority to profitability in regard to the output mix to be pursued by major investments. Yet both those reforms in the 1960s and these in the 1980s encouraged reliance on profitability in getting individual enterprises to choose efficient technologies for their outputs. Under the incentive that they could have control over a portion of their profits, enterprise managers would be led to invest in a more efficient technology that would generate more profits.

(3) Finally, in the case of military outputs, there is a tendency within the Soviet economy to prioritize their production. This is understandable in light of the history of efforts by capitalist states to contain and roll back bureaucratic planning. The threat of Nazism and finally Hitler's invasion of the USSR led to a military buildup for a patriotic defense of the fatherland. After World War

II, the spread of bureaucratic planning to Eastern Europe and to China posed a challenge to the ambition of the United States to become the global leader. The result was the adoption by the United States of the policies of massive retaliation and containment. These threatening policies were met with another Soviet military buildup. With military threats mounting around the USSR, military production was destined for a special place in its economic system.[11]

Currently accounting for 12–15 percent of annual production, military production is expected to meet the military customer's standards, whereas the production of consumer goods remains deficient in both supply and quality. A military representative is stationed in defense-related plants and has the authority to reject anything below prescribed standards. In 1987 the State Committee for Standards ordered quality inspectors into nonmilitary enterprises with the power to reject inferior products as counting for plan fulfillment. So long, though, as defending bureaucratic planning remains the economy's goal, it will be a war economy *sui generis*, and hence military production will be prioritized.

4. Soviet political morality

I turn now to the pattern of justice in the USSR. How is the Soviet pattern of justice affected by the society's being an other to capitalism? Something new appears because of this that we did not find in the capitalist case. The novelty is that within the pattern of justice there is a dominant element. In contrast, within capitalist states the pattern of justice is a hodgepodge of elements. The dominant element within the Soviet pattern is the rejection of capitalism as unjust. Capitalism is assumed to be the unlimited greed of the few and the unlimited private accumulation of productive resources through profits. Justice calls for limiting this unlimited activity, and thus the goal of the Soviet economy, which is to defend against the spread of capitalism, is a just goal. Here the function of the state coincides with its form, or so it would seem.

It only seems that they coincide since there is more to Soviet justice than its dominant element. There is first the residue of the radical justice of the October Revolution. This shows up, as I noted, in the negative control of the working class in the workplace. It shows up in the commitment to a high level of employment. And it shows up in the guarantee of important welfare rights. There was a second impulse affecting the pattern of justice;

266

the millions of survivors of the Stalin terror who returned from the camps after his death became a powerful constituency for democratic reforms. Though these reforms had only a short existence under Khrushchev, they have been revived under Gorbachev. Moreover, this survivors' movement of the 1950s left a permanent legacy in the form of significant limits on state terror and of efforts to improve the standard of living.

The connection between the dominant element and these others is that the dominant element is used to limit the other elements of justice. Equality, welfare, civil rights, legal justice, and worker control are subject to review against the standard of limiting capitalism. The conservative position that was able to restrict the reforms of the 1950s opposed the elevation of "ethical-moral problems above those of the state and patriotism."[12] The conservatives wanted the defense against capitalism to be the touchstone of all political morality. But, though limiting capitalism is the dominant element, it modulates rather than eliminates the other elements in the Soviet pattern of justice.

If the justice of opposing capitalism were the only element in the pattern, there would be no limits on the sacrifices demanded of the people. There would be even greater abuses of bureaucratic power, and the state's ability to govern and hence to defend the system against capitalism would be undermined. There are, though, the other elements, stemming from October and from the reforms of the 1950s, that restrict the sacrifices. These restrictions make up what is called the Soviet social contract. Yet, so long as the justice of opposing capitalism remains the dominant element, it can act as a filter to eliminate popular political control as an element of justice.

In the capitalist case there are, to be sure, efforts to make the limiting of communism the dominant element in the state's pattern of justice. Communism is represented as the unlimited domination of the individual by the state, and thus limiting it appears as an appropriate goal of justice. But these efforts remain marginal in regard to the major movements that have fashioned state justice in the more developed capitalist societies. Of course, the communist tag gets tied to everything from the progressive income tax to the Equal Rights Amendment. Yet the elements in the pattern of justice are modulated not by reference to the injustice of communism but through concern for profits and for the reproduction of the economy. And in the capitalist state's pattern of justice neither pursuit of profit nor the reproduction of the economy becomes a dominant element since neither is seen as an element of justice at all, though both are subject to limitation by justice. At bottom there is the fact that the goal of the capitalist economy, unlike that of the Soviet economy, is the process of accumulation and not the limiting of some external system. Until this is changed, the economic framework of capitalism will not support projecting the injustice of communism into a dominant position in the pattern of justice.

5. Soviet global justice

The Soviet Union, like the United States, exercises partial rule over other states, and along with this partial rule goes a conception of global justice. Peace and prosperity are also the central elements in Soviet global justice, but they are interpreted in a way that reflects the Soviet Union's nature as an other to capitalism. The USSR promises peace and security to the nations in its orbit based on its particular foreign policy.

(1) The Soviet Union promises peace based on its cautious and defensive foreign policy in relation to the more aggressive U.S. foreign policy. This more aggressive stance suited the vision that an American Century would follow World War II. We can derive this difference from the USSR's status as other to the capitalist world. Peace for a state in the orbit of the USSR will then be peace that is possible within a general struggle to protect the centralist forms of organization within the Soviet Union and its empire from the threat of capitalism, whether the threat appears as internal – Solidarity in Poland – or external – U.S. intervention in Vietnam. The Warsaw Pact is a military means of providing this protection in Eastern Europe. Soviet sponsorship, since the 1950s, of sections of the international peace movement with the aim of moderating capitalist militarism has been an ideological means of providing this protection. Peace for a state in the orbit of the United States will be peace that is possible within a general strategy to attack communism wherever it arises outside the bounds more or less agreed to by the great powers during World War II. This general strategy led to actions at the Bay of Pigs, in Vietnam, in Chile, in Grenada, and in Nicaragua. In both orbits, peace is pocked with hostilities. In fact, as long as Western imperialism is committed to attack communism everywhere it arises, the Soviet promise of peace for states coming into its orbit is empty. Its defensive posture would assure peace only in the absence of a commitment in the West to roll back communism everywhere it arises.

268

(2) The Soviet Union promises prosperity based on exchanging the outflows of surplus experienced under capitalist imperialism for balanced development within the Soviet bloc. In effect, prosperity is defined in terms of escaping from capitalist economic domination into a path of development that insures improvements in the lives of the majority. Compared with its neighbors in the Caribbean, it can be claimed that as regards poverty, health care, literacy, and employment Cuba has made real strides after its escape from capitalist domination. The record is naturally uneven – compare Poland with the more prosperous German Democratic Republic – as it is among countries within capitalist imperialism.

Where nationalist struggles are under way within the capitalist empire there is enormous appeal to the idea of limiting capitalism – limiting the insecurity its aggressive foreign policy creates and limiting the misery its partial and distorted development creates. The Soviet Union is the only major power committed to limiting capitalism, and thus some degree of involvement with it in those struggles is inevitable. This is the opening for the various forms of domination the Soviet Union exercises over countries like Cuba, South Yemen, Syria, and Vietnam. Peace and prosperity interpreted in terms of limiting capitalism help make possible the partial rule the Soviet Union exercises over its empire.

Why, then, has the Soviet pattern of global justice made so little progress in undermining capitalist imperialism? First, a conception of prosperity based on ending capitalist economic domination does not, by itself, project a positive plan of development. Does the Soviet past suggest an appropriate plan of development? The rapid industrialization that worked in the USSR has little relevance to much smaller countries with scarce resources. Moreover, Moscow's aid programs are not adequate for development plans that will satisfy the ambitions of nationalist elites. Thus, on the completion of the Aswan Dam project, Anwar Sadat took Egypt out of the Soviet camp. Salvador Allende was actually rebuffed by Moscow in December 1972 when he asked for relief for Chile's deep financial crisis.[13] The Soviet Union seems reluctant to adopt any more Cubas, where development has depended on a continual flow of aid.

Second, ending capitalist imperial rule does not, of itself, call for popular control of the state. Where it intervenes, the Soviet Union wants to settle accounts with capitalism on its own terms. Thus, until recently, the Soviet model of bureaucratic state power comes to be fostered among the states that have turned to the USSR in their struggles against capitalist imperialsm. This conflicts with

269

the deep desire of many participating in those struggles to put an end to the arbitrary power of their own national ruling group. When, however, populist or proletarian elements challenge the state, the response of the Soviet Union has too often been either to go over their heads in order to work with an undemocratic nationalist elite or to crush them altogether. In Europe alone, this happened in Spain in 1936, in France in the 1940s with the resistance, in Hungary in 1956, in Portugal in 1975, and in Poland in 1981.[14] The Soviet pattern of global justice, based on undercutting capitalist domination, is only a weak base indeed for legitimating its partial rule over the states it dominates.

6. The basis for the superpower rivalry

In concluding, I wish to return to the theme that the rivalry – understood here as an economic, political, and ideological rivalry – between states is understandable only in the global framework of economic domination. How does this apply to the rivalry between the United States and the USSR? Recall that there is another important aspect of the global framework besides economic domination. This is the aspect I have summarized by saying that some economies are *the other* of the remaining economies, since they pursue the goal of holding out against these remaining economies. These economies are not just different; they actually complement one another in an antagonistic manner. Because of this complementarity, they can fall within a unitary global framework.

To return to that theme of the importance of the global framework for state rivalry and to apply it to the superpower rivalry, we must first be clear about how the Soviet economy relates to the Soviet state. The fact that its economy is part of the state fails to deprive the economy of its role as a framework.[15] Specifically, it is only within the framework of this economy that the way the Soviet state functions to reproduce the economy is determined, for the way the state reproduces the economy will depend on the goal of the economy. The state's role in controlling foreign trade, in setting investment priorities, and in giving primacy to the military depends, as we saw, on the economy's goal of holding out against capitalism. Just because the economy is run by the state does not mean that the state will cease to have the function of reproducing the economy, and it certainly does not mean the economy ceases to be a useful abstraction.

Putting all this together leads toward superpower rivalry as follows. (1) The place of the Soviet economy in the global framework is fixed by its being an other to capitalism. (2) Ultimately, this place influences the kinds of state institutions that will be used for the reproduction of the Soviet economy. (3) These institutions for protection against capitalism will provide part of the basis for the way the Soviet Union relates to capitalist states. (4) So, in light of (1) and (2), (3) will mean specifically that these institutions will make rivalry with the outward-thrusting United States almost inevitable.

This enables us to carry one step further the account in Chapter 19 of the military competition based on the demands of imperial state sovereignty. That account did not give a basis for the economic and political rivalry between imperial states. This rivalry was assumed as an inevitable relation between such states rather than derived in each case within the global economic framework. But the economic and political rivalry itself does not follow from the very conception of imperial sovereignty. There are several reasons for this. On the one hand, sovereign imperial powers may expand into areas of the world that are sufficiently distant from one another that there is no geographical basis for conflict. On the other hand, these powers may form alliances with one another that commit each of them to supporting, rather than contesting, the other's subjection of certain nations.

There is no general formula for deriving rivalry, but that between the United States and the USSR can be derived from the need of the Soviet Union to hold out against an expanding capitalism. This need leads the Soviet Union to view with favor and in some cases to support struggles around the world for liberation from capitalist imperialism. It hopes thereby that the states emerging from such liberation struggles will decrease the odds favoring capitalism. The rivalry between the United States and the USSR expresses itself in this search by the USSR for collaborator states through favorable treatment of struggles for liberation from capitalist imperialism.

Superpower rivalry then tends to focus on third states, in accord with the Orwell thesis. Their rivalry over third states takes its specific form from two special factors. First, the selection of nations over which the imperial powers come into conflict does not derive from the fact that such nations are at the intersection of two blindly expanding empires. Rather, such nations will have been selected due to their potential as collaborators with the USSR in its effort to protect its system from the capitalist market. Second, those states selected for their potential as collaborators with the USSR will be

271

ones whose political character has been affected by a struggle against capitalist imperialism. Of course, the thrust of these struggles need not be toward a pro-Soviet policy. But the struggles provide, in the context of a world with both capitalism and communism, an opening for those who wish to promote a pro-Soviet policy. In Eastern Europe the antiimperialist struggles against nazism provided such an opening. Yet this opening was exploited for the creation of states collaborating with the Soviet Union only through heavy-handed intervention by the Soviet Union. In Cuba and in Vietnam, in contrast, such collaborator states have deeper roots in their own struggles against capitalist imperialism.

This rivalry coming from three-cornered conflicts has become the basis for an unprecedented military competition. The sovereignty of each superpower requires that it have the military might to overcome interference with its operations, both domestic and imperial. The Soviets tried to match the might of the United States in hopes of making it harder for the Western powers to keep nations in their camp that have experienced struggles against capitalist imperialism. After the immediate post–World War II period, recruitment to the Eastern camp has been more cautious. But a continuation of the effort to attract collaborator states remains a key element in keeping bureaucratic planning viable in a world where the capitalist economy is still dominant.

Part Five

A reflection on the transition
to a new kind of state

Contradictions gnaw at the state and are the source of changes in it. The contradiction between justice and the economy is manifest when the justice needed to make governance possible undermines the economy the state functions to promote. There is also the contradiction between state justice as publicized policy and state justice as an actual institutionalized tendency. The global justice of the imperial state is billed as a policy of peace but ends up as a tendency toward hostilities. In addition, state justice will fall short of the standards of radical justice. Specifically, the subsistence justice of the welfare state will fall short of the radical demand for egalitarian redistribution. Repression also enters into this expanding circle of conflict. State justice aspires to secure universal acceptance for the state; yet tensions between different interests make it impossible to realize this aim and necessary to use repression in order to rule. Each of these contradictions emerges within the framework of an economy that promotes or at least sustains divisions among classes, races, and sexes.

How does the state adjust to these contradictions? When, on the one hand, state justice, by answering the demands of radical justice, becomes so strong that it is undermining the economy, the state might well retreat from justice to greater repression. The ensuing struggle between social groups and the state could lead to a defeat for the existing state along with the emergence of a new form of state. But the use of repressive force is not the only way to such a transition. A popular mobilization in defense of the original strong form of state justice might be so rapid and widespread that the state sees the futility of organizing a campaign of repression against it. This form of state justice, by eroding still further the original economic system, may lead to a new form of state.

When, on the other hand, state justice fails to answer the demands of radical justice, there might still be a recognition of the

273

need for reforms calculated to end an insurgency for radical justice. Residual pockets where the radical demands are still raised will be isolated by ending the broader insurgency and can then be contained by repression. What, though, if strengthening state justice through these reforms should begin undermining the economy? No progressive fraction of the ruling group will then be forthcoming in the cause of reform. The possibility of a successful reform movement would have to be based on an alliance of nonruling groups. If the reform alliance prevails and subsequently the state fails either to undermine the reforms with inaction and legal stratagems or to destroy the reform alliance by repression, a new kind of state will develop.

In this concluding part of my study of the state, I will focus on several conceptions of radical justice, their foundations, and the transitions they imply to new kinds of states. There is a liberal conception of radical justice that emphasizes equality not just in rights but also in goods. The anarchist faces state justice with a conception of radical justice that opposes what the anarchist assumes is the inevitable elitist organization of the state. The socialist will propose a form of radical justice that emphasizes bargaining between mass organizations and the state for the transitional period and widely shared control of production as a long-term goal.

21

Liberal egalitarianism

The focus of this chapter will be the liberal conception of radical justice. This conception is called liberal because of the specifically liberal conception of human nature it assumes. It might be thought that this liberal conception of justice had already become the state's pattern of justice in modern liberal democracies, leaving no room for a liberal critique of state justice in them. In fact, liberals have plenty of room for finding fault with actual state justice in liberal democracies on the basis of liberalism's conception of human nature.

1. Human nature and the right to equality

Of fundamental importance for liberal theory is the idea that humans are actors guided by personal interests. These personal interests are also called private to emphasize that they differ from social interests. An individual will be said to have a social interest provided, first, it is satisfied only when a similar interest on the part of others in the relevant social group is satisfied and, second, it is satisfied by a joint effort with them. A personal, or private, interest need not satisfy either of these two requirements.

By making personal interests the basis for humanity, human beings are regarded as basically discrete in the sense that they are what they are apart from links with others of the sort they would have if social interests were part of their nature. The personal interests of different humans will of course differ, but all humans on this view share the common nature of being actors guided by personal interests. To satisfy their nature, each of them will need access to resources generated from the environment. But, since all are alike in having their own personal interests, their nature calls for equal treatment for all of them as regards these resources.[1] As we shall see, matters would be more complicated if humans were considered to have social interests by nature, since social interests involve a shared satisfaction. But with only personal interests to

275

consider, distributing resources concerns itself exclusively with getting resources to humans with their discrete natures.

Equal treatment is a responsibility humans can execute when they come together to review how resources are being distributed by their economy. They review this distribution in anticipation of calling upon one another to make adjustments in it that would favor greater equality. This social coordination called for by equal treatment is ultimately institutionalized by the state in its capacity as a redistributor. The consequence of ignoring equal treatment as regards the distribution of resources is that humans are no longer taken to have the same nature. If, for example, those with a stronger acquisitive instinct are allowed to have more just because they happen to have this instinct, then in effect people are distinguished according to whether they are acquisitive or not and are allowed different shares of resources on this basis.[2] This clearly subverts the liberal view that humans are alike in nature and should be treated equally because of this. Their differences are adventitious and cannot be used as a basis for treating them unequally. The liberal conception of human nature has, then, a built-in bias against any inequality in the distribution of resources.

This liberal conception of human nature implies immediately a right to equality: Each person has a right to equal treatment by society as regards resources in his or her effort to realize personal interests. Liberal egalitarianism is the position that there is such a right. The agency for insuring this equality of treatment, despite unequal treatment from the economy, a status system, or force, is to be certain institutions of the surrounding society, including of course the state's distributive mechanisms. These institutions are to do more than prevent interference with the realization of personal interests. Such noninterference is far from sufficient for liberal egalitarianism and by itself is the basis only for libertarianism, which being based ultimately on the inviolability of property, is not troubled by striking inequalities. Rather, equal treatment has the positive connotation of requiring institutions to be so structured that they counteract sources of inequality. The equal treatment of liberal egalitarianism becomes a form of radical justice. Institutions that tolerate inequalities will be challenged by the changes brought about by the radical justice of the liberal. The liberal conception of human nature then leads to a radical conception of justice that Ronald Dworkin calls the principle of rough equality, which says "that roughly the same share of whatever is available is [to be] devoted to satisfying the ambitions of each."[3]

2. Social interests and inequality

Suppose we substitute for the liberal conception of human nature one that goes beyond merely personal interests. In this new conception, humans are to be actors guided not just by personal interests but also by interests in the kind of life they create with those around them.[4] People take an interest in their family, their community, their class, their state. These interests are not personal since for them to be satisfied requires more than one person being satisfied through their mutual efforts. If I have an interest in class solidarity, I can satisfy that interest only if others in my class develop a similar interest and only if through our joint efforts their interest in class solidarity as well as mine is satisfied. Yet one cannot base an argument for equal shares on the fact that humans have such overarching social goals, as well as the discrete personal goals emphasized by the liberal. If our nature is to be actors with personal goals alone, then equal shares are required. Once, though, we go beyond personal goals, the distributional issue is no longer how we divide resources among individuals. There is the additional question as to how much goes to social projects. Can this really make a difference?

The argument that, since humans are alike as actors with personal interests, they should be treated equally as regards resources depended on the discreteness of beings with that kind of nature. Now that a social element is added to their nature, humans are no longer basically discrete. For the fulfillment of its potential, the nature of any human is linked to the fulfillment of the potential in the nature of certain others. Such a linked realization does not typically take place simply by distributing the same resources to everyone who is linked together. Instead, resources are put at the disposal of a social project these individuals are jointly engaged in.

Suppose the social project is to develop a community through paving streets that connect it with a nearby highway. Some houses are much farther from the highway than the majority. Thus we might say that the project involves unequal distribution since people who are more remote get a greater stretch of pavement than is required by those neighboring the highway. Moreover, those more remote benefit more since it is a greater hardship to have to traverse a longer stretch of unpaved road. The value of developing the community cannot, though, be realized by running the pavement only partway to the remote houses merely to satisfy an equality based on having a common human nature.

277

True enough, humans are alike in having both personal and social interests. But this commonality no longer does the trick of implying equal treatment as regards resources. We have just seen part of the basis for this claim. It is that social interests call for distributions to projects and hence do not of themselves call for equal distribution to persons. What, though, about the remaining aspect of humans, their personal interests? A possible solution might be to rectify any inequalities introduced by social projects through compensating inequalities in the distribution of resources to satisfy personal interests. If the remote members of the community got more paving in the project of community development, perhaps they should get less income with which to satisfy their personal needs. Unfortunately, this solution poses a challenge to the social interests themselves. It does this by placing strong restrictions on the willingness of humans to engage in social projects. Humans would become willing to engage in social projects only if any sacrifices they make for the benefit of others in the project are compensated for. Those who dwell near the highway will then need the assurance that those more remote will take a cut in income before they are willing to undertake the road paving. To get this assurance prior to cooperating on social projects is to get assurance that there will be no free riders. But there is no obvious way of getting this assurance in the absence of an initial willingness to engage in social projects. So the proposed solution, which makes cooperation conditional upon compensating inequalities, undercuts cooperation by introducing the intractable free-rider problem and thereby undercuts social interests themselves.

It is not open to the liberal to object to all this by saying that social projects that threaten to introduce inequality should be eschewed since equality is mandated by human nature. This objection simply begs the question of human nature, for it assumes the presocial conception of human nature that is being challenged by a social conception of human nature. Starting from this social conception of human nature does *not* lead us to equality; if there is a basis for equality it lies elsewhere. On this social conception, equality will have a basis only if it promotes the goals of certain of the social projects humans take an interest in.

3. Inadequacy of the liberal view of human nature

The reason, of course, that we look to a conception of human nature that includes social interests is that the liberal's conception is

278

impoverished. It abstracts from the overarching goals that come from group membership and falsifies even personal interests by treating them as though they could be accounted for apart from these overarching goals. Our dietary, artistic, and other interests are never purely personal but reflect group membership. As members of groups, we are not like investors who buy stock in a company in oder to protect and enhance the values they antecedently possess.[5] Rather, the values we wish to protect and enhance are ones we pursued not as isolated individuals but only as members of groups already.

The liberal conception of humans makes it difficult to deal successfully with certain important moral issues. This is one indication of its impoverishment. Moral issues need to be debated against the backdrop of assumed group interests, without which a fixed point for the discussion is lacking.[6] Yet the liberal supposes that it suffices to be cognizant of the way the personal interests of different actors lead to conflicts. The liberal discussion of the abortion issue illustrates the problem. What is the responsibility of a woman to a fetus she is carrying as a result of voluntary intercourse accompanied by the knowledge that it could well lead to a pregnancy?

An uncertainty enters here in regard to the interests of the fetus. Does the fetus have personal interests at all, and if so what are they? Recall that personal interests guide self-interested actors. The liberal method of starting with the conflicting personal interests of different actors is, at least here at the outset, inapplicable since the fetus does not appear to be guided by anything. In this uncertainty, where do we look? The discussion must shift from focusing on the interests of the fetus to the significance of carrying the fetus for the interaction between groups. Only after this can we hope to return to the interests of the fetus.

Reproduction has become a focal point for conflict between groups because a number of groups have a sizable stake in controlling reproduction. The modern medical profession had a stake in it when it was endeavoring to exclude midwives from medical practice. Midwives had regularly practiced abortions, and an attack on midwives could be mounted by making abortions illegal. In 1859 the American Medical Association railed against "snuffing out life in the making." In the United States, as states passed laws against abortion in the mid 1800s, women saw their control over the reproductive process ebbing away. As male heads of households found their authority over their wives and daughters threatened by the

279

spread of wage work for women, it was some compensation for male authority that women were being denied control over the reproductive process. The various sides on the issue cluster about the efforts of the respective groups to assert their control over the process of reproduction.[7] The side that maintains that a woman has a right to choose to terminate a pregnancy clusters about the efforts of feminists who rightly see that, if women cannot wrest control of the reproductive process from male institutions, then women stand little chance of winning liberation generally.

Now we can return to the fetus itself. The interests of one or another of the groups competing for control over reproduction are appealed to in liberal thinking to resolve the uncertainty about the fetus's interests. The fetus's interests get interpreted in light of the interests of the respective groups. If the liberal then goes on to use any one of these interpretations of the fetus's interests in order to resolve the conflict between the fetus and its interests and the mother and her interests, the liberal is merely substituting a constructed agent with discrete interests for the reality of group conflict over control of reproduction. The point of resorting to a construct is simply to try to engage the liberal method of dealing with conflict.

Suppose the liberal uses such a construct to support a prochoice position. In this case the interests assigned to the fetus will be those of a merely prepersonal sentient being. From the prochoice position this is as far as one can go in order to engage the liberal method. These interests will not be interpreted as those of a self-interested agent and hence not of a being with the rights of a person. The basis for this interpretation behind the prochoice position is in fact the interest of women as a group in asserting control over reproduction as a key factor in their liberation.

Suppose, though, the liberal takes the construct of a fetus with interests to include interests of a private kind that can guide a self-interested agent. This would be done in order to support an anti-abortion position. It is equally clear in this case that this construct arises not from a direct examination of the personal interests of the fetus but from the interests of male institutions in asserting control over reproduction as a key to the domination of women. In neither case has the liberal avoided social interests in constructing the interests of the fetus in order to deal consistently with the morality of abortion. [8]

Though impoverished, the liberal conception of human nature is not arbitrary. It is in fact derived from the idea of the market. The

280

market is a mechanism for relating actors in a way that ignores any social links they might have. The market is a vehicle for satisfying their personal, not their social, interests. But surely our community could go to the market to buy its paving project from a construction company. This, though, is not all there is to it, since the community must tax itself to raise the money to pay the company. Can taxing be viewed as a set of market exchanges within the community? Does each community member exchange money for paving? As noted, these will not be equal exchanges since those farther from the highway get more paving. If, though, we make the exchange equal in order to be able to say there is a market behind social-interest satisfaction, then we need assurances of the equality of the exchanges before there is cooperation in the tax scheme. But this we cannot have without a willingness to cooperate in the first place. This willingness takes us beyond market exchanges, showing that the market is not an adequate vehicle for satisfying social interests. As far as the market is concerned, there are only personal interests, and no personal interests are alien to it. Since humans do have social interests, the market derivation of the liberal view of human nature is a source of its impoverishment. A view of humans as actors with personal interests is both adequate to market behavior and suggested by the market. Clearly, though, tensions exist between the egalitarianism of this view of humans and the inequalities generated by the market.[9]

4. The liberal equalizing state

The common assumption of liberal thought has been that the state serves to reproduce the market, whether the principle of ownership is capitalist or socialist. It is admitted by liberals that a market is not designed to eliminate the hardships resulting from the inequalities it generates. The state must then play a dual role: The state that preserves the market will also need to intervene on behalf of the equality derived from the conception of human nature motivated by the market. This gives rise to obvious tensions within liberal theory. But these tensions have not made it retreat from its reliance on the structure of the market in shaping its view of human nature.

How can measures be taken to curb the inequalities the market does nothing about? When people compete in the market, some have enormously greater advantages than others, through luck, inheritance, training, gender, and physical fitness. Guaranteeing

281

rough equality of market competitors would reduce the inequality of outcomes. Complementing the state's function by such a guarantee creates a powerful pair: We have the market, as the institution the state functions to reproduce, and we have egalitarian justice, as the form of ruling that counteracts the hardships resulting from the market. The liberal conception of human nature provides this form of ruling – a pattern of egalitarian justice – which when implemented would seem to allow the state to continue pursuing its function of reproducing the market.[10] When this egalitarian justice comes into play, the state must undergo a transition to an equalizing state. This would redirect existing liberal democracies in fundamental ways.

The dynamic, though, behind liberal reform leading to the equalizing state is not theory but deprivation. There is a contradiction between the demand for more equality as a demand of those who are deprived of resources and the capitalist state's conception of justice as subsistence justice. The popular demand for equality rejects the official conception of subsistence justice as inadequate. This leaves the state with a deficit of legitimacy. The roots of this popular demand are not in the liberal conception of human nature but in the hardships directly and indirectly associated with inequality. The key thing for the liberal is to respond to this popular demand in a way that promises to reform the state without altering its function of preserving the market. Of course, the demand for equality will not be the only demand that comes from dominated groups. There will also be the demand for control over production. Marxists as opposed to liberals make the demand for equality less central than the demand for lower-class control of production.[11]

The popular demand for equality is of itself not completely determinate. It admits of interpretation in several ways, one of which is in terms of the liberal model of human nature. Using this model as background helps to channel the demand for equality within the market. The reason this model helps is that the market is designed to satisfy personal interests in an optimal way and to accommodate an unlimited variety of such interests.[12] So the market is an optimal context within which humans with a nature composed of personal interests may seek equality. The demand for equality then leads to reforms that leave the state as guardian of the market. In sum, though the dynamic behind it is the popular demand for equality, liberal egalitarianism is not derived from this alone; it comes from that popular demand by way of the liberal model of human nature.

Suppose, however, the popular demand for equality had been interpreted by using the contrasting model that blends group and personal interests together to make the stuff of humanity. This model would actually stand in the way of channeling the demand for equality within the market.[13] Take the interest that blacks have in ending the system of race-based income inequality. A market system may be able to insure that my personal interest in musk-scented after-shave lotion and your interest in cologne-scented after-shave lotion are both satisfied. But market remedies for black inequality in respect to whites have an air of unreality since they assume blacks can solve their problem by acting alone rather than together as a group, thereby ignoring the social rather than the individual nature of the forces against them. The equalizing state, as a state promoting the market, would not result from the demand for equality together with the social model of humans.

5. Contradictions of the liberal equalizing state

The problems for the liberal conception of human nature mentioned in Section 3 might all be brushed aside on the ground that this conception helps promote freedom. To insist that humans are in part determined by groups is to play into the hand of schemes to subvert personal interests and give primacy to the interests of groups. Liberalism devotes iteself to avoiding this subjection of the individual to the group. Never mind that an emphasis on personal interests gives primacy to the availability of an after-shave lotion for every taste while demoting the importance of the liberation of an oppressed group; this is the price to be paid if the individual is not to be submerged within the group and is to realize his or her proper freedom.

Though there is surely something desirable about freedom in this limited sense, the liberal view of human nature leads to an equalizing state that ends in contradiction. In view of the tension mentioned earlier, the equalizing state of liberalism proves incapable of reproducing the market. This creates a difficulty since the market seems best designed of all systems to satisfy the large variety of personal interests coming from persons with discrete natures. But without the market, liberal freedom is severely restricted. One cannot appeal to its nature because this freedom calls for a market that a state respecting this conception of human nature undermines. What can liberalism do to protect the market, given that it also has a need for the state? The state is needed as the

283

means of enforcing the equalization of resources called for by the fact that none of those personal interests is inherently more worthy than any of the others. As we shall see, the reason this equalizing state is incapable of reproducing the market is that it destroys the motivation for market behavior.

Consider what a state with an equalizing role would be like. The state of liberal egalitarianism is a strongly interventionist state. It has, after all, egalitarian justice as a form of ruling and thus commits itself to eliminating hardships resulting from inequality. In a passionate affirmation of liberal egalitarianism, legal theorist Bruce Ackerman concludes that "there is no reason to think the invisible hand will ever lead us to the promised land without any assistance on our part. The end of exploitation will come only through self-conscious political action."[14] For him political action takes place within the context of the liberal state, which "*is* deeply committed to the ideal of free exchange." In what ways is Ackerman's state interventionist? He rejects the noninterventionist night-watchman state on the ground that it is a cover for maintaining existing unfair advantages. So, before it can take action on other matters, the liberal state should act to reduce inequalities. A structural budget is designed to fight inequality; according to Ackerman, genetically normal white capitalist males will, because of their multiple privileges, be taxed so as to make a large contribution to the structural budget. Handicapped, minority, noncapitalist females will, because of what they lack, be favored recipients of budgetary expenditures. Resources will be redistributed in a way that provides the less well-off with equal educational, financial, market, and inheritance rights in relation to those who were the most well-off. The market and bad judgment can still introduce inequalities, but these would be even greater without attempts to curb inequalities among competitors. Attempts to implement such an equalization would require special compensation for the handicapped, affirmative action in hiring, trust busting, and confiscatory inheritance taxes. And all this by a liberal state that "*is* deeply committed to the ideal of free exchange."

The structural budget provides the justice needed for the state to rule where there is a popular demand for equality. Rawls would implement this justice through state agencies that gather and spend the funds of the structural budget.[15] He has a stabilization branch that guarantees full employment, an allocation branch that – by subsidies and taxes – insures that prices measure bene-

284

fits and costs, a transfer branch that makes up for the market's inability to guarantee an income sufficient for need, and a distribution branch that prevents great concentrations of wealth and provides funds for public goods. Together these agencies transform the state into an equalizing state, one that by its form of rule is committed to implementing the greatest possible equality of civil and political rights and the greatest possible equality of goods and services. Since these agencies are part of a liberal state, they implement a form of rule coupled with the function of preserving the market.

Wherein lies the incompatibility of such equalizing institutions with the function of preserving the market? It is not enough to say that the administrative measures of these institutions add an impurity to the exchange process; perhaps the variety added by an impurity is exactly what is needed to strengthen the market. The key issue is, rather, how an equalizing state affects the basic motivation for keeping the market alive. This motivation is not captured by presenting the market as a formalism of supply and demand tending toward an equilibrium at which consumers are satisfied, within their means, at least cost. This market efficiency is not enough to explain why those with initial advantages would limit themselves to the market if they could increase their advantages more outside the market. That they are willing to limit themselves to the market is an indication that the market itself is capable of increasing those advantages, that is, of increasing power and control.

Power and control, not efficiency, are the basic incentive for using the market. There is an incentive to employ a market system on the part of those who estimate their power and control will be enhanced by its use. Those who enhance their power and control will do so through at least a relative loss of power and control by others; so this incentive operates on the expectation of inequality. Not surprisingly, this incentive is inoperative for the least well-off; what meager resources they command do not enhance their power and control relative to the most well-off when they are disposed of on the market. Their position is often strengthened more by the welfare state than by the free market. The most well-off, by contrast, enhance their power and control more when they expand their holdings by investing the returns of their enterprise than when decisions over these returns are transferred to others in order to promote competitiveness, stabilization, and redistribution.

Equalizing measures are an impurity within the market, but more importantly they undercut the prospect the market offers of

285

increasing power and control. C. B. Macpherson puts it nicely: "Competition in this [possessive] market, unlike that in the simple market in products [where labor is not for hire], is a means by which men who want more may convert more of the powers of others to their use than others convert of theirs."[16] This is a point that applies both where there is private ownership and where there is public ownership of the means of production. With private ownership, control over returns goes to private owners, whereas with public ownership control over returns goes to the officials making allocative decisions.[17] Neither private owners nor public allocators will have an incentive to support a market that, like one limited by an equalizing state, will not enhance their power and control. When the market is restricted so that it is no longer a useful mechanism for increasing the power and control of those who have become dominant, they will turn to more effective ways of increasing their power and control. But before they abandon the market, they will use their power to end the state's equalizing role so that the market can recover its potential for increasing power.

Look at some of the ways the power motive is weakened, ways the equalizing state has a negative impact on the ability of the market to increase the power of those who have it. Full-employment programs limit the power of employers in relation to employees by making it more difficult to reduce wages with the threat of unemployment. An increased tax burden on property income and on inheritances limits the amount by which the power of the most well-off is increased by the market. And finally, when the equalizing state subsidizes items of need, it is diverting resources that would otherwise be used for increasing power through higher-yield enterprises.

The irony of the liberal equalizing state is that is promotes equality to gain legitimacy but promotes inequality to perform its function of reproducing the market system. When the state raises the banner of market efficiency, the least well-off anticipate a worsening of their condition. When there was talk of using the market in Poland in 1981, workers understood this would mean unemployment and still higher prices. When the market was used as a basis for attacking welfare measures in the United States in the early 1980s, workers and pensioners understood that this would mean increasing poverty. This contradiction of the equalizing state is too blatant for that state to become the goal of a broad-based movement. The popular demand for equality might find expression in the effort to transform the current state into some other form of state but decidedly not into an equalizing state. The equalizing

286

state deserves a place among radical conceptions of the state. But it is a stillborn conception promoted by academic political moralists working in isolation from popular demands.

6. A false abstraction

How could such a blatant contradiction ever have arisen? Can the market itself be the basis for both a conception of equality and a conception of inequality? It can be treated as a basis for both only because two of its aspects are artificially pulled apart.

On the one hand, there is the atomizing effect of the market. The market substitutes for the bonds of community interest the self-interest of the individual characterized by personal interests.[18] A morality that serves this social atomization will have to be one that makes no distinctions among individuals or their personal interests. The atomization effected by the market legitimates itself, as an alternative to community, through a morality that claims equal treatment for all.

On the other hand, there is the goal of aggrandizement. Once the bonds of community interest are broken by atomization, those who would increase their power via the market no longer have to face collective foes, but only the isolated individuals in their way. In this manner, market atomization serves the concentration of power.

The morality of equality was then a mistake made by artificially abstracting atomization from the goal of aggrandizement it served. The atomization of humans was not arbitrary in the context of the market, but it could not be pulled out of the market, leaving behind the aggrandizement possible in the market, without making it a misleading concept. The morality of equality came in only by refusing to keep an eye on the class reality of the market, on its power relations.

The response to all this may well be that we can have equality without the market and capture consistency that way. Doesn't the liberal conception of human nature as an aggregate of personal interests stand on its own without the market? Liberal egalitarianism as an ideal would, then, cease to be tied to the state's protection of the market, even though contemporary liberal political moralists, like Ackerman, Dworkin, and Rawls, all assume the market at the base of their reasoning. The problem with this is that it leaves an arbitrary conception of human nature, one tied to no social reality. To make the liberal conception of human nature worthy of consideration, it must be linked with some actual social

287

tendency. The only tendency with which it is compatible is the atomizing tendency of the market. Thus liberal egalitarianism would become a merely ideal conception of radical justice, in the sense of Chapter 5, were it not linked to the market and the state promoting the market.

22

Revolutionary anarchism

For the anarchist, the state itself is an abomination; it deals un-
fairly with its subjects not by accident but unavoidably. A transformation based on an anarchist sense of radical justice is not one to
an equalizing state or to a socialist state; it leads away from the
state altogether. Once social democratic and communist states
proved their potential for equaling the unfairness of earlier forms
of the state, the anarchist logic was revived in the minds of many of
those who felt a social transformation was needed. This logic underlies the thinking of those in the late 1960s and early 1970s who
pressed the liberating force of what were called autonomous movements without considering it necessary for a state to integrate
these movements. Is the state, in fact, so infected with its brutal
past that a socialist state would be but one more abomination?

1. The anarchist's essentialist critique of the state

A commitment to liberty lies behind anarchist critiques of the
state. In these critiques the state appears as an authority that
crushes both individual and collective liberty. Since it conflicts
with liberty, state authority cannot be fully legitimate.[1] Anarchists
might admit that liberty would be restricted to some degree, apart
from the state, by society itself, which even in the best of cases
needs repression for self-protection. Supposedly, though, the state
goes beyond this by crushing liberty unnecessarily. There are numerous ways the modern state in particular violates liberty. Anarchists often refer to the following three.

First, there is the iron law of bureaucracy according to which,
beginning with the industrial epoch, states have become more and
more dominated by their own bureaucracies. Democracy ceases to
signify popular political control as the bureaucracy gains more
control over the state. This is the *fonctionnairisme* that Proudhon
said leads to the absorption of all local and individual life into the
machinery of administration.[2]

289

A second criticism locates the essence of the state in the physical repression of dissidents and in the armed pursuit of its interests against other states. Those who call for an armed state as a necessity for security are reminded of its role in actually increasing the level of insecurity. For Emma Goldman, the anarchist pursuit of liberty can take place only when it is recognized that all forms of government rest on violence.[3] The Bolshevik state, like others, rested on coercion, which naturally evolved "into systematic violence, oppression, and terrorism."

A third attack on the state points to its reification.[4] The state is supposed to be an instrument rather than an end in itself, but it nonetheless does come to defend, through its sovereign power, its own power to act as an instrument. This makes of it a thing in itself that reacts hostilely to any challenge and works ceaselessly to enhance its image.[5]

The revolutionary anarchist accepts these three criticisms as a basis for the implication that an acceptable transformation should lead away from the state altogether.[6] The same criticisms could, though, be used to make a conservative point. According to these criticisms, no attempt at transforming the state to meet the demands of radical justice will succeed. The conservative concludes it is wasted effort to undertake a transformation of the state at all. The revolutionary anarchist and the conservative critic of the state thus share an important premise. Each believes that in essence the modern industrial state is inevitably flawed, however it might be changed. Reforms would not alter the roots of those features of the state that render it so vulnerable to criticism.

I shall speak of this as the essentialist view of the state. Essentialism holds that things of a given kind have a common essence. In this case, states have a common essence of being incompatible with freedom. Anything that follows from the essence is a necessary feature, thereby making it necessary that the state is flawed. The opposed view is empiricism, which rejects essences. The consistent empiricist would thus allow the state to assume a variety of forms as circumstances change. The variety is wide enough so that the state can be reformed to avoid the criticisms above. For the empiricist there are no real necessities and hence no impossibilities. It should then be possible to transform existing states into benign ones with a minimum of adjustments. I will argue that there is a middle position between essentialism and empiricism.[7] In this middle position, essences are accepted, as they are not by empiricism, but they are not the same throughout a kind, as they

290

are for essentialism. However, the revolutionary anarchist position is an essentialist one since it takes the three criticisms of the current state to follow from an essence common to all states and hence to reveal the impossibility of the reform of any state.[8] From an empiricist perspective, though, those criticisms do not cut so deep since the state is malleable enough to avoid them after reforms. On the middle position, it is granted that the crushing of freedom follows from the essence of contemporary states, without granting that all conceivable states must have an essence of this sort. For the middle position, then, there are structural restraints, unrecognized by the empiricist, limiting what can be done to reform contemporary states.

An essentialist position on the state could have several dimensions to it. There is the *organizational dimension,* along which it is claimed that certain organizational structures are essential to the state. We are familiar with the theme that the organization of the state is inevitably directed by only a small number of people.[9] This leads to a high degree of bureaucratic centralization, repression, and reification of power. A state organization to be set in motion by masses of people is allegedly an impossibility or at least highly unstable. A corollary is that there is an intense competition among elites for state power. This is the dimension of greatest interest to the anarchist.

There is also an *economic dimension,* along which it is claimed that the state can promote only certain kinds of economy. What kinds of economy are these? Here the theme is that the state can function to promote only those economies in which a small number of people control the producers, who constitute a much larger number. Again we have a theme that asserts a close relation between the state and a minority. Economic systems without the exploitation of producers will then exist only in nonstate societies. Finally, there is the *dimension of social struggle,* along which it is claimed that the state is an instrument for advancing only certain forms of social struggle. The theme here repeats once more the state's bias toward a minority: The state functions to support the struggles of dominant classes to realize their interests, only when they are minority classes.

Socialists, of both the Marxist and non-Marxist persuasions, have for some time denied the economic theme and the theme of social struggle. They suppose that a state could serve a nonexploitative economy and the interests of a majority class. But what good is this if the state remains an elitist organizational structure?

291

The anarchist can point to numerous ills resulting from elite organization. A socialist state will not escape from these ills. Whatever its advantages – resulting from economic and social changes – it is in the end to be rejected because it is a state. Denying that the state is essentially a servant of an exploitative economy and of the interests of a social minority is not enough to make the socialist state acceptable. The socialist can, then, no longer afford to ignore the claim that the state must be organized along elitist lines.[10] Indeed, even the economic and social gains that the socialist state allegedly promotes will be eroded by its elitist organization. So, the anarchist argues, to preserve those gains there can be no state.

Socialists did break with essentialism by thinking that, though it may in the past have been in the nature of things that the state supported a dominant minority, the state need not always have such an essence. They affirmed the possibility of a state that would serve the interests of a majority. They justifiably did not accept historical verification of the state's support of minorities as the basis for a common essence for all states. The spell of enthusiasm had been broken, but only long enough for the essentialists to prepare their counterattack based on the unavoidability of elite organization of the state.

2. Socialism as shared control over production

Before testing this counterattack, I want to sketch out a few of the salient features of the socialist ideal. This ideal has been shared by many revolutionary anarchists as a part of their radical conception of justice. Revolutionary anarchism raises the issue as to whether a society that comes close to realizing this ideal can be ruled by a state. If we can show that the socialist ideal can be realized along with a state, then the anarchist's essentialism about the state is wrong.

It is odd that in some formulations of it socialism presupposes the state. This is the case when socialism is understood as a social system within which the state has taken control over the means of production. But just what state is it that takes control? The problem is that there is no neutral conception of the state available to insert here. We are unable to say without circularity that the state referred to in this formulation is a state that reproduces a socialist society, for here a socialist society means nothing more to us than *a society with a state* that controls the means of production. Inevita-

292

bly, we would have to fall back on a conception of the state gotten by surveying past and present states. The conception of the state resulting from such a survey is one within which minority control of the economy, minority interests, and minority rule are promoted. So if socialism presupposes the state, that state will be thought to promote a dominant minority.

The reason such a formulation is odd is now obvious: Socialism, as we noted, makes a break with past and present states by challenging their bias toward dominant minorities. This challenge is forgotten when socialism defines itself in terms of a conception of the state that inevitably contains a bias in favor of dominant minorities.

A conception of socialism should, then, be formulable without presupposing the state, and thus without making socialism immediately objectionable to the revolutionary anarchist. This requirement can be satisfied with the idea of shared control. *In a socialist society, control in matters relating to production is widely shared among producers in such a way that the shares of control are not diminished because of social status.* Diminution of control because of one's gender or one's race, being based on social status, would be unallowable within socialism. The sharing of control among producers would tend to eliminate class distinctions since the share of control of those who are not producers would tend to vanish. Excessive male or white control of production tends to vanish, not because class distinctions tend to vanish but only because the share among producers, however decided, is not decided on the basis of social status.

Producers in a socialist society form a "community of free individuals" in the double sense that by sharing control they are not locked into a production process controlled by another class for its ends and that by not having their shares diminished by social status they do not dominate one another in the production process.[11] This freedom in regard to production is valued not in itself but only in relation to a conception of humans that differs fundamentally from the liberal conception of Chapter 21, according to which different humans were motivated by various aggregates of personal interests.

The new conception of humans posits a different motivation for them. Now the motivating factor for humans is "the universal development of the individual."[12] The notion of universal development refers to the fact that individuals develop by extending the scope of their community rather than merely by increasing the

293

number of personal interests they satisfy. They make progress in shedding provincial antagonisms and in grasping the special needs of different peoples. Through the sharing of control in production, when production itself is, as a result of its development, no longer a local but a universal process, the individual is connected with individuals across the globe. The sharing of control develops producers universally as production becomes more interconnected. The community of free producers thus promotes the realization of this new conception of human nature. Without shared control, the producer is only a tool in global production and hence does not develop universally by becoming part of a global community.

The notion of shared control is given social importance through the struggles of lower classes and oppressed groups against their lack of control over matters related to production. Their struggle is one not of isolated individuals but of individuals who recognize that the effectiveness of their present struggle requires a commitment to a sharing of the control they wrest from others. It is crucial, then, not to replace the idea of "shared control" with that of "equal control," which suggests an equality of the liberal sort that depends on the discreteness of individuals as centers of personal interests. Shared control is control within an entire process of production. This process itself will set the degree of the equality of the sharing. Socialist justice posits this shared control of production as a holistic condition behind distribution, which is absent in liberal justice.

3. Political dominance and state organization

We come back now to the question of the elite organization of the state. I shall argue that a true socialist state will not be elitist, since that would be incompatible with the political dominance within it of the majority. But the revolutionary anarchists's essentialism makes minority political dominance the rule. Even if we ignore this essentialism, there is the anarchist objection – to be dealt with in Section 4 – that liberty is crushed not just by politically dominant minorities but also by majorities. Dissidents are repressed by ideology if not by force, whether it is a minority or a majority that has political dominance.

To respond to the anarchist view of state organization, I appeal to the class base of the socialist state. The essentialism of the revolutionary anarchist abstracts from this class base. It is through political dominance that the state's class base is revealed. When

294

one or several classes jointly gain political dominance, they get the backing of the state for their basic class interests.[13] Among their basic interests will be their interest in displacing from economic dominance those minority groups that were economically dominant in order to share economic dominance jointly themselves. Getting the backing of the state is, of course, qualified by the demands of justice; the state backs the basic class interests of a politically dominant group within the limits of state justice. Through justice the socialist state will also back certain of the interests of hitherto economically dominant groups but normally not the interests of any of them in regaining economic dominance. It was noted in Chapter 13 that a group that is politically dominant need not be a ruling group. But the policies and personnel selected by a ruling group will, within the limits of state justice, accord with the interests of a politically dominant group. We can assert that unless the lower classes – or some one of them – gain political dominance there will never be a socialist state, one that promotes the development of a socialist society, that is, a society in which those lower classes share economic dominance. Specifically, unless the working class moves into political dominance there will be no state that promotes socialism, that is, no socialist state.

How does this relate to the essentialism of the anarchist? This view – that states must function through organizations directed by elites – makes sense in application to a hypothetical socialist state only if the factor of political dominance is ignored. The political dominance of groups making up a majority dictates a form of state organization that is not elitist. The reason for this is that one of the things a politically dominant majority will either have or press for is widely shared control of production. The majority has been restricted in its control, and an expansion of control is consistently one of its demands. But a state whose elite organization restricts a wide sharing of political power will also attempt to restrict a wide sharing of economic control. For an economy controlled by producers is a fertile base for the organization of councils that will challenge the rule of an elite.

It is easy enough to ignore political dominance in its relation to state organization. Political dominance has always been the dominance of minority classes and never the dominance of majority classes. Thus there has been no enduring break in the elitist organization of the state. When we do posit a break in the character of political dominance, so that we are no longer dealing with the dominance of a minority class, the familiar inference to elitist orga-

295

nization is no longer valid. The political dominance of the working class favors organizing the state in such a way that its direction is widely shared.

Why would anyone think that an elitist state could promote socialism? Briefly, by abstracting from political dominance; for, as noted, a necessary condition for a socialist state is the political dominance of the working class. Since elitist organization of the state would attempt to restrict widely shared control of production by producers, it is incompatible with political dominance of the working class, and it hence makes the socialist state impossible. So long, though, as we allow the abstraction from political dominance – which means at bottom considering state rule without its grounding in the reality of class – it is prefectly possible to imagine cases where elites rule in order to promote socialism.[14] Benign elites actually could broaden the segment of the population controlling production. But since the abstraction is a falsifying one, socialism cannot be promoted very far under elite rule.

The Soviet state has been the centerpiece in the view that a socialist state is inevitably top-down. The rise of the political power of the working class, which was manifest in the taking of state power by the soviets in October 1917, was quickly reversed. In conditions of economic collapse, many workers returned to the countryside; in fighting to save the revolution from internal and external attack, the Red Army came to rely on the old czarist officers' corps; a political alliance of workers and peasants couldn't get off the ground, as detachments of workers and poor peasants, with nothing to offer in exchange, collected grain from other peasants; and the party, as an instrument of political dominance, integrated fewer and fewer workers and slipped under the control of a new social group. Formal notice was taken of this reversal of the political rise of the working class by the formation of the so-called Workers' Opposition in the party by Alexander Shlyapnikov and Alexandra Kollontai in 1920.[15] Without its becoming political dominant, there would be a socialist state in name only.

This diagnosis of the Soviet state differs from that which emphasizes its lack of representative democracy. According to the Eurocommunist critique of the Bolshevik revolution, the degeneration of the revolution resulted from its failure to maintain representative democracy.[16] That critique emphasizes organizational structure. In contrast with the revolutionary anarchist, the Eurocommunist thinks a socialist state need not be contradictory. All that is required is to thwart elitist organization with parliamentary forms. If organization were the nub of the matter, this "solution" to the problem of the socialist state would be plausible. Mere organizational structures are, though, not all we must be concerned with. Representative democracy can quickly become a talk shop while elite control becomes the underlying reality. This happens when a turn in the tide of the class struggle erodes the political dominance of the working class. It is, of course, important to find the proper mix of direct democracy of the true soviet type with representative democracy of the classical parliamentary type. However, this is not the primary thing: Without the political dominance of the appropriate social elements, no state, parliamentary or otherwise, pursues the development of socialism. Thus, when working-class political dominance has failed to occur or be maintained, due to factors of the sort that reversed the rise of its political power in the USSR, it is senseless to look to organizational forms to explain the collapse of a socialist state.

4. The protection of liberty in the socialist state

What might some of the institutions of a socialist state actually look like? So far we have imposed two constraints on such institutions. The first has to do with the function of the state, which is to promote the development of socialism. The second constraint has to do with the political dominance of the working class within such a state. Political dominance of the working class was seen to be incompatible with organizing the state so that it would be ruled by only a small number. Control over the decisions giving direction to the state must then be widely shared.

It is easy to see that there is a third constraint on the socialist state, one having to do with justice. The political dominance of the working class does not relieve the socialist state of the necessity of ruling for all. A strong opposition from other classes or even from parts of the working class itself, such as occupational, racial, and gender groups, would undermine the development of a socialist society. Such an opposition would make it difficult for the socialist state to perform its special function. It is imperative to guarantee rights for such groups and to build those rights into the institutions of the socialist state.

In view of these constraints, the socialist state is less vulnerable to the charge that it, like elite-run states, crushes liberty. Bureaucracy, repression, and the reification of power become qualitatively less than in minority-run states. There ceases to be a basis for the

297

horror of the state from which the anarchist argument derives its appeal.

First, in the case of the military, these various constraints lead to drastic changes. Military policy for the imperial state is set in bodies like the National Security Council of the United States and in the Defense Council of the Soviet Union, whose recommendations go to the Politburo. These bodies typify the elite direction of the imperial state. Where military production is a sizable factor in a national economy, elite control of military policy conflicts both with the broadly shared control of production demanded by socialism and with the broadly shared political control implied by working-class political dominance. Institutions like the National Security Council and the Defense Council would not, then, be possible within our constraints. At the very least, larger bodies such as the Congress and the Supreme Soviet would have to capture control over military policy. But this is only a beginning. The military of the imperial state is run by an elite, a fact that cannot be reconciled with political dominance of the working class. The election of military officers, the formation of military soviets, and the integration of military units within the population are elementary demands of a socialist republic.

Of course, it is ludicrous to think of such a democratized military winning imperialist wars or conducting nuclear arms races. This makes a socialist state vulnerable in a hostile world. But seeking invulnerability in a hostile world will erode the political dominance of the working class, violate socialist justice, and make the goal of the state something other than socialism. How then can the revolution be saved? At crucial times, state power is not worth the effort since by capturing it one gives up the goals one wanted it for. The socialist movement must at such times return to unofficial status within popular bodies. This is not for the reason the anarchist gives; it is not because state power is inherently elitist, but it is because an all-out defense of state power against elitist states tends to rest on elitist power.

Second, to the extent that the socialist state uses repression, the repression results not from an arbitrary repressiveness inherent in it but from a legitimate need for self-defense. What, though, is legitimate self-defense? Part of the answer comes from noting that the socialist state is committed to promoting widely shared control of production. To repress a minority will, though, inevitably involve restricting its share of the control of production. For otherwise it could use its economic power to try to win back the rights

298

denied to it by repression. So the economic function of the state will itself protect minorities from arbitrary repression. And this function will then add weight to the demand, under state justice, for protecting minorities. Political dominance by a majority will not leave minorities unprotected since it is political dominance in a state aiming at widely shared economic control. Self-defense is legitimate only where there is a grave threat both to this goal of shared economic control and to the goal of widely shared political control. To be effective the repression used in such a case may need to be organized centrally and hence be state repression. But it is no more repressive than if it were the spontaneous action of unofficial groups defending their widely shared economic control.

Third, the enormity of the problem of reducing the authoritarianism of contemporary states should not be underestimated. Offe suggests that the possibility of a socialist state is more real at present due to the recent shift in the capitalist state from reliance on institutionalized forms entirely within the state to reliance on policy-making bodies of a corporatist nature at the periphery of the state.[17] These corporatist bodies are closer to society, and through them the state reduces its relative autonomy from the society. When control of production is widely shared in the society, this reduction of state autonomy promotes widely shared political control and undercuts elite control. Offe is right that there is contracting out of policy making to joint labor–management boards, to community investment boards, and to blue ribbon commissions to study the best way for a state to intervene.

This reliance on corporatist bodies is, though, not a substitute for the more institutionalized state but only an adjunct to it. Also, such bodies coopt elites from various social sectors to get the full cooperation of these elites with the institutionalized state. It is, then, hard to imagine that such bodies could be genuine transmission belts from below to the state. In 1986 in the United States a Carnegie task force formulated policy on professionalizing schoolteaching without a single practicing schoolteacher in its ranks. Such corporatist bodies could promote non-elite political control only as a result of an alteration of the state itself. Only when the core institutions of the state encourage a broader sharing of political power will the contracting out of policy making be more than an effort to get wider support within the elite for a state already directed by a section of that elite.

The anarchist challenge cannot be met by Offe's appeal to a new corporatism. To meet it we must move from the organizational level at which we speak of corporatism to the political level at which we speak of class dominance. It is the political dominance of the working class in a socialist state that prevents the consolidation of ruling institutions that by lying beyond mass control would destroy a socialist state.

23

Democracy and the transition to socialism

I shall try to drive a wedge between two familiar views of the possibility of democracy in the transition to socialism. One of these views is that after the triumph of a revolution an authoritarian state is inevitable. The tasks set by the transitional period call for authoritarian decisiveness. The other view is that the group that assumes power loses legitimacy unless it promotes full direct democracy in the form of a system of councils. The revolutionary triumph was, after all, based not just on such a group but also on a broad movement for enhanced participation.

1. A false dichotomy

The Leninist view of *The State and Revolution* gives support to each of these views, without however making clear how they are to be reconciled. On the side of organizational structure, his model contains a hierarchy of councils – of soviets – rooted in the activity of popular bodies. The highest soviet is linked to this base through the democratic selection of delegates. On the side of tasks to be accomplished, his model contains a list of repressive tasks that can be performed only by what he calls a dictatorship. The transition must begin the construction of a socialist society, and this calls for confronting the counterrevolution and insisting upon discipline.[1]

Commitment to the Leninist model has created the illusion that full-blown direct democracy is on the agenda for a transitional period. The illusion has dangerous results. For when it gives way in the face of postrevolutionary events, those who had been committed to the model proceed with its repressive tasks. Observers outside the revolutionary country who are themselves committed to the same model have a pat answer to the undemocratic turn of events. They expected direct democracy to have been in place on the morning after the triumph of the revolution. Since it wasn't, the lower classes must have been betrayed by their leaders.[2]

It is worth considering what form of democratic organization

301

might coexist with state functions called for by a transition to socialism. The model I will suggest poses a less ambitious ideal for democracy within the transition. Nonetheless, it preserves a democratic base adequate to prevent aborting the transition to socialism. It is only by abandoning the ideal of full-blown direct democracy for the transition that it can be reintroduced later on. The price paid for insisting on full-blown direct democracy at the outset without a fallback to a less ambitious ideal for democracy may well be the authoritarian state.

Instead of assuming that councils constitute the state, my model puts mass organizations, which are outside the state, in a bargaining relation with the state. Separating the two does not leave the state uncontrolled. Through bargaining with mass organizations, the power of the state is restricted. The power of the mass organizations is not state power, as it would be in a council system. This general theme will be developed through the example of Nicaragua in the 1980s.

The Sandinista revolution has been the focus of attention during the 1980s for all those interested in the nature of the transition to socialism. That revolution has increased the political power of the lower classes and decreased that of capitalists and landowners. A continuation of this empowerment of the lower classes would indicate that a transition to socialism is under way. There has been plenty of advice from inside as well as outside Nicaragua on how best to carry through the transition to socialism. This advice falls along a spectrum between two extreme positions.

At one extreme there is the view that the revolutionary state needs to assert itself more decisively.[3] The state is staffed at the top by those who through their role in overthrowing the Somoza regime and in beginning the restructuring of society are, in this view, best able to carry through the revolution. The state should not then have to tolerate opposition from the church, dissident unions, minorities, and capitalist political parties. Not only this, but the state should not have to encourage the growth of genuinely independent mass organizations; their independence might lead them to take initiatives at odds with the priorities of the state.[4] When one adds that the revolution has been under attack from U.S. imperialism, it is clear that a state is needed that can ignore the immediate demands of the mass organizations and suppress organizations opposed to the revolution.

At the other end of the spectrum of advice there is the view that the revolutionary state should be run by a system of councils repre-

302

senting urban workers, rural workers, women, and neighborhoods.[5] The councils for these sections of the nation would feed into a general council that would not bargain with an already constituted state but would itself be the central body of the state. Only this system will make the classes supporting the revolution truly politically dominant and prevent the state from being run by a ruling elite for any ends it chooses. Those who offer this advice are aware that a state is necessary in the transitional period and even afterward. But their conception of such a state is one that has already begun the process of withering away. It has begun to lose the relative autonomy characteristic of presocialist states. Councils rule the country directly, and state ministries are reduced to doing the bidding of these councils. There is then less room for a gulf to open up between agencies of the state and the initiatives of the politically dominant classes. The restriction on worker takeovers of plants, the pressure to keep wages from going up,[6] and the bans on strikes provoked by the CIA-backed war have all been pointed to as ways the Nicaraguan state asserts its autonomy at the expense of the power of the lower classes.

Neither form of advice is useful in the case of the Nicaraguan revolution, and we might suspect that neither is useful in the case of other revolutions in this period, even revolutions in countries more developed than Nicaragua.

Emphasizing state autonomy, with the first form of advice, can sever the connection between the state and the demands of the revolution. By isolating itself from the mass organizations and by taking action to destroy any oposition, the state will tend to postpone the realization of the demands deriving from the revolution and to give primacy to the consolidation of its own power. But then it will have to rule not on the basis of a pattern of justice rooted in revolutionary demands but on the basis of a new and more limited pattern of justice compatible with its consolidating its power.

Emphasizing the direct rule of the lower classes through councils, with the second form of advice, may incapacitate the state for tasks that are essential in the transition to socialism. Wars against counterrevolutionaries must be fought; productivity increases must be orchestrated to counter shortages resulting from boycotts; wage and price policies must be implemented. These tasks call for a state with a high degree of autonomy, rather than for a state that is withering away. Emphasis on direct rule often comes from the alarmist attitude that without direct rule the interests of the lower classes will be held hostage by an elite until it realizes its own interests.

303

There is certainly need for constant scrutiny of state leadership. But such an attitude of alarm is not fully justified when not only are the interests of the lower classes given primacy by the state but the mass organizations of those classes are sufficiently independent to challenge an attempt by the state to make other interests primary. Pressure from the mass organizations can effectively dissuade a state leadership – coming from outside the lower classes and forming the state as armed rebels rather than as class leaders – from overturning the revolutionary agenda in favor of one that merely consolidates the power of the leadership.[7] The state leaders will then continue to work in the context of the revolutionary demands. A major advance toward realizing these demands still counts as a victory even though this progress is made by a state that separates itself from the lower classes. Of course, direct rule through councils remains one of the demands to be realized, though in the circumstances it cannot be the first of the demands to be realized.

2. A third way: bargaining

The transition to socialism is not, then, advanced either by cynical power politics or by purist participatory politics. Between these extremes lies *the politics of bargaining*. Bargaining helps win popular support for state measures, in particular for measures limiting the losses of some and the benefits of others – for the state's pattern of justice. The mechanism for this is the free bargaining between the popular bodies emerging from the revolution and the state led by revolutionary figures.

The function of the revolutionary state is to facilitate the transition to socialism, but its effectiveness in doing this depends on its being held to something approximating the conception of justice that motivated support for the revolution. It is held to this standard through the process of bargaining with the mass organizations. It is assumed that these organizations, like the councils of the council state, are internally democratic. This, though, is only one dimension of democracy in the transitional state. Bargaining of itself adds a second dimension to democracy in the transitional state, for it restricts the power of the state when it has to accept, more or less fully, initiatives coming from below. Unless the power of the state is restricted through bargaining, the internal democracy of the mass organizations will be snuffed out and there will be no basis for a transition to the higher expression of democracy in the council state.

304

The transitional state may be democratized in a third way through a parliamentary system. But a parliament without mass organizations is not sufficient for holding the state to the task of the transition. Bargaining with the mass organizations keeps the state from forgetting that it is not its own interests but those of the lower classes and the oppressed that are to be advanced by the transition. The social context created by the revolution becomes the context in which democracy operates. Accordingly, the form of democracy will be modified to accommodate itself to this new context. Mass organizations of the lower classes and the oppressed become a major feature of this context, and it is not then surprising that democracy accommodates to this feature.[8]

Purism wants nothing to do with bargaining with state leadership and is not satisfied until the old institutions of the state have been replaced by councils and the administrative bodies set up by them. There is no juxtaposition of state leadership and mass for the purist, and even the idea of mass organization is suspect since it implies a center of leadership outside the mass. For the purist, bargaining is a compromise that falls short of those limits on benefits and losses that the mass organizations themselves would impose. Why stop with the state's conception of transitional justice when one can demand direct rule itself?

In contrast, cynical power politics wants to be able to manipulate the popular bodies – the mass organizations and a parliamentary assembly if there is one – in order to assure a successful transition without the interference of well-intentioned citizens, whose level of consciousness also suffers from being in transition.[9] Cynicism wants nothing to do with bargaining with popular bodies, which can only blur the goal and impede the process. It allows a minimal pattern of state justice, according to which limits on benefits and losses for the duration of the transition are to be set by the necessity of the leadership's retaining state power. This is a minimal pattern since it puts the popular demands of the revolution on ice for the duration.

The politics of bargaining has a central place as revolutions seize state power. The conflicts within the revolutionary camp itself make bargaining an attractive political method. There will be different views on the pace of nationalizations, on land reform, on the scope of the market, on the degree of autonomy allowed to minorities, on the extent of press censorship, and on strikes. Bargaining over these issues diffuses rumors of conspiracies and deters defections that would result from power plays.[10]

305

The existence of these conflicts affects the issue of state justice because the conflicts concern the distribution of benefits and losses. If the leadership is to be able to rule it cannot simply impose a pattern of justice. Yet the leadership cannot passively accept a pattern of justice advocated by the mass organizations. A revolutionary leadership will, then, need to set in motion a bargaining process in relation to these conflicts if it is to be able to rule without abandoning the revolution.[11] A pattern of justice that facilitates rule will reflect the demands of the revolution with distortions due to bargaining with a leadership bent on consolidating state power. Even when there is bargaining, the radical justice of the earlier phase will be in continuity with, but not identical with, the state justice of the later phase of the revolution.

There is certainly a parallel between bargaining in a transitional state and interest-group pressure in a capitalist democracy. But the differences are essential for characterizing the transitional state. First, there is a class difference. Mass organizations represent lower classes and oppressed groups. In a capitalist democracy interest groups also represent dominant classes and oppressing groups. Second, there is a difference in state autonomy. The transitional state, its leading party, or both will work at a regional and national level with mass organizations. The state integrates itself to some degree with the society rather than waiting for petitioners while standing fully above society.[12] Third, there is a difference in equality. The transitional state bargains with mass organizations knowing that it depends on them, rather than on its ministries alone, to implement policies either agreed to directly or agreed to pending approval of a parliament. In a capitalist democracy, the state itself has the power to implement its policies. Fourth, there are differences in goals. The transitional state bargains with a mass organization on the basis of a shared commitment to promote the interests of the lower classes and the oppressed over those of dominant groups.

These four differences between bargaining and pressures suggest that bargaining will typically not be a matter of generating proposals outside the state and then looking for sponsors within the state who are willing to fight for those proposals. Rather, bargaining generates proposals that often shape government policy directly and then provide the framework for government-sponsored legislation.

There are anticipations of this view of the transition to socialism in the work of Rosa Luxemburg. Much of her writing was devoted to the revolutionary party under capitalism rather than to the tran-

306

sition to socialism. There is, though, a continuity between her views on the party under capitalism and her comments on the Bolshevik state. The party, she says in 1899 in *Social Reform or Revolution*, must work between "two reefs: abandonment of the mass character or abandonment of the final aim." A rigid adherence to either mass character or final aim to the exclusion of the other would be disastrous; yet the proper blend of each at a given time is arrived at not by a formula but through interaction between a class and its leadership.

In 1906 in *Mass Strike* she rejected the slogan that the economic trade union struggle was separate from the political party struggle. The trade union struggle needs political direction whereas the political struggle needs a mass base. Thus the trade unions were to be integrated into the revolutionary party. The trade unions, nonetheless, are not to accept passively the political lead of the party but are to be a factor in the determination of tactics and policy. Conversely, the party is not to abdicate its leadership role to the trade unions. The party must lead since, among other things, not only trade unions but also organizations of the oppressed, with apparently divergent goals from the trade unions, will be integrated into the party. The party must then "know how to subordinate the present pains of this colorful herd of recruits" to the ultimate goal of a society without oppression, as she put it in "Organizational Questions of Russian Social Democracy" in 1904.

All of this gets carried over into her comments on the Bolshevik state made in 1918 in "The Russian Revolution." The "spiritual transformation" required for living a socialist life could not, she thought, be carried through by decree. That transformation would be a historical product in which "the whole mass of the people must take part." To move from egoism to social instinct, from inertia to mass initiative, it is necessary to return to "the broadest democracy." For her the dictatorship of the working class must be "the work of the *class* and not of a little leading minority in the name of the class." But there is no hint of an objectionable purism here, since she has already made it clear that leadership and participation are complementary.[13]

3. The transitional state

To get a better understanding of the politics of bargaining, we need to discuss the nature of the state itself within the transition to socialism. At the structural level, there are both the function and the form of state rule to consider. As to its function, the transitional state will promote the emergence of a new social order: socialism. It does this while extending the empowerment of the lower classes. In the new order after this transition there will be widely shared control of production, a control that is not diminished by gender, race, or other forms of social status. Promoting the emergence of this new order will involve altering the previously existing social order in ways necessary to bring about the new order. Of itself, this does not imply that there is a continuously increasing broadening of control through the transition period. There may be shifts up and down in increased breadth of control as the state maneuvers to destroy the main institutions that are obstacles to the new order and to destroy armed forces attempting to reestablish the old order.

The form of state rule in the transition period makes up, partially at least, for this wavering on continuously broadening control of production by the lower classes. It forces limits on the *means* rather than concentrating on the *goal*. Here the form of rule is determined by the requirements of governability – the requirements that must be met if the state is to be able to take the measures it decides upon for realizing its goal. If the transitional state cannot implement the measures it has adopted for promoting the emergence of socialism because of inertia or opposition, it must adjust to this situation not by taking repressive measures that would very likely thwart the goal of increased control but by looking for institutions that will legitimate itself. These institutions will guarantee certain limits on the sacrifices to be made by the people and on the prerogatives to be enjoyed by the state. The state cannot enjoy unlimited power to demand sacrifices to realize its goal of promoting the emergence of socialism.

When a revolution has occurred, the demand by the lower classes for more widely shared control will itself be one of their foremost demands, as it clear from all revolutions of the twentieth century. Assuming this demand is not immediately and fully met, the lower classes will not rule directly through councils and there will be a separation of the state from the lower classes. The demand for greater control will be raised by popular bodies in face of such a transitional state. Governability will, then, require that limits be put on the state by giving these popular bodies a role in determining the road ahead. The limits, worked out by these bodies in bargaining with the state, will reflect, weakly perhaps, the demand for control raised by the popular bodies. Beyond this there will be institutional guarantees of greater equality and more adequate social services. In addition, the interests of small popular groups will be respected as a necessary condition of taking seriously the state's commitment to ending exploitation and oppression. All of this is required by governability and thus makes up the state's form of rule. Since these requirements of governability put limits on the benefits and the losses that people may enjoy or suffer, they make up the state's concrete pattern of justice. It is not a justice administered from on high but a justice arrived at by bargaining.

In addition to the structural level of function and form, there is the level of social forces. Revolutions make otherwise tidy maps of class alliances obsolete, and a transitional state is pressured by novel mixes of social forces. Normally there is no one class that is politically dominant in a transitional society. Instead, expressions such as "the popular classes" or "the masses" are used to signify that it is an alliance of classes, exclusive of the large capitalists and their militarist allies, that has political dominance. The popular classes, that is, get the backing of the state for their interests, at least within the limits of state justice. Political dominance translates, at the level of structure, into the state's functioning to promote a certain social goal. The interests of most of the popular classes cannot be realized without an end to capitalism and the beginning of widely shared control. So the political dominance of the popular classes translates into the revolutionary state's functioning to promote the emergence of socialism. Its so functioning may be, as in Nicaragua in the mid 1980s, less than explicit, but so long as it puts the interests of the popular classes first, including their interest in empowerment, the state is promoting the emergence of socialism. State subsidies for capitalist enterprises have entailed sacrifices for workers and peasants. These are, though, tactical losses rather than a strategy of making capitalists politically dominant. In revolutionary Nicaragua, procapitalists like Alfonso Robelo and Arturo Cruz understood the political dominance of the *clases populares*. They refused to participate for long in the state's internal politics because without the political dominance of the capitalist class it was futile to do so.

A ruling group, as distinct from the politically dominant alliance, has direct control of the state. It controls access to top positions in the state in a manner that goes beyond merely filtering out advocates of interests opposed to those of the politically dominant alliance. A ruling group can see to it that militants from the politically dominant alliance are barred from top state positions. A ruling group must represent its policies as truly in the interest of everyone. But a politically dominant alliance may have the support of the state even though that alliance, but not the state, may represent its policies as opposed to the interests of some classes. In modern times, ruling groups have achieved and sustained their position with the help of political parties. The ruling group in Nicaragua is composed mostly of Sandinistas; it has used the Sandinista National Liberation Front (FSLN) to bolster its power.

The transitional state will need to make investments to raise the standard of living and to reduce dependence on the economies of other states. Assuming it has the funds, how does it invest? Does it keep labor-intensive production in order to assure jobs for the growing population, or does it insist on maximum growth through a balanced capital-intensive production?[14] It is true that the increase in unemployment from an emphasis on capital-intensive production would be of limited duration. Peasants would be forced off the land, and backyard industry would collapse now and in the immediate future; thereafter there would be an increased capacity for supporting more workers through the production of a greater mass of consumer goods. On the basis of the state's function of providing a transition to greater popular control, can it, then, be argued that the immediate and short-term sacrifices of employment are justified? Suppose, though, the demands of radical justice included a call for land distribution and expanded employment. Then impatience on the part of the state for capital-intensive production will clash with the call for land and jobs that helped to unite the opposition to the old regime and the support for the new one.

There are no abstract resolutions of this problem. The state can argue that it would be difficult to promote the emergence of socialism at the slow pace allowed by labor-intensive production. Yet the mass organizations can argue that jobs and land were among the motivating factors of the revolution. To ignore either argument might destroy the transitional process. Ignoring the argument of the state would run the risk of eliminating the goal of socialism, whereas ignoring the argument of the mass organizations would run the risk of either making it impossible for the state to rule or forcing the state to back up an autocratic rule with repression. To avoid what Luxemburg calls these "reefs" of abandoning the goal or the mass character of the revolution, bargaining must mediate between the impatience of state leaders and the righteousness of the militants. In Nicaragua, the initial emphasis on forming state and cooperative farms that were to be mechanized gave way by the mid 1980s to an acceleration of the distribution of individual titles.[15] By this shift it was hoped that both the political loyalty and the greater productivity of peasants previously holding insufficient land would be guaranteed.

It must not be thought that, because the state is open to bargaining on such issues, it thereby loses the autonomy it needs. This would undercut the view being developed here that the appropriate relation is an interaction between autonomous forces. Compromises can be reached through bargaining that support the state's ability to rule and still go a certain way toward satisfying the demands of radical justice.

Take, for example, the demand for rapid and sizable increases in personal consumption. This demand will have to be dealt with even in a context like that of Nicaragua in the 1980s where the disruption of the economy by the civil war mounted by the contras and by the boycott imposed by the United States has created shortages in most essentials. Because of the shortages, workers' wages could not rise universally without depriving the peasantry of essential resources. Yet strikes by workers in only selected areas of the economy for higher wages would, if successful, fly in the face of the revolutionary aim of greater equality. What is the possibility of a compromise that takes cognizance of the shortages and of the nation's vulnerable position in relation to imperialism?

The Sandinista Workers' Central (CST), the largest trade union federation, focused on winning the support of trade unionists for greater equality and for improved services, rather than cash wages. The struggle for equality included the struggle not just to get equal pay for equal work but also to break down the sex barrier to certain jobs – one of the goals of the mass organization of women – and to end the dictatorial power of the doctors in the health field – one of the goals of the union of health workers, which is in another labor federation. The struggle for improved services included the struggle to obtain transportation to and from work provided by the employer, free lunches at work, and buildings for day-care centers.[16] These measures did not prevent workers from suffering from the shortages. Still, distributional justice was realized not just by the cash wage but by a broad range of measures that together both increase a sense of solidarity and put less strain on the economy.

4. Bargaining and justice

It is tempting to assume that one can say in advance what the state's pattern of justice in the transition period should be. The utilitarian thinker would be tempted to sacrifice the short-term advantages of the mass organizations to the long-term prospect of maximizing utility through building the base for future production. But contractarian thinkers object to such an answer as unfair to those who must make the sacrifices. Their answer is based on having each generation through history consider what would be a fair contribution for it to receive from its immediate predecessor.[17] The socialist society at the end of the transition could not demand great sacrifices from the society within the transition without being willing to make similar sacrifices for its followers. So the contractarian would have us believe that some common formula could in principle be agreed to between all generations. This formula would regulate the bargaining between the state and the mass organizations in the transition period.

This reassuring outcome is possible, though, only after abstracting from the conflict between state leaders and popular organizations in the depiction of the various generations. In short, it abstracts from the very conflict that, in the transitional period at least, gives rise to the question of sacrifices for the future. The utilitarian position does, of course, make an equally grave mistake; it emphasizes the goal pursued by state leaders and downplays the sacrifices of the popular organizations. But the way to rebut the utilitarian is not to ignore the conflict between the state and the populace as the contractarian does when speaking about internally homogeneous generations. If their conflict is ignored, there might be the possibility of a hypothetical agreement on how much each generation is to save for the future. But the agreement will unravel in the actual context in which things are changing under the influence of the conflict between these two social forces. The reason is that the state and the masses of a given generation disagree on precisely how much to sacrifice for the future.

The only formula useful for guiding bargaining is that the shared goal of ultimately spreading control be preserved. This will mean, first, that the bargaining itself should not degenerate into dictation by the state leadership, either directly or through making the mass organizations its mouthpiece. And it will mean, second, that the goals of an initial radical justice, which motivated the revolution, should not be treated as uncompromisable but should be compromised in a way that allows governability. The state's pattern of justice resulting from this formula for bargaining will deal not only with the distribution of goods and services but also with the distribution of control in the process of determining the pattern of justice itself. In fact, bargaining under this formula leads to a pattern of state justice that makes bargaining itself an element of this pattern.

Consider now the broad issues to which this Luxemburgist politics of bargaining will typically be applied in a transitional situation. Among them are the following: How deeply should the state intervene in the market in order to promote greater equality?[18] Are the mass organizations sufficient guarantees of popular democracy without a parliament based on universal suffrage?[19] Will the transition be aborted if the working class fails to gain hegemony over the other groups in the politically dominant alliance? Must the ruling group cease to act merely in the name of the working class and finally become a working-class rather than a multiclass group? We must not be led blindly by classical models in answering these questions.

Consider, for example, the view that the demands of democracy are met by mass organizations even in the absence of a parliament. The only alternative to this classical model is not the familiar social democratic view that mass organizations are an impediment to the full expression of the democratic will in a parliament. Leftist Eurocommunists have elaborated an intermediate alternative which, on the one hand, curbs the reformism of a parliament with pressure from autonomous mass organizations and, on the other hand, curbs the tendency of mass organizations to degenerate into transmission belts for the policies of a leading party with the more atomistic representation of a parliament.[20] But to decide the appropriate mix between mass organizations and parliament, whether in the Chile of 1970 with its parliamentary tradition intact or in the Nicaragua of 1979 where the old state institutions had crumbled, calls for interaction between those who have taken over the state and the mass organizations that they promoted or that emerged spontaneously.

Even the classical model of working-class hegemony within the revolutionary alliance needs to be treated cautiously. On the one hand, hegemony within an alliance may mean that the interests of *some group* in it become interests shared by all the groups of that alliance. But if this is what is meant there is no impossibility in several of the allied groups becoming hegemonic together. At least for those groups whose interests are consistent with one another,

313

each can make the interests of the others its own. When several groups are hegemonic within an alliance, we can speak of a "federated" rather than an "exclusive" hegemony. However, those groups of the alliance with interests that clash with those of this hegemonic section of the alliance will remain in the alliance only so long as this clash remains latent.

On the other hand, hegemony might mean that the interests of *only one group* in the revolutionary alliance have become the interests of the entire alliance. This exclusive transformation of the corporate interests of one group onto a broader plane is a thing of the past. Luxemburg's "colorful herd of recruits" to the transition to socialism is the reality of the day. Each group of the herd makes the interests of the others its own so that there is not an exclusive but a federated hegemony. A place is then made among those groups for the demands of overcoming a variety of forms of oppression. Widely shared control that would perpetuate these forms of oppression would not be wide enough to satisfy the goal of socialism.

The oppressed will not be put off any longer with the promise that their demands will be met at the far end of the transition to socialism. If their interests are not accepted by the working class but it asks them to accept its interest in widely shared control in production, then the working class wants exclusive hegemony, not federated hegemony. Again, abstract formulas are not what is needed to insure that such an exclusive form of hegemony is avoided. It can be avoided if there are strong movements of the oppressed that, despite their large overlap with the working class, insist on their autonomy both in respect to the state and in respect to the working-class movement. Their acceptance of the goals of the working class will come from a reciprocal acceptance by the working class to strive for an end to oppression. Without such a reciprocal acceptance, the demands of the oppressed will be relegated to the level of the optional. Part of the remedy is bargaining between the state and the mass organizations of women and minorities. The other part is the creation of a federated hegemony within the colorful herd itself. Together these remedies will insure that the attack on oppression begins in the transition period rather than being indefinitely postponed.

314

24

The socialist state

The distinction between justice and goal, between the state's form of rule and its function of reproducing an economy, will be the window through which I shall view the socialist state. There are of course other perspectives, but this one clarifies a fundamental difference between the socialist state and other states. It makes clear that the conflict between justice and goal manifest in contemporary states has a different character in the socialist state. The socialist economy itself imposes limits on losses and benefits. These limits are integrated into the socialist state's pattern of justice. Moreover, since relative autonomy for the state implies a conflict between form of rule and economic functioning, there is a reduction of the autonomy of the state when it becomes a socialist state. The attenuation of the conflict between justice and goal depends, though, on the transformation of the economy from one that allows unrestricted benefits, as well as losses, to an economy that has built-in limits on benefits and losses. A pattern of justice is built into the socialist economy without having to be imposed on it by the state.

1. The downward spiral

The contemporary state has a tendency toward crisis due to the conflict between justice and goal. Where such a crisis is evident it will involve a process of interaction between justice and goal that weakens the state's ability to realize either one. On the one hand, there is a weakening of the power of the state to reproduce the economy as a result of the concessions it must make in order to be able to rule; on the other hand, there is a weakening of the ability of the state to rule as a result of the pressure on it to reproduce the economy. Justice weakens the reproductive power of the state, and conversely the reproductive power of the state weakens justice. These trade-offs between justice and the economy are not mere zero-sum trade-offs, which would be harmful enough but would in principle allow a weakening of, for example, the economy without

315

the birth of a political movement that undermines governability. Rather, the trade-offs begin a process that involves losses in *both* the areas of justice *and* the economy. Losses in the area of justice are not always a matter of there being less democracy or less welfare. The pattern of justice may promise with time more democracy and more adequate welfare. So when such improvements are blocked there are losses in the area of justice and hence of governability. As the crisis drags on, the state prepares for wide-scale repression. Such preparations are the response of state sovereignty to the challenge of continuing to reproduce the weakened economy in the face of resentment caused by inadequate concessions. The desperation of the state is intensified by the fact that concessions are, of course, not the only factors weakening the economy; the economy has its own internal tendency to crisis, one that is reflected in periodic recessions and long waves of relative stagnation.

A transition to socialism becomes possible where the contemporary state is made desperate by the downward spiral of justice and the economy. In this transition the basis is laid for a new relation between justice and the economy, one that minimizes the conflict. Where the conflict leads to a downward spiral its roots are easy enough to uncover. They are the limitless character of the economy. In the first book of the *Politics* Aristotle had pointed out that acquisition through trade is limitless; yet it is not just a market economy but also an economy whose goal is defense against the market that puts no limits on losses and benefits. In both cases those who demand justice do so in an economic context that places no limits on the losses they can suffer and no limits on the gains others can make. Promoting the economic system is at odds with constraining it in order to limit losses and benefits. Of course, the economic system distributes losses and benefits not randomly but in patterns corresponding to class divisions. Thus, in promoting the economy the state cannot pretend to be ruling for all. To rule for all it must impose limits on losses and benefits that distort the normal behavior of the economic system. In contrast, we can expect that the downward spiral of justice and the economy resulting from this conflict will lead to a search for a form of economy that is not limitless but of itself imposes restrictions on losses and benefits.

There is more to a socialist transformation than a new form of economy. Political dominance must have passed to the lower classes. Until it does, the transformation to a state that pursues an economic goal that embodies limits on benefits and losses will remain in the future. A transition period is precisely one in which these lower classes gain political dominance and begin to shape such a goal.

Yet, properly speaking, the state of the transition period is not a socialist state, for in the transition period the bifurcation between justice and goal has not yet been attenuated. There is still an economic system without inherent limits on benefits and losses. Proclaimed limits on aggrandizement will tend to be ignored, not just as a tactic for preventing the flight of capital and of managerial skill but because the economy is either still capitalist or a fledgling bureaucratic planned system. Only in the socialist system yet to be produced will there be inherent limits. Popular bodies in the transition period must, then, demand concessions from the transitional state in order to limit the sacrifices the lower classes are called on to make. The downward spiral of weakened justice and a weakened economy might even make the transitional state desperate enough to abort the production of socialism. As we saw, bargaining between the state and the popular bodies can avoid this result. Such bargaining is, moreover, a real possibility in view of the participants' sharing the goal of producing socialism.

Prior to the transition period in capitalist countries, there will be a period of downward spiral with growing desperation on the part of the state. The state during this downward spiral may even be unable to fulfill its function of reproducing capitalism. Function and performance are, though, different, and hence a capitalist state presiding over the weakening of capitalism is a distinct possibility. Moreover, the decline of capitalism is one thing, and the emergence of a state whose role it is to produce socialism is quite another.[1] Once caught in the downward spiral, the capitalist state may be unable to perform its function, but that does not make it a transitional state with the new function of bringing about the emergence of socialism.

The main question in regard to the period of downward spiral is not the familiar one as to whether the institutions of the capitalist state can then be taken over pretty much as they are to constitute the transitional state. Institutional questions are secondary to political ones. The main question is whether a transitional state with its goal of preparing the basis for socialism can replace the capitalist state without the political dominance of those classes and groups whose interests lead to building socialism. Clearly, the political dominance of these classes and groups is vital.[2] Their coming to political dominance, however that may transpire, is a revolutionary break with the reformist course, which is content to leave

317

the equation of political dominance unchanged. Unless, that is, the lower classes and groups are powerful enough to get the state to prioritize their interests, the state will remain with an unchanged function.

2. The socialist economy

It is time to turn from its preconditions to socialism itself. What is the socialism that the socialist state functions to reproduce? The concept of socialism here is a modified productionist one. The original Marxist emphasis on production in the concept of socialism is retained. Socialism, as defined in Chapter 22, is widely shared control in matters of production. The modification comes from the insistence that the sharing of control not be limited by discrimination based on social status, such as gender and race. Today people frown on productionist conceptions of almost anything and describe socialism in terms rather of the freedom to have a say in decisions affecting one's life.[3]

Productionist conceptions allegedly reduce all the good things in life to mere economics. But, given my commitment to the framework of historical materialism, my motivation cannot be reductionism. The productionist base acts in explanation merely as a framework for formulating connections of a causal sort and not as itself a universal stimulus cause. Despite having a productionist conception of socialism, I am opening the possibility of dealing with the socialist state as something, strictly speaking, undetermined by socialism itself, in the same way that I spoke of the capitalist state as undetermined by capitalism. The stimulus causes that fashion the socialist state will do their work in the context of a socialist environment. In a different one they might do quite different work.

In contrast, if socialism is a generalized freedom, then the concept of socialism mixes everything together – economics, politics, and culture. That concept may do a good job of summing up the desired condition. And there is an analogous concept of capitalism that mixes everything together and sums up our present condition. But for purposes of understanding, it is imperative that we abstract from within these omnibus conceptions the key features that are to constitute an explanatory framework. The productionist framework of socialism is one within which the broader liberationist aspirations of the socialist can be worked out without the obstacles contained in the capitalist framework.[4]

318

Socialism in the modified productionist sense is the name of certain productive relations. As noted in Chapter 10, productive relations have both a strictly economic component and a component of control as well. To realize economic productive relations, there must be institutions of control. What, though, are the economic productive relations of socialism? Corresponding to each of the tendencies making up the hypothetical model for capitalism is a tendency characteristic of a socialist economy.

(1) In place of wage labor remunerated on the basis of the exchange value of labor power, there is under socialism labor that receives a distribution from the common product proportional to the time it contributes to that product.[5] (2) Whereas the surplus under capitalism is accumulated in a private manner by either individuals or corporations, it is accumulated under socialism by labor as a group, that is, by labor collectively. (3) Instead of the overall product of society coming from only one segment of it, the wage laborers, under socialism it comes from the able-bodied adult society as a whole. (4) In place of the law of value as the basis for the allocation of investable funds, there is a law of planning whose main priority is the satisfaction of prominent social needs.[6] Finally, (5) rather than productivity increases being behind a tendency for the rate of profit to decline and hence behind crises with cutbacks in production, under socialism those increases are associated with increasing abundance.

3. Socialist control

The reproduction in reality of this abstract scheme requires the element of control. According to this scheme, labor collectively will make decisions about investing surplus. No group is then to be allowed to substitute itself for labor in this role. This requires that tendencies to make such a substitution be strictly controlled. Once the surplus passes to a group like this, planning ceases to be thoroughly democratic, since it will be carried out by a special body controlling the surplus. We could then get a form of bureaucratic planning made familiar by the Eastern bloc. To prevent such a distortion of the socialist economy, there must be mechanisms of control for insuring widespread decision-making power over investment and other facets of production as well. The requirement follows from (2) in Section 2. We recall that under capitalism mechanisms of control, such as a high ratio of supervisors to workers or a technology that reduces worker autonomy, are designed to further

319

private accumulation. In contrast, socialist mechanisms of control will work to keep planning democratic.

Under the general principle of allocation by planning, it is conceivable that a limited market would be allowed, just as under the law of value as a general principle there may be a limited use of planning. In the context of planning, market mechanisms, which would relieve pressures for the plan to be omniscient, will be controlled by general goals relating both to how widely distributed certain goods are to be and to how investable capital is to be allocated among certain priorities. Thus, with planning as the dominant theme, the motivation to use the market to increase initial advantages, which promotes the inegalitarian results of the market, would be held in check.[7]

The council system provides a mechanism for democratic planning. It is through this system that labor decides collectively on matters such as the investment of surplus. But councils cannot be limited to enterprise councils since they oversee only small segments of the interconnected process of production. Accumulation of surplus and its allocation do not occur enterprise by enterprise but take place by and for labor as a whole. The problem is not dealt with simply by adding neighborhood councils and councils of the oppressed. Enterprise councils and all these others must be the base of a pyramid of councils in which only general priorities are decided at the apex, thus allowing for decision making on matters of greater detail at the various lower levels.[8]

Institutions of control, which are behind the full productive relations of socialism, limit benefits in two directions. The first has to do with allocation. Since accumulation is by labor as a whole, there are no individuals or corporations who are the direct beneficiaries of the surplus of production. (Exceptions to this restriction can be allowed provided they leave democratic planning intact.) Those who benefit from the surplus do so not directly but only as a result of democratic planning. The second has to do with distribution. The duration of labor, not authority over others or a skill that is highly marketable, is the basis of remuneration for work. This limits income differentials within the working group. (Again, exceptions are allowable provided they leave solidarity intact.)

What about limits on losses? Planning is directed at the satisfaction of outstanding social needs. If employment, care for the elderly, disability compensation, literacy in less developed areas are the outstanding social needs, then investable funds will find their way toward these problems. This will happen in the nature

320

of the economy – which includes both the economic and the control relations of production – and not as an artifact of class struggle, which will be the case where the economy itself imposes no limits on the losses some may have to suffer. This is what it means to say that a pattern of justice is incorporated within an economy. When the socialist state takes up the task of reproducing the socialist relations of production, it is not attempting to reproduce a process that allows limitless benefits for some and limitless losses for others. There are already built-in limits within the economy it supports.

The socialist economy's most distinctive reduction of losses concerns alienation and exploitation. In capitalism there is a relative lack of control by producers over the surplus they produce. This alienation from the product is limited by a system of council-made investment decisions. Also, in capitalism there is a relative lack of control by producers of the extent of the surplus labor time they work. They are exploited by having little say over whether and how much they will work beyond the time needed to reproduce their labor power. This exploitation is limited by a system of council-made work decisions. Controls will be needed to insure the protection of these limits on alienation and exploitation built into the socialist economy.

4. Attenuated state autonomy

We have seen that there are distinctive controls needed to entrench socialism. We have said little about the institutions embodying these controls. The socialist state enters here as an institution imposing certain of these controls. (The capitalist state plays an analogous role in regard to capitalist controls.) More specifically, the council system, as the core of the socialist state, will participate in the effort to establish the appropriate controls.

The issue now to be addressed concerns state autonomy. State controls imposed to entrench the economy are a sign of resistance to its becoming entrenched. If everyone were convinced of socialism in a socialist society, a state would need to exist only for protection from outside aggression. We cannot suppose everyone will be convinced; there will be groups and individuals within the society demanding that they be allowed to satisfy interests at odds with the encompassing socialism. Such demands are a stimulus for limits on losses and benefits that are not covered by the limits coming directly from the economy. The limits on losses and benefits coming from the socialist economy are only part of the full pattern of justice of the socialist state. The controls the state imposes in order to carry out its economic function will have to be less strict if the state is to be able to perform as ruler of all.

But couldn't the socialist state ignore the demands of opposition- ists and still remain socialist? There would be a fatal conflict result- ing from doing this. The voice of such oppositionists in the councils and other bodies of governance would be discounted by a flat re- fusal to make concessions to their demands. They would in effect be excluded from the widely shared decision making characteristic of socialist democracy, thereby limiting how widely that decision making is shared. If, though, the opposition chooses a combat by arms, it is unlikely to be placated with concessions but will be satisfied only with the overthrow of the socialist state itself.

Once it takes the demands of oppositionists into account, a pat- tern of justice is created that, though it derives much from the socialist economy, also contains elements derived from opposition- ist pressure. Socialist justice must be a justice of toleration, for otherwise the socialist state will lose the appeal it has as a means of ruling by widely shared decision making. The opposition will harden, and a repressive and paranoid state will emerge. Eventu- ally, those suspected of being oppositionists will be harrassed so that there is no longer the excuse that repression is just for the class enemy. This state ends by no longer promoting socialism. Still, with a justice of toleration, conflict emerges between the promotion of the economy and socialist justice. The promotion of the economy will demand controls that have to be weakened in order to conform to socialist justice. The autonomy of the state will not then end with the socialist state, though this state certainly will attenuate that autonomy, due to the limits derived from the economy itself.

This attenuated autonomy is an important gain. To understand exactly what it is I shall first ask if it means doing away with the "separation" of the state from society. In discussing the nature of the state that the Paris Commune of 1871 attempted to overthrow, Marx said it was "separate from and independent of society."[9] The metaphor of separateness can be misleading if we do not keep in mind the full extent of its ambiguity.

First, separation admits of interpretation through the frame- work model. There is the separation from that framework itself of those things whose variations a framework helps explain. In this sense, the state, whose changes are understood within an economic framework, is inevitably separate from society, as the embodiment of the economic framework. This is a separation that belongs to the level of our methodology and comes about on the basis of a conceptual abstraction that pulls apart things that are interlinked. Not just the French Second Empire of Louis Napoleon Bonaparte from 1852 to 1870, to which Marx was referring, but also the socialist state will be separate, in this sense, from the relations of production. So attenuated autonomy is no diminution of this separation.

Second, there is the separation of the state's reproductive activity from the needs of *the large majority* in the society. Separateness here means that the state functions at cross-purposes to the majority. The French Second Empire illustrates this conflict in an advanced form. To rule, the state must adjust to those who require limits by adopting a pattern of justice. The initial separation between state functioning and the needs of the majority then gets internalized within the state as a conflict between its function and its pattern of justice. Despite state justice, there will be unmet needs creating tensions that call forth repression, which is the most apparent manifestation of this kind of separation of the state from society.

Where a minority group is economically dominant, the state will manifest this second kind of separation from society. In contrast, through its incorporation of limits on benefits and losses from the economy, the socialist state will not exhibit the same kind of separation of its function from the needs of the majority. This opens up the possibility of yet another type of separation.

So, third, without a separation from the majority, there may still be a separation from *several small minorities*. It is only sometimes excusable to identify the society with its majority component. In this third case, the needs of reproducing the economy conflict with the needs of minorities. There is still the conflict between state justice and the state's economic role. However, the important difference is that this conflict no longer exists for those aspects of state justice demanded by the majority as such. This third form of separation is equivalent to our attenuated autonomy.

5. The wayward majority

The basis for attenuated autonomy is conflict with the needs of minorities. But there may well be needs of the majority itself that conflict with the socialist economy. As to minorities, the state will have to deal with the organized opposition of antisocialists. Such

323

an opposition is, if it cannot be pacified by state justice, a sufficient basis for a state military, organized, of course, in a way that is compatible with the aim of reproducing the socialist relations of production. But such an opposition is not the only root of socialist state autonomy. This is apparent if we concentrate on the special problems resulting from the diversity within the revolutionary alliance, which, as in the transition phase, is politically dominant. These problems seem to take the form of a conflict between the state's function and needs of the majority.

Socialism does not put an end to this diversity. Racial and sexual identity will not have disappeared, though instead of being associated with oppression these identities will be associated with distinguishing features in which their bearers take pride and which they strive to develop. The division of labor will not have disappeared, and as a consequence there will remain distinct groups of rural and urban workers, of operatives and laborers on the one hand and those who provide technical, medical, or educational services on the other hand. These groups in the politically dominant alliance could allow their focus on reproducing socialism to become diffuse due to conflicts arising from their diversity. Dedication to widely shared decision making in production is threatened by the traditional sectional rivalries between these groups.

It should not be thought that diversity in the revolutionary alliance is a sufficient basis for the socialist state in contrast to socialist anarchy. Consumption demands pressed by operatives and laborers may be at odds with the prominent needs of social workers in recreation facilities, schools, data analysis centers, and urban planning offices. The resolution of such conflicts does not, though, call for a state that plays magistrate.[10] Traditional societies resolved analogous disputes through their elders. One generates an argument for the state here only when one reads class conflict into this talk of diverse interests.

The need for a socialist state is to be found not in nonclass diversity itself but rather in the inherited tendency to handle conflicts between diverse groups through elites. A group readily turns over to its leadership, its lawyers, and its experts the winning of a conflict with another group. A socialist society will inherit this tendency to rely on elites from millenia of minority domination. To increase chances of winning disputes, groups will grant enormous power to their elites. This tendency is at odds with the social goal of widely shared decision making and ultimately at odds with the socialist goal of producers running all facets of production.

324

To preserve these socialist aims, formal means are needed to combat this tendency toward elitism. Toleration of those promoting a leadership/mass dualism would only promote this undermining of socialism. A smooth-functioning council system might, though, reduce the attractiveness of elitism. But some system of state controls would appear likely in order to prevent elitism from undermining socialism. Does this mean that attenuated autonomy was only a dream? The state's goal in this case is, after all, opposed to the interests of a potential majority of those who support elitist resolution of conflicts. I wish to sketch an argument showing how even here the socialist state's autonomy is quite minimal.

Were the socialist state to prevent a majority from realizing its elitist tendencies, we would face a paradoxical situation. Suppose the state resorts to coercion in order to combat a tendency of the majority to support elitist control of the means of resolving disputes. This would indeed imply a separation of the second kind and hence unattenuated autonomy of the state from the society since the state's goal would conflict with the needs of the majority. The goal of the state being to encourage widely shared control of production, the majority finds itself in opposition to the socialist state. By assumption, though, the majority has political dominance in respect to a socialist state, and hence this state should promote its interests. It is this that causes the trouble. Far from recognizing this dominance, the state makes only token concessions to the elitist sympathies of the majority in order to govern. The state remains the major force for socialism while the majority, its engines roaring in reverse, demands elitist justice. The majority's having to demand limits on the state's pursuit of widely shared control of production contradicts its political dominance. How it this paradox resolved?

The theory of human nature, on which much of political morality ultimately rests, is relevant to resolving the paradox. If human nature is fixed and it includes the tendency to support elitism, then the socialist state will not only find itself in a battle with elites rising out of the allied groups but also find itself as one elite among others. If, though, human nature is not fixed and the tendency to support elitism is a carry-over from a time when minority control fit with the economic productive relations, then the tendency to support elitism has only a precarious existence in the framework of the socialist economic relations. Defying the tendency to support elitism does not go against a feature of the socialist framework as it would against a feature of the capitalist framework. Defying that

325

tendency may then be successful in eradicating elitism from socialist society.

The more flexible view of human nature holds promise for resolving the paradox. Consider the historical process by which the allied groups become politically dominant. The outcome of that process is that the state advances the interests of the politically dominant alliance, and hence the alliance should have no quarrel with the state's goal of promoting a socialist economy. This goal is not one that comes from outside the struggles of the alliance, and for this reason the state adopts it. This goal will represent for those groups the integrating theme of their struggles through the previous periods. It is their "general will," not in an ideal but in a historical sense of a common determination they have arrived at through joint action and joint discussion over generations.[11] The general will is not, then, the creation of an agreement of the assembled groups but something that emerges as the mature expression of what those groups have become in their struggles. It is an expression of what those groups are and what the nature of their members is.

If all this is true, how are we to interpret the elitist tendencies? These tendencies, which use the conflicts based on the diversity of the allied groups to concentrate rather than share control, are an expression of a past in which the opposition to elite-run society adopted the elitism of the society it opposed. The socialist state can act to eradicate this holdover from the past without placing itself in opposition to the general will of the society. The socialist state does not then separate itself from the majority. What it attacks is not the common determination that has made the society and its members what they are. State controls are used only against features that are holdovers from elite-run societies, which conflict with what society and its members have become. It is only on the view of human nature as fixed that it becomes impossible for the socialist state's autonomy to be attenuated.

In combating elitist tendencies the state will engage in one of its age-old tasks, that of modifying behavior. Both the tendency to allow oneself to be dominated by an elite and the tendency to strive to form a controlling elite will be weakened if the state is constituted by and defends implacably institutions that promote political participation and that open governance to the widest possible inspection. In short, a council system is a deterrent to elitism, but at first it may not be sufficient to prevent it. Lenin pointed out that the socialist revolution is not to be delayed because as they are now

326

people "cannot dispense with subordination."[12] The socialist state will need to destroy elitism but in a way that conforms to the limits set by state justice.

The attenuation of autonomy eliminates enormous areas of conflict. These are areas of conflict that would both increase the intrusion of the state into society and weaken it through further conflicts created by this intrusion. The attenuation of the distinction between the state's form and its function would be the basis for a genuine withering away of the state. Assuming socialism has spread internationally and become economically dominant domestically, conflict between groups becomes manageable without a downward spiral that generates more conflicts. The elitist tendencies that come to the fore to benefit from these conflicts can then be reduced and possibly eliminated as damaging social forces without stopping the withering away. With all this accomplished, the remaining tasks of the state can be performed without the existence of a body that rules over society. An economy that is not opposed by the demands of justice and that is not part of a system of competing national units has less need for a state to reproduce it. The state as protector of the economy withers away, while the residual tasks of analyzing information and of coordination that the state had performed become tasks performed within an institution of planning. The democratic planning decisions become accepted as features of the social fabric in somewhat the same way that the price determinations made by the capitalist market were generally accepted as features of the social fabric. But the scope of my work ends where alternatives to the state begin.

Conclusion

State, class, and democracy

How might one evaluate the theory of the state I have presented? The implicit perspective from which the theory is developed is not a neutral one, since it is that of those interested in promoting a version of radical justice. The same theory could conceivably have emerged from some other perspective. But the first order of business in evaluating a theory is to see how it stands up within the project it was devised to serve. I shall suggest some of the ways my theory of the state – in which the state is the center of conflict between justice and the economy – facilitates the task of those promoting radical justice.

1. Nature of the state

It will be helpful to begin by drawing together all the different strands of my theory into a single formula. In the formula the features of justice and the reproduction of the economy will of course have a prominent place, but here it is imperative to emphasize that there are other important elements in my theory as well. In it the features of justice and reproduction are integrated with the institutions that are essential for realizing them, institutions that jointly make up the state as an institution. Moreover, all of these elements – justice, reproduction, and institutions – will be integrated within a materialist framework in which the pressures of various groups are important stimuli.

The modern state rules over a heterogeneous population

(1) in order to reproduce the population's economy
(2) by means of a collection of institutions
(3) that must be able to employ a monopoly of force and to adopt and implement a pattern of justice
(4) but that are being continually refashioned within the framework of the economy by a variety of stimuli.

329

This formula emphasizes that what a state does is to rule – that is, to control a group-divided population in order to realize a dominant goal. Clause (1) of the formula picks out this dominant goal as economic reproduction. Clause (2) emphasizes that the state has its concrete manifestation in bodies operating by set procedures. Clause (3) mentions the contrasting elements of force and justice in the state's form of rule. Clause (4) deals with the matter of determination; it specifies the way in which our theory of the state is a materialist one. An economic framework is the context for changes in both institutions and the form of rule. Specifically, pressures from nondominant groups are among the stimuli for changes in official justice.

It is understood that the economy for the sake of which the state rules need not be a purely national economy. It may be a segment of the international economy with a national base. Consequently, the pattern of justice need not be limited to a national one but may include the peace and prosperity of an empire.

Should there not be a moral goal assigned to the state rather than the economic one in our formula? In view of the involvement of the state in affirmative action in order to overcome discrimination, in view of its involvement in the protection of the population from unsafe working conditions, and in view of its involvement in making more health care available to the needy, there would appear to be a good case for looking at the state as a promoter of a moral goal. Closer study of these and other progressive state activities reveals them to be not so much part of a goal as part of the price paid for stable governance. They thus fall under (3), rather than calling for correcting (1) in our formula for the state.

Our formula limits the state's goal to reproduction of the economy without suggesting that its role is the common good or moral improvement. In this regard it agrees with one of the basic themes underlying the liberal theory of the state. That theme is that the state is in the business not of imposing a conception of the good on people but only of providing preconditions for individual conceptions of the good to be realized. Of course, in our theory there is no requirement that the individual good be furthered, except insofar as this is needed for governance.

Ruling through force is given a less central place in our formula than in Leninist theories of the state. Stable rule calls for a pattern of limits on losses and benefits that will legitimate the state. Legitimacy is thereby raised to the level of an essential feature of the

330

state by our theory. This is done, however, without using this fact to reject a materialist view of the state.

The materialist roots of legitimacy can be seen as follows: First, it is the interests of lower groups rather than abstract ideals that lie behind official justice. The state imposes limits on benefits and losses as an imperative of ruling rather than because doing so is a means of realizing an ideal of human nature. The use of force is also an imperative of ruling, though one designed to win acceptance by awe or fear rather than by a promise of well-being. The element of justice is, however, indeterminate apart from popular pressure, and when it is determinate it will reflect the interests of the lower groups bringing pressure to bear on the state.

Second, our formula makes clear through (4) that justice – as a means to legitimacy – is determined within a materialist context. Ruling through justice is given its specific character not just by the pressures for realizing the interests of nondominant groups but by the way the economic framework allows these pressures to act.

Our formula for the state implies that the limits making up justice are connected to the class struggle. This is quite simply because these limits set by justice conflict with the unlimited character of the economy. Justice will then be granted reluctantly. The state's reluctance to grant it reflects not just its structural tendencies to promote the economy but pressure from the economically dominant class. The state is then at the intersection of conflicting class forces when it comes to the imposition of measures of justice.

There can be no successful promotion of radical justice without an awareness of the connection between the official justice it aspires to replace and the class struggle. To push beyond official justice to the more adequate realization of the interests of dominated groups called for by radical justice is not then a matter of getting the state to recognize that it has been neglectful of its true goal of human realization. On the contrary, what is needed is a revolutionary situation. Either the economically dominant class must be drastically weakened so that the state no longer gets counterpressure from it to the pressures from the lower classes; or the state must be reconstituted so that its institutions function naturally for a different goal. Yet theories of the state that ignore the conflict between justice and the economy make it seem too easy to realize radical justice. This can be taken as a partial confirmation of our theory.

331

2. Class politics

The formula for the state in Section 1 emphasizes the materialist framework for the state, including its aspect of justice. The importance of emphasizing the materialist framework for official justice is that it challenges the widespread view of the pattern of justice as a practical expression of an ideal justice. On the materialist view of the state, justice is a working out of the class struggle between popular pressures for limits on benefits and losses and the demands of economic reproduction. Even radical justice is brought to earth within the materialist perspective. It is not an ideal justice in opposition to official justice but an expression of group interests modified by taking the point of view of ruling sometime in the future.

In particular, the materialist perspective avoids the pitfalls of both liberal egalitarianism and revolutionary anarchism. These views project conceptions of radical justice but in such a way that radical justice becomes a species of ideal justice. Liberal egalitarianism sees radical justice as deriving from the equal individuals of the liberal theory of human nature. The group nature of individuals, however, undercuts this form of egalitarianism. There is a parallel problem with revolutionary anarchism, for it assumes as a yardstick for justice an ideal that makes the state an abomination. Humans are of such a nature that they are violated by the state as such. Yet the possibility of a state based on non-elite control makes the anarchist worry seem less real. Such a possibility emerges in a materialist framework in which the state is taken not in the abstract but as fitting the circumstances of an economy run by popular participation.

The fundamental way the state is conditioned by a materialist framework still needs to be emphasized. We already saw that the basic task of a state is set not by some conception of what is best for a people but rather by class realities. This leads to the point that there is no state without a class program promoted by its ruling group. It is in this way that the materialist framework fundamentally conditions the state. The basic aspect of such a class program is the reproduction of the economy. The inevitability of such a class program has to do with what I called the inertial aspect of a materialist framework. The framework favors policies and institutions that favor it.

Moreover, a conception of radical justice can be implemented only by means of a class program. It is interesting to consider the

332

common feature shared by those cases in which the United States happens to support opposition groups to right-wing regimes. This support tends to be for groups with a class program that presents no challenge to capitalist relations of production even though these opposition groups adopt a form of radical justice. At times the bourgeois character of the program is masked by nationalist or other aspects of the opposition.

U.S. support for the bourgeois opposition to Somoza in his last days in Nicaragua continued after his overthrow in the form of support for the counterrevolutionaries. The unwillingness of the anti-Somocista bourgeoisie to accept the fact that its minor role in the overthrow of Somoza gave it no claim to have its program for a bourgeois republic adopted led it to turn to the United States to create an armed opposition to the Sandinistas.

A similar consideration is operative in the case of the anti-apartheid movement in South Africa. In the event that the apartheid regime should fall, the U.S. government would be prepared to favor the accession to power of the Inkatha Party of KwaZulu leader Gatsha Buthelezi. Inkatha, though it has a program for the rights of the black majority, apparently has no class program. In contrast, the African National Congress's Freedom Charter projects a view of an egalitarian future. The silence of Inkatha on the economic issue constitutes in fact an acceptance of capitalist relations of production for South Africa and an acceptance of the role of South Africa in Western imperialism.

Turning to the opposition groups to the left of those that get U.S. sympathy or backing, we find that they too have class programs. They cannot sustain a nationalist program without an attack on the powerful elements of the bourgeoisie tied to imperialism. An environmentalist opposition can realize its program only by extending investment rights in a way that drastically reduces the control of capitalists over capital. A women's party could not become a ruling party just on a gender program. It would either adopt an economic program acceptable to the dominant economic group or present an alternative program that might be more compatible with its gender program. Our theory of the state is partly confirmed by its making clear why there is a class program as part of the program of existing ruling groups and also as part of the program of groups aspiring to rule on the basis of a radical justice.

A materialist theory of the state starts from the recognition that in political change a materialist framework is bedrock. It is not something that plays the same role as historical stimuli; it is a

333

structural form of determination. From here the theory advances to the recognition that the state, as formed and perpetuated in the materialist framework, is a collection of institutions that plays a role in reproducing that framework. This expresses the inertial tendency of the framework. It is only one step farther to the recognition that class is primary in state politics. It is primary in the sense that a class program is at the center of the politics of a ruling group. The asymmetry between class and other programs is obvious; a racial or an environmental program is not a program for a ruling group without at least the implicit inclusion of a class program, though the converse is not necessarily true. The root of this asymmetry is the state's role in reproducing the economy. A class program is a program for fulfilling that role.

3. Paradox of justice

My concern has been theory rather than prognostication. But to conclude I wish to mention a tendency within the modern state that makes its legitimation a more and more difficult achievement. This suggests a rocky future for the state, unless there are fundamental changes toward greater popular participation.

The problem has the form of a paradox. There is pressure for limits on losses and benefits, and the state is the dominant mechanism for setting such limits and enforcing them. The state sets and enforces limits not as a direct response to popular demands but as a mediated one. Its economic function and the interests of the ruling group modulate the response. Since the response is not a direct reflex, state justice may even appear to be an expression of an inner progressive essence of the state. But the crucial fact is that the administration and enforcement of justice, in our broad sense, require an ever larger state apparatus. Administration becomes the most obvious face the state turns to the public. The citizen's loss of power due to the rise of state administration is an obstacle to justice. There is then the paradox that the state, in the process of implementing justice, becomes a chief obstacle to its own justice.

This is true at least where effective restrictions on state power embodying the spirit of democracy are part of the state's justice. The democratic spirit insists on wider forms of participation, whether or not these forms become part of official justice. So, more accurately, the paradox is that the modern state's implementation of justice is an obstacle either to its own official justice or to a common form of radical democratic justice. This paradox affects

334

capitalist as well as bureaucratically planned societies. The paradox impacts both on the welfare recipient who complains of the control over people's lives exercised by the apparatus of putting a floor under poverty and on the conservative who objects to the encroachment of the state on the freedom of enterprise.

The democratic spirit may be more intense at some times than at others. But its pressure is felt everywhere. The intrusive state may quash it for a time with repression, yet it cannot end it. The democratic spirit takes different forms at different times. It takes the form of abstention from politics as a protest against the manipulation of participation by party elites and ruling groups. Such an alienation from politics is a predictable result of an emphasis on strong leadership that devalues participation. When, though, the demand for participation is intense, the problem arises for the state of what to do with it. Sacred agendas would have to be rewritten as real democracy replaced formal democracy. To prevent this the state maintains tight control over matters of official justice, thereby blocking the realization of the democratic aspect of justice. The resulting tensions weaken legitimation, making it still harder for the state to rule.

It is easy to find illustrations of both manifestations of the democratic spirit. Alienation from politics is associated with various forms of lawlessness; the civil war in the inner cities of the United States with its great toll in human life is an example of the failure of legitimation of the state. Moreover, the way in which the National Democratic Front of Cuauhtémoc Cárdenas captured the support of many Mexicans manifested the way the administration of the gains of the Mexican Revolution by the one-party state had placed an obstacle before democracy.

One way out of the paradox of justice is to call a halt to extending and deepening justice. The state would not have to get progressively more intrusive as it would if justice were continually extended and deepened. Another way out is a devolution of power in the administration of justice without otherwise changing the state as it now exists. Yet both paths are of doubtful effectiveness. Solutions to the problem of governability in industrial nations along the lines of fascist or quasi-fascist restrictions on justice have not proved stable and have resulted in temporary setbacks for dominant economic groups. A halt to the extension and deepening of justice would in all likelihood call for such a repressive regime and hence offer no long-term solution to the paradox. The alternative of initiating a devolution of power would call for a willingness to make economic reproduction hostage to greater justice in the form of greater democracy. This is not something that would be impossible for the state to do. But outside a desperate situation the forces aligned against such a devolution would be irresistible.

It is fair, then, to say that the state possesses little potential for reforming itself in order to avoid the tensions of the paradox of justice. To avoid the paradox, something on the order of the state that is transitional to socialism seems called for. In the transitional state there is bargaining between popular and state bodies. This amounts to more than the advisory power of official committees made up of persons antecedently known to play politics according to present rules. Popular bodies in a transitional state would, in contrast, be independent of the state and would not only bargain over policy with the state but also play a crucial role, along with the state, in its implementation. Our theory of the state receives further confirmation by suggesting this possible escape for radical justice from the paradox of justice.

The route to avoiding the paradox of justice is not, then, the reform of states subject to it but the empowerment of those whose participation in those states is at best formal. This empowerment does not come from voter registration drives, which by themselves merely enhance the legitimacy of a state that is an obstacle to justice. The empowerment can take place only if there is a general awareness of the need to change the political situation so that the lower classes and the oppressed become politically dominant. They will be politically dominant when they see to it that their interests become a priority for the state. So long as the priority interests of the state are those of a small minority, there will be no possibility of democracy in anything like the full sense.

Armed with the goal of making themselves politically dominant, the lower classes together with the oppressed groups can do battle for democracy. Only when they are politically dominant will they be able to insist on an official justice that the state will not undercut in the very process of implementation. For then, through bargaining with the state, popular bodies become party to the formulation and implementation of justice.

Notes

Introduction: Can the state rule without justice?

1. Nigel Harris, *The Mandate from Heaven: Marx and Mao in Modern China*, Quartet, London, 1978, pp. 161–6.
2. Jean Esmein, *The Chinese Cultural Revolution*, trans. W. J. F. Jenner, Doubleday, Garden City, N.Y., 1973, Chapter 7.
3. If, as Wood interpreted him, Marx held that a state's justice corresponds to the existing mode of production, then my thesis that a state's justice may conflict with the existing mode of production is not Marxist (Allen Wood, "The Marxian Critique of Justice," *Philosophy and Public Affairs*, 1, no. 3, Spring 1972, pp. 244–82). This interpretation of Marx has, though, been widely disputed. Buchanan, for example, interprets Marx as thinking that capitalism was unjust even according to its own, and its state's own, standard of justice. My thesis that a state's justice may conflict with the existing mode of production would be Marxist on Buchanan's reading of Marx (Allen E. Buchanan, *Marx and Justice*, Littlefield, Adams, Totowa, N.J., 1982, Chapter 4).
4. Daniel Bell, *The Coming of Post-Industrial Society*, Basic, New York, 1973, pp. 451–5.
5. See, e.g., Alasdair MacIntyre, *After Virtue: A Study in Moral Theory*, University of Notre Dame Press, Notre Dame, Ind., 1981, Chapters 7 and 8; Mary Hesse, *Revolutions and Reconstructions in the Philosophy of Science*, Indiana University Press, Bloomington, 1980, Part 3; and Milton Fisk, *Ethics and Society: A Marxist Interpretation of Value*, New York University Press, New York, 1980, Chapter 3.
6. John Rawls, *A Theory of Justice*, Harvard University Press, Cambridge, Mass., 1971, Section 9. More recently, Rawls has made it clearer than it was in *A Theory of Justice* that the starting point for moving to equilibrium is "the intuitive ideas that are embedded in the political institutions of a democratic society." Thus we learn that overarching principles of justice going beyond any social circumstances, including the democratic tradition, are not at all the goal of his modified rationalism (John Rawls, "Justice as Fairness: Political Not Metaphysical," *Philosophy and Public Affairs*, 14, no. 3, 1985, pp. 223–51).
7. Ernest Barker, *Principles of Social and Political Theory*, Oxford University Press, Oxford, 1951, Book 4, Chapter 5. Barker thinks that setting

337

limits on the various groups in a society can realize genuine social cohesion. He ignores the tension that would be generated between such limits and the state's role in protecting the status of a dominant group. The state's role in protecting the dominant group normally leads to its setting limits that are insufficiently rigorous to end group conflict and begin genuine social cohesion.

8. Aristotle *Politics* 1278b–1279b. Aristotle objected to tyranny, oligarchy, and "democracy" since each promoted the interests of only a fraction of the society. A just constitution would be "directed to the advantage of the whole body of citizens." But it would advantage citizens only according to their contribution to the state itself (1281a). The just state in this way puts limits on benefits and losses, whereas benefits are unlimited for the favored group and losses are unlimited for the disfavored group under, say, oligarchy or "democracy."

9. Antonio Gramsci, *Selections from the Prison Notebooks*, trans. Q. Hoare and G. Nowell Smith, International Publishers, New York, 1971, p. 182.

10. E. P. Thompson, *The Heavy Dancers*, Pantheon, New York, 1985, pp. 49–60.

11. Lucy Mair, *Primitive Government: A Study of Traditional Political Systems in Eastern Africa*, Indiana University Press, Bloomington, 1962, pp. 50, 63.

12. Marvin Harris, *Cows, Pigs, Wars, and Witches*, Random House, New York, 1975, pp. 111–30.

13. Precisely such omnipotence has been ascribed to ruling classes by Richard W. Miller, *Analyzing Marx: Morality, Power, and History*, Princeton University Press, Princeton, N.J., 1984, Chapter 3. For him a ruling class has sufficient power to enable the state to stop activity counter to its long-term interests as an economically dominant class. This supposes a greater degree of freedom than most ruling classes have enjoyed. When they attempt to secure their political power, there is nothing in the nature of things to guarantee that they can always do so in ways that promote their long-term economic interests.

14. Claus Offe, " 'Ungovernability': The Renaissance of Conservative Theories of Crisis," in his *Contradictions of the Welfare State*, ed. J. Keane, MIT Press, Cambridge, Mass., 1984, pp. 81 ff.

1. A challenge to materialism

1. E. P. Thompson, *Beyond the Cold War: A New Approach to the Arms Race and Nuclear Annihilation*, Pantheon, New York, 1982, pp. 41–80.

2. E. P. Thompson, "On Peace, Power, and Parochialism," *The Nation*, September 24, 1983. Thompson says, "The sequence that is leading the world toward nuclear war is not made up only of technologies and

things (missiles, task forces); it is also made up of ideological and political preparations. . . . It is ideology, even more than military-industrial pressures, that is the driving force of Cold War II. . . . We may call that ideology 'imperialist.' . . . But in naming it imperialism we should avoid reducing the problem to simplistic preconceptions. . . . The rhetoric of the cold war legitimates the whole operation." One need not give ideology primacy in quite this way in order to admit that economist accounts don't get off the ground.

3. Milton Fisk, *Nature and Necessity: An Essay in Physical Ontology*, Indiana University Press, Bloomington, 1973, Chapter 3, Section 3; Chapter 10, Section 3. These sections provide arguments for the holistic rather than atomistic systems in explanation in physical science.

4. Nikolai Bukharin, *Historical Materialism: A System of Sociology*, University of Michigan Press, Ann Arbor, 1969, Chapter 3, Section b. In contrast, Karl Marx himself employed a distinction between agency, direct impulse, stimulus, pretext, on the one hand, and cause in a more structural sense, on the other, leaving himself free to admit many kinds of agents without abandoning materialism. See, e.g., *Capital*, Volume 1, Chapter 1, Section 4, where he speaks of the supremacy of Catholicism in the Middle Ages, and chapter 10, Section 4, where he discusses the extension of the working day in the fourteenth century.

5. This is the form of economist argument given by Ernest Mandel, *Late Capitalism*, trans, J. De Bres, Verso, London, 1975, Chapter 9, Section 3.

6. As an illustration of atomist economism, consider the following exchange (Alexander Cockburn, "Can Capitalism Be Saved? A Chat with Sweezy and Magdoff," *The Nation*, June 9, 1984). COCKBURN: "But many left and liberal groups tell workers that if they built houses instead of missiles, they, and capitalism, would be better off. That just isn't true, is it?" SWEEZY: "I agree." MAGDOFF: "But the lack of replacement of capital goods for civilian use or the lack of modernization are due not to military spending but to the stagnation . . ."

I hope that Sweezy and Magdoff are not telling us to be immobilized before the arms race. Yet if, as they seem to say, the economic relations of capitalism are the only factors needed to determine spiraling arms spending, then indeed transitional demands – such as those for conversion to peaceful production – that will not lead directly to a socialist economy are not capable of curbing arms spending. Short of socialism, those opposed to the arms race have, then, no option but to wait for a *deus ex machina*. A contextual rather than an atomist approach to economic determination would, though, avoid this immobilization, because the economic context frames, without making inevitable, the decisions of the state. Under popular pressure, the state could then subsidize peaceful projects to make them viable in a period of stagnation, just as it now subsidizes arms production. (See the debate on economic conversion between Gordon Adams and his critics Lloyd J. Dumas, Suzanne Gordon, and Kevin Bean in *Bulletin of the Atomic Scientists*, 42, no. 2, 1986, pp. 24–8, and no. 6, pp. 45–51.

7. Bruce Russett, *The Prisoners of Insecurity: Nuclear Deterrence, the Arms Race, and Arms Control*, Freeman, New York, 1983, Chapter 4.

8. Louis Althusser, "Ideology and Ideological State Apparatuses," in his *Lenin and Philosophy and Other Essays*, trans. B. Brewester, Monthly Review, New York, 1971, p. 162. Althusser's formulation of ideology captures the referential element in it: "Ideology represents the imaginative relationship of individuals to their real conditions of existence." Liberal theorists have also emphasized this important referential element by noting that ideology relates people to troublesome realities through novel symbolic combinations (Clifford Geertz, *The Interpretation of Cultures*, Basic, New York, 1973, Chapter 8).

9. See the critique of Althusser's view of ideology by Paul Hirst, *On Law and Ideology*, Humanities, Atlantic Highlands, N.J., 1979, Chapter 3.

10. Sidney Lens, *The Day before Doomsday: An Anatomy of the Nuclear Arms Race*, Beacon, Boston, 1977, Chapter 8.

11. Harry Magdoff, *The Age of Imperialism: The Economics of U.S. Foreign Policy*, Monthly Review, New York, 1969, Chapter 5.

2. A framework for the state

1. Wilfrid Sellars, "The Language of Theories," in his *Science, Perception, and Reality*, Humanities, Atlantic Highlands, N.J., 1963, p. 121.

2. As an example of a materialism that is both atomist and empiricist, see G. A. Cohen, *Karl Marx's Theory of History: A Defense*, Princeton University Press, Princeton, N.J., 1978, Chapter 6. I criticized Cohen's atomistic empiricism some time ago from the perspective adopted in the current chapter (Milton Fisk, "The Concept of Primacy in Historical Explanation," *Analyse und Kritik*, 4, 1982, pp. 182–96). Cohen's philosophical outlook has become integral to that of the "analytical Marxism" school, which also ignores the contextual tier of explanation and can consequently find no place for a genuine notion of dialectic. John Roemer, for example, in his essay "Should Marxists Be Interested in Exploitation?" (in *Analytical Marxism*, ed. J. Roemer, Cambridge University Press, Cambridge, 1986, pp. 260–82) imagines a situation in which the poor work less than the rich and survive on the surplus transferred to them from the rich. It is the rich who are exploited here, since they transfer some of the fruit of their labor to the poor. So for Roemer exploitation is not a clear indicator of a distribution of less wealth to the exploited. This is all of a piece with Hume's imagining causes without their accustomed effects; atomistic empiricism is behind all these imagined possibilities. Indeed, where the historically given context for em-

pirical factors is imagined away, then, as Hume pointed out, anything can follow from those factors. Cohen, Elster, and Roemer are teaching us this lesson again, two and one-half centuries after Hume's *Treatise of Human Nature*. But if the capitalist context that has been given by history is to be the background for connections, then exploitation of the rich by the poor is simply a nonstarter. Hegel and Marx made clear that they rejected atomistic empiricism because they were interested in how context constrained empirical connections. Of course, they would have agreed that if the context is imagined away anything might follow. But then what's the point of doing it?

3. Milton Fisk, "Materialism and Dialectic," *Critique* (Glasgow), 12, 1979–80, pp. 97–116. The demarcation I argued for in this article sets materialist theories apart on the ground that their basic concepts are of extensive – that is, divisible – magnitudes.

4. Maurice Dobb, *Studies in the Development of Capitalism*, International Publishers, New York, 1947, Chapter 2, Sections 2 and 3.

5. Marvin Harris, *Cultural Materialism*, Random House, New York, 1979, p. 72; also Geoffrey Hellman, "Historical Materialism," in *Issues in Marxist Philosophy*, Volume 2, ed. J. Mepham and D.-H. Ruben, Harvester, Brighton, 1979, pp. 143–70.

6. For the basis for a similar perspective in regard to quantum physics, see Hanry Margenau, *The Nature of Physical Reality*, McGraw-Hill, New York, 1950, Chapter 17.

7. It is one thing to say that there is no way of demonstrating the correct structure causes. It is quite another to say, with Hook, that this is due to empirical equivalence (Sidney Hook, *Towards the Understanding of Karl Marx: A Revolutionary Interpretation*, Day, New York, 1933, Chapter 15). Hook's view differs from the one here in that he posits the empirical equivalence of competing theories, such as neoclassical economies and the Marxian theory of value, that are nonetheless different since they are formulated within different class perspectives. Hook's empirical equivalence assumes the pre-Kuhnian view that different value perspectives can generate theories whose comparison is not plagued with incommensurability problems.

8. Michael Mandelbaum, *The Nuclear Revolution: International Politics before and after Hiroshima*, Cambridge University Press, Cambridge, 1981, pp. 141–2.

9. Elaborating on Henry Luce's idea of the American Century, published in *Life* in 1941, Secretary of Defense James Forrestal wrote to the Senate Armed Services Committee in December 1947, "As long as we can outproduce the world, can control the sea and can strike inland with the atomic bomb, we can assume certain risks otherwise unacceptable in an effort to restore world trade, to restore the balance of power – military power – and to eliminate some of the conditions which breed war" (cited in Gregg Herken, *The Winning Weapon: The*

Atomic Bomb in the Cold War, 1945–1950, Random House, New York, 1982, p. 237.

10. Even those who see the centralized economy as internally in serious crisis also recognize that this crisis is made much worse by the external pressures of the market and geographical restrictions. See, e.g., Marshall I. Goldman, *U.S.S.R. in Crisis: The Failure of an Economic System*, Norton, New York, 1983, Chapter 5, Section 3.

3. The revolt against theory

1. Antonio Gramsci, *Selections from the Prison Notebooks*, trans. Q. Hoare and G. Nowell Smith, International Publishers, New York, 1971, pp. 333–5. We need not worry that Gramsci was recommending fairy tales as devices for advancing interests. Not just any account of the world will do, since an account that gains adherents must show signs of being fruitful in the long haul and over the full range of their interests.
2. One of the political motivations for rejecting an underlying materialist theory has been the recognition that there are multiple forms of struggle, forms associated with sexism, racism, nationalism, environmentalism, and pacifism. Thus, if historical materialism is – wrongly, I believe – taken to give preference to economic stimulus causes, it provides no basis for understanding and aiding these struggles (Stanley Aronowitz, *The Crisis in Historical Materialism: Class, Politics, and Culture in Marxist Theory*, Bergin, South Hadley, Mass., 1981, p. 68). A number of such criticisms of a preferred kind of causation are poststructuralist in origin, having come as a direct response to Althusser's attempt to revitalize the notion of the economy's being "determining in the last instance" (Barry Hindess and Paul Q. Hirst, *Mode of Production and Social Formation*, Macmillan, London, 1977, pp. 49–57). Anticipating the objection that this rejection of a structural level leads "to the worst sort of pluralism" in regard to causation, those who reject theory speak darkly of "a single, textured, layered analysis" (Ronald Aronson, "Historical Materialism: Answer to Marxism's Crisis," *New Left Review*, 152, July–August 1985, p. 92).
3. A model that, like Wright's, postulates two-way connections between economic structures, class struggle, state structure, and state interventions certainly avoids economist reductionism. Distinguishing the connections between these factors, as Wright does, into various kinds of causation – limitation, transformation, mediation, selection, reproduction, and functional compatibility – helps to avoid the further reduction of connections to one kind. It also enables us to know what connections to look for when the model is used in the analysis of concrete phenomena. But, though the geometry of the model is appealing, there is an arbitrariness about the whole thing, insofar as the

connections themselves remain unexplained. Without a unifier that embeds the network of connections, the model provides a guide to investigation without any indication of why it should work (Erik Olin Wright, *Class, Crisis, and the State*, New Left, London, 1978, Chapter 1). A popular version of the model of interconnected factors is to be found in Michael Albert, Robin Hanel, et al., *Liberating Theory*, South End, Boston, 1986. See the exchange between Albert, "Why Marxism Isn't the Activist's Answer," and Milton Fisk, "A Basis for Solidarity," *Monthly Review*, 39, no. 7, December 1987, pp. 43–55.

4. This theme is developed in Milton Fisk, "The Instability of Pragmatism," *New Literary History*, 17, no. 1, 1985, pp. 23–30.

5. As Plotke puts it, "the history of real societies appears as the product of a group of interlocking processes, each with its distinct forms. Particular conjunctures arise out of the meshing of these processes, not as the *expression* of one through the others" (David Plotke, "The United States in Transition, I." *Socialist Review* (U.S.), 10, no. 6, 1980, p. 88). Sensing a problem of unity with this view, Plotke hastens to tell us that the political is the process with unifying power, even though it is just one among the interlocking processes and hence does not get "expressed" through the economic and ideological processes. This solution, though, raises all the problems of atomist empiricism. Jessop, after surveying recent trends in the theory of the state, comes to the conclusion that one "must insist on the multiplicity of possible causal mechanisms" (Bob Jessop, *The Capitalist State*, New York University Press, New York, 1982, p. 228). He too assumes that Marxism holds an atomist conception of privileging economic determination. But, without this assumption, privileging economic determination is not vulnerable to his arguments.

6. According to Offe, "In an era of comprehensive state intervention, one can no longer reasonably speak of 'spheres free of state interference' that constitute the 'material bases' of the 'political superstructure'; an all-pervasive state regulation of social and economic processes is certainly a better description of today's order" (Claus Offe, "Political Authority and Class Structure," *International Journal of Sociology*, 2, no. 1, 1972, p. 78). Offe does not go as far as those who advocate the "state monopoly capitalism" thesis, which would collapse the distinction between the state and the economy altogether (Ben Fine and Laurence Harris, *Re-Reading "Capital,"* Macmillan, London, 1979). Poulantzas maintained somewhat obscurely that though the economy and the state are today not "external" to one another there is still a "relative separation" of the two (Nicos Poulantzas, *Classes in Contemporary Capitalism*, trans. D. Fernbach, New Left, London, 1975, p. 105, n. 14).

7. Michael Ryan, *Marxism and Deconstruction*, Johns Hopkins University Press, Baltimore, 1982, Chapter 4. Ryan's formulation here is in the manner of the French critic Jacques Derrida in, e.g., "Structure, Sign,

and Play in the Discourse of the Human Sciences," in *Writing and Difference*, trans. Alan Bass, University of Chicago Press, Chicago, 1978, pp. 278–93.

8. Milton Fisk, "The State and the Economy," *Midwest Studies in Philosophy*, 7, 1982, pp. 287–300, Section 2.

9. Compare Ryan's charge that the idea of primacy is an authoritarian and phallocratic one (*Marxism and Deconstruction*, p. 101) with the view of Iris Young ("Socialist Feminism and the Limits of the Dual Systems Theory," *Socialist Review*, nos. 50–1, March–June 1980, pp. 169–88) that a joint economic–gender system can have primacy. Young rightly rejects the claim that there are two isolated contexts, an economic context and a gender context. But her positive contribution does not represent the only choice. She says, "*We need . . . a thoroughly feminist historical materialism, which regards the social relations of a particular historical social formation as one system in which gender differentiation is a core attribute.*" However, the distinction between stimulus and structure cause makes it possible to employ economic structure causes as a framework for the causal efficacy, at the level of stimuli, of gender differentiation. Gender oppression is then fully recognized without the need for blending gender and economics in a unitary structure cause.

10. Jürgen Habermas, *Knowledge and Human Interests*, trans. J. J. Shapiro, Beacon, Boston, 1971, pp. 308–11. Another attack on my reaffirmation of historical materialism will come from the quarter that rejects science for being a form of domination over nature (Aronwitz, *Crisis in Historical Materialism*, pp. 55–61). Yet the framework model of historical materialism leaves ample room for a variety of agents at the stimulus level, including agents who take the side of environmental concerns by rejecting an unconditional domination of nature.

11. Mary Hesse, *Revolutions and Reconstructions in the Philosophy of Science*, Indiana University Press, Bloomington, 1980, Chapter 7. Habermas makes an effort to respond to these criticisms in *Theory of Communicative Action*, Volume 1, trans. T. McCarthy, Beacon, Boston, 1984, pp. 109–10.

12. Hilary Putnam, *Reason, Truth, and History*, Cambridge University Press, Cambridge, 1981, Chapter 5.

13. Laudan adopts a strong form of the intellectualist myth. He says, "My exclusive preoccupation will be with what I call '*cognitive progress,*' which is nothing more nor less than *progress with respect to the intellectual aspirations of science*. Cognitive progress neither entails, nor is entailed by, material, social, or spiritual progress" (Larry Laudan, *Progress and its Problems*, University of California Press, Berkeley and Los Angeles, 1977, p. 7). For a critique of attempts to draw a sharp line between scientific method and interpretation, see Richard Rorty, "Method, Social Science, and Social Hope," in his *Consequences of*

Pragmatism, University of Minnesota Press, Minneapolis, 1982, pp. 191-210.

14. Louis Althusser, "On the Materialist Dialectic," in his *For Marx,* trans. B. Brewester, Random House, New York, 1970, pp. 203, 213. A revival of emanationist essentialism, in as cogent a form as the theory permits, has been made by Scott Meikle, *Essentialism in the Thought of Karl Marx,* Open Court, La Salle, Ill., 1985.

15. Paul Hirst, *On Law and Ideology,* Humanities, Atlantic Highlands, N.J., 1979, p. 139. Hirst's critique of Althusser eliminates some of the revolutionary implications of the view that the economy is determining in the last instance, which are not sacrificed by using the framework model.

16. For example, the attack on essentialism by Ernesto Laclau and Chantal Mouffe in their *Hegemony and Socialist Strategy: Towards a Radical Politics* (Verso, London, 1985, Chapter 3) ignores the possibility of a contextualist essentialism and thereby leads them to adopt a politics that does not call into question the liberal capitalist state.

4. State autonomy

1. Alan Wolfe, *The Limits of Legitimacy: Political Contradictions of Contemporary Capitalism,* Free Press, New York, 1977, Introduction.

2. Nicos Poulantzas, *Political Power and Social Classes,* trans. T. O'Hagan, Verso, London, 1978, pp. 147-56. What Poulantzas calls different "forms of state" and which traditionally were referred to as different "constitutions" are different ways of defining the limits of justice necessary for ruling.

3. This economic determinist view is implicit in the interpretation of the capitalist ruling class by Richard W. Miller, *Analyzing Marx: Morality, Power, and History,* Princeton University Press, Princeton, N.J., 1984, Chapter 3. He neglects the degree to which struggles behind the setting of limits to losses and gains have actually changed the capitalist ruling class's long-term economic interests in regard to property and workplace control.

4. Those quotations as well as the surrounding account of changes toward a centralized military bureaucracy are taken from Stephen Skowronek, *Building a New American State: The Expansion of National Administrative Capacities, 1877-1920,* Cambridge University Press, Cambridge, 1982, pp. 100, 118.

5. Quoted in Howard Zinn, *A People's History of the United States,* Harper and Row, New York, 1980, p. 292.

6. Bob Jessop, *The Capitalist State,* New York University Press, New York, 1982, pp. 183-5.

7. Skowronek, *Building a New American State,* p. ix. Skowronek claims to

find political negotiations adequate for an account of the shift to a military bureaucracy, but he himself resorts to setting these negotiations in an economic framework to make his account feasible.

8. Samuel Bowles and Herbert Gintis, "The Crisis of Liberal Democratic Capitalism: The Case of the United States," *Politics and Society*, 11, no. 1, 1982, pp. 51–93. For Bowles and Gintis, it was the participation of the working class in the U.S. democratic process that by the 1970s brought about a shift of shares in the social product unfavorable to capital. Others who advocate complete state autonomy from the internal perspective emphasize not the ability of the working class to use the state against capital but the ability of state managers themselves to maximize their power at the expense of the interests of the capitalist class. See Fred Block, "Beyond Relative Autonomy: State Managers as Historical Subjects," in *Socialist Register*, ed. R. Miliband and J. Saville, Merlin, London, 1980, p. 229; also Theda Skocpol, "Political Response to Capitalist Crisis: Neo-Marxist Theories of the State and the Case of the New Deal," *Politics and Society*, 10, no. 2, 1981, pp. 155–201. As against these authors, it would seem that state managers occupy a position in opposition to capital more frequently because they must devise a way of ruling in a class-divided society than because of their own interests. Moreover, it would seem that, if we abstract from such a necessity of ruling, state managers would only infrequently have conflicts with capital, indicating that they are functionally linked with capital.

9. Claus Offe as well emphasizes the importance of the private accumulation of capital in shaping what are nonetheless relatively antonomous state activities. However, his overly empiricist method leaves no room for an economic framework within which this shaping can be understood. He confuses the empirical fact of the politicization of the economy with the methodological impossibility of a useful abstraction of an economic framework from the politicized economy. See my review of Offe's *Contradictions of the Welfare State* in *Noûs*, 21, no. 4, 1987, pp. 609–11.

10. Poulantzas, *Political Power and Social Classes*, pp. 284, 285, 297.

11. By 1978 Poulantzas had given up the claim that a correspondence must exist between state and economy. His view in *State, Power, and Socialism* (New Left, London, 1980) is that class struggle, not an inevitable correspondence, sets not only the state's form but also its function. There is, though, an intermediate position: The state's stable economic function may restrain class struggle without determining an outcome that exactly corresponds with that function. This intermediate position would not support Poulantzas's optimistic assessment of the democratic road to socialism.

12. Anthony Giddens, *A Contemporary Critique of Historical Materialism*, Volume 1, *Power, Property, and the State*, University of California Press,

Berkeley and Los Angeles, 1981, p. 220. In recognizing the power of struggle-imposed limits against economic self-interest, Giddens says, "The state can in some part be seen as an emancipatory force."

13. Nora Hamilton, *The Limits of State Autonomy: Post-Revolutionary Mexico*, Princeton University Press, Princeton, N.J., 1982, Chapter 9.

14. Karl Marx regarded his own materialism as compatible with the state's failing the economy. In "The Rule of the Pretorians," *New York Tribune*, March 12, 1858, Marx said in regard to Louis Bonaparte's France, "The army is no longer to maintain the rule of one part of the people over another part of the people. . . . It is to represent the *State* in antagonism to the *society*." For a discussion of this autonomist strand in Marx's thought on the state, the best source is Hal Draper's *Karl Marx's Theory of Revolution*, Volume 1, *State and Bureaucracy*, Monthly Review, New York, 1977, Chapter 18.

15. Milton Fisk, "Dialectic and Determination," *Critique* (Glasgow), 13, 1981, pp. 79–101. The contrast between a "static" and a "dialectical" framework model is drawn in this article. A dialectical framework model includes contradictory features.

5. Ideal justice

1. Franz Neumann, *Behemoth: The Structure and Practice of National Socialism, 1933–1944*, Harper and Row, New York, 1966, Part 3, Chapter 2, Section 8.

2. Plato *Republic* 434C, 540, 590–1.

3. See Edmund Pincoffs, *The Rationale of Legal Punishment*, Humanities, Atlantic Highlands, N.J., 1966, pp. 2–16.

4. Neumann, *Behemoth*, pp. 294, 432.

5. Alan Wolfe, *The Limits of Legitimacy: Political Contradictions of Contemporary Capitalism*, trans. T. O'Hagan, Verso, London, 1978, Chapter 6. Wolfe discusses the problem of the coexistence of rationality and irrationality within the state in terms of what he calls the dual state, which in the United States came into existence with the covert state created by the National Security Act of 1947. While one side of the dual state proclaimed its democratic character, the other, covert side dealt with third-world populations through the CIA and even instituted domestic repression.

6. Aristotle *Politics* 1280a.

7. In a survey of recent writing on Marx and morality, Norman Geras ("The Controversy about Marx and Justice." *New Left Review*, 150, March/April, 1985, pp. 47–85) claims that at least Marx's implicit view was that there is a justice that allows "the free development of all." If this were true, then Marx would be an advocate of a form of ideal justice. In this case the form of justice would be validated by the fact

that it would promote general self-realization. I agree with Allen Wood ("Justice and Class Interests," *Philosophica*, 33, no. 1, 1984, pp. 9–32) that the touchstone for radical Marxian justice is the interests of the proletariat. In contrast, an ideal of general human realization could not be given content from the standpoint of any class due to the conflict between the interests of that class and those of other classes. If in place of such an ideal justice we accept a radical justice based on the interests of a specific class, then an important qualification must be borne in mind. A form of justice emerging from the interests of the proletariat, or from those of any class, will express those interests only as modified by the needs of ruling. This modification introduces the element of universality normally associated with justice, without eliminating much of the sectoral content of a class-based justice.

8. Machiavelli sees quite clearly what is at stake in gaining legitimacy: "And well-organized states and wise princes have, with great diligence, taken care not to anger the nobles and to satisfy the common people and keep them contented; for this is one of the most important concerns that a prince has" (*The Prince*, trans. P. Bondanella and M. Musa, Oxford University Press, Oxford, 1984, Chapter 19). Unfortunately, his positivism goes too far to allow him to countenance a distinction between acceptable and accepted rule, once he has rejected ideal justice.

9. Ernest Barker, *Principles of Social and Political Theory*, Oxford University Press, Oxford, 1951, Book 6, Chapter 5; see also Barker's introduction to his translation of the *Politics* in *The Politics of Aristotle*, Oxford University Press, Oxford, 1958, Introduction, Chapter 3.

10. Samuel Bowles and Herbert Gintis, *Schooling in Capitalist America*, Basic, New York, 1976, Chapter 6.

11. Nicos Poulantzas, *Classes in Contemporary Capitalism*, trans. D. Fernbach, New Left, London, 1975, Part 3, Chapter 4, Section 4.

12. One example of pluralist reform was the struggle to form a black studies program with teeth in it at San Francisco State University (William Barlow and Peter Shapiro, *An End to Silence: The San Francisco State Student Movement in the '60s*, Pegasus, New York, 1971, Chapter 5).

13. I argue in Part 3 of *Ethics and Society: A Marxist Interpretation of Value*, New York University Press, New York, 1980, against the "compatibility assumption" by developing a social conception of human nature. See also the argument of Richard W. Miller in Chapter 2 of *Analyzing Marx: Morality, Power, and History*, Princeton University Press, Princeton, N.J., 1984, against the view that in a class-divided society social goals such as freedom and self-development admit of a single interpretation on which a political choice of a just social order could be based.

14. John Rawls, *A Theory of Justice*, Harvard University Press, Cambridge, Mass., 1971, p. 513.

6. Property and Justice

1. Thomas Hobbes, *Leviathan*, Part 2, Chapter 24. Hobbes says, "Seeing therefore the introduction of *propriety* is an effect of *commonwealth*, which can do nothing but by the person that represents it, it is the act only of the sovereign; and consisteth in the laws, which none can make that have not the sovereign power."
2. John Locke, *The Second Treatise of Government*, Chapter 5, Section 28. Locke says, "He that is nourished by the acorns he picked up . . . certainly appropriated them to himself. . . . That labor put a distinction between them and common . . . and so they became his private right."
3. Maurice Dobb, *Studies in the Development of Capitalism*, International Publishers, New York, 1947, Chapter 4, Section 3.
4. Robert Nozick, *Anarchy, State, and Utopia*, Basic, New York, 1974, p. 157.
5. Locke, *Second Treatise*, Chapter 8, Section 98; Chapter 11, Section 140.
6. For a different division of property, see C. B. Macpherson, "The Meaning of Property," in *Property: Mainstream and Critical Positions*, ed. C. B. Macpherson, University of Toronto Press, Toronto, 1983, pp. 1—13.
7. Gunnar Adler-Karlsson, *Reclaiming the Canadian Economy*, Anansi, Toronto, 1970, p. 53. Marx himself derives private property from control when he derives it from alienated labor, in which the worker "begets the dominion of the one who does not produce over production and over the product" ("Estranged Labor," in *The Marx–Engels Reader*, 2nd ed., ed. R. C. Tucker, Norton, New York, 1978, pp. 78—9).
8. John Maynard Keynes, *The General Theory of Employment, Interest, and Money*, Macmillan, London, 1936, pp. 378—9.
9. According to Morton J. Horwitz, in the early period of the United States "Property rights came to be justified by their efficacy in promoting economic growth" ("The Transformation in the Conception of Property in American Law, 1780–1860," *Chicago Law Review*, 40, 1973, pp. 248–61). On the question of the relation of the law to property, I am rejecting the view that the law simply institutionalizes conceptions of property already existing in "civil society." The picture is more complex since, to govern, the state must change property conceptions from those that might be justified purely on the basis of what is useful for the economy. Moreover, when as in the cases Horwitz describes, the needs of the economic system are changing rapidly, corresponding changes in the forms of control making up property may not take place spontaneously within civil society, thus requiring action of the courts to put those forms of control in place. The picture is more complex precisely because it falls between the Hobbesian statist and the Lockean economist views of property.
10. An alternative procedure is to take property inequality as basic for

purposes of accounting for a pattern that involves surplus making and taking. This is the procedure adopted by John Roemer, "New Directions in the Marxian Theory of Exploitation and Class," *Politics and Society*, 11, no. 3, 1982, which summarizes his *General Theory of Exploitation and Class*, Harvard University Press, Cambridge, Mass., 1982. There are several reasons for avoiding this approach. First, it is unable to account for the complex changes in property relations we have been discussing. Those changes occur within a single pattern of economic activity, a single form of surplus taking. Second, the control relations of property are given no goal without being embedded in a pattern of economic activity. My wish is to tie control to a purpose rather than to appeal simply to a brute motive to control facets of production. Third, the property-first procedure is ambiguous without methodological clarification. If all that is meant is that property is first because controls are a necessary condition of surplus taking, then likewise surplus taking is first because without it there is no need for property to protect it. If, however, what is meant is that inequality in property is the stimulus cause for being exploited, this may be admitted in the sense that controls set up surplus taking as a stable procedure. This is not, though, of fundamental theoretical importance, for stimulus causes act within frameworks. If the framework is the abstract economic one, then surplus taking, not property, is part of that framework. Hence, surplus taking has a theoretical priority over property. As noted earlier, Roemer's atomist methodology makes no room for such a distinction as that between stimulus and framework.

11. Milton Fisk, "Property and the State: A Discussion of Robert Nozick's *Anarchy, State, and Utopia*," *Noûs*, 14, 1980, pp. 99–108.

12. Frances Fox Piven and Richard A. Cloward, *The New Class War: Reagan's Attack on the Welfare State and Its Consequences*, Pantheon, New York, 1982, pp. 14, 123.

13. John Paul II, *Laborem Exercens*, Part 3, Sections 13–15, in *National Catholic Reporter*, September 25, 1981. John Paul says here, "From this point of view the position of 'rigid' capitalism continues to remain unacceptable, namely the position that defends the exclusive right to private ownership. . . . The principle of respect for work demands that this right should undergo a constructive revision. . . . Therefore . . . these many deeply desired reforms cannot be achieved by an *a priori* elimination of private ownership of the means of production."

7. Repression and radical justice

1. Milton Fisk and Jim Hurd, in *Socialist Worker* (Cleveland), 37 and 38, May and June 1980.

2. On the connection between outrage and justice, see Barrington Moore,

Jr., *Injustice: The Social Bases of Obedience and Revolt*, Sharpe, White Plains, N.Y., 1978, Chapter 12.

3. Feudal decentralism, which allowed a fragmentation of force among the barons, might seem to be an anomaly on this view that the state aspires to a monopoly of force. But even in feudal times any threat from the lower orders in the communes cemented the nobility and the monarchy in a common front against urban rebellion. The 1357 tax revolt led by the provost of merchants, Etienne Marcel, of Paris against the dauphin Charles was suppressed in 1358 after the nobles had been provoked into supporting the dauphin. An attack on wages and a poll tax sparked the urban–peasant revolt of 1381 led by Wat Tyler and the socialist priest John Ball that was quickly put down by Richard II of England with the aid of the nobility. The *comunero* revolt of 1520–1 in Castile was put down by the army of Charles V backed by the aristocracy. The urban and peasant revolts of the 1580s and 1590s in France united the ruling class so that Henry IV could suppress the revolts. When it comes to putting down the class enemy, examples like these confirm the feudal state's aspiration to a monopoly of force.

4. See John Rawls's formulation of what he calls "Hobbes's Thesis" (*A Theory of Justice*, Harvard University Press, Cambridge, Mass., 1971, Section 38). "By enforcing a public system of penalties," Rawls says, "government removes the grounds for thinking that others are not complying with the rules." It is the need for adherence to rules of justice and not the need to guarantee state power that for Rawls is the basis for state coercion.

5. Lucy Mair, *Primitive Government: A Study of Traditional Political Systems in Eastern Africa*, Indiana University Press, Bloomington, 1962, pp. 35–43.

6. Ibid., pp. 131–6.

7. E. P. Thompson, " 'Rough Music': Le charivari anglais," *Annales: Economies Sociétés Civilisations*, 27, no. 2, 1972, pp. 285–312.

8. Antonio Gramsci, *Selections from the Prison Notebooks*, trans. Q. Hoare and G. Nowell Smith, International Publishers, New York, 1971, pp. 136–43; also p. 259.

9. Jeffrie Murphy points out that in the absence of general consent to state rule liberal theories that attempt to justify state punishment on grounds of restoring justice fail ("Marxism and Retribution," *Philosophy and Public Affairs*, 2, no. 3, 1973, pp. 218–43). My hypothesis is that in actual societies, which are class divided and thus lack general consent to state rule, the only justification for state punishment is the strengthening of state rule, a justification that succeeds for the powerful but hardly for those who withhold consent.

10. *Boston Globe*, October 17, 1982, pp. 1, 25, 27.

11. Doreen J. MacBarnet puts much of the content of this distinction between repression for sovereignty and corrective justice in terms of that

between actual law and legality ("The Police and the State: Arrest, Legality, and the Law," in *Power and the State*, ed. G. Littlejohn, B. Smart, and N. Yuval-Davis, St. Martin's, New York, 1978, pp. 196–216).

12. John Stuart Mill took explicit note of this connection between outrage and justice through the mediation of a sense of social existence in Chapter 5 of *Utilitarianism*, Hackett, Indianapolis, 1979, p. 51.

13. Edward Westermark notes that morality is formed on the basis of a need for limits in a social order. On this basis he has moral resentment building specific moralities (*Ethical Relativity*, Routledge and Kegan Paul, London, 1932, pp. 72–3).

14. Frederick Engels points up this double tension in one of his formulas for the state: "And the modern state too is only the organization with which bourgeois society provides itself in order to maintain the general external conditions of the capitalist mode of production against encroachments either by the workers or by individual capitalists" (*Anti-Dühring*, International Publishers, New York, 1939, Part 3, Chapter 2, p. 304). Individual capitalists are the problem when their economic interests are restrained by state justice, and workers are the problem when their radical justice conflicts with state justice.

15. Howard Zinn sums this up nicely: "The system [in the United States] responded to workers' rebellions by finding new forms of control – internal control by their own organizations as well as outside control by law and force. But along with the new controls came new concessions. These concessions didn't solve basic problems; for many people they solved nothing. But they helped enough people to create an atmosphere of progress and improvement, to restore some faith in the system" (*A People's History of the United States*, Harper and Row, New York, 1980, p. 393).

16. Penny Lernoux, *Cry of the People: The Struggle for Human Rights in Latin America – The Catholic Church in Conflict with U.S. Policy*, Penguin, New York, 1982, pp. 243–80. Also Penny Lernoux, "Brazil, the Banks, the Third World," *The Nation*, November 5, 1983, pp. 434–6.

17. Philip S. Foner, *History of the Labor Movement in the United States*, Volume 5, *The A.F.L. in the Progressive Era (1910–1915)*, International Publishers, New York, 1980, Chapter 3. This provides an account of progressive movement reforms at the local as opposed to the federal level.

8. Justice and materialism

1. The Trilateral Task Force on the Governability of Democracies, *The Governability of Democracies*, Trilateral Commission, New York, 1975. In Chapter 3, Samuel Huntington discusses a "democratic distemper"

that hinders the political system from carrying out its traditional policies.

2. Evgeny B. Pashukanis, *Law and Marxism*, trans. B. Einhorn, Ink Links, London, 1978, p. 161. Allen Wood, "The Marxian Critique of Justice," *Philosophy and Public Affairs*, 1, no. 3, Spring 1972, follows the spirit of Pashukanis's program.

3. See the critique of the reduction of law to mere bourgeois justice by Colin Sumner, "The Rule of Law and Civil Rights in Contemporary Marxist Theory," *Kapitalistate*, 9, 1981, pp. 63–91.

4. Richard A. Posner, *The Economics of Justice*, Harvard University Press, Cambridge, Mass., 1981, Chapter 4.

5. When Allen Buchanan speaks of "justice in capitalism" it is not clear which justice he means. Is it bourgeois justice, official state justice, or ideal state justice? He speaks about the notion of justice prevailing "in capitalist ideology." Again, which ideology is it? It is important to ask for distinctions here since his central theme is that, as regards justice, capitalism is subject to criticism primarily because it is not just by its own standards (*Marx and Justice*, Littlefield, Adams, Totowa, N.J., 1982, Chapter 4). This claim is not true for either bourgeois or official state justice, if we ignore certain unsystematic failures of enforcement. Ideal state justice fits the claim best. But identifying it as ideal, and hence as depending on the compatibility assumption about human nature in conflicting groups, would have enabled Buchanan to make clearer why capitalism could not come up to this standard of justice. Also, it would have suggested that there was indeed an alternative – official state justice – which could be realized in a capitalist society.

6. Edward P. Thompson, *Writing by Candlelight*, Merlin, London, 1980, p. 153. Thompson's own rejection of the economist view of justice leads him to defend the rule of law as something that depends in no way on the economy or the class struggle. See the able critique of this idealist thrust of Thompson's thought by Bob Fine, *Democracy and the Rule of Law: Liberal Ideals and Marxist Critiques*, Pluto, London, 1984, Chapter 7.

7. Herbert G. Gutman, *Work, Culture, and Society in Industrializing America*, Random House, New York, 1977, p. 52.

8. Emile Durkheim, *Leçons de sociologie: physique des moeurs et du droit*, Presses Universitaires de France, Paris, 1950, Lesson 6.

9. Jürgen Habermas, *Legitimation Crisis*, trans. T. McCarthy, Beacon, Boston, 1975, Part 2, Chapter 7.

10. Nicos Poulantzas, *Political Power and Social Classes*, trans. T. O'Hagan, Verso, London, 1978, Part 2, Chapter 1, Section 3. Poulantzas points out that the state has the double role of (*a*) fragmenting all classes so that members of no class see their class relations to members of their own or another class and (*b*) then uniting these isolated agents under

the "general interest." In each of these roles the state promotes the development of a key moral idea – the idea of individualism, on the one hand, and the idea of the superiority of the "general interest" in relation to particular class interest, on the other hand.

11. Like the critical theorists and the discourse theorists, Stanley Aronowitz derives a rejection of historical materialism from his denial that the working class must play the chief role in social change. Actually, he goes beyond denying it a chief role and minimizes its role in order to emphasize cultural, sexual, and racial themes. (See his "Socialism and Beyond: Remaking the American Left," *Socialist Review* [U.S.], 69, 1983, p. 39.) But the framework-model interpretation of historical materialism gives the economy, and through it class, explanatory primacy without thereby implying that class will play the chief role as a political agent in the struggle to end class and other forms of domination. (See Milton Fisk, "Why the Anti-Marxists are Wrong," *Monthly Review*, 38, no. 10, 1987, pp. 7–17; and 39, no. 7, 1987, pp. 50–5.) In particular, under this interpretation, historical materialism does not imply that the working class must initiate, lead, or carry through struggles to end domination. Despite this lack of necessity for playing the role of chief agency, the working class can be seen to have, through the structural role given it by the framework model, a central place in determining the political basis for compromise among groups in an effective alliance. This is incompatible with the way Aronowitz, for example, minimizes its role.

12. E.g., Jon Elster, *Making Sense of Marx*, Cambridge University Press, Cambridge, 1985, pp. 232–9, 402–27.

13. Claus Offe, "The Theory of the Capitalist State and the Problem of Policy Formation," in *Stress and Contradiction in Modern Capitalism*, ed. L. N. Lindberg et al., Heath, Lexington, Mass, 1975, pp. 125–44. The conflict Offe notes between functional need and the political form best able to realize that need parallels the conflict emphasized here between functional need and the distributional form best able to motivate the effort needed to realize that need.

9. Equality and liberty

1. C. L. R. James, *The Black Jacobins: Toussaint L'Ouverture and the San Domingo Rebellion*, 2nd ed., Random House, New York, 1963, pp. 139–42.

2. Albert Soboul, *The French Revolution, 1787–1799*, trans. A. Forrest and C. Jones, Random House, New York, 1975, p. 322.

3. John Crook, *Law and Life of Rome*, Cornell University Press, Ithaca, N.Y., 1967.

4. For a libertarian view of justice for labor, see Tibor R. Machan, "Some

Philosophical Aspects of National Labor Policy," *Harvard Journal of Law and Public Policy*, 4, 1981, pp. 67–160. Anthony T. Kronman criticizes the view that what counts as noninterference could be settled apart from introducing a norm for distribution ("Contract Law and Distributive Justice," *Yale Law Journal*, 89, 1980, pp. 472–97). In fact, such a norm would reflect a solidaristic conception of liberty and equality.

5. For a good statement of the need for solidarity as a basis for a broad view of equality, see R. H. Tawney, *Equality*, Unwin, London, 1964, Chapter 1.

6. For Rawls's justice-as-fairness and stability arguments, see *A Theory of Justice*, Harvard University Press, Cambridge, Mass., 1971, Sections 3 and 76.

7. Daniel Bell saw that Rawls really broke with "liberal universalism" and adopted a principle of unequal burden for the wealthy and administrative determination of distribution (Bell, *The Coming of Post-Industrial Society*, Basic, New York, 1973, p. 448). In his "Justice as Fairness: Political Not Metaphysical" (*Philosophy and Public Affairs*, 14, no. 3, 1985, pp. 223–51), Rawls offers an interpretation of his work that makes it seem that he could agree that his postliberal justice was based on solidarity rather than universalism. This interpretation of Rawls is pursued further by Richard Rorty, "The Priority of Democracy to Philosophy," in the *Virginia Statute of Religious Freedom*, ed. M. D. Peterson and R. C. Vaughan, Cambridge University Press, Cambridge, 1988, pp. 257–82.

8. For the debate between liberal liberty and workers' freedom, see David Schweikart, *Capitalism or Worker Control? An Ethical and Economic Appraisal*, Praeger, New York, 1980, Chapter 5.

9. Ernest Barker solves such a conflict of freedoms in favor of the owner with the claim that the struggle for acquisition is essential for personal development. How those who struggle simply for a living wage and not for wealth are to fulfill themselves is not made clear (*Principles of Social and Political Theory*, Oxford University Press, Oxford, 1951, p. 158).

10. The formulation of equality in terms of equal well-being instead of equal resources is elaborated by Bruce Landesman, "Egalitarianism," *Canadian Journal of Philosophy*, 13, March 1983, pp. 27–56. However, Wood has denied that the principle "to each according to his or her needs" is an equality principle at all on the dubious ground that one cannot determine in advance what distribution of resources will satisfy the principle (Allen Wood, "Marx and Equality," in *Issues in Marxist Philosophy*, Volume 4, ed. J. Mepham and D.-H. Ruben, Harvester, Brighton, 1981).

11. Barrington Moore, Jr., *Social Origins of Dictatorship and Democracy*, Beacon Press, Boston, 1967.

12. Amartya Sen, *Levels of Poverty: Policy and Change*, World Bank, Washington, D.C., 1980, Chapter 6.
13. Roy A. Medvedev, *On Socialist Democracy*, Norton, New York, 1975, pp. 38–162.

10. Class and the limits of control

1. On this distinction between difference and distinctness, see Milton Fisk, "Dialectic and Ontology," in *Issues in Marxist Philosophy*, Volume 1, ed. J. Mepham and D.-H. Ruben, Harvester, Brighton, 1979, pp. 117–43.
2. Perry Anderson, *Lineages of the Absolute State*, Verso, London, 1974, p. 403.
3. Geoffrey Kay and James Mott, *Political Order and the Law of Labour*, Macmillan, London, 1982, pp. 97–110.
4. Morton J. Horwitz, *The Transformation of American Law, 1780–1860*, Harvard University Press, Cambridge, Mass., 1977, pp. 207–10.
5. Marx, *Capital*, Volume 1, Chapter 10, Sections 5 and 6.
6. See the discussion of capitalist control by John Westergaard and Henrietta Resler, *Class in a Capitalist Society: A Study of Contemporary Britain*, Penguin, Harmondsworth, 1976, pp. 142–3. These authors make clear that the power of capitalism to realize its goals depends to a great extent upon the widespread, habitual acceptance of capitalist economic relations. "The dull compulsion of economic relations completes the subjection of the laborer to the capitalist" (Marx, *Capital*, Volume 1, Chapter 28). This might be taken as a vindication of the idea of economic control *sui generis*. However, habitual acceptance only "completes the subjugation of the laborer" and thus depends on the force and the norms that allow the habit to start and then continue.
7. The definitions of economic productive relations for feudalism and industrial state-run economies need to highlight economic goals without relying on market mechanisms for their realization. In the feudal economy, the goal of surplus generation is the consumption of a nonproductive class. The surplus is generated mainly from the land by one division within the population, and it goes by labor services, deliveries in kind, or rent in cash to another division within the population for its consumption. That those who deliver do so on the basis of being tied personally to a noble is a fact about the control needed for realizing this economic goal and is thus a fact about feudal classes rather than about the economic productive relations themselves (*pace* Perry Anderson, *Lineages of the Absolute State*, p. 401). Likewise, as will be indicated in Chapter 20, the contemporary state-run economies give one division within the population, as a group, the use of the surplus of the industrial establishment. The goal of this allocation is to defeat

attempts to undermine it by economies based on private appropriation of the surplus. Having the power of the state is a condition for that division within the population – the bureaucratic class – to realize this defensive goal.

8. Marx says, "The more the capitalist has accumulated, the more he is able to accumulate" (*Capital*, Volume 1, Chapter 24, Section 1).

9. Ronald L. Meek, *Studies in the Labor Theory of Value*, 2nd ed., Monthly Review, New York, 1975, p. 179. For a critique of the labor theory of value, see Robert Paul Wolff, *Understanding Marx: A Reconstruction and Critique of Capital*, Princeton University Press, Princeton, N.J., 1984, pp. 163–78.

10. See Chris Harman's defense of this tendency in "Marx's Theory of Crisis and Its Critics," *International Socialism*, 11, 1981, p. 37.

11. For a historical account that interprets changes in the forms of control of the labor process as responses to specific forms of worker opposition at the workplace, see Richard Edwards, *Contested Terrain: The Transformation of the Workplace in the Twentieth Century*, Basic, New York, 1979, Chapters 2 through 4.

12. In contrast, for an account of class that attributes to the capitalist class a *monopoly* over the work process, the means of production, and investment, see Erik Olin Wright, *Class, Crisis, and the State*, Verso, London, 1979, pp. 72–3. In his more recent book, Wright has taken a quite different view (*Classes*, Verso, London, 1985, Chapters 3 and 4). In defining classes for capitalism, he abandons his earlier appeal to control. Following Roemer, he appeals to a differential distribution of ownership to define classes. This view has the problem that ownership itself must be understood as a form of control over facets of production – labor, organization, surplus, skills. The perspective of my framework model yields a diagnosis of Wright's inability to come up with a theory of class without a central flaw. He sees rightly that controls alone do not distinguish a working class from an oppressed nonclass group. This he takes as a sufficient basis for abandoning controls for a property criterion for class, which in fact fails to move him beyond a reliance on controls. Instead of abandoning controls, he would have done well to take them along with a structural economic background. Then controls over class groups could have been distinguished from controls over nonclass groups. The controls over labor that account for class are precisely those that are adequate to reproduce the structural background of exploitation. The same cannot be said of controls over nonclass groups.

13. Elster regresses to the Weberian view of class after posing objections to the idea that class is based on exploitation and on power relations. Thus, for him, class becomes a matter of having to take one's chances on the market with a certain set of assets (Jon Elster, *Making Sense of Marx*, Cambridge University Press, Cambridge, 1985, p. 326). Some

357

assets make one a capitalist, and others qualify one as a worker. Control over these assets is taken as a given without any elaboration. In contrast, within my framework model, control emerges on the background of productive economic relations – including exploitation – through specific historical challenges to those relations. Thus neither exploitation nor power alone but both together provide an avenue to understanding class. (For a critique of the Weberian view of classes, see Rosemary Crompton and Jon Gubbay, *Economic and Class Structure*, Macmillan, London, 1977, Chapter 2.)

14. *Pace* Nicos Poulantzas, *Classes in Contemporary Capitalism*, trans. D. Fernbach, New Left, London, 1975, p. 187.
15. Irving Bernstein, *The Lean Years: A History of the American Worker, 1920–1933*, Houghton Mifflin, Boston, 1960, p. 199.

11. On functional explanation

1. Nicos Poulantzas, *Political Power and Social Classes*, trans. T. O'Hagan, Verso, London, 1978, pp. 140, 287.
2. Thomas Hobbes, *Leviathan*, Part 2, Chapter 17.
3. Frederick Engels, *The Origin of the Family, Private Property, and the State*, ed. E. B. Leacock, International Publishers, New York, 1972, pp. 229–30.
4. Lucy Mair, *Primitive Government: A Study of Traditional Political Systems in Eastern Africa*, Indiana University Press, Bloomington, 1962, Chapter 10.
5. For a critical history of institutionalism or "organization theory," see Graeme Salaman, *Class and the Corporation*, Fontana, Glasgow, 1981, Chapter 6.
6. Charles Lindblom, *Politics and Markets: The World's Political and Economic Systems*, Basic, New York, 1977, Chapter 13.
7. For a clear exposition of the concept of a *Rechtsstaat*, see Elías Díaz, *Estado de derecho y sociedad democrática*, Cuadernos para el Diálogo, Madrid, 1979, Chapters 1 and 3.
8. G. W. F. Hegel, *Science of Logic*, Volume 2, Section 2, Chapter 1(C)(b), "Laws," trans. W. H. Johnston and L. G. Struthers, Allen and Unwin, London, 1929, Volume 2, p. 364.
9. G. A. Cohen, *Karl Marx's Theory of History: A Defense*, Princeton University Press, Princeton, N.J., 1978, Chapter 9.
10. John Roemer, " 'Rational Choice' Marxism: Some Issues of Method and Substance," in *Analytical Marxism*, ed. J. Roemer, Chapter 9. For a view of choice that connects its elements with the social background, see Milton Fisk, *Ethics and Society: A Marxist Interpretation of Value*, New York University Press, New York, 1980, Chapters 13–15. Cohen speaks of the role of belief and purpose under the heading of "elaborations" of functional explanation in *Marx's Theory of History*, pp. 287–8.

11. Jon Elster, "Further Thoughts on Marxism, Functionalism, and Game Theory," in *Analytical Marxism*, ed. Roemer, Chapter 10.

12. Milton Fisk, *Nature and Necessity: An Essay in Physical Ontology*, Indiana University Press, Bloomington, 1973, Chapter 3, Section 3. This source provides a general discussion of the sort of "essentialism" on which the framework model rests. It is shown that rejections of essentialism have a positivist root and make explanatory science impossible. This applies to all rejections of essentialism, whether inspired by existentialism, language analysis, or deconstruction.

13. In contrast, "ideal justice" – Chapter 5 – is a primary need, and hence the state exists to promote it. It is not a great oversimplification to say that the state serves justice in the doctrine of Part 2 of John Rawls, *A Theory of Justice*, Harvard University Press, Cambridge, Mass., 1971.

14. Poulantzas, *Political Power and Social Classes*, Part 3, Chapter 2, Section 1.

15. Anthony Giddens, *A Contemporary Critique of Historical Materialism*, Volume 1, *Power, Property, and the State*, University of California Press, Berkeley and Los Angeles, 1981, p. 18.

12. Power and function

1. Richard W. Hurd, "How PATCO Was Led into a Trap," *The Nation*, December 26, 1981, pp. 696–8.

2. See the threefold division of power in Steven Lukes, *Power: A Radical View*, Macmillan, London, 1974, Chapter 4.

3. Stephen Skowronek, *Building a New American State: The Expansion of National Administrative Capacities, 1877–1920*, Cambridge University Press, Cambridge, 1982, p. 27.

4. See the discussion of the critique of the liberal state from the standpoint of the Nazi theory of the totalitarian state by Franz Neumann, *Behemoth: The Structure and Practice of National Socialism, 1933–1944*, Harper and Row, New York, 1966, Part 1, Chapter 1.

5. Howard Zinn, *A People's History of the United States*, Harper and Row, New York, 1980, Chapter 10.

6. Philip S. Foner, *History of the Labor Movement in the United States*, Volume 1, *From Colonial Times to the Founding of the American Federation of Labor*, International Publishers, New York, 1947, Chapters 22–4.

7. As before, hegemony is taken here in what I guess to be Gramsci's sense of it when he applies it to the state (Antonio Gramsci, *Selections from the Prison Notebooks*, trans. Q. Hoare and G. Nowell Smith, International Publishers, New York, 1971, pp. 210, 242, 333).

8. On the reflexive character of state power and how it leads to the mystique of state power, see Lawrence Krader, *Formation of the State*, Prentice-Hall, Englewood Cliffs, N.J., 1968, Introduction.

9. See, e.g., John Stuart Mill, *Considerations on Representative Govern-*

ment, Chapter 5, in *Collected Works of John Stuart Mill*, ed. J. M. Robson, Volume 19, University of Toronto Press, Toronto, 1977.

10. A precondition of the state's successful defense of its power is the monopoly of force. If this monopoly is not totally realized, it must at least be partially realized. The monopoly of force was partially realized through the feudal mechanism of possession of the land on the condition of a pledge by the landholder of military service at the side of the king. Also, it was partially realized through a system of feudal hostage practiced in the Tokugawa shogunate starting in the seventeenth century in Japan. The Japanese barons could in some cases field almost as many samurai as the shogunate. This dispersion of force was compensated for by the requirement that the barons set up alternate residences in the capital city of Edo where, in their absence, they had to leave members of their families as hostages (Perry Anderson, *Lineages of the Absolutist State*, Verso, London, 1974, pp. 435–61).

11. For some reason Giddens thinks that Marxists cannot give force the role it is due in the state. In particular, he thinks they fail to have an appreciation of the monopoly of force, which is the trademark of the Weberian state. Marxists are portrayed as completely caught up in a market model, which excludes physical force. The account in the text should be an indication that Giddens is wrong in his general claim that a Marxist account of the state's need for force is impossible, and wrong also in his particular claim that considerations of territoriality and nationality are at the bottom of talk about force (Anthony Giddens, *A Contemporary Critique of Historical Materialism*, Volume 1, *Power, Property, and the State*, University of California Press, Berkeley and Los Angeles, 1981, Chapter 8). Rather, the need for reproduction and stability are behind the state's need for force.

12. Poulantzas shows that he cannot shake an attachment to reductive materialism when he claims that state institutions are power centers only insofar as the power of social classes is organized in them (Nicos Poulantzas, *Political Power and Social Classes*, trans. T. O'Hagan, Verso, London, 1978, p. 115).

13. Alan Wolfe, *The Limits of Legitimacy: Political Contradictions of Contemporary Capitalism*, Free Press, New York, 1977, Chapter 2.

14. Quentin Skinner, *The Foundations of Modern Political Thought*, Volume 2, *The Age of Reformation*, Cambridge University Press, Cambridge, 1978, pp. 241–54.

13. Democracy, its bright and its dark sides

1. Alexander Hamilton, John Jay, and James Madison, *The Federalist Papers*, ed. Clinton Rossiter, New American Library, New York, 1961, Number 10.

2. Madison's solution to this problem is subtler than John Stuart Mill's, who in Chapter 6 of *Considerations on Representative Government* (in *Collected Works of John Stuart Mill*, ed. J. M. Robson, Volume 19, University of Toronto Press, Toronto, 1977) advocated a weighting system for admission to a representative assembly that would give the majority class no more votes in it than the class of employers.

3. Aristotle *Politics* 1286a.

4. For the role of special bodies − the Brookings Institution, the Committee for Economic Development, the Committee on Foreign Relations, the National Civic Federation − in building the political power of the bourgeoisie in the United States, see G. William Domhoff, *The Higher Circles: The Governing Class in America*, Random House, New York, 1970, Chapter 6.

5. In this threefold distinction, economic power equates with what was discussed in Chapter 10 as control over the economic productive relations. For elaboration of the view that power at each of the three levels is associated with class struggle at the economic, ideological, and political levels, see Nicos Poulantzas, *Political Power and Social Classes*, trans. T. O'Hagan, Verso, London, 1978, pp. 113–14.

6. Herbert G. Gutman, *Work, Culture, and Society in Industrializing America*, Random House, New York, 1977, Chapter 5.

7. Charles Lindblom, *Politics and Markets: The World's Political and Economic Systems*, Basic, New York, 1977, Chapter 15. He remarks that "government officials . . . would like to remove from politics those highly divisive issues on which businessmen would be loath to yield. Since theirs is the task of seeing to it that business performs, they do not want the fundamentals of private enterprise to become lively political issues" (p. 205).

8. Bob Jessop, "Capitalism and Democracy: The Best Possible Shell?" in *Power and the State*, ed. G. Littlejohn, B. Smart, and N. Yuval-Davis, St. Martin's, New York, 1978, p. 33.

9. G. E. M. de Ste. Croix, *The Class Struggle in the Ancient Greek World: From the Archaic Age to the Arab Conquests*, Cornell University Press, Ithaca, N.Y., 1981, pp. 287–93. Also M. I. Finley, *Politics in the Ancient World*, Cambridge University Press, Cambridge, 1983, pp. 42–7.

10. It would, for example, be difficult to contend that the constitutionalism of Jean Gerson of the early fifteenth century, which derived from his support of the conciliar tradition in the church as a basis for ending the Great Schism, had genuinely democratic implications. On Gerson's constitutionalism, see Quentin Skinner, *The Foundations of Modern Political Thought*, Volume 2, *The Age of Reformation*, Cambridge University Press, Cambridge, 1978, pp. 114–23.

11. The bourgeois rising of Paris under Etienne Marcel was an attempt to get the dauphin Charles to accept rule by a Council of the Estates and to levy no tax not voted by the Estates-General. The nobility, who

resented these conditions, was pushed by subsequent events to active support for the monarchy. See Barbara W. Tuchman, *A Distant Mirror: The Calamitous 14th Century*, Ballantine, New York, 1978, Chapter 7.

12. Poulantzas rightly points out the willingness of the capitalists to give up a measure of economic power for the purpose of retaining political power (*Political Power and Social Classes*, Part 3, Chapter 1).

13. R. H. Tawney, *Equality*, Unwin, London, 1964, p. 202. The history of the British Labour Party in the half-century after Tawney wrote shows that he underplayed the dark side of democracy. Had he taken account of the dark side, he would have seen that it was essential to resist the almost complete institutionalization of the political class struggle that has since occurred in Britain.

14. Welfare capitalism

1. Jim Campen, "Economic Crisis and Conservative Economic Policies: U.S. Capitalism in the 1980s," *Radical America*, 15, Spring 1981, pp. 33–54.

2. Goran Therborn, "The Prospects of Labor and the Transformation of Advanced Capitalism," *New Left Review*, 145, May–June 1984, pp. 5–38.

3. David Thomson, *England in the Nineteenth Century (1815–1914)*, Penguin, Harmondsworth, 1950, Chapter 10.

4. Quoted in Domhoff's account of elite group pressure for social legislation (*The Higher Circles: The Governing Class in America*, Random House, New York, 1970, p. 215).

5. P. G. Peterson, "Social Security: The Coming Crash" and "The Salvation of Social Security," *New York Review of Books*, December 2 and 16, 1982.

6. Karl Marx, *Theories of Surplus Value*, Volume 2, Progress, Moscow, 1968, Chapter 17, pp. 470–546; and John Maynard Keynes, *The General Theory of Employment, Interest, and Money*, Macmillan, London, 1936, Chapter 2, Section 6.

7. Paul A. Samuelson, *Economics: An Introductory Analysis*, 5th ed., McGraw-Hill, New York, 1961, p. 376.

8. Martha Derthick, *Policymaking for Social Security*, Brookings Institution, Washington, D.C., 1979, Chapter 5.

9. Frances Fox Piven and Richard A. Cloward, *The New Class War: Reagan's Attack on the Welfare State and Its Consequences*, Pantheon, New York, 1982, pp. 114–18.

10. Milton Friedman and Rose Friedman, *Free to Choose*, Avon, New York, 1979, Chapter 4.

11. John D. Stephans, *The Transition from Capitalism to Socialism*, Macmillan, London, 1979, p. 174.

12. A word is in order on the notion of subsistence. The norm for subsis-

tence is not just a physical one, so justice as subsistence is not merely an expression of physical human nature. It is also an expression of both the struggle of the lower classes and the development of technology. As the "general will" evolves, a standard of subsistence evolves as part of it.

13. Lester Thurow, *The Zero Sum Society*, Penguin, Harmondsworth, 1981, p. 160.
14. Ian Gough, *The Political Economy of the Welfare State*, Macmillan, London, 1979, pp. 111–13.
15. Amartya Sen, *Policy and Change*, World Bank, Washington, D.C., 1980, Chapter 7.
16. Jürgen Habermas, *Legitimation Crisis*, trans. T. McCarthy, Beacon, Boston, 1975, Part 2, Chapters 6 and 7.
17. James O'Connor, *The Fiscal Crisis of the State*, St. Martin's, New York, 1973, Chapter 6.
18. Gough, *Political Economy of the Welfare State*, pp. 116–21.
19. Friedman and Friedman, *Free to Choose*, p.115.

15. The new mercantilism

1. Norman Fischer, *Economy and Self: Philosophy and Economy from the Mercantilists to Marx*, Greenwood, Westport, Conn., 1979, Chapter 1. See J. W. Horrocks, *A Short History of Mercantilism*, Dent, London, 1925.
2. O'Connor, for example, rejects his earlier functional analysis of *The Fiscal Crisis of the State* for a positivist conjunctural analysis. James O'Connor, "*The Fiscal Crisis of the State* Revisited," *Kapitalistate*, 9, 1981, pp. 41–61.
3. John Maynard Keynes, *The General Theory of Employment, Interest, and Money*, Macmillan, London, 1936, Chapter 24.
4. Because we are using the framework model, the injection of considerations of nationality into a functional explanation of state support for accumulation in no way detracts from the materialist character of such an explanation. To play a role, nationality need not feature among the economic tendencies of the framework. On the importance of nationality in explanation, see Anthony Giddens, *A Contemporary Critique of Historical Materialism*, Volume 1, *Power, Property, and the State*, University of California Press, Berkeley and Los Angeles, 1981, Chapter 8.
5. Taking on the position of world economic leader requires a stronger sense of internationalism, but such a position depends on the economic productivity of the leading nation. See David A. Lake, "International Economic Structures and American Foreign Economic Policy, 1887–1934," *World Politics*, 35, no. 4, 1983, pp. 517–43.
6. Marx's treatment of the role of the state in the "primitive accumula-

tion" of capital remains relevant to the discussion of state funding of large-scale expansion. See *Capital*, Volume 1, Part 8.

7. Anwar Shaikh, "Political Economy and Capitalism: Notes on Dobb's Theory of Crisis," *Cambridge Journal of Economics*, 2, 1978, pp. 233–51.

8. Nigel Harris, *Of Bread and Guns: The World Economy in Crisis*, Penguin, Harmondsworth, 1983, Chapter 4.

9. This overproduction view has long been championed by Paul Sweezy; see the editorial "Supply-Side Theory and Capital Investment," *Monthly Review*, 34, April 1983, pp. 1–9. Cf. Milton Fisk, "Rate of Profit and Class Struggle," *Radical Philosophers' Newsjournal*, no. 5, August 1975, pp. 1–37 (see esp. Section 4).

10. For this interpretation of the 1920s, see Chris Harman, "The Crisis Last Time," *International Socialism*, 13, 1981, pp. 1–28. The overproduction thesis of the depression is stated by Antonio Carlo, "The State's Crisis in the 1930s," *Telos*, 46, Winter 1980–81. For a variation on this view, see James N. Devine, "Underconsumption, Over-investment, and the Origins of the Great Depression," *Review of Radical Political Economy*, 15, Summer 1983, pp. 1–27.

11. Milton Fisk, *The Roots of the Stagnant Economy* (pamphlet), Hera Press, Cleveland, 1978, pp. 19–34.

12. Maurice Dobb, *An Essay on Economic Growth and Planning*, Routledge, London, 1960, pp. 7 and 17. Also Charles Lindblom, *Politics and Markets: The World's Political and Economic Systems*, Basic, New York, 1977, pp. 152–7.

13. Alan Wolfe points out that the inability of "the accumulative state" of the early nineteenth century, with its mercantilist support for capital, to survive the development of the working class was due to its lack of a legitimating conception (*The Limits of Legitimacy: Political Contradictions of Contemporary Capitalism*, Free Press, New York, 1977, p. 40).

14. A third way, which is more basic, results from the fact that, though injections of capital have a short-term potential for creating employment growth, they have a long-term potential for reducing the average rate of return, as a result of reducing the ratio of labor to constant capital. See Ernest Mandel, *Late Capitalism*, trans. J. De Bres, Verso, London, 1975, Chapter 9, Section 4.

15. Milton Fisk, "U.S. Labor and Foreign Competition," *Against the Current*, 5, no. 1, 1989, pp. 19–25.

16. See the editorial "Production and Finance," *Monthly Review*, 35, May 1983, pp. 1–13.

16. Organized labor and the state

1. G. William Domhoff, *The Higher Circles: The Governing Class in America*, Random House, New York, 1970, Chapter 7.

2. Nicos Poulantzas, *Political Power and Social Classes*, trans. T. O'Hagan, Verso, London, 1978, pp. 299–320. Poulantzas denies that parties have the relative autonomy characteristic of the state. But his analysis actually shows only that the degree of autonomy of parties varies inversely with the degree of autonomy of other state institutions.

3. Antonio Gramsci, *Selections from the Prison Notebooks*, trans. Q. Hoare and G. Nowell Smith, International Publishers, New York, 1971, p. 155.

4. Philip S. Foner, *History of the Labor Movement in the United States, Volume 2, From the Founding of the A. F. of L. to the Emergence of Imperialism*, International Publishers, New York, 1955, p. 338. For a nuanced interpretation of Gompers that confirms the view in the text, see Stanley Aronowitz, *Working Class Hero: A New Strategy for Labor*, Pilgrim, New York, 1983, Chapter 1.

5. Philip S. Foner, *History of the Labor Movement in the United States, Volume 5, The AFL in the Progressive Era (1910–1915)*, International Publishers, New York, 1980, Chapter 5. For an account of the relation of the CIO in its formative years to the Democratic Party, see David Milton, *The Politics of U.S. Labor: From the Great Depression to the New Deal*, Monthly Review, New York, 1982, Chapters 5 and 6.

6. Mike Davis relies too heavily on this pregiven disunity in his account of the failure of labor to form a third party (*Prisoners of the American Dream*, Verso, London, 1986, pp. 40–51).

7. Adolfo Gilly, *La revolución interrumpida, México, 1910–1920: una guerra campesina por la tierra y el poder*, Ediciones "El Caballito," Mexico City, 1971, pp. 182–6.

8. Nora Hamilton, *The Limits of State Autonomy: Post-Revolutionary Mexico*, Princeton University Press, Princeton, N.J., 1982, pp. 145–62, 240–4.

9. Ralph Miliband, *Parliamentary Socialism: A Study in the Politics of Labor*, Allen and Unwin, London, 1961, Chapters 3 and 4.

10. On the origin of the USSR trade unions' loss of economic independence, see E. H. Carr and R. W. Davies, *Foundations of a Planned Economy, 1926–1929*, Volume 1, Macmillan, London, 1969, Part 1, Chapter 20, Section a.

11. Bob Arnot, "Soviet Labour Productivity and the Failure of the Shchekino Experiment," *Critique* (Glasgow), 15, 1981, pp. 31–56. For a less negative view of Soviet unions than is presented in the text, see David Lane, *Soviet Economy and Society*, New York University Press, New York, 1985, pp. 25–45.

12. Milton Fisk, "The American Labor Movement's Politics of Futility," *Changes: Socialist Journal*, 6, nos. 9–10, 1984, pp. 8–11.

13. Quoted in Art Preis, *Labor's Giant Step: Twenty Years of the CIO*, Pathfinder, New York, 1972, p. 357.

14. On labor's effort to win these measures in the United States, see David

Greenstone, *Labor in American Politics*, Knopf, New York, 1969, pp. 75-7, 337-43. For an update on U.S. labor's legislative efforts, see Richard B. Freeman and James L. Medoff, *What Do Unions Do?* Basic, New York, 1984, Chapter 13.

15. Colin Crouch, "The State, Capital, and Liberal Democracy," in *State and Economy in Contemporary Capitalism*, ed. C. Crouch, St. Martin's, New York, 1979, p. 23.

17. Global justice

1. René Descartes, *Rules for the Direction of the Mind*, Rule 5; see *Ouevres de Descartes*, Volume 10, ed. C. Adam and P. Tannery, Vrin, Paris, 1966, p. 381.
2. Ernest Barker, *Principles of Social and Political Theory*, Oxford University Press, Oxford, 1951, Book 4, Section 7. Barker takes as adequate a definition of the state as "a juridically organized nation" (p. 56).
3. John Rawls, *A Theory of Justice*, Harvard University Press, Cambridge, Mass., 1971, Sections 38 and 58. On international relations, Rawls says, "Now at this point one may extend the interpretation of the original position and think of the parties as representatives of different nations who must choose together the fundamental principles to adjudicate conflicting claims among states. . . . These representatives are deprived of various kinds of information. . . . They know nothing about the particular circumstances of their own society, its power and strength in comparison with other nations." The global justice arrived at by Rawls here is ideal (Chapter 5) rather than a requirement of ruling, and the assurance that other states conform to this justice would depend on Rawls's introducing a superstate.
4. Nikolai Bukharin, *Imperialism and World Economy*, Merlin, London, 1972, Chapter 4: "The state grew on the economic foundation; it was only an expression of economic connections." An updated version of Bukharin's 1917 account is given by Nigel Harris in *Of Bread and Guns: The World Economy in Crisis*, Penguin, Harmondsworth, 1983, Chapter 1.
5. Leon Trotsky, "Thoughts on the Progress of the Proletarian Revolution," in his *The First Five Years of the Communist International: 1919–1924*, Volume 1, Pathfinder, New York, 1972, pp. 50–63.
6. James Petras, "Marxism and World Historical Transformations," *Contemporary Marxism*, 9, Fall 1984, pp. 18–34. Petras comments, "Surplus appropriated from the metropole and the less developed countries has created new dynamic areas and sets of relations in which regional linkages of domination and subordination begin to pre-empt the global patterns established earlier by the metropolitan countries."
7. Tony Cliff, *State Capitalism in Russia*, Pluto, London, 1974, Chapter 7.

8. Michael Mandelbaum, *The Nuclear Revolution: International Politics before and after Hiroshima*, Cambridge University Press, Cambridge, 1981, Chapter 3. This enthusiastic account of the market model proceeds with no awareness of the shakiness of its foundations. Mandelbaum pushes the model to cover Smithian laissez-faire and Keynesian managed-market stages of international relations. Thus the balance-of-power equilibrium represented by the 1713 Treaty of Utrecht was reached through laissez-faire, whereas the Quadruple Alliance of 1815 and the United Nations of 1945 resulted less haphazardly from managing the anarchy between states.

9. The differences between Roemer and Elster on this point illustrate the issues involved. See John Roemer's " 'Rational Choice' Marxism: Some Issues of Method and Substance" and Jon Elster's "Marxism, Functionalism, and Game Theory," in *Analytical Marxism*, ed. J. Roemer, Cambridge University Press, Cambridge, 1986, pp. 191-201, 202-20.

10. For a classic statement of such "realism," see Reinhold Niebuhr, *Moral Man and Immoral Society: A Study in Ethics and Politics*, Scribner, New York, 1932, Chapter 4.

11. George Orwell, *1984*, Harcourt Brace Jovanovich, New York, 1949, Part 2, Chapter 9.

12. Richard R. Fagen, "Theories of Development: The Question of Class Struggle," *Monthly Review*, 35, no. 4, September 1983, pp. 13-24.

13. Thomas E. Weisskopf, "Imperialism and the Economic Development of the Third World," in *The Capitalist System*, 2nd ed., ed. R. C. Edwards, M. Reich, and T. E. Weisskopf, Prentice-Hall, Englewood Cliffs, N.J., 1978, pp. 508-9.

18. The imperial state

1. *A Documentary History of the United States*, ed. R. C. Heffner, New American Library, New York, 1952, Chapter 24.

2. Charles P. Kindleberger, *The World in Depression: 1929-1939*, University of California Press, Berkeley and Los Angeles, 1973, Chapter 14.

3. The idea of combined and uneven development is at odds with both a stage theory of development and that form of the theory of third world dependency that emphasizes the development of underdevelopment in the third world. For the stage theory, there is no combined development of nations but only the separate development of each nation through the same trajectory the original capitalist countries went through. For that form of dependency theory, the development of the original capitalist countries necessitated blocking the development of others, which became underdeveloped. In contrast, combined and uneven development occurs when some less developed economies take leaps and hence skip traditional stages as a result of linkages with the

more developed economies in the global system, without there being as a result of this development a final evening out – though the various economies may change their rank in the developmental ranking – since there are unequal starting places as well as different class and material factors affecting subsequent development. (See Leon Trotsky, *The History of the Russian Revolution*, Volume 1, trans. M. Eastman, Sphere, London, 1967, Chapter 1. Also see Michael Lowy, *The Politics of Combined and Uneven Development*, New Left, London, 1981. For a critique of stage and dependency theories from the prespective of "combined and uneven development," see Steve Zeluck, "On Third World Development," *Against the Current*, 2, no. 2, Spring 1983, pp. 23–32.) The global economic framework in my account is proposed as a way of articulating the view of combined and uneven development.

4. Norman Girvan and Richard Bernal, "The IMF and the Foreclosure of Development Options; The Case of Jamaica," *Monthly Review*, 9, no. 33, February 1982, pp. 34–48.

5. For a discussion of these World Bank data, see Fidel Castro, *The World Economic and Social Crisis: Report to the Seventh Summit Conference of Non-Aligned Countries*, Council of State Publishing Office, Havana, 1983, Chapter 10.

6. André Gunder Frank, *Capitalism and Underdevelopment in Latin America*, Monthly Review, New York, 1969, p. 9.

7. James F. Petras et al., *Class, State, and Power in the Third World: With Case Studies on Class Conflict in Latin America*, Allenhead, Osmun, Montclair, N.J., 1981, pp. 17–20.

8. Rob Hager, "State, Tribe, and Empire in Afghan Interpolity Relations," in *The Conflict between Tribe and State in Iran and Afghanistan*, ed. R. Tapper, Croom Helm, London, 1983, pp. 83–118.

9. Robert Brenner, "The Origins of Capitalist Development: A Critique of Neo-Smithian Marxism," *New Left Review*, 104, July–August 1977, pp. 25–92. Compare with André Gunder Frank, *World Accumulation, 1492–1789*, Monthly Review, New York, 1978.

10. Ernest Mandel, *Late Capitalism*, trans. J. De Bres, Verso, London, 1975, pp. 60–73. In following Mandel and others like Barratt Brown in making differential productivity the structural root of imperialism in the global system, I am assuming that this is the structural root in the sense of the framework model, allowing thereby for a historical account of imperialism in which the political is relatively autonomous.

11. On productivity-based conceptions of economic domination, as distinct from political domination, see Stephen D. Krasner, "State Power and the Structure of International Trade," *World Politics*, 28, no. 3, 1976, pp. 317–47; and David A. Lake, "International Economic Structures and American Foreign Economic Policy, 1887–1934," *World Politics*, 35, no. 4, 1983, pp. 517–43.

12. Fernando H. Cardoso and Enzo Faletto, *Dependency and Development*

in Latin America, trans. M. M. Urquidi, University of California Press, Berkeley and Los Angeles, 1979, pp. xx–xxi, 159–66. Their conception of the link between development and economic domination makes use of the framework model and avoids thereby a crude determinism. For a summary of the three forms of economic domination, see Marta Harnecker and Gabriela Uribe, *Imperialismo y dependencia* (*Cuaderno de educación popular*, no. 6), Editorial Nuevos Horizontes, Mexico City, n.d.

13. Michael Barratt Brown, *The Economics of Imperialism*, Penguin, Harmondsworth, 1974, Chapter 10.

14. On the primacy of the role of bank capital, over direct investment, in development in the 1960s and 1970s, see Jeff Frieden, "Third World Indebted Industrialization," *International Organization*, 35, no. 1, 1981, pp. 407–31.

15. Form and function of the imperial state are embodied in specific agencies, which may only be extensions of the agencies servicing the economy within national boundaries. The U.S. Departments of Commerce, Treasury, and Agriculture are economic agencies of the imperial state, whereas the Department of Defense, the Central Intelligence Agency, and the Defense Intelligence Agency are branches of the repressive apparatus of the imperial state, and the U.S. Information Agency and the Peace Corps are ideological agencies of the imperial state. See Petras et al., *Class, State, and Power in the Third World*, p. 16.

16. Marx, *Capital*, Volume 1, Chapter 15, Section 7. For Marx's change, see Suniti Kumar Ghosh, "Marx on India," *Monthly Review*, 35, no. 8, January 1984, pp. 39–53. On the thesis that imperial relations are compatible with development toward equal status on a world scale, see Bill Warren, *Imperialism: Pioneer of Capitalism*, Verso, London, 1980; and Albert Szymanski, *The Logic of Imperialism*, Praeger, New York, 1981.

17. Cheryl Payer, *The Debt Trap: The International Monetary Fund and the Third World*, Monthly Review, New York, 1974, Chapter 3; and Robin Broad, "The Transformation of the Philippine Economy," *Monthly Review*, 36, no. 1, May 1984, pp. 11–21.

19. Peace through strength

1. See, for example, Albert Einstein's discussion of the state in *Einstein on Peace*, ed. O. Nathan and H. Norden, Schocken, New York, 1968, p. 471.

2. In saying this I am not accepting the view of Max Weber that the state is fundamentally "a human community that (successfully) claims the *monopoly of the legitimate use of physical force* within a given territory" ("Politics as Vocation," in *From Max Weber: Essays in Sociology*, ed. H.

H. Gerth and C. W. Mills, Oxford University Press, Oxford, 1946, p. 78). This leaves out the functional and hegemonic power of the state, for which, in any event, the monopoly of force is a bulwark.

3. Stephen Skowronek, *Building a New American State: The Expansion of National Administrative Capacities, 1877–1920*, Cambridge University Press, Cambridge, 1982, Chapters 4 and 7.

4. Fernando Claudin, *The Communist Movement*, Penguin, Harmondsworth, 1975, pp. 321 ff.

5. Michael Mandelbaum, *The Nuclear Revolution: International Politics before and after Hiroshima*, Cambridge University Press, Cambridge, 1981, Chapter 4.

6. Bruce Russett, *The Prisoners of Insecurity: Nuclear Deterrence, the Arms Race, and Arms Control*, Freeman, New York, 1983, pp. 178–90.

7. George F. Kennan, *The Nuclear Delusion: Soviet–American Relations in the Atomic Age*, Pantheon, New York, 1983, Chapter 12. Kennan opposed the imperialist view of the 1950 National Security Council document 68 that the interests of the United States are global with his modified imperialist view that the United States should commit itself only where it has "vital interests," namely, in Western Europe and Japan.

8. This conformity to the principle of superiority is not unconscious but is pushed along by the aspirations of state leaders. Thus, in arguing for the hydrogen bomb in 1950, the joint chiefs of staff said, "The public expects the Department of Defense to take action necessary to regain the favorable balance previously held [when the USSR had no atomic bomb]" (quoted in Gregg Herken, *The Winning Weapon: The Atomic Bomb in the Cold War, 1945–1950*, Random House, New York, 1982, p. 318). And defense secretary Caspar Weinberger's Defense Guidance of 1982 says, "Should deterrence fail and strategic nuclear war with the U.S.S.R. occur, the United States must prevail and be able to force the Soviet Union to seek the earliest termination of hostilities on terms favorable to the United States" (*New York Times*, May 30, 1982).

9. Robert Axelrod has claimed that, in a situation that conforms to the prisoners' dilemma setup, cooperation is a better strategy than indefinitely making second-best choices (*The Evolution of Cooperation*, Basic, New York, 1984, Chapter 3). Imperial states, however, deny themselves the benefits of this better strategy, as far as military competition goes, because their imperial sovereignty excludes cooperation even of the limited kind discussed by Axelrod. Cooperation would require that they forgo imperial sovereignty and hence cease to press their claims to partial rule over their peripheries. Imperial rivalry is, then, a structural constraint, making Axelrod's recommendation of cooperation irrelevant to avoiding the struggle for superiority.

10. As Paul H. Nitze put it, "To have advantage at the utmost level of violence helps at every lesser level. In the Korean War, the Berlin

Blockade, and the Cuban missile crisis, the U.S. had the ultimate edge because of our superiority at the strategic nuclear level" (*Is SALT II a Fair Deal for the United States?*, Committee on the Present Danger, Washington, D.C., May 16, 1978, p. 40).

11. Colin Gray and Keith Payne, "Victory Is Possible," *Foreign Policy*, 39, Summer 1980, pp. 14–27. The key question in the debate in the United States on "self-inhibition" in the use of a nuclear retaliatory force is whether the USSR could destroy enough of the U.S. *counterforce* arsenal in a first strike to make it impossible for the United States in a second, retaliatory strike to destroy enough of the remaining Soviet strategic arsenal to leave much of the U.S. population and industry safe from a third strike. A credible critique of the USSR's potential for such a disabling first strike is made by Andrew Cockburn, *The Threat: Inside the Soviet Military Machine*, Random House, New York, 1984, Chapter 12.

12. For an overblown version of this thesis, which was criticized in Chapter 2, see E. P. Thompson, "Notes on Exterminism, the Last Stage of Civilization," in his *Beyond the Cold War: A New Approach to the Arms Race and Nuclear Annihilation*, Pantheon, New York, 1982, pp. 41–80. For a critique of Thompson that emphasizes the link between the arms race and imperialist intervention, see Mike Davis, "Nuclear Imperialism and Extended Deterrence," *Against the Current*, 3, no. 3, Winter 1985, pp. 23–31.

13. On taking risks, see Milton Fisk, "The Logic of the Arms Race," in *Nuclear Weapons and the Future of Humanity*, ed. A. Cohen and S. Lee, Rowman and Allanheld, New York, 1985, pp. 457–79.

14. Barry M. Blechman and Douglas M. Hart, "The Political Utility of Nuclear Weapons," in *Strategy and Nuclear Deterrence*, ed. S. E. Miller, Princeton University Press, Princeton, N.J., 1984, pp. 273–97.

20. The Soviet Union as other

1. According to National Security Council document 68 of 1950, "The Soviet Union . . . is animated by a new fanatical faith, antithetical to our own, and seeks to impose absolute authority over the rest of the world" (quoted in Gregg Herken, *The Winning Weapon: The Atomic Bomb in the Cold War, 1945–1950*, Random House, New York, 1982, p. 328). Since its founding in 1976, the Committee on the Present Danger – including figures such as Paul Nitze, Richard Pipes, and Eugene Rostow – has based itself on an identical view (Jerry W. Sanders, *Peddlers of Crisis: The Committee on the Present Danger and the Politics of Containment*, South End, Boston, 1983, Chapter 5).

2. John Kenneth Galbraith, *The New Industrial State*, New American Library, New York, 1967, Chapters 9 and 25. For the view that the USSR

was not just converging toward capitalism but already was capitalist by the 1930s, see J. R. Johnson [C. L. R. James], "Russia and Marxism," *The New International*, 7, 1941, p. 214.

3. This applies to the Soviet phobia of the Michael Harrington–Irving Howe wing of the U.S. social democracy, which had its roots in the views of Max Shachtman (*The Bureaucratic Revolution: The Rise of the Stalinist State*, Donald, New York, 1962). Shachtman's undialectical view that the USSR could be characterized without being internally related to capitalism led him in the end to see the USSR as an independent threat rather than as a threat that is parasitic on the existence of capitalism.

4. For the conception of dialectic involved here, see Milton Fisk, "Dialectic and Ontology," in *Issues in Marxist Philosophy*, Volume 1, ed. J. Mepham and D.-H. Ruben, Harvester, Brighton, 1979, pp. 117–43.

5. E. H. Carr, *Socialism in One Country, 1924–1926*, Volume 1, Macmillan, London, 1958, Chapter 6.

6. E. H. Carr and R. W. Davies, *Foundations of a Planned Economy, 1926–1929*, Volume 1, Macmillan, London, 1969, Chapters 26 and 29; and Carr, *Socialism in One Country*, Volume 1, Chapter 9.

7. Carr and Davies, *Foundations of a Planned Economy*, Volume 1, p. 837, n. 2.; and Alec Nove, *An Economic History of the U.S.S.R.*, Penguin, Harmondsworth, 1969, p. 188.

8. Marshall I. Goldman, *Gorbachev's Challenge: Economic Reform in the Age of High Technology*, Norton, New York, 1987, Chapter 3.

9. Marshall I. Goldman, *U.S.S.R. in Crisis: The Failure of an Economic System*, Norton, New York, 1983, Chapter 5; and Christopher E. Stowell, *Soviet Industrial Import Priorities*, Praeger, New York, 1975, p. 239.

10. Alec Nove, *The Soviet Economic System*, Allen and Unwin, London, 1977, Chapter 6; and Howard J. Sherman, *The Soviet Economy*, Little, Brown, Boston, 1969, Chapter 12.

11. Alan Wolfe, *The Rise and Fall of the Soviet Threat: Domestic Sources of the Cold War Consensus*, South End, Boston, 1984, Chapter 8.

12. Quoted by Stephen F. Cohen, "The Stalin Question," in *The Soviet Union Today: An Interpretive Guide*, ed. J. Cracraft, Bulletin of the Atomic Scientists, Chicago, 1983, p. 31.

13. Robin Edmonds, *Soviet Foreign Policy, 1962–1973: The Paradox of Super Power*, Oxford University Press, Oxford, 1975, pp. 122–3.

14. In Portugal the USSR-backed Portuguese Communist Party supported capitalist development while incipient soviets were forming in Lisbon suburbs and Setúbal and plantations were being transformed into cooperatives in Alentejo. On the incompatibility of the Polish Solidarity with bureaucratic power in Poland, see Colin Barker and Kara Weber, "Solidarność: From Gdansk to Military Repression," *International Socialism* (Great Britain), 15, 1982, Chapter 6.

15. For an alternative that gives primacy to the political, see Włodzimierz Brus, *Socialist Ownership and Political Systems*, Routledge and Kegan Paul, London, 1975.

21. Liberal egalitarianism

1. John Locke's proviso that, after the acquisition of property by the labor of one individual, "enough and as good" be left for others can be viewed as based on such a conception of human nature (*The Second Treatise of Government*, Sections 27 and 36).
2. Nagel adopts a variant of the classical liberal egalitarianism developed here (Thomas Nagel, "Equality," in *Readings in Social and Political Philosophy*, ed. R. M. Stewart, Oxford University Press, Oxford, New York, 1986, pp. 257–69). His version takes the private interests of each person into account but assigns resources, not equally but according to a schedule of the *urgency* of the needs of different persons. The need of a disabled person for mobility might, for example, be more urgent than a student's need for a postgraduate education. This qualification of equality by urgency introduces an element familiar in welfare liberalism but not to be found in classical liberalism based on the market model. We could, though, easily substitute Nagel's conception of human nature, which involves prioritizing needs by urgency, for the classical liberal conception in order to get a more sophisticated radical justice that is still in the liberal egalitarian vein.
3. Ronald Dworkin, "Liberalism," in *Public and Private Morality*, ed. S. Hampshire, Cambridge University Press, New York, 1978, pp. 113–36.
4. See the discussion of the contrast between "simple private value" and "social value" in Robert Paul Wolff, *The Poverty of Liberalism*, Beacon, Boston, 1968, Chapter 5.
5. R. H. Tawney, *Religion and the Rise of Capitalism*, Harcourt, Brace, New York, 1926, Chapter 3, Section 3. In view of the inability of the liberal view of humans and its contemporary counterpart, methodological individualism, to resolve the problems I discuss here, the insistence of thinkers like Jon Elster (*Making Sense of Marx*, Cambridge University Press, Cambridge, 1985, Chapter 1) that only methodological individualism is intellectually rigorous appears as a form of self-flagellation.
6. This general problem about the inadequacy of liberal individualism for morality has implications for the liberal contract theory of the state. Francisco Suárez, in his *Treatise on the Laws and God the Law-Giver* of 1612, criticized contract theory on the Aristotelian ground that individuals "simply by forming a kind of aggregation" cannot grant authority to a sovereign since to do this they have to "be capable

of being regarded, from the moral point of view, as a single unified whole." Quoted in Quentin Skinner, *The Foundations of Modern Political Thought*, Volume 2, *The Age of Reformation*, Cambridge University Press, Cambridge, 1978, p. 165.

7. Milton Fisk, "Abortion Rights and Socialism," *Against the Current*, 2, no. 4, 1987, pp. 30–6 and 42–3.

8. For a critique of the view that women's liberation in particular can be grounded in the liberal conception of human nature, see Alison Jaggar, *Feminist Politics and Human Nature*, Rowman and Allanheld, New York, 1983, Chapter 3.

9. Richard Sennett and Jonathan Cobb, *The Hidden Injuries of Class*, Random House, New York, 1973, p. 255.

10. Milton Fisk, "The State and the Market in Rawls," *Studies in Soviet Thought*, 30, 1985, pp. 347–64.

11. In this regard, see Allen Wood's argument for the view that equality is not central for Marx in his "Marx and Equality," in *Issues in Marxist Philosophy*, Volume 4, ed. J. Mepham and D.-H. Ruben, Harvester, Brighton, 1981.

12. C. B. Macpherson, in *The Political Theory of Possessive Individualism: Hobbes to Locke* (Oxford University Press, Oxford, 1962, p. 78), points out in regard to Hobbes that "it is only a society as fragmented as a market society that can credibly be treated as a mechanical system of self-moving individuals." Here humans with their distinctive personal interests are themselves modeled as mechanical systems with their distinctive motions.

13. The breakdown of what Jürgen Habermas calls "privatism" creates a "motivational crisis" since the breakdown is dysfunctional in respect to the state's effort to reproduce the market (*Legitimation Crisis*, trans. T. McCarthy, Beacon, Boston, 1975, Part 2, Chapter 7).

14. Bruce A. Ackerman, *Social Justice and the Liberal State*, Yale University Press, New Haven, Conn., 1980, Chapter 8.

15. John Rawls, *A Theory of Justice*, Harvard University Press, Cambridge, Mass., 1971, Section 43.

16. Macpherson, *Possessive Individualism*, p. 55.

17. For the view – opposed to that in the text – that market socialism is inconsistent with the pursuit of equality, see Arthur Di Quattro, "The Market and Liberal Values," *Political Theory*, 8, 1980, pp. 183–202. See also Włodzimierz Brus, *The Market in a Socialist Economy*, trans. A. Walker, Routledge and Kegan Paul, London, 1972. For a critique of market socialism, see Milton Fisk, "Market Socialism: A Matter of Priorities," *Against the Current*, 3, no. 1, 1988, pp. 34–9.

18. Karl Marx, *The Grundrisse*, trans. M. Nicolaus, Penguin, Harmondsworth, 1973, p. 157. Marx says, "The less social power the medium of exchange possesses . . . the greater must be the power of the community which binds the individuals together."

22. Revolutionary anarchism

1. Robert Paul Wolff, *In Defense of Anarchism*, Harper, New York, 1970, pp. 18–19.
2. *Selected Writings of P.-J. Proudhon*, ed. S. Edwards, trans. S. Fraser, Doubleday, Garden City, N.Y., 1969, p. 104. Also Paul Goodman, "Contemporary Decentralism," in *Patterns of Anarchy*, ed. L. I. Krimerman and L. Perry, Doubleday, Garden City, N.Y., 1966, pp. 379–86.
3. Emma Goldman, "The Psychology of Political Violence," in *Red Emma Speaks*, ed. A. K. Schulman, Random House, New York, 1972, pp. 210–33.
4. As the functional and hegemonic powers of the state are thwarted in the situation of permanent and generalized crisis, its soverign power is enhanced in hopes of ending the stalemate. Alan Wolfe says, "With the exhaustion of alternatives, public administrators become entrapped in their own symbolic world, which is increasingly divorced from the needs and concerns of the society at large" (*The Limits of Legitimacy: Political Contradictions of Contemporary Capitalism*, Free Press, New York, 1977, p. 274).
5. The reified state defends its power not by the organization of its citizens but by their "disorganization," which leaves them incapable of advancing their own interests. See Jeremy Brecher, *Strike!*, South End, Boston, 1980, pp. xiv–xvi, 306–8.
6. The "revolutionary anarchist" is to be distinguished from the "laissez-faire anarchist." The former attacks the state as such, whereas the latter preserves the state insofar as the state protects the inequalities won through enterprise and attacks only the institutions of justice that would moderate those inequalities. For laissez-faire anarchism, see Robert Nozick, *Anarchy, State, and Utopia*, Basic, New York, 1974, Chapter 5.
7. Milton Fisk, *Ethics and Society: A Marxist Interpretation of Value*, New York University Press, New York, 1980, Chapter 8, Section 1.
8. Alan Ritter notes this anarchist essentialism in his study of classical anarchism, *Anarchism: A Theoretical Analysis*, Cambridge University Press, Cambridge, 1980, pp. 131–2.
9. As one of the elements of politics, Charles Lindblom lists "Top authority engaged both in directing the hierarchy and in a struggle to maintain itself" (*Politics and Markets: The World's Political and Economic Systems*, Basic, New York, 1977, p. 122).
10. See E. O. Wright's criticism (*Class, Crisis, and the State*, New Left, London, 1978, p. 214) of the Lenin of *The State and Revolution* (*V. I. Lenin: Collected Works*, Volume 25, Progress, Moscow, 1964, Chapter 5, Section 4) for having neglected the complexity of the organizational problems of a proletarian state.

11. Marx is clearly referring to socialism when, in discussing the fetishism of commodities, he says, "Let us now picture to ourselves, by way of change, a community of free individuals, carrying on their work with the means of production in common, in which the labor-power of all the different individuals is consciously applied as the combined labor-power of the community" (*Capital*, Volume 1, Chapter 1, Section 4).

12. Karl Marx, *The Grundrisse*, trans. M. Nicolaus, Penguin, Harmondsworth, 1973, p. 542. In contrast with this internationalist conception of Marxist self-realization, there is Jon Elster's individualist conception of it (*Making Sense of Marx*, Cambridge University Press, Cambridge, 1985, pp. 88, 397, 527).

13. On political dominance, see Antonio Gramsci, *Selections from the Prison Notebooks*, trans. Q. Hoare and G. Nowell Smith, International Publishers, New York, 1971, p. 18; and Nicos Poulantzas, *Political Power and Social Classes*, trans. T. O'Hagan, Verso, London, 1978, p. 114.

14. Thus a Marxist critique of the organization theories of the followers of Durkheim and Weber that emphasizes, from a functionalist perspective, the goal of reproducing a social structure is not enough. There must in addition be the political perspective that emphasizes the class struggle for political dominance. This difference is not emphasized in Graeme Salaman's otherwise instructive handling of those organizational theories from a Marxist perspective (*Class and the Corporation*, Fontana, Glasgow, 1981, Chapter 6).

15. E. H. Carr, *The Bolshevik Revolution, 1917–1923*, Volume 1, Macmillan, London, 1950, Chapter 8. Also Daniel Guerin, *Anarchism: From Theory to Practice*, trans. M. Klopper, Monthly Review, New York, 1970, p. 93.

16. Eurocommunists implicitly accept the equation between direct democracy and terror to be found in G. W. F. Hegel's critique of "the general will" (*Phenomenology of Spirit*, trans. A. V. Miller, Oxford University Press, Oxford, 1977, Chapter 6, B, Section 3). See Santiago Carrillo, *Eurocommunism and the State*, trans. N. Green and A. M. Elliott, Lawrence Hill, Westport, Conn., 1978, p. 156; Nicos Poulantzas, "The State and the Transition to Socialism," *Socialist Review* (U.S.), 38, March–April 1978, p. 20; and Fernando Claudin, *Eurocommunism and Socialism*, trans. J. Wakeham, New Left, London, 1978, p. 79.

17. Claus Offe, "European Socialism and the Role of the State," in his *Contradictions of the Welfare State*, ed. J. Keane, MIT Press, Cambridge, Mass., 1984, p. 249.

23. Democracy and the transition to socialism

1. V. I. Lenin, *The State and Revolution*, in *Lenin: Collected Works*, Volume 25, Progress, Moscow, 1964, pp. 404, 426.

NOTES TO PP. 301-5

2. Mike Gonzalez, "The Nicaraguan Revolution: Classes, Masses, and the Sandinista State," *International Socialism*, 2, no. 17, 1982, pp. 39–90.

3. In Nicaragua the Popular Action Movement–Marxist Leninist and its union federation, Workers' Front, have advocated more nationalizations and an end to bourgeois participation in the elections.

4. Luis Serra, "The Sandinista Mass Organizations," in *Nicaragua in Revolution*, ed. T. W. Walker, Praeger, New York, 1982, pp. 95–113. Serra quotes an editorial of January 2, 1980, from the Sandinista newspaper *Barricada:* "The passivity which . . . has quieted some mass organizations should be broken and they should struggle to maintain their class independence from the state. . . . their behavior should manifest itself in concrete actions that tend to transform and strengthen the state, without passively waiting for all of the decrees . . . to fall from heaven."

5. Dan La Botz, "State, Party, Masses: Who Rules?" *Against the Current, 7,* 1987, pp. 39–45.

6. The Sandinista Workers' Central (CST) and the Sandinista National Liberation Front (FSLN) have both countered demands for higher wages by emphasizing social benefits (Marifeli Perez-Stable, "The Working Class in the Nicaraguan Revolution," in *Nicaragua in Revolution*, ed. Walker, pp. 133–45). See the more pessimistic view of Carlos Vilas that the mass organizations have suffered a loss of autonomy during the contra war ("The Mass Organizations in Nicaragua," *Monthly Review*, 38, no. 6, 1986, pp. 20–31).

7. Petras emphasizes that the class background of revolutionary leaders is less important for their social identity than the intensity of class struggle in their society (*Class, State and Power in the Third World, with Case Studies on Class Conflict in Latin America*, Allenhead, Osmun, Montclair, N.J., 1981, pp. 159, 175).

8. On the role of the capitalist class in Nicaraguan politics, see Carlos Vilas, *The Sandinista Revolution*, Monthly Review, New York, 1986, pp. 145–7; and G. Invernizzi, F. Pisani, and J. Ceberio, *Sandinistas: entrevistas a Humberto Ortega, Jaime Wheelock, y Bayardo Arce*, Vanguardia, Managua, 1986, Number 10, "Burguesía sin hegemonía," pp. 173–94.

9. The basic tension in the mass organizations in Nicaragua stems from their being charged both with implementing state policy and with representing their constituents to the state (Richard Fagen, "Revolution and Transition in Nicaragua," *Socialist Review* [U.S.], 59, September–October 1981, pp. 16–17). On the manipulation of mass organizations in noncapitalist countries, see Clifford Du Rand, "Toward a Theory of the State in Socialism: The Case of China," *Monthly Review*, 36, no. 2, June 1984, pp. 21–37.

10. On the bargaining between the FSLN and the National Union of Farmers and Ranchers (UNAG), see "Movimiento Cooperativo: los campesinos dan un nuevo giro," *Envío*, 6, no. 72, 1987, pp. 13–38.

11. At first, the Nicaraguan mass organizations – urban and peasant unions, neighborhood bodies, women's groups, youth groups – were represented in the legislative process by participating in the Council of State, and in policy making by their presence on the Programmatic Coordinating Commissions (Institute for Central American Studies, "The Council of State and the Mass Organization," in *The Nicaragua Reader: Documents of a Revolution under Fire*, ed. P. Rosset and J. Vandermeer, Grove, New York, 1983, pp. 273–7). However, after the elections for the National Assembly in November 1984, representation passed to a geographic basis. The mass organizations retained political influence through their own initiatives and through the state's reliance on them.

12. For the way both the state and the FSLN work with mass organizations at the regional level, see Gary Ruchwarger, *People in Power: Forging a Grassroots Democracy in Nicaragua*, Bergin and Garvey, South Hadley, Mass., 1987, pp. 152–60.

13. *Selected Writings of Rosa Luxemburg*, ed. D. Howard, Monthly Review, New York, 1971, pp. 131, 253, 303; and Rosa Luxemburg, *"The Russian Revolution" and "Leninism or Marxism?,"* ed. B. D. Wolfe, University of Michigan Press, Ann Arbor, 1961, pp. 71, 78.

14. Maurice Dobb, *Economic Growth and Planning*, Monthly Review, New York, 1960, Chapter 3.

15. "Interview with Jaime Wheelock," *Barricada International*, August 21, 1986.

16. Kim Moody, "Nicaraguan Revolution: Struggling for Survival," *Changes*, 6, 1984, pp. 8–13. For a more general view on trade-offs through bargaining, by which I have been strongly influenced, see James Petras, "Problems in the Transition to Socialism," *Monthly Review*, 35, May 1983, pp. 14–24. On the determination of economic policy by the class goals of the revolution, see José Luis Coraggio, "Economics and Politics in the Transition to Socialism: Reflections on the Nicaraguan Experience," in *Transition and Development: Problems in Third World Socialism*, ed. R. R. Fagen, C. D. Deere, and J. L. Coraggio, Monthly Review, New York, 1986, pp. 143–70.

17. John Rawls, *A Theory of Justice*, Harvard University Press, Cambridge, Mass., 1971, Section 45.

18. On state and market in Nicaragua in the mid 1980s, see Barbara Goldoftas, "Feeding Nicaragua: Meeting Basic Needs in a Mixed Economy," *Dollars and Sense*, 104, March 1985, pp. 9–13; and R. Bakker, O. Mendoza, M. Spoor, and E.-J. Visser, "Política de precios y de comercialización en Nicaragua, 1979–1987," typescript, Department of Agricultural Economics, University of Amsterdam, 1988.

19. Michael Lowy, "Mass Organization, Party, and State," in *Transition and Development*, ed. Fagen et al., pp. 264–79.

20. See the criticism of pure soviet democracy by Fernando Claudin, *Euro-*

communism and Socialism, trans. J. Wakeham, New Left, London, 1978, p. 129. In contrast to Claudin's support for parliaments alongside mass organizations, the Communist Party of Nicaragua labeled the elections to a National Assembly in November 1984 "a concession to imperialism."

24. The socialist state

1. E. O. Wright slips over this difference between the decay of capitalism and the rise of an alternative (*Class, Crisis, and the State*, New Left, London, 1978, Chapter 5).
2. There are prescriptions from the Left on how to overcome the economic decline of the United States by restrictions on corporate control of production (Samuel Bowles, David M. Gordon, and Thomas E. Weisskopf, *Beyond the Wasteland: A Democratic Alternative to Economic Decline*, Doubleday, Garden City, N.Y., 1983, Chapter 6) and on how to overcome the assaults on society by that part of the capitalist class associated with monopoly capital (Santiago Carrillo, *Eurocommunism and the State*, trans. N. Green and A. M. Elliott, Lawrence Hill, Westport, Conn., 1978, Chapter 4). They offer useful suggestions for reform goals that if pursued will elevate the struggles of the lower classes. They fail, though, to insist that, unless those classes become politically dominant, the pursuit of these reform goals will only aggravate the downward spiral of capitalism, risking increased repression without, however, bringing socialism closer.
3. "From Capitalism to Socialism," in *The Capitalist System*, 2nd ed., ed. R. C. Edwards, M. Reich, and T. E. Weisskopf, Prentice-Hall, Englewood Cliffs, N.J., 1978., p. 518.
4. It is also by getting beyond the capitalist framework that liberation theology sees the possibility of a genuine human liberation (Gustavo Gutierrez, *A Theology of Liberation*, trans. C. Inda and J. Egleson, Orbis, Maryknoll, N.Y., 1973, Chapters 3 and 9).
5. Karl Marx, *Critique of the Gotha Programme*, ed. C. P. Dutt, International Publishers, New York, 1966, Part 1, Section 3, pp. 8–9.
6. For a survey of issues relating to the topic of socialist planning, see Howard Sherman, *Radical Political Economy*, Basic, New York, 1972, Chapter 14. I cannot agree with the unargued view of Alec Nove that because planning is hierarchical it must therefore be undemocratic and elitist and hence contrary to the spirit of socialism (*The Economics of Feasible Socialism*, Allen and Unwin, London, 1983, pp. 32–9). See the response to Nove on this point in Milton Fisk, "Market Socialism: A Matter of Priorities," *Against the Current*, 3, no. 1, 1988, pp. 34–9.
7. See the debate between Hillel Ticktin and Włodzimierz Brus, "Is Mar-

ket Socialism Possible or Necessary?" *Critique* (Glasgow), 14, 1981, pp. 13–40.

8. Ernest Mandel, "In Defense of Socialist Planning," *New Left Review*, 159, 1986, pp. 26 ff.

9. Karl Marx, *The Civil War in France*, Foreign Language Press, Peking, 1970, pp. 69, 167. These passages contain Marx's most explicit discussion of the state.

10. But see Otto Sik, *The Third Way: Marxist Leninist Theory and Modern Industrial Society*, trans. M. Sling, Wildwood House, London, 1976, p. 206. Carmen Sirianni thinks that relative scarcity makes nonclass conflicts of this sort inevitable. This may be true. But his conclusion that there will thus have to be state coercion to settle such conflicts fails to follow ("Production and Power in a Classless Society," *Socialist Review* [U.S.], 59, September–October 1981, pp. 33–82).

11. For this historical conception of the "general will," see Ernest Barker, *Principles of Social and Political Theory*, Oxford University Press, Oxford, 1951, Book 5, Section 3. For him, though, the general will extends throughout a domain, including even those who are not politically dominant, whereas here it extends to the politically dominant alliance with no assurance of its going beyond that.

12. V. I. Lenin, *The State and Revolution*, Chapter 3, Section 4, in *Lenin: Collected Works*, Volume 25, Progress, Moscow, 1964, p. 425.

Index

382

Derrida, Jacques, 343 n. 7
determination
  in atomistic materialism, 18–19
  in the framework model, 31–5
  in the last instance, 48
determinism, 145
deterrence
  extended, 253–4
  self-inhibition, 254
  and superiority, 254
development
  combined and uneven, 235, 367 n. 3
  limited and distorted, 235, 238
  and imperialism, 234, 244
  and investment, 235, 241–2, 244–5
Devine, James N., 364 n. 10
Díaz, Elías, 358 n. 7
difference in nondistinctness, 128
Di Quattro, Arthur, 374 n. 17
distinctions, 42–4, 127–8
Domhoff, G. William, 361 n. 4
domination
  class, 10, 59, 172, 294
  economic, 223–4, 239–43, 295, 323
  forms of economic: commercial, 241;
    financial, 241; technological, 241–2
  low productivity the basis for, 240
  among nations, 224
  and partial rule, 228, 240–3
  political, 242–3, 294–7
Draper, Hal, 347 n. 14
Du Rand, Clifford, 377 n. 9
Durkheim, Emile, 111–12

economism
  and the arms race, 20–1
  and justice, 107–10
economy
  capitalist, 131–2
  in conflict with justice, 50, 55, 106–7,
    321–2
  control abstracted from, 130–1
  and division of labor, 131
  as economic productive relations,
    130–2
  international, 195
  and the political, 127–30
  reproduction of, vii, 12, 155, 157, 172
  and the state, 127–8, 200–1

education
  and justice, 74
  reforms of, 75–6
  and the state, 76–7, 299
Edwards, Richard, 357 n. 11
egalitarianism, 275–6
Einstein, Albert, 369 n. 1
elites, 6, 292, 294–8, 324–6, 379 n. 6
Elster, Jon, 357 n. 13, 367 n. 9, 373 n. 5
eminent domain, 138
empiricism, 30–2, 290
employment
  effect on of capital flight, 202
  promoted by justice as mutuality,
    194–5
  and rate of profit, 200
Engels, Frederick
  capitalists and the state, 352 n. 14
  institutions of the state, 142–3
equality
  changes in, 115–17, 186–7
  in the French Revolution, 115–16
  and liberalism, 74, 118, 275–6
  of opportunity, 124
  popular demand for, 282, 286
  second to shared control, 294
  social, 124
  and subsistence justice, 186
  of well-being, 124
essentialism
  anarchist, 289–91
  emanationist, 47–8
  and structure causes, 49
ethics, political, ix, 10, 65, 101, 112
Eurocommunism, 296, 376 n. 16
explanation
  causal, 18
  framework model of, 19, 30
  functional, 147–50
  materialist, 19, 27
  primacy in, 38, 40–5, 344 n. 9, 354 n. 11
  realist view of, 30
exploitation, 129, 131, 321, 340–1 n. 2

Fagen, Richard R., 377 n. 9
Faletto, Enzo, 368 n. 12
feminism, 44, 280
feudalism
  economy's relation to politics in,
    127–30, 356 n. 7